The Dictatorship of Sex

The Dictatorship of Sex

Lifestyle Advice for the Soviet Masses

Frances Lee Bernstein

NORTHERN ILLINOIS UNIVERSITY PRESS / DeKalb

Published by the Northern Illinois University Press, DeKalb, Illinois   60115

Manufactured in the United States using acid-free paper

Design by Julia Fauci

STUDIES OF THE HARRIMAN INSTITUTE, COLUMBIA UNIVERSITY

The Harriman Institute, Columbia University, sponsors the Studies of the Harriman Institute in the belief that their publication contributes to scholarly research and public understanding. In this way the Institute, while not necessarily endorsing their conclusions, is pleased to make available the results of some of the research conducted under its auspices.

Library of Congress Cataloging-in-Publication Data

Bernstein, Frances Lee.

The dictatorship of sex: lifestyle advice for the Soviet masses / Frances Lee Bernstein.

   p.   cm.

Includes bibliographical references and index. ·

ISBN-13: 978-0-87580-371-5 (clothbound : alk. paper)

ISBN-10: 0-87580-371-7 (clothbound : alk. paper)

1. Sex customs—Soviet Union. 2. Communism and sex—Soviet Union.

3. Soviet Union—Social life and customs. 4. Soviet Union—History—1917–1936.

I. Title.

HQ18.S65B47 2007

306.770947'09042—dc22

2006026557

For Eliot, my comrade in arms

Contents

List of Illustrations

Acknowledgments

During the long years it took to complete this book, it often seemed that what kept me going was the prospect of thanking in print those who had sustained me during the process. I'm relieved to finally be able to do so. To my late grandfather Ned—the family's black sheep musician, whose trumpet, jazz records, and wash-and-wear shirts were confiscated at the Soviet border in 1932—I owe my first exposure to stories of life in Russia.

At Brown University, Barbara Monahan and Tom Gleason nurtured my growing obsession with all things Russian. Mark von Hagen encouraged my pursuit of graduate work on gender and sexuality at Columbia University and, together with Richard Wortman, served as perceptive readers of my thesis. At Columbia I had the privilege of working closely with Atina Grossmann, ever generous with her time and intellect.

A number of colleagues read chapters, shared documents, and challenged me with their observations and questions: Greta Bucher, Andrea Chandler, Hera Cook, Michael David-Fox, Elizabeth Feder, Bruce Grant, David Hoffmann, Peter Holquist, Mark Johnson, Paul Josephson, Christina Kiaer, Yanni Kotsonis, Natalia Lebina, Anne Lounsbery, and Kate Transchel. Laurie Bernstein, Roger Davidson, Lesley Hall, Stephen Kotkin, Robert Nye and Mary Joe Nye, the late Roy Porter, Don Raleigh, Roger Smith, and Elizabeth Wood provided encouragement over the years. Since our long-ago meeting at a Moscow archive, Bill Husband has been a steadfast advocate, not to mention an inspired dining companion. His confidence in me has meant a great deal.

Chris Burton, Michael David, Dan Healey, Kiril Rossiianov, and Irina Sirotkina always responded thoughtfully to my endless queries about medical history. Ken Pinnow, my fellow student of Russian pathologies, has been a valued sounding board and friend since our first days of graduate school.

Too rarely is intellectual acumen combined with extreme *Menschlichkeit*. At an early stage of this project I had the great fortune of making contact with Eric Naiman and Susan Gross Solomon. Both have been unstinting in their attention, read countless versions of these chapters, and written more letters of recommendation than anyone should ever need. As my unofficial *Doktormutter*, Susan balanced rigorous appraisals with unconditional support. Much of what I know about the history of Soviet medicine I credit to her efforts. My ongoing conversations with Eric on all manner of deviance and bodily disruptions span several time zones and a herd of unruly cattle, and I have been inspired by his broad understanding of culture and commitment to interdisciplinarity.

Dan Todes and the other members of the Department of the History of Science, Medicine, and Technology rescued me, in more ways than one, with a glorious year as a postdoctoral fellow at Johns Hopkins University. ACTR sponsored the bulk of my research for this project; I also received postdoctoral support from the Kennan Institute, the Social Science Research Council, and the International Research Exchanges Board. My colleagues at Drew University have been unfailing in their enthusiasm and will be almost as happy as I am to see the finished product.

Helena Goscilo and Ron Myer were careful and astute readers of the manuscript. My thanks to the staff of Northern Illinois University Press—especially to Mary Lincoln—for their professionalism, skill, and patience.

Portions of Chapters 1, 2, and 3 have been published in, respectively, *Eros i pornografiia v russkoi kul'ture*, ed. Marcus Levitt and Andrei Torporkov (Moscow: Ladomir, 1999); *The Politics of Russian Modernity: Knowledge and Practices, 1800–1950*, ed. David Hoffmann and Yanni Kotsonis (London: Macmillan, 2000); and *Everyday Life in Early Soviet Russia: Taking the Revolution Inside*, ed. Christina Kiaer and Eric Naiman (Bloomington: Indiana University Press, 2005). An early version of Chapter 4 appeared in *Russian Review* 57 (April 1998): 191–217 and in *Sex, Sin, and Suffering: Venereal Diseases in European Social Context since 1870*, ed. Lesley Hall and Roger Davidson (London: Routledge, 2001).

In Russia I benefited from the assistance of many individuals and institutions. I am indebted to Misha Poddubnyi for his help in finding sources, negotiating archives, making contacts, and, most importantly, for his friendship. Mark Borisovich Mirskii provided a cordial introduction to the Moscow community of historians of medicine. Nikolai Borisovich Korostelev invited me to his seminar on the history of medicine and entertained me with stories of his own experiences as a health educator. My life is far richer for having known the late Georgii Vladimirovich Arkhangel'skii, whose on-the-spot psychiatric diagnoses of total strangers brightened many a dark day in the *pervyi zal*. The late Viktor Petrovich Danilov facilitated access at two Moscow archives. I thank the many librarians and archivists who took an interest in my work, in particular the staffs of the Medical Bookstore and the reading rooms of the State Archive of the Russian Federation (formerly TsGA) and the State Venereological Institute. At the Medical Museum of the Russian Academy of Medical Sciences I was shown a warm welcome by its historians and by Igor Borisovich Buteev, who photographed most of the posters appearing in this book. The Moscow office of the Fulbright representative kindly provided me with a typewriter and (unwittingly) my future husband. Anna Guenina made sure I was well fed and culturally engaged. Lena Morozova's home and family became my own.

I will never be able to adequately express my appreciation to my family and especially to my parents, Joan Kosta and Joel Bernstein, for their boundless love and devotion. My boys, Lev and Louis, have done their best to ensure that I keep my work life in perspective. Knowing that Jennifer Smith was watching over them made it easier to tear myself away and get back to the computer. My husband, Eliot Borenstein, has read every word of every draft more times than either of us would care to remember, always with good humor and great insight. This book is far richer for his input and presence; for this reason, as well as for so many others, I dedicate it to him.

Preface

My great-grandfather Alex Bernstein traveled frequently to Moscow during the 1920s and 1930s as a fur importer who was instrumental in setting up the first purchase of skins from the new regime after the Russian Revolution. Of his adventures there, two anecdotes in particular—both recounted by my grandfather (himself a rare visitor to the USSR in 1932, thanks to his father's connections)—hold special interest for me. The first, the stuff of family legend, involves my five-foot-two-inch great-grandfather hectoring Stalin about his deplorable treatment of the Jews. The second story is far more plausible: as a guest at the National Hotel in the mid- and late 1930s, Alex was repeatedly awakened by attractive young women knocking on his door to ask if he wanted company. These propositions occurred several years after the Soviet government's claim to have definitively "solved" the problem of prostitution.

My grandfather first related this story to me after learning that I planned to write my master's thesis on the social history of Russian prostitutes. Not long into my research, however, I concluded that a focus on the prostitutes themselves was unfeasible, given the available sources. So I shifted gears in a way that enabled me to pursue an interest in the topic through emphasis on a group that left a much richer paper trail: the medical profession. In the years after the Russian Revolution, physicians devoted considerable energy to the battle against prostitution and the venereal disease that usually accompanied it. My thesis focused on medical efforts to transform infected prostitutes into model workers through political education

and job training, even as doctors sought to vilify prostitution by linking it with a debauched and discredited prerevolutionary era.

As I gathered materials for my thesis I became aware that the battle
against prostitution—and in particular the emphasis placed on inform-
ing and mobilizing the public to participate in this campaign—was part
of an even more ambitious medical agenda: a fundamental reeducation
of the entire population on the subject of sex. "Sexual enlightenment,"
as this body of health information and sex advice was called, would correct the carnal mistakes of the past and provide a blueprint of "scientifically approved" intimate behavior for the inhabitants of this new world.
This book documents the history of sexual enlightenment from its in-
ception during the first years of Bolshevik power to the early 1930s,
when discussion of sexuality (medical or otherwise) disappeared from
public discourse. Aside from the obvious interest generated by any book
on a sexual theme, the story outlined here is important because it links
the medical mission to make the population sexually healthy with the
broader revolutionary crusade to transform reality after 1917. The sheer
quantity of sexual enlightenment materials produced during the decade
(countless plays, posters, pamphlets, advice columns, traveling exhibits,
poems, and lecture series) will doubtless be surprising to those more familiar with the prudish and evasive treatment reserved for sexual matters in later periods of Soviet history. On the contrary: far from being
taboo, a forthrightness about sex (in the right hands) was considered evidence of the modernity of the state and especially its embrace of science as a foundation of its ideological system.

In part, this is a history of one segment of the medical profession
and the way it navigated the new political and institutional landscape.
I describe how doctors staked their claims to the (extremely popular)
territory of sexuality; established networks, institutions, and professional associations; and sought to shape a new specialty, all against the
backdrop of Communist power and a new supervisory authority, the
People's Commissariat of Public Health. More fundamentally, it is the
story of sexual enlightenment itself, and the body of knowledge that
served as the basis of the physicians' teachings. I do not address the actual sexual behavior or practices of the populace; just as with my
abortive master's thesis topic, the kind of sources necessary for such an
approach are regrettably missing. Rather, my prism for viewing
postrevolutionary sexuality is through the eyes of these newly Soviet
doctors. Medical observations and diagnoses may tell us little about
the patients but reveal much about their physicians. Thus I examine
doctors' definitions of normal and deviant sexuality, their assessment
of the causes of and solutions to the sexual problems facing Russian society, and the concerns and values that shaped their responses. The
medical perspective is especially valuable because sexual enlighten-

ment established an attitude toward sexuality that would prove remarkably enduring in the following decades, long after the experiment itself had been terminated.

It would take over half a century for the taboo on sexuality to be lifted. As a graduate student working on my dissertation, I was a direct beneficiary of the climate of openness that characterized the years following the collapse of the Soviet Union, especially when a fortuitous elevator breakdown in the archive and a gas leak in the library left me with a lot of free time on my hands. Showing up at a number of medical institutes and treatment facilities that had either never encountered or barred foreign researchers in the past, I received uniformly gracious welcomes and full access.

Without exception, every institution with which I came into contact suffered financial hardship due to rapid inflation and drastic cuts in governmental funding. A noble colleague single-handedly rescued a number of my sources from the trash when the main repository for health education for the entire Soviet Union—the Institute of Sanitary Culture—was closed, its building sold to a popular magazine, and its priceless library thrown into the street. The Medical Museum of the Russian Academy of Medical Sciences, from whose rich collection most of the images featured in this book are drawn, has since also shut its doors to the public due to lack of support.

Even as documents were being declassified, finding their physical location became something of a scavenger hunt due to the bureaucratic fallout of the political changes following 1991. When the collection I had used extensively a few years earlier disappeared from its previous location, I was told it had been transferred to the jurisdiction of a different ministry and moved to a new site many hours from the capital. After several wasted months of inquiries and a few gratuitous official meetings, I learned that the materials had been incorporated into a new archive and had merely shifted to a different section of the very same complex where I had examined them before.

The archival documents I did have access to provided a wealth of information on the institutional structure of medical care in the years after the Revolution, and especially on the interactions between the various research and treatment facilities and the new health commissariat. Sadly, many of the holdings of individual institutes were lost when much of Moscow was evacuated during World War II. Rich as any of my archival findings are, my most valuable resources, the enlightenment materials themselves, were located in the various public libraries. This is not surprising, given the subject matter, but it serves to remind us of the historical treasures occasionally available in plain sight.

The Dictatorship of Sex

Introduction

A revolution will occur not only in the spheres of politics and the economy, but also in the sexual sphere.

—DR. A. USPENSKII, *POLOVAIA ZHIZN' I EE OTKLONENIIA*

• In the years following the Bolshevik Revolution, as so many of the long-vexing "questions" plaguing Russian society (the woman, peasant, nationality, and Jewish questions, to name a few of the most important) were declared resolved, one in particular continued stubbornly to assert itself, defying resolution by way of the radical egalitarianism and various revolutionary decrees that were supposed to have taken care of the others, at least on paper. This was the sex question (*polovoi vopros*), which had first emerged in the late nineteenth century out of civil society's growing pains, and which was implicated in the increasingly anxious (and politically charged) interactions between educated society and "the people," teachers and students, experts and patients, and finally, the authorities and the populace. Imperial Russia clearly had sex on the brain, as well as on the boulevard, in the school, and at the meeting. Syphilitic husbands, masturbating youths, underage prostitutes, and sexually liberated new women troubled a great many minds.[1]

With the mobilization for war and the country's spiral into crisis, the sex question receded into the background, only to reemerge with a vengeance in the heady days of the new revolutionary order. Indeed, the sexual experimentation that followed the Revolution and the fleeting sexual encounters associated with the Civil War period provoked grave concern throughout society. With the 1921 transition to the New Economic Policy (NEP) of limited, small-scale private enterprise, this so-called sexual nihilism assumed the dimensions of a "sexual crisis." Prostitution, widely believed defeated by the Revolution, had "reappeared," reaching "epidemic" proportions thanks to rampant female unemployment. Simultaneously, medical observers noted a dramatic increase in venereal disease, impotence, masturbation, and casual sex, particularly among the young, as well as the proliferation of dubious advice literature, titillating public lectures, and self-styled miracle cures that exploited widespread sexual anxieties. Writing in the mid-1920s, the first People's Commissar of Public Health Nikolai Semashko could still declare, "the sex question is a painful [*bol'noi*] question." Surveying postrevolutionary society, Semashko deplored the profligate, disordered state of sexual relations and bemoaned the obsession with sexual topics that plagued daily life. Only medicine, the commissar unequivocally concluded, could treat these ills and make the construction of the new society possible.[2]

Soviet doctors were ready and willing to heed Semashko's call, as they had been engaged in this very activity for the last several years. Responding to the pervasive sense of chaos, they had begun to develop a popular health advice program known as "sexual enlightenment" (*polovoe prosveshchenie*), which established a model of sexual conduct for the men and women who would build socialism. In NEP-era Russia, sexual behavior had ramifications that extended far beyond the bedroom; indeed, the sex question is crucial to any understanding of the political and ideological debates that dominated center stage in the 1920s, and which are usually understood to have been resolved by fiat with Stalin's consolidation of power.[3] Sexual mores were clearly of great import to the project of creating the new world and all its inhabitants, and the Communist Party— through the Young Communist League (Komsomol), the Women's Section (Zhenotdel), and its own ideologues and moralists—grappled with these issues throughout the decade. But the discourse of sexuality and health would be framed far more thoroughly and consistently by those professionals who felt it was in their purview, and who had no intention of leaving such questions to the Party to decide. The doctors who defined and redefined sexuality for the revolutionary era were motivated both by the desire to contribute to a socialist society and the pressing need to assert and maintain the independence and integrity of their profession and their institutions. Thus the sex question lies at a complicated intersection between revolutionary ideology and institutional consolidation.

The medical profession's attempt both to solve the sex question for a new way of life and to carve out a niche for itself in the changing matrix of postrevolutionary social institutions is at the heart of this analysis of the rise and fall of Soviet sexual enlightenment. The study traces the program's evolution from the founding of the People's Commissariat of Public Health (*Narkomzdrav*) in 1918 to the abrupt cessation of such discussions in the early 1930s, drawing on a wide arsenal of educational tools to examine the medical practices, programs, and propaganda that defined sexual norms in the new state. Investigating the production of sexual knowledge reveals a great deal about the tortured attempts of professionals in the early Soviet period to accommodate the multiple demands and constraints imposed by modernity, communism, and science.

This book also affords a different lens through which to contemplate a central historiographic conundrum of Russian studies, namely the relationship between the supposedly "liberated" 1920s and the "repressive" 1930s. Stalin's consolidation of power in the early 1930s clearly involved the assertion of what are understood to be "traditional" values: pronatalism and a decidedly nonegalitarian family structure, hostility to sexual experimentation and unconventional practices, and a harsh crackdown (including forced "reeducation" in labor colonies) on those unwilling to comply.[4] What may not be so apparent is how developments in the previous decade facilitated this shift.

In recent years several works have called into question the idea that the mid-1930s marked a "Great Retreat" from the principles of socialism in favor of a reassertion of traditional values.[5] Focusing on ideas rather than on the people who espoused them has enabled these scholars to see the continuities between the 1920s and 1930s that are easily eclipsed by the often violent fate that befell many individuals and institutions during this era. Thus writing about the "civilizing mission" of advice books and etiquette manuals in the campaign for cultured behavior (*kul'turnost'*), Catriona Kelly detects little change between the ideals promoted in the early days of the Soviet regime, including "health, self-education, discipline, and conformity to collective norms," and those encouraged in the 1930s. Similarly, in his study of the values underpinning official Soviet culture, David Hoffmann shows not only that many cultural norms associated with the 1930s had already been advanced during the 1920s, but that they also had a great deal in common with contemporaneous European trends. Hoffmann draws on Katerina Clark's notion of a "cultural ecosystem," in which "over time and through interaction with political trends and social conditions, some cultural concepts flourished, others adapted, still others withered and died." In this light, the reversal posited by Timasheff becomes instead "a tilt toward certain preexisting strands within the existing cultural ecosystem."[6]

The sexual knowledge produced by medical enlighteners and the methods used to assert their professional authority over sexuality in the 1920s would pave the way for the state's adoption of repressive policies toward sex during the 1930s. Indeed, the very behaviors promoted by sex educators—"normalcy" as the absence of deviance, restraint, abstinence, and concern for the collective at the expense of the individual—bore a striking resemblance to the values preached by the Party in the 1930s. That such norms were encoded in a public examination of sex whose prominence and state support (financial and otherwise) would make it the envy of progressives abroad makes sexual enlightenment even more noteworthy. Focusing on this body of information allows us to consider the participation of physicians in the origins of Stalinism even as it rejects a simplistic estimation of them either as victims of a steamrolling state or as Stalin's willing henchmen. Ironically, the doctors' successful elaboration of these behaviors made the sexual enlighteners superfluous as soon as the values they championed were absorbed into the Party's own agenda, one that now could be advanced without competing experts and overt references to the problematic subject of sex.

A Dictatorship of Sex for the Dictatorship of the Proletariat

The phrase "dictatorship of sex," borrowed from a 1920s advice pamphlet, refers to the emphasis sexual enlighteners placed upon biological sexual difference and to the gender distinctions they attributed to this difference. Much like their counterparts in the Party and the Komsomol, medical educators saw no contradiction between an avowed commitment to sexual equality and the advocacy of gender-specific roles and responsibilities.[7] In their analysis, health and societal well-being depended upon the reassertion of the traditional distinctions between women and men that were threatened by the upheavals of the revolutionary years.

Positing a sexual dictatorship based upon "irrefutable" biological truths also enabled physicians to justify their authority over this domain against the claims of competing professionals and institutions, and in particular the Bolshevik Party. Participants in the revolutionary project, public health physicians subscribed to an ideology that was nonetheless distinct from Bolshevism, regardless of whether individual practitioners were Party members. Ultimately what united and defined them was the invocation of a vague "science" that differed radically from the Marxist faith in science held by so many intellectuals at the time. The Soviet doctors who worked so hard to defend their role in the new order resorted to a peculiar, hybrid strategy: on the one hand, their stress on the sexual body's place in a healthy state was a clear attempt to accommodate science with socialism; on the other hand, the source of their specialized authority resided in their reprocessing of scientific trends and disciplines from "bourgeois" Europe, deliberately transforming theories and fields that might be suspect from a Leninist standpoint, or which had long since lost their prominence in the countries that produced them.

The term "dictatorship of sex" also alludes to the rigid and proscriptive nature of sexual advice in the years following the Revolution, thereby calling into question the standard assessment of the 1920s as an age of tolerance and experimentation.[8] In sharp contrast to contemporaneous "sex reform" movements throughout Europe, Soviet sexual enlightenment had no room for pleasure and sexual fulfillment. Sexual normalcy (or its equivalent, sexual health) was defined negatively as the absence of a series of deviant and dangerous behaviors, and education focused on those forms of expression that were to be avoided. The physicians' insistence on conceiving of "healthy" sexuality in purely negative terms is the key to understanding the sudden disappearance of the sexual enlightenment movement at the end of 1931. When health concerns were subordinated to the goals of production during the Five-Year Plans, an educational program whose origins lay in an implicit connection between sex and disease ceased to be an acceptable topic for public discussion.

A Soviet Sexual Science

Doctors were far from alone in their attempts to shape behavior during these years, given the commitment to wholly remake reality that was a fundamental objective of the Bolshevik Revolution. Language, hygiene, leisure, time management—all aspects of existence were subject to scrutiny and radical alteration in the battle for a new lifestyle (*bor'ba za novyi byt*) waged during the first decade of Soviet power.[9] At the same time the country's medical educators also belong to a longer and broader trajectory linking their efforts with those of European and prerevolutionary Russian experts to intervene in the lives of the populace for purposes of mobilization and control, key features of the modern state. Like their European counterparts, Soviet doctors were engaging in what Michel Foucault sees as the transformation of sex into discourse: the process in which scientific knowledge and professional authority set the framework for discussing, understanding, even experiencing sexuality, medicalizing sex in order to discipline the body and manage populations.[10]

This is not to say that sexual enlighteners enjoyed the same authority and influence as their European counterparts; in the Western European context that Foucault himself examined, the process of disciplining sexuality in the modern era owed a great deal to the rise of liberal democracy and the autonomous powers of professional institutions, features lacking in Russia both before and after the Revolution. But to acknowledge, as Laura Engelstein reminds us, that the political context impinged upon professional authority is not to suggest that the Soviet medical disciplinary regime was without power, or that the body of knowledge advanced by health educators was without influence. Bolshevism may indeed have eventually "harnessed professional disciplines to its own repressive ends," but this does not mean that physicians did not pursue a similar vision independently, albeit with highly different methods.

Sexual enlighteners arrived at this position all on their own, and it is precisely this commonality that facilitated the shift in authority on sex in the 1930s.[11]

Despite their endorsement of such policies as the decriminalization of homosexuality and prostitution and the legalization of abortion, physicians were not advocates for personal choice and free sexual expression, a position held by certain progressive jurists and women's activists, among others. That they were identified with this camp by foreign supporters—at least in part because of their own expressions of encouragement for this viewpoint when applied to other countries and voiced abroad—perhaps helps explain why observers like Reich and later Timasheff would describe the 1930s as a retreat.[12] Before the Revolution, and then again after 1931, sexuality was regulated through prohibitions and punishments. The medical response to the sex question in the years from 1918 to 1931 represents a fundamentally different kind of control. Sex, viewed primarily as an issue of health, was managed rather than prohibited through the expert treatment of specialists and a program of education promoting a sexuality firmly harnessed to heterosexual reproductive monogamy. Yet it is of great significance that sexual enlighteners' negative understanding of sexual behavior was shared in the 1920s by many of the same organizations (such as the Party and the police) that would assume authority over this domain in the early 1930s. Despite a fundamental qualitative difference in the forms of control derived from this negative model, a common legacy of attitudes toward sex underlies these eras and links them both with the prerevolutionary past.

Early Soviet Russia was a society seemingly obsessed with sex. Nonetheless, the medical discourse on sexuality was distinct from the competing and overlapping voices that discussed, debated, or exploited the subject during this era, if for no other reason than that the physicians themselves claimed this to be the case. Enlighteners' jurisdiction over the fashionable topic stemmed from their "unique" relationship to science. The Revolution may have provided the conditions for sexual health, they suggested, but it would be achieved only under the personal guidance of medical experts.

While a medical degree was the crucial imprimatur, a doctor's specialization was of little importance; most writers treated the same variety of topics, regardless of their particular areas of expertise. Indeed, the body of sex education literature is characterized by an overwhelming sense of sameness. Authors similarly identified what was wrong with contemporary sexuality and the reasons behind current problems, agreeing not only on the substance of the sex question but also on the proper means to resolve it. Furthermore, the content of enlightenment changed little, if at all, over the course of the decade.

The similarity of their contributions is especially noteworthy in light of some significant and potentially divisive differences in the individual backgrounds and biographies of the physicians. All of the authors for whom biographical information is available completed their medical education before the Revolution. Those who received their training at one of the empire's medical schools were subject to a uniform curriculum and examination process.[13] A number spent some time studying or working abroad as well, and chief among this group were those who had been expelled or arrested for revolutionary activity, including such prominent "old Bolsheviks" as V. M. Bronner and N. A. Semashko.[14] Nonetheless, there is no appreciable difference between the sex advice produced by doctors educated abroad and the pamphlets, books, and articles written by those who never crossed the imperial borders.

Other potential sources of variety based on the doctors' background prove to have an equally limited effect on content. Judging by the last names of the physicians involved, the group was ethnically rather homogenous: over half of the doctors are clearly of Jewish descent. Not surprisingly, this is another issue that the sexual enlightenment literature passes over in silence, but reasons why Jews were overrepresented in this particular medical subfield are easy to imagine. As in Germany and in the United States, the treatment of sexual disorders and diseases made fields like venereology and urology low-status professions, so the barriers to entry would be far lower than in the more prestigious branches of medicine. But the most significant factor may well have been sociopolitical, a combination of heightened social engagement and alienation from the established order—the same factors that contributed to Jewish overrepresentation in radical and revolutionary movements.[15] Venereologists, epidemiologists, and specialists in sanitary medicine all by definition would have shared a commitment to the category of the social. Given the tsarist regime's reluctance to address issues of sexual hygiene, even the most modest public health agenda advocated by these doctors would be likely to identify them with the Left. The fact that so many of these physicians trained before 1917 threw themselves so enthusiastically into socialist public health would seem to bear this out.

A scholar of the Soviet sexual enlightenment movement could also search in vain for dissenting approaches to the sex question based on gender. Here, too, the doctors are a markedly uniform lot: the overwhelming majority of them are men. Nevertheless, one might expect even the few women doctors to provide a different perspective, if for no other reason than that they may have experienced personally "female complaints," in addition to childbirth and (perhaps) orgasm. But no such alternative viewpoint is to be found. While these female physicians did at times address exclusively female audiences, the content of their advice did not vary from that given by the men. If anything, the women doctors were even more dismissive of the role of pleasure in sexual relations. Yet even this distinction is one of degree rather than quality.

Representing themselves as the voice of science gave doctors a credential lacked by other interested parties. A magazine advertisement for

"What One Needs to Know about Sexual Life" (one of the many series on the sex question dating from the 1920s) demonstrates how physicians represented the need for such knowledge and the significance of their particular contribution:

> In a collection of easily accessible brochures, this popular scientific series offers basic information about human sexuality, as it is understood at the present time by science. The goal of the publication: the "sexual literacy" so necessary to contemporary youth, the struggle against the ignorance and indolence that reigns among our young people.[16]

The series held out the promise that "what one needed to know" would be both understandable and unimpeachable—the fruits of science's most recent discoveries. The title also staked physicians' claim *to* the sex question: among the items one needed to know were the identity and qualifications of the most appropriate providers of this information. Typical of the kinds of titles found in this body of writings, the name of this series of pamphlets is also an apt appraisal of the sexual enlightenment project as a whole. While the project offered new, absolutely vital information, the name nonetheless suggested the limits imposed on this knowledge. Everyone should know certain things about sex, but no more (or less) than what the authors considered necessary. There was also information that people were not meant to know (suggesting an important parallel between sexual literacy and the campaign for political literacy), and educators made explicit distinctions between the appropriately and inappropriately curious, between seekers of crucial knowledge and seekers of thrills.

To be sure, scientific credentials are no guarantee of good science. That the imprimatur of science was more important than the substance was proved several times in this literature, which had its fair share of errors and inconsistencies, according to the scientific standards prevailing at the time. Narkomzdrav was barely able to meet the most basic and urgent health needs of the population during these years, much less provide the kind of professional oversight to serve as a check on inaccuracies or to verify the medical qualifications of writers. Suspect credentials and questionable information and recommendations were likewise present in European and American sex advice, so it is no wonder that they would turn up in Soviet enlightenment as well, given the Western origin of most sexual science.[17] To the extent that it was politically possible, many members of the Russian medical profession were eager participants in the international exchange of ideas in the early twentieth century, traveling or studying abroad, reading and publishing in foreign journals, and attending international conferences. However, as important as it is to acknowledge that Soviet doctors had a place in the international scientific community after the Revolution, it is equally imperative to note what is distinctive about their medical writings on sex. On the grounds of fact and accuracy, much of the substance of the enlighteners' writing can be easily dismissed with the benefit of hindsight, but to do so would miss the point: Soviet medical professionals had a number of models and paradigms available to them at the time, and the choices they made, particularly in fundamental questions of "nature vs. nurture," shaped and reflected the discipline's sense of normalcy, health, and social order.

One striking aspect of sexual enlightenment is that much of the medical thinking it drew on was already out of date elsewhere. This adherence to outmoded research might be explained in part by a certain lag in scientific ideas originating abroad being incorporated into medical thinking and practice, or perhaps by the questionable credentials of some of the writers. Furthermore, while some physicians did enjoy the benefits of international contacts, many others and especially those living far from the capital cities had very limited access to current medical journals, a situation made even more precarious by the disruptions in mail and communications networks during the early years of Soviet rule. Even while entertaining these possibilities, it is nonetheless likely that the use of dated scientific information and the rejection of certain ideas currently advanced elsewhere (or the promotion of theories that had been discredited abroad) was sometimes deliberate, to further promote the gendered, negative model of sexual behavior outlined above.[18]

The goals of this campaign highlight another important difference between Western sex advice and sexual enlightenment, namely the Soviet program's collectivist orientation. Rejecting the liberal individualism that was central to the shaping of the sexual self in the modern West, Soviet sex education, along with the countless other initiatives attempting to transform behavior after the Revolution, sought to instill an "illiberal subjectivity."[19] In emphasizing communal obligation at the expense of individual satisfaction, even in this most personal realm of sexual expression, doctors counseled Russians to put the needs of the collective first.

This discussion suggests that Soviet physicians' relationship to their European counterparts and to Western science more generally was decidedly complex. As in other areas of Soviet life, mention of the "West" as a rhetorical device was an important feature of medical writing. Domestic writings on sex for a popular audience pointed to Europe's decadence and degeneration and its similarities to Russia's own reviled past. Despite this criticism, however, even here enlighteners cited specific Western specialists to bolster their arguments. In Russian medical literature geared toward its own community, the anti-Western invective is all but absent. Europe, and especially Germany, represented a point of comparison against which to measure the Soviet Union's medical progress. Soviet medical accounts in foreign publications, meanwhile, concentrated on the USSR's achievements and progressiveness, matching the enthusiasm with which their endeavors were hailed by sex reformers in these same countries.[20] While the influence of the Soviet sexual project on Western activists and theorists is beyond the scope of this study, the benefit that accrued to the Soviet medical establishment both at home and abroad as a result of this attention is worthy of note. This interest, which served to legitimate its endeavors during the 1920s, ultimately contributed to the demise of sexual enlightenment by the early 1930s.

As Catriona Kelly has cautioned, advice literature does not reflect reality but rather presents idealized norms of conduct.[21] Thus rather than use these sources to make assumptions about how Russians actually conducted their sexual lives, I examine how the medical profession represented such behavior and proposed its own sexual vision in response. While it might be possible to conjecture about some people's sexual proclivities based on writers' recommendations about specific acts to avoid, even here caution is recommended: in their jostling for authority with other institutions, in the attendance at their lectures, in the purchase of their pamphlets, and in the waiting rooms of their clinics, physicians certainly benefited from the assumption of widespread promiscuity and sexual chaos that needed to be explained and controlled.

While the subject of children's sex education generated significant medical attention during the decade, I have confined my focus to the enlightenment directed at adults and "youth," a cohort ranging in age from the teen years through the early to midtwenties.[22] I have likewise restricted my scope to Russian-language sex advice, published primarily in Russia and to a lesser extent Ukraine, where Khar'kov had an especially active medical community. While some of the same publications and posters were translated for use in enlightenment work in other parts of the country, others were composed with specific nationalities and regions (alleged to have their own special sexual problems and concerns) in mind. As a number of historians have shown, enlightenment work conducted beyond European Russia had a distinctly different agenda, and medical analyses of "native" sexuality were likewise colored by a range of assumptions originating in these populations' supposed backwardness.[23]

*A*fter a brief examination of the institutions that struggled to establish authority over the subject of sex in Chapter 1, the rest of this book explores both the themes with which sexual enlightenment was preoccupied and the particular kinds of scientific knowledge whose appropriation facilitated the physicians' model of a sexually healthy society. Sexual enlighteners drew on the fields of endocrinology (Chapter 2) and psychoneurology (Chapter 3) as the foundation of a binary model of sexual behavior, using "scientific evidence" about the glands and the nerves to reinforce traditional notions of gender in their approaches to male and female sexual dysfunction and to insist on a normative and highly restrained heterosexuality as the solution to social upheaval. The results of their gendered understanding of health and illness are literally on display in Chapter 4, which shows how the educators encoded their conceptions of femininity, masculinity, and proper sexual behavior in health posters to be distributed throughout the Soviet Union. Such visual aids concurred with the more detailed advice given by public health practitioners to young people and to married couples, as seen in Chapters 5 and 6.

In all cases, sexual enlighteners were at great pains to make sure that sex play an extremely limited role in the lives of Soviet citizens. Squandering sexual energy meant depleting the body's precious resources, distracting young people from vital social tasks. The unmarried were counseled to sublimate their libido as much as possible, eventually choosing healthy partners who would understand that the primary purpose of marital sex was to produce healthy offspring. Having safely steered clear of the perils of carnal excess, birth control, and abortion, the married couple could reproduce, raise a family, and dispense with sex altogether. By promoting such a narrow vision of acceptable sexuality and in particular its culminating sexless-sex model, medical education in the 1920s facilitated the more drastic and coercive policies on sexuality pursued in the 1930s, after this sphere had been removed from the medical profession's jurisdiction.

Disciplining the Sex Question in Revolutionary Russia

If you consider that in no other realm is such an enormous amount of energy spent as it is on sexual excess, if you take into account the vast number of human victims who are either the direct or indirect result of such excesses . . . then the importance of a serious approach to the sex question becomes understandable, in terms of making ideas about sexual experiences healthy, in terms of educating young people, in terms of preparing the younger generation that will replace us.
—DR. I. M. TKACHENKO, *O POLOVOM VOPROSE*

• In the autumn of 1920, Klara Zetkin conducted one of her famous interviews with Vladimir Il'ich Lenin in his Kremlin study. The point of departure of their discussion was the subject of women's rights and the international women's movement, but conversation soon turned to sexuality. Speaking about the situation in Germany, Lenin noted that evening discussion sessions intended for political and educational work among women workers focused primarily on the problems of sex and marriage. Even in the midst of counterrevolution, he complained, communist women "consider it their foremost duty to enlighten working women on questions in this sphere." Lenin railed in particular against an extremely popular pamphlet on the sex question written by one such communist activist, which cited the theories of Freud "to give it a scientific veneer." He continued:

> I have no confidence in sex theories expounded in various articles, scientific papers, pamphlets, and the like—briefly, in that specific literature which has sprung up so luxuriantly on the dung heap of bourgeois society. I do not trust those who are constantly and persistently absorbed in problems of sex, like that Indian fakir is in the contemplation of his navel.[1]

After being reassured by Zetkin that such topics were no longer popular at educational sessions in Germany, Lenin turned his attention to the situation in his own country. He observed that in Russia, both adults and especially young people were caught up in similar discussions, struggling to replace the discredited bourgeois values of the past. He promised that "in the sphere of marriage and sexual relations a revolution is approaching in keeping with the proletarian revolution." But in the meantime, young people "suffered greatly from the messy state of sex relations . . . one would hardly say it was a good thing that in these years sex problems, violently pushed into the limelight by natural causes, were becoming the central feature of youth psychology. The consequences are sometimes nothing short of fatal." To bring youth the joy of life and cheerfulness that they would never find in the sexuality that permeated society, Lenin encouraged them to adopt a variety of physical and intellectual pursuits. "That," he asserted, "will mean more to the youth than eternal lectures and discussions on sex problems."[2]

Just a few years after this interview, Soviet society amassed its own collection of pamphlets, articles, lectures, and posters on the sex question, much of it produced as sexual enlightenment by members of the medical profession. The explosion of popular sex education was made possible by a number of factors, including the relaxation of censorship after the Revolution, the rise of a relatively free press and independent publishing houses, and the free-market conditions that reigned during NEP.[3] The proliferation of sexual enlightenment owed to the population's seemingly unquenchable thirst for knowledge and guidance and the efforts of physicians to meet this challenge.

In asserting their authority over the realm of sexuality, medical educators encountered many of the dilemmas and concerns raised by Lenin. The task was to produce information considered revolutionary (not bourgeois), legitimate (not unscientific), and most important of all, necessary: helping to solve the sexual problem rather than exacerbate it. During the 1920s, physicians attempted to "discipline" the sex question through the commissariat's efforts to claim jurisdiction over sex-related social issues. On the one hand, the process involved establishing sexual enlightenment as part of the official health agenda of the new state. On the other, it necessitated providing guidance (whether desired or not) to all physicians who sought an audience based on their claims of expertise in sexual matters. Ultimately, whether a particular pamphlet, article, or lecture was deemed appropriate and sufficiently "scientific" by Narkomzdrav depended upon the author's relationship to the new commissariat. The health commissariat sought to control the content of sex advice to properly structure the conduct of its audience, but disciplining the doctors, both in the sense of creating a new cadre of sex specialists and of regulating their behavior, was similarly crucial to the agenda.

Yet this represents only part of the story. Despite the commissariat's best efforts to direct the flow of information, the number of popular educators identifying themselves as doctors who wrote or lectured on sex extended far beyond Narkomzdrav's control. The claims of Health Commissar Nikolai Semashko and other Narkomzdrav representatives notwithstanding, little in fact separated officially sponsored enlightenment endeavors from those produced by other doctors. Nor should one assume a rigid separation between Narkomzdrav as state agency and the physicians who staffed it, on the one hand, and those doctors who implemented (or ignored) their suggestions, on the other. Many of the Narkomzdrav-affiliated figures referred to in this book moved freely from official business to clinic or lab and back again. Behind the monolithic authoritative image it sought to project was an institution comprised of individuals who, in addition to supporting its overall mission, presumably continued to advocate for and work in their own disciplines and to represent these professional interests and affiliations in their work on behalf of the commissariat.[4]

Regardless of the institutional affiliations (or lack thereof) of its authors, enlightenment literature posited sexuality and hence sex education as a medical problem best left to the care of trained professionals. Although the commissariat ultimately provided little in the way of concrete recommendations about methodology or content, there is a high degree of uniformity to the material. Indeed, while the center expressed considerable frustration over its inability to regulate the literary output of individual physicians, there was no mention made on the subject of duplication, a not surprising omission given the restrictive boundaries of "what each reader was supposed to know." No doubt this common outlook is attributable in part to the educators' training, and to the modernizing ethos of medical professionalization that Russian doctors shared with their foreign counterparts. Moreover, the conventions of the genre (favoring simplified, easily accessible information), not to mention assumptions about the intellectual capacities of the intended audience, discouraged diverse approaches to the topic.

Yet the sexual knowledge produced and popularized by these writers was shaped by other factors as well. Their work expressed a strong commitment to the revolutionary creation of a new lifestyle (*byt*) as the basis for Russia's future society. Whether physicians had trained in venereology, hygiene, or psychiatry, they approached their educational mission as social doctors, specialists committed to the health of society as a whole.[5] Regardless of individual political involvement or party affiliation, educators extolled the Bolshevik Revolution for making their endeavor possible by providing the means to improve the social conditions to which they attributed bad health. Illness (which included unhealthy sex) would be treated through preventive medicine and education, in conjunction with the transformation of the environment. Yet even as they advocated a code of sexual behavior that would have appealed to Lenin, enlighteners took pains to distinguish the science that justified their efforts from that which underpinned Marxism. Science legitimized their focus on sexuality, underscored their authority, and served as the "evidence" and basis of their teachings.

The Origins and Institutionalization of Soviet Sexual Enlightenment

As much as the Bolshevik regime wanted to claim exclusive credit for bringing public health issues to national prominence, the reality is more complicated. Although the People's Commissariat of Public Health at its July 1918 inauguration was hailed as a purely Soviet phenomenon, plans to organize a health ministry were well under way before October.[6] Adult sex education, another purportedly Soviet innovation, likewise had its prerevolutionary antecedents. According to Engelstein, translations of classic pedagogically oriented texts on sexual themes (such as Jean Jacques Rousseau's *Emile* and Simon-André Tissot's dissertation on masturbation) were available to the (small) reading public in the mid-eighteenth century. A hundred years later, works combining "sexual diagnosis and home cure" (such as the anonymous *No More Onanism, Venereal Disease, Nocturnal Emissions, Male Impotence, or Female Infertility*) could also be found. By the turn of the twentieth century, one could purchase a number of popular pamphlets on sexual topics, many written by physicians. At the same time, the need for sex education was widely discussed in the medical and pedagogical literature, with the scope of this instruction to be limited to school-age boys and young men.[7]

In 1897, at the First All-Russian Congress for the Prevention of Syphilis, physicians identified (adult) education as a crucial element in the battle against the disease. Yet such opportunities were severely hindered by censorship laws, which prohibited doctors from conducting public discussions on the topic. Educators were permitted to lecture only from previously approved texts, which reportedly dated from twenty to thirty years earlier. Writing in 1927 about the history of this period, the venereologist V. M. Bronner recalled the stipulations governing the granting of permission for such lectures. Presented to the police for preliminary approval, a lecture also had to be delivered in police presence, to ensure that the speaker did not deviate from the text. When the presenter did stray from the script, the police would stop the talk and break up the gathering; neither extemporaneous elaborations nor even answers to audience questions were permitted.[8] The conference delegates therefore petitioned the authorities for more freedom in conducting educational endeavors, and in particular for permission to engage the population in discussion as a method of disease prophylaxis. Yet in view of the government's opposition to all forms of free speech, its suspicion of public gatherings, and the medical profession's gradual assertion of professional identity and ensuing radicalization, it is not surprising that these proscriptions remained in effect until the fall of the autocracy in 1917.

Given these constraints, and despite appeals by individual physicians, it was only after the February Revolution that the medical profession revisited the subject of sex education on an institutional level. In a lecture delivered at the All-Russian Meeting for the Fight against Venereal Disease, sponsored by the Pirogov Society and held in June 1917, Dr. I. M. Malyshev and Professor A. I. Liants described the conditions that made such educational initiatives imperative. Of the situation in Moscow, the doctors claimed that rates of venereal disease in the city had reached "alarming" proportions, greatly exacerbated by the conditions of war. Gonorrhea was spreading rapidly and was a potential cause of not only death and disability but also sterility, thereby contributing to a likely demographic crisis. Increasing rates of infection led the doctors to argue that syphilis occupied a "position of honor among such scourges of humanity as tuberculosis and alcoholism, and no other epidemic can compare with it in terms of the number of its victims." This was a decidedly pointed comparison: although the problems of alcoholism and tuberculosis had received the attention of both government and society in the past, the speakers maintained that the same could not be said for venereal disease. As a cause it was virtually ignored by the various volunteer groups and philanthropic societies, who approached the issue only in terms of the "white slave trade," and it was battled by the government only indirectly, through the regulation of prostitutes. Therefore in addition to the efforts made to combat prostitution, Malyshev and Liants insisted on the need for "energetic propaganda" against venereal disease, to be conducted among both the common people *(prostoi narod)* and the intelligentsia. Physicians were encouraged to use every means at their disposal: lectures, discussion groups, drawings, brochures, visual aids, and museum exhibits to familiarize the public with the "proper understanding" of these diseases.[9]

The speakers also called the conference's attention to the role of pornography in the corruption of the young, leading them on the path to venereal infection. "Society should remember that pornographic literature and various pornographic images, abundantly available in films, theatrical farces, etc., greatly contribute to the early debauching of youth." They therefore recommended that older students be exposed in a "rational" and "careful" manner to the fundamentals of sex, with a particular emphasis on the safety of abstinence.[10]

In its resolutions, the conference expressed strong support for the speakers' recommendations. In addition to the decision to repeal the regulation of prostitution, the conference elected a fifteen-person central committee charged with directing the country's fight against venereal disease, including among its tasks the elaboration of an educational agenda. By April 29, 1918, this group had been absorbed into the All-Russian Commission for the Fight against Venereal Disease of the Union of Medical Boards. In October this authority was incorporated in turn into the structure of the new Commissariat of Public Health.[11] The Central Commission for the Fight against Venereal Disease was institutionally located within the commissariat's Subsection for the Fight against Venereal Disease. It held its first meeting in late October 1918, under the leadership of V. A. Zuev.

The need for a program of sex education was expressed in the commission's earliest pronouncements, both in terms of the general fight against venereal disease and in relation to the more specific problem of prostitution. In its first progress report to the Narkomzdrav board, the group identified the production of agitation and propaganda (agitprop) and the "normal" introduction of sexual enlightenment as crucial to its mission to educate the population and prevent the spread of disease. Similarly, at a meeting devoted to the subject of prostitution on February 6, 1919, the commission reiterated that the prevention of sexually transmitted ailments would figure prominently in its work.[12] That the sex education movement originated as a tactic in the battle against venereal disease was crucial to its later development and ultimately its fate. Initially, education focused on disease prevention, the avoidance of prostitutes, and for younger members of the population, the advocacy of abstinence; this approach was gradually expanded as other medical specialists incorporated sexual enlightenment into their broader campaigns to improve everyday life.[13] Nonetheless, the initial link between sexuality and sickness persisted, shaping sexual enlightenment's content as well as its representation of sexual health and normalcy.

The commission devoted a considerable portion of its first budgetary allotment to educational work, yet in the initial years of its activity attention was more focused on understanding contemporary sexuality than on changing it. On September 4, 1919, Dr. Gel'man, an acknowledged "expert" in the field, delivered a presentation on the sexual hygiene of youth. Five months later, the prominent Russian zemstvo physician D. N. Zhbankov appeared at the commission's February 27 meeting and urged it to publish the responses to a survey he had supervised over a decade earlier.[14] Commissioned in 1909 by the Pirogov Society to investigate the sex lives of the young, the project was terminated by the police, who also confiscated a large portion of the findings.[15] Of the 325 pages of responses that had been saved, over a hundred contained the "confessions" of female students in several Moscow institutions of higher education. It was these documents that Zhbankov proposed the commission publish, explaining that the Pirogov Society (still in existence) was unable to do so for both technical and financial reasons. Zhbankov praised the richness of the materials, "the likes of which have never been printed either in Russia or in Western Europe."[16]

The commission chose two members to assess the documents and report back at a later meeting. In their presentation and the general discussion that followed it at the March 20, 1919, meeting, the members of the commission agreed with Zhbankov's evaluation of the material's worth.[17] Referring to the general ignorance on matters relating to sex, revealed by the students' responses, one doctor pointed to the survey as proof of the need for a program of sex hygiene among young people. However, one of the physicians who issued the preliminary report, Dr. Bogrov, expressed concern that Zhbankov's survey might have an "unfavorable influence on the younger [*podrastaiushchee*] generation," since "negative phenomena" were simply described without the provision of any practical information about how to fight against such behaviors. He urged the committee to publish a limited portion of Zhbankov's survey, with access restricted to doctors, pedagogues, and social activists.[18] Eventually the commission resolved that the findings appear "in a solid, scientific journal without a wide readership and in this way stay out of the hands of the simply curious." They recommended that the materials be published as soon as possible, either in a collection devoted to venereology or alternatively in a psychiatric journal, since "there is a lot of psychopathology evident in the survey's confessions." Entitled "About the Sex Lives of Women Students," Zhbankov's study eventually appeared in 1921, in the journal of the Ukrainian Commissariat of Health. It was soon followed by many other surveys assessing the sexual behavior of different segments of the population (students, medical personnel, factory workers, and so on), the results of which were frequently cited by enlighteners in their work.[19]

The commission's discussion of the Zhbankov survey offers a preliminary glimpse at how medical educators would approach sexuality over the course of the decade. In their analysis, ignorance of sexual matters was equated with pathology, hence the choice of a venereological or psychiatric journal as the preferred publication site for the study. The desire to exclude the "simply curious" and prevent "unfavorable influence" suggests a concern with issues of access that would remain a central preoccupation of sexual enlighteners. Sex education, it would seem, was not meant for everyone; moreover, the advice provided to its intended recipients would be delivered carefully and accompanied by the editorial commentary necessary to ensure the proper direction. Such instruction ultimately occupied a much larger percentage of content than any specific details about "the facts of life."

Over the next few years, although individual health workers incorporated information on sex into their professional activities, there was little specific direction from the center on how to approach the issue. The lack of attention was due in part to the confusion involved in organizing the new commissariat, the instability of its relationship to the local health departments, and the priority given to addressing the health epidemics and emergencies that accompanied the wars and Revolution.[20] The introduction of NEP in 1921 and the transfer of financial obligations to local budgets led to severe cutbacks in funding for work in education and a marked decrease in activity. For instance, sex education was on the agenda of the First All-Russian Congress of Sanitary Enlightenment, scheduled to take place March 15, 1921. On March 3, the Committee of Councils of Worker, Peasant, and Red Army Deputies canceled this and all other congresses (except for the Tenth Party Congress and the Congress of Railroad Workers) until further notice, owing to "housing and production difficulties."[21]

A month later, the director of Narkomzdrav's Subsection for the Fight against Venereal Disease, V. A. Pospelov, complained that the delivery of public lectures on venereal disease and related topics had been almost completely suspended. Expressing the need for new lecturers, he reported that the subsection would be sending letters to the city's venereologists and other specialists, asking them to participate and to indicate the hours, days, and subject matter of their proposed presentations. Yet as of the following November, the central commission nonetheless concluded that endeavors in this realm remained unsatisfactory. In their work plan for 1923, therefore, they emphasized the need to increase sexual enlightenment activity and to provide behavioral guidelines for the population and teaching aids for medical educators.[22]

In addition to the central commission, several other medical organizations under the jurisdiction of Narkomzdrav identified sex education as central to their activity. These were principally the State Venereological Institute (GVI) and the State Institute of Social Hygiene (GISG).[23] Sexual enlightenment also developed as a subfield of sanitary enlightenment, the broader program of health and hygiene education that emerged as a new medical specialty after 1918 (see Chapter 4). Thus health educators working for the commissariat's Division of Sanitary Enlightenment or the Institute of Sanitary Culture, to name only a few, would be charged with producing materials on specific sex-related topics, often coordinating their efforts with one another and the other institutions mentioned above.

Within GVI and its journal, *Venereology and Dermatology* (*Venerologiia i dermatologiia*), the subjects of sexuality and sexual enlightenment were the responsibility of the Division of Social Venereology, identified as a "new Soviet field" in the journal's first issue. The division oversaw the publication of pamphlets, posters, and leaflets; conducted lectures for patients and at factories and clubs throughout the city; supervised its labor clinic for prostitutes (*trudovoi profilaktorii*), which combined treatment for venereal disease with job training and education; and arranged exhibits on venereal disease and the sex question at city health clinics (see Figure 1.1).[24] The division also oversaw the activities of the Committee for Making Labor and Lifestyle Healthy (KOTiB), a voluntary organization comprising workers from neighboring factories who engaged in "social work" at the institute. The principal figure at GVI associated with sex education was V. M. Bronner, who served as editor in chief of its journal and head of the Social Venereology Division.[25]

The Institute of Social Hygiene (GISG) likewise devoted considerable attention to issues of sexuality. Founded as the Museum of Social Hygiene in 1919 within Narkomzdrav's Division of Sanitary Enlightenment, it was given independent institutional status in June 1923. Like GVI, the institute was committed to establishing "Soviet social hygiene" as a scientific discipline and subject in medical school curricula.[26] It published its own scholarly journal, *Social Hygiene (Sotsial'naia gigiena)*, and a considerable amount of popular literature on the sex question. GISG was particularly active in establishing ties with foreign groups and individuals interested in these matters. At the Copenhagen meeting of the World League for Sex Reform in 1928, for instance, the report on the sexual problem in the USSR was delivered by the institute's representative at the congress.[27]

Organizationally, GISG's work in this area was centered on what by 1927 would be called its Sexology Office. The office organized its responsibilities into three divisions: research on the sexual behavior of the population (this division conducted many of the surveys on sex during the decade); questions of sexual enlightenment and education; and the problem of prostitution. The Sexology Office also designed the section on sexual hygiene for a Narkomzdrav-sponsored exhibition on health protection in 1928. The display included segments on heredity and eugenics, infertility and its causes, abortion (reasons, statistics, and the fight against it), the hygiene of maternity, and birth control. Associated with the office was a scientific sexology study group—composed of specialists working in the field of sexology, as well as other interested individuals including physicians, biologists, pedagogues, and pedologists—that met to formulate educational methodology and discuss participants' work in this area.[28] Among the social hygienists most closely connected to sex education were G. A. Batkis and Commissar Semashko.

There was a great deal of overlap and cooperation among the Narkomzdrav institutions engaged in sexual enlightenment. Physicians from both GVI and GISG served on the Central Commission for the Fight against Venereal Disease and its subdivision, the Council for the Fight against Prostitution. As of 1922, both the commission and the council were chaired by Bronner. The central commission was given the responsibility of organizing the exhibits on venereal disease, prostitution, and the sex question at the Museum of Social Hygiene.[29] In 1925, the State Institute of Social Hygiene, the State Venereology Institute, and the State Neuropsychiatric Dispensary joined forces in establishing the Counseling Center for Sexual Hygiene (see Chapter 3). Finally, physicians from other disciplines

СИФИЛИС

Figure 1.1—Venereal Disease Clinic Lecture, Moscow, mid-1920s. Photo no. 14210, Poster and Photograph Collection (NITs "Meditsinskii muzei" RAMN).

working on the sex question participated in a variety of specialist confer-ences addressing the topic, including meetings of sanitary enlighteners, physical culture specialists, pedologists, forensic medical experts, psy-choneurologists, and especially meetings organized by venereologists, who retained the institutional "leadership" position in this realm.

It was not until June 1923, at the First All-Union Congress for the Fight against Venereal Disease, that the center first tackled the issue of sex edu-cation on an official and programmatic level. The timing of this focus was influenced by several developments subsequent to the first appearance of sex education on the Narkomzdrav agenda. As Bronner himself explained at the congress, it had taken the commissariat until then to recover and stabilize financially after the introduction of self-financing in 1921.[30]

In October 1918 the country's first Code on Marriage, the Family, and Guardianship was ratified, legalizing divorce and making both marriage and divorce easily obtainable.[31] As a result, marriage and divorce rates in-creased markedly, especially in the cities, prompting the accusation that many "abused" the new laws. As Wendy Goldman relates, the Marxist framers of the code had been guided by the belief that marriage and law, like the state itself, would eventually disappear, no longer necessary in the socialist future. While communal dining rooms, public laundries, and child care facilities liberated women from their domestic burdens, increased educational and employment opportunities would guarantee their financial independence. "Free union would gradually replace marriage as the state ceased to interfere in the union between the sexes. . . . The family, stripped of its previous social functions, would gradually wither away, leaving in its place fully autonomous, equal individuals free to choose their partners on the basis of love and mutual respect."[32]

Yet it soon became apparent that the socialist vision of free union embodied in the 1918 code had "tragic, unforeseen consequences," especially for the mothers, housewives, and unskilled workers who were abandoned without any other means of support. When NEP was introduced, it resulted in widespread economic instability. The high rates of unemployment and cutbacks in social services associated with this financial policy further exacerbated women's dire economic position, leaving many (especially those with children) no recourse but the streets and prostitution. Doctors feared that these developments were producing an epidemic of venereal disease, significantly increasing the already high levels recorded in conjunction with the demobilization of soldiers at the end of the Civil War. Doctors also worried about the general loosening of morals believed to have occurred during wartime and now exacerbated by the debauchery and vice on view in the bars and cafes open since 1921.

Irrespective of whether Russians believed in the existence of a sexual and moral crisis, they were nonetheless extremely interested in the sex question. Furthermore, many individuals and organizations had already mobilized to meet this demand for information. As early as 1920, a reviewer in *Book and Revolution* (*Kniga i revoliutstiia*) commented on the collections on the sex question that flooded the marketplace and sold out immediately, regardless of their quality, which was usually "dubious."[33] Thus the physicians who had appointed themselves society's sex educators now lagged behind and competed with others for this privilege.

Of the many presentations at the congress calling for a more systematic and structured response to venereal disease and sex education, the report by I. D. Strashun, the director of Narkomzdrav's Division of Sanitary Enlightenment, was the most specific in its recommendations for control over the process of education.[34] Strashun proposed that educators make use of a wide array of venues and approaches in order to reach the population. Each of his suggestions emphasized the dominant role of the doctor as the mediator of this knowledge. In youth clubs, for example, physicians would organize and direct study groups and conduct lectures on the sex question and sexual hygiene. Excursions to houses of enlightenment and special movable exhibitions, both accompanied by medical personnel, would be made available to the public. While the participation of such organizations as the Zhenotdel and the Komsomol was encouraged, Strashun stressed that the supervision of this education must lie with the departments of sanitary enlightenment and the venereological dispensaries and that their leadership role be legally mandated.

Strashun explained that the presence of doctors was necessary to ensure that the topic of sex be handled in a scientific manner. In addition to the regulation of content, publicity for educational initiatives also had to meet certain standards of appropriateness. He specified that popular lectures be organized "without loudly publicized, sensationalist advertisements." Although he commended the use of agitational trials, he nonetheless advised that such productions avoid the appearance of a sensation or spectacle.[35] Recalling the central commission's desire to prevent access to the "simply curious," the underlying message of Strashun's remarks was that sex education should not be too sexy. Sensationalism tainted the educators themselves and the educational content and, it seems, encouraged the wrong kind of audience.

In another paper at the congress, on the subject of medical ethics, the venereologist N. L. Rossiianskii criticized those physicians who profited from the ignorance and embarrassment of the population regarding venereal diseases. Unqualified doctors interested only in making money lured patients to their offices with showy ads promising quick and discreet treatment. In order to combat this phenomenon, he recommended that the advertisement of venereal disease treatment be banned from newspapers and public spaces. He also urged that individual practitioners be prohibited from publishing popular works on sex and venereal disease without the express permission of Narkomzdrav, since "some doctors, by way of advertising, publish popular books . . . whose contents have not been confirmed scientifically and are completely inappropriate."[36]

The conference reaffirmed this position in its resolutions. It decreed that the center take charge in publishing "appropriate" popular literature and visual aids such as albums, posters, and slides. To deal with the vast amount of popular literature produced "solely for commercial gain" rather than in the interests of enlightenment, the conference resolved that the publication of such works without the appropriate permission of the health commissariat was "impermissible"; it also voted for a complete ban on advertisements by venereologists.[37] Concluding that the "successful fight against prostitution and venereal disease would be possible only if the young generation were given the correct sex education," the congress urged that Narkomzdrav and the People's Commissariat of Enlightenment *(Narkompros)* begin to elaborate "without delay" a methodology of sex education corresponding to "contemporary conditions." The attendees also selected sex education as one of the programmatic questions on the agenda of the second congress, to be held in Khar'kov in May 1925.

At a planning session for the Khar'kov conference, the organizational bureau elaborated on the expectations for the coming meeting. Sex education would be considered at the congress on a purely informational (nonbinding) level, to acquaint attendees with current research and thinking on the "sex problem." Focusing attention on the matter would raise awareness of the need for a special gathering of "competent" experts who would use the congress's resolutions as directives for its future work. Presentations would be divided into four categories: the biological bases of sexuality both normal and pathological, the sex problem as a social problem, current thinking on the subject of sexual pedagogy, and research on the sex question.[38]

Over the course of several days at the second All-Union Congress, sessions were held on a variety of sex-related topics. Yet of the eighteen presentations directly addressing the subject of sexuality, only one report, by the social hygienist G. A. Batkis, provided specific suggestions for educators. Batkis divided the content of sexual enlightenment for adults into three sections: the biology of sexual attraction, the sex question as a social problem, and sexual hygiene as both a public (*obshchestvennyi*) and an individual concern. As a general rule, he endorsed the practice of communicating scientific material in "popular form" as long as such popularization was strictly materialist in its approach, did no damage to the material's "scientificity," was devoid of "tendentious teleology," and explained the question's social side from a Marxist viewpoint.[39]

In his remarks on the biology of sexual attraction, Batkis asserted that there was no place for "anthropomorphically idealized interpretations" in discussions of sexual attraction in animals, or for that matter in comparisons between animal and human behavior. Moreover, explanations of the role of the endocrine glands in sexual attraction were to focus on their connection to and interrelationship with the external environment. This portion of his advice was ignored (see Chapter 2).

With respect to sexual hygiene, Batkis stipulated that any treatment of the topic should be based upon the principles of public behavior. He recommended, however, that educators restrict their remarks to the level of general behavioral criteria—such as responsibility before the collective for one's health or for the expense of one's energy—without attempting to provide detailed public norms for different aspects of sexual life. Instructors were to emphasize the harmful effect of early sexual activity on the overall development of the organism and the need for abstinence until the attainment of full sexual and physical maturity. They were to take care not to treat masturbation "as a special disease and specific source of diverse pathological conditions." The subject of birth control was to be approached "objectively," taking into consideration its significance in the fight against abortion. Specific questions about sexuality were to be handled individually, in separate medical consultations. Finally, Batkis considered it mandatory that the discussion of personal sexual hygiene be combined with the hygiene of maternity and eugenics.[40]

As for instructional models, Batkis warned educators to approach popular publications cautiously and to question their "scientific value." To review such works, he proposed the publication of a guidebook, to be edited by the leading scientific institutions in the field. He also recommended the creation of a methodological bureau for sexual enlightenment workers, and the introduction of the topic into medical school curricula.[41]

The call for methodological guidance in matters of sex education was reaffirmed in the resolutions of the congress, which concluded "with satisfaction":

> The sociopolitical enviroment of the life of workers in the USSR provide extensive possibilities for the correct and appropriate expenditure of energy by the population, and especially by the younger generation, thus creating favorable preconditions for the practical realization of the new sexual pedagogy's tasks.

Two years after the first congress, it was no longer just a "necessity" but "a matter of urgency" that the appropriate institutions of health, education, and political enlightenment come together to address the growing need for leadership in this field.[42] Yet, while individual educators continued to lecture and lead discussion groups, and health organizations continued to produce significant quantities of educational material, it was not until 1930 that such a meeting took place.

On May 31, 1930, a group of physicians convened at the Institute of Social Hygiene to lay the groundwork for a scientific center for sexual pedagogy. Plans for this bureau had grown out of the preparations begun by educators for the 1931 meeting of the World League for Sex Reform, scheduled to be held in Moscow.[43] According to its charter, the new center would provide the organization and direction that sexual enlightenment so urgently required. The aim was to coordinate popular and scientific publications, produce methodological materials, supervise the various sexology research projects, and conduct sex education training classes for teachers, parents, doctors, and youth group leaders. Other proposed objectives included developing ties with regional scientific institutes and serving as a central repository for relevant works produced throughout the country and abroad. Most important, the scientific center would finally put an end to the needless duplication of sex enlightenment projects and efforts, by facilitating contacts with the many institutions and individuals working in this area. Included in the bureau's proposed membership roster were representatives from the Komsomol, the Institute of Social Hygiene, the Institute of Methods for Work in the Schools, the Institute for the Study of Criminality, the Institute of Scientific Pedagogy, the Venereological Institute, and the commissariats of Public Health and Enlightenment.[44]

Yet this organizational effort occurred too late. By May 1930 the reverberations of the Cultural Revolution were already being felt throughout the scientific world, even though sexual enlightenment publications and endeavors continued for another year. The founding meeting of the scientific center for sexual pedagogy appears to have been its last; the institution left no further trace in either archival or published sources. Medical publications were similarly reticent about the reasons behind the change in location for the World League for Sex Reform meeting, which convened in Brno in 1932 instead of in Moscow.[45] The health ministry did not broach the subject of sex education again until the 1940s, prompted once more by the upheavals and diseases of wartime.

Controlling the Sex Question — Doctors and the Problem of Sexy Science

"The sex question has become, one might say, a trendy topic." Thus began a 1925 *Izvestiia* editorial by Commissar Semashko, entitled "How Not to Write about the Sex Question."[46] A commentary on the "misfortune" that occurs "when cobblers begin to bake pies," this article in effect established *who* should not write about the sex question. Remarking upon the stupidity and vulgarity evident in many of the ubiquitous lectures, debates, and publications on sex, Semashko nonetheless dismissed these as part of the phenomenon surrounding any "hot" issue. The commissar reserved his criticism for those who should have known better: "It is much sadder when the crudest, most unforgivable mistakes come from the pens of comrades whose opinions people are accustomed to heeding." He had two groups of cobblers and comrades in mind. The first were Party members. Referring to Martin Nikolaevich Liadov's *Questions of Everyday Life*, Semashko declared that everyone would have been better off if its author had limited his scholarly attention to the history of the Party. He continued:

> What particularly confused Comrade Liadov is A. Zalkind's article, "The Sex Question from the Communist Point of View" (oh, how easily the phrase "from a communist point of view" is bandied about here, it's almost criminal!) . . . And this is called the "communist" point of view! (undoubtedly, Comrade Zalkind admired his own "class analysis" when he wrote this absurdity)![47]

Semashko's comments speak to a jurisdictional conflict with Party ideologues for control over the domain of the sex question. In part this was a disagreement over method; the medical approach to sexuality stressed education rather than the flat-out condemnation and prohibition characteristic of Party writings on sex. Also at issue was the overt linking of sexuality with the rhetoric of communism and, more important, with Party writers' invocation of science. While Semashko expressed disapproval at Zalkind's exploitation of the language of communism, most troublesome was the fact that it was used to justify bad science. Zalkind and Liadov argued that sexuality had become unnatural; they identified the sexual depravity of Russia's youth as the most alarming evidence of sexuality's separation from nature.[48] As evidence of the unnatural state of contemporary sexual relations, they pointed to the fact that women menstruated monthly, unlike animals, whose period of heat (*techka*) occurred once a year. Semashko dismissed this and similar analyses of the immorality of the young, which likewise relied on faulty science, as "complete nonsense and sophistry. . . . Without a knowledge of biology in general and the role of the endocrine glands, in particular, one shouldn't put pen to paper or open one's mouth to pronounce judgments regarding the sex question."[49]

When Party writers (with their own distinct and well-established basis of authority) invoked scientific language and theories, they threatened doctors' control of this particular area of knowledge and hence their jurisdictional claims. This conflict may also explain the infrequency of references to the Party in medical publications on sex, although many sexual enlighteners, including Semashko, were Bolsheviks. The Bolshevik Revolution may have made it possible to approach life from a scientific viewpoint, but medical legitimacy in the realm of sex hinged upon fluency in the higher language of science.

Semashko identified the second group of cobblers as physicians, a point that explains why the psychiatrist Zalkind merited particularly harsh criticism. His sin was further compounded because his work appeared in a collection edited by another doctor: "The collection was published under the editorship of Doctor (no joke: Doctor!) Kalmanson." In a second editorial in *Izvestiia*, entitled "Ignorance and Pornography beneath the Mask of Enlightenment, Science and Literature," Semashko's attack on those members of the medical profession engaging in inappropriate sex education became even more vituperative:

> The bacchanalia of publications on the "sex question" continues. Into the book market is thrown literature that is sometimes dirty, sometimes outrageously ignorant. . . . And what is most shocking of all is that this trashy literature takes refuge under the bold name of enlightenment, scientific research, and similarly lofty goals.[50]

Much of Semashko's invective focused upon a series of brochures by medical authors entitled "The Sex Question in Easily Accessible Sketches" and published by the Odessa firm The Torch-bearer (Svetoch). He criticized their content as unscientific and their presentation as sensationalist, accusing the publishers of trying to attract readers: "With titles one screaming louder than the next . . . each is filled with lewd details and lewd drawings. On every booklet a warning in red (what else) states: 'with illustrations.'" Other doctors were charged with following Svetoch's cue, publishing books containing bad science, primarily for profit. Concerning *Questions of Sexual Life*, by Dr. Zdravomyslov, Semashko wrote: "From a booklet by one remarkable doctor (ha ha) we learn, for example, that for 'sexual frigidity' 'spraying a solution of eau de cologne' is recommended. . . . And this nonsense sustained a second printing!!!"

Yet scientific ignorance comprised only half the target of Semashko's criticism. He singled out for attack another "zealous attempt at 'scientific research' in the sphere of sex": a survey distributed among students at a technical high school in Riazan', which had been compiled under the supervision of a local sanitary doctor.

> Reading this survey, one involuntarily asks the question: How in the world is this all being done in broad daylight, almost under the nose of Moscow? If the author apparently finds some pleasure in the "scientific study" of the responses, then why in the world isn't he being treated for nymphomania, instead of being given the disgraceful opportunity to corrupt the young in broad daylight?

In seeking to protect both the purity of science and the reputation of the medical profession, Semashko confronted a central dilemma of sexual enlightenment: how to discuss sex without being accused of promoting it, and thereby engaging in pornography. The answer provides the key to the nature of the sex education program, and yet another explanation for its origins within the anti–venereal disease movement. With very few exceptions, the idea of sexual satisfaction was rarely mentioned by Soviet sex educators, and the mechanics of the sexual act, if discussed at all, were dealt with on a purely physiological level. Instead, enlighteners promoted the idea of sexual restraint, with the needs of collective health clearly outweighing a concern for individual pleasure in sexual matters. This "desexualization" of sexual enlightenment only increased the implied connection between sex and sickness.

There was a second motivation behind Semashko's interest in protecting the reputation of the medical community. Such "ignorance and pornography" not only reflected badly on the profession but also displayed an independence of action and thought that challenged the authority of the center to control the medical personnel presumably under its jurisdiction. In other words, it was the fact that these activities occurred "under the nose of Moscow," "in broad daylight" without the sanction or approval of the center, that so threatened Semashko. That the issue in this case was less one of content than of opposition to local initiative becomes clear when the Riazan' survey is compared to another survey on sex produced under the jurisdiction and with the strong approval of Narkomzdrav. Conducted by Dr. Gel'man in 1922 among students at Sverdlovsk Communist University, this "approved" survey asked almost the same questions, in a very similar format, as those of the Riazan' questionnaire:

Questions from the Riazan' survey

Do you lead an active sex life? If not, why?

At what age did you begin to have sex?

How often do you have sexual intercourse?

Do you feel satisfied with sexual intercourse? If not, why?

What do you think is better—a long-term sexual relationship or frequent short-term ties?

If you are married, do you have extramarital sexual relations?

Are you in a long-term relationship with one man (woman), with two, with three, more?[51]

Questions from the Gel'man survey

Have you had sexual intercourse?

How old were you when you first had sexual intercourse?

Are your sexual relationships with a man/woman of a long-term or short-term nature?

If to this point you have not begun sexual activity, what has kept you from this: lack of sexual desire, circumstances, absence of love, moral considerations, fear of venereal diseases or other reasons?

If married, do you have sexual relationships on the side?

What would you like your sex life to be: marriage, a long-term, free relationship, short-term relationships, casual encounters, using prostitutes?[52]

Moreover, the published study based on this survey included extensive excerpts from the answers themselves. For instance, Gel'man commented on the provocative, unscientific, and superficial tone of the majority of sexual enlightenment publications. He observed that not even the famous Forel's *The Sex Question*, which many of the respondents had reported reading, was free from such "unnecessary moralizing and sentimental Philistinism." It was not surprising, therefore, that a few students were aroused by the book, with one describing how he began to masturbate under its influence. Gel'man then proceeded to list other authors who had had a similar effect on the respondents (Weininger, Zola, Pisemskii), perhaps providing curious minds with ample suggestions for future, titillating reading. Yet Gel'man's book enjoyed universal praise and was favorably cited on numerous occasions by

Semashko himself. Similarly, many of the very same illustrations that Semashko labeled lewd in The Torch-bearer series found their way into more scholarly Narkomzdrav-endorsed publications of the period.[53]

In fact the "accessibility," financial and otherwise, of the pamphlets produced by The Torch-bearer (whose name Semashko noted ironically) and similar publications was a dominant concern of Narkomzdrav at this time. Three months earlier a report of Narkomzdrav's own publishing division to the commissariat's board raised the issue of the harm done to state medical publishing by such private popular medical presses as Svetoch, Kosmos, *Practical Medicine* (*Prakticheskaia meditsina*), and *Contemporary Problems* (*Sovremennye problemy*). The publishing section sought a major budgetary increase to meet the growing demands for popular literature on health issues and to compete financially with the huge, inexpensive editions of this type of medical literature, "a part of which is extremely dubious from the point of view of Soviet ideology," put out by these houses. The board approved the increase in order to fund bigger editions that could be produced at lower prices, explaining that "expanding production at the present time is especially justified by the need to compete against private publishers of popular sanitary enlightenment literature."[54]

The records of the publishing division indicate that Narkomzdrav did indeed follow through with its intentions to increase the publication of popular health works. During the 1927–1928 year, for instance, its publication plan included nine different popular titles on the sex question, adding up to 260,000 copies, and thirteen thousand posters. For the same time period, Narkomzdrav's Division for the Protection of Mothers and Infants *(Okhmatmlad)* proposed seven popular works totaling 85,000 copies. Along with its list of titles, Okhmatmlad's report to the board included a code to identify the appropriate audience for each publication: (a) midlevel office personnel and advanced readers; (b) workers; (c) women workers and women peasants; (d) peasants; (e) youth, Komsomol members, and attendees of worker schools (*rabfakovtsy*). The State Medical Publishing House (GMI) also devoted considerable attention to this issue. Listed in its plan for 1929 were twenty brochures on the sex question, for a total of 177,000 copies, likewise broken up into categories targeting specific segments of the population, and ten thousand posters.[55]

Semashko and Narkomzdrav's concerns about the quality of available works were shared by popular health publications. Thus journals not only explored sexual questions on their own pages but also attempted to control the information on sexuality that readers received beyond their publications. An article in the popular *Hygiene and Health of the Worker and Peasant Family* (*Gigiena i zdorov'e rabochei i krest'ianskoi sem'i*) on "How to Make Your Sexual Lifestyle Healthy" cautioned readers to avoid boulevard literature and to choose books "written by experienced specialists." The author then assigned the following homework, along with a recommended reading list:

1. Read the literature on sexuality listed at bottom. Try to see the films: "Love in Nature," "Abortion," "Gonorrhea," and "The Truth of Life."

2. Organize a debate or discussion with your comrades about sexuality and wage a battle against abnormal displays [of sexuality] using concrete examples taken from the lifestyles of your comrades.

3. For questions related to sexual experiences, see a doctor. Remember about the dangers to health associated with early sex.[56]

Similarly, health journal columns entitled "What to Read on the Sex Question" promised to help readers wade through the "inappropriate rubbish, geared toward unhealthy curiosity," and to avoid unscientific, profit-motivated works, the majority of which were "inaccessible" to the working class.[57] For the most part, the featured pamphlets received favorable recommendations. Writers briefly described a work's subject matter and noted the publisher, number of pages, and price. Reviews also indicated the kind of language used (popular, scientific), and the most appropriate audience for the work.

Dr. Nestrukh's *Sexual Attraction in Nature*, for instance, received a favorable review: "This booklet explains the basis of sexual attraction in animals and humans. [It has] good illustrations, is presented in an interesting manner, and is accessible to the reader with little preliminary training." Although it provided important information, Professor Okinchits's *Miscarriage and Birth Control Methods* was deemed "insufficiently popular," understandable therefore only to the "intelligent reader." "Not a bad-looking publication," it was nonetheless considered expensive at thirty kopecks (most approved publications ranged from fifteen to twenty kopecks). On the other hand, Dr. Bremener's *What Everyone Should Know about Syphilis* was recommended to the semi- and fully literate, as well as to those barely able to sound out syllables, since it presented information in a form of agitational verse. The work was published on "good paper in large print" and cost twelve kopecks. The uninitiated reader interested in learning about male sexual disorders was advised to read *Sexual Impotence* by Dr. Iakobzon, a "leading specialist on the sex question." For the more advanced reader, Professor R. M. Fronshtein's brochure on the same subject was recommended.[58]

Only one journal identified publications of which it disapproved. Echoing the concerns raised earlier that year by Commissar Semashko, *Hygiene and Health* also denounced Svetoch's Sex Question series as a calculated, provocative "hack-job": "Under no circumstances can the majority of brochures in this series be recommended. . . . [Like Semashko,] we must also caution the proletarian reader away from such literature and only approve of scientifically accurate brochures, written by qualified specialists and popularizers."[59] Svetoch's pamphlets were not recommended by any of these journals, although *Path to Health* (*Put' k zdorov'iu*) and *Toward a*

New Lifestyle (*Za novyi byt*) included works from Kosmos and *Contemporary Problems*, both of which had been criticized as "dubious" by Narkomzdrav's publishing division.

Defining the Sex Question

Devoting considerable attention to the subject of how not to (and who should not) write about the sex question, authors were far more vague in specifying precisely what the sex question was. Dr. Ivanovskii defined it as embracing such issues as how a normal sex life should correctly proceed, the forms that sexual cohabitation (between a man and a woman) might assume, the meaning of marriage, and the significance of the family in contemporary society. Yet such definitions were a rarity; readers interested in gaining a precise understanding of the sex question were left to extrapolate from analyses of what had made it "painful" and how to treat it. They might also deduce an answer by considering what topics were not covered in sexual enlightenment and hence were excluded from the sex question. Sex with children, coercive or violent sex, anal sex, and oral sex were all listed by Dr. Rozenblium as "deviant" sexual practices. Yet because they were far beyond sexual enlightenment's boundaries of sexual normalcy, such behaviors were rarely considered, or even named, by educators. One of the only writers to mention these "perversions," Rozenblium quickly concluded: "We will not spread any more information about possible forms that sexual perversions can take. This is not interesting or important to us."[60]

What was the source of the sex question's current "sickness"? On the simplest level, it was attributed to a basic lack of knowledge. The characterization of others' works as dubious or pornographic was a standard feature of sexual enlightenment, yet writers were similarly quick to respond to critics who would challenge the need for information on sex or accuse education of contributing to the problem. Medical authors asserted that premarital sex, sexual precocity, and even abortion and venereal disease were not the consequences of familiarity with the sex question but, rather, a product of the masses' "profound ignorance" in this sphere. It is precisely education, according to Dr. Sigal, that "removes from the sex question the taint of dirtiness, illuminates it from a scientific point of view and provides the chance to examine it soberly, as one examines the acts of digestion, breathing, and other processes in the life of the human organism."[61]

With the prerevolutionary value system discredited, young people sought the "proper path" to sexual knowledge; writers warned that if such guidance were not provided by specialists, it would be given by the street, through the examples of "excess and perversions." In countless pamphlets authors justified their works by focusing upon the dangers of ignorance and hence the need for such scientific intervention. For example, in the introduction to his 1926 brochure *Questions of Sexual Life*, Dr. Ia. I. Zdravomyslov—whose transparently allegorical name (literally "Dr. Healthy-Thinker") turns out to be felicitous rather than a pseudonym, and who was himself singled out by Semashko for his own "scientific ignorance"—pledged to provide scientific responses to "the masses of the population, as they awake from the slumber of age-old ignorance, doggedly searching for answers and explanations [about sex]."[62]

At the same time, however, sexual enlighteners acknowledged the need to tread carefully in this realm. An editorial on the sex question in the popular health journal *Path to Health* made a distinction between appropriate and inappropriate sexual curiosity. The piece described the two types of letters received at the journal on the subject of sex. The first expressed "the desire to know, to understand, to pull back the curtain of 'sweet secrecy' with which bourgeois lust has surrounded questions of sex." Such a motivation was deemed "legitimate and healthy." Not so the second group of letters, which exhibited the desire "to dig into the 'secrets' of sex, tickle one's nerves, glance through a chink in the wall at what goes on behind closed doors." This heightened sense of curiosity was diagnosed as "sick, unhealthy" and was attributed to "an improper upbringing, a withdrawal from public life, and the desire to lock oneself away in the confines of one's petty inclinations." The editorial nonetheless warned seekers of the curious and the provocative that they would be disappointed in the volume, which was devoted in its entirety to the sex question, as the publication was not intended for such ends and would not satisfy them. This knowledge was meant instead for those workers and peasants who were genuinely committed to providing the proper sex education for their children, to making family and marriage hygienic, and to preventing the spread of venereal disease. In sum, it aimed "to make private and public life healthy." When "the Revolution pulled back the curtain on questions of sex, [a]ll that had been hidden became visible," the piece observed. Now, therefore, the population's sexual depravity was as apparent as its sexual ignorance.[63]

An unhealthy interest in the sex question was only one manifestation of Russia's sexual "crisis." To fully comprehend the "unhealthy state of contemporary sexuality," Dr. Mandels noted the "countless crimes, committed due to sexual attraction; the prevalence of venereal disease among the working class; premature sexual activity on the part of young people; countless divorces and failed marriages concluded thoughtlessly; and the pervasiveness of various sexual deviations, such as masturbation."[64] Others added further evidence to the list, citing sexual excess, casual sex, the abandonment of women and children, and pervasive prostitution. Such unbridled sexuality, according to Dr. Glezer, exhausted young people, weakening their will to fight. He asked: Was such behavior beneficial to the Revolution, to the construction of socialism? The answer was an emphatic no; "this type of sexual life is fatal to the proletarian class, ushering the battle for the new, free, better world not toward life, but toward death."[65]

Such disordered and unhealthy sexuality allegedly interfered with the ability to work and sapped the strength and energy that people might otherwise have devoted to society.[66] That the state lacked the financial means to contend with the consequences of this depraved behavior (especially pregnancy) explained for Semashko why the sex question had become so "acute."[67] While the commissar advocated the use of abortion and birth control to prevent the birth of children parents did not want or could not support, other physicians considered the availability of such procedures and products as further contributing to the crisis. Separated from its biological function, contemporary sex had become unnatural, "solely a source of pleasure."[68] Glezer warned that this desire for sexual satisfaction was "capitalistic" and went a long way toward explaining why the contemporary West faced the demise of its culture. Now Russia confronted a similar dilemma: "Society is in need of fighters," Dr. Uspenskii wrote, but those who devote too much attention to sex are unable to fight, shirking their communal obligations. Significantly, several authors compared those engaged in such irresponsible, wanton promiscuity to parasites.[69]

Enlighteners traced this depravity to those vestiges of the former morality and way of life that still lingered after 1917. Dr. Sigal maintained that in this transitional era, whatever sincere attempts people made to acquire sexual knowledge were matched by examples of "sexual nihilism," reminiscent of the "love leagues" that sprang up after the failed 1905 Revolution. Only one physician, looking on the bright side, interpreted this state of affairs as a positive development. Speaking at the Second All-Union Congress in Khar'kov, Dr. L. V. Pisareva contended that

> The current intensification of the sex question . . . is closely related to the occurrence of the Great Revolution, to the revolutionary rupture of the old way of life, and is conditioned by the process of profound reassessment of values currently taking place as a result of the Revolution. The intensification of the sex problem thus accompanies every great shift in the social structure of a society.[70]

Others were far less optimistic. Of special concern were those young people, Komsomol members in particular, who linked sexual behavior to the Revolution and justified their "licentiousness" by invoking Marxism.[71] Perhaps most troubling was the phenomenon of male Komsomol members ("of course, the unbalanced ones," noted Glezer) branding young women who were not sexually active or interested in casual sex as "petty-bourgeois," a serious charge in Komsomol circles. Like Lenin, Glezer interpreted the frequent changing of sexual partners (under the heading of "free love") as "deeply bourgeois" and indicated a lack of understanding of the Revolution.[72] A few educators were more forgiving. Dr. Rozenblium ascribed this "old morality" to the period of transition, assuring readers that "on the whole, a new relationship between the sexes" was emerging in the youth organization.[73]

Sanitary enlighteners also followed Lenin's lead in assigning particular blame for the youths' "madness" to the "glass of water theory," widely (and mistakenly) attributed to Aleksandra Kollontai.[74] Kollontai was a prominent Bolshevik activist and champion of women's issues who headed the Zhenotdel from 1920 to 1922.[75] Her alleged advocacy of free love was traced to her 1923 article "Make Way for Winged Eros" and to *The Love of Worker Bees*, a collection of fiction published the same year.[76] That "Make Way for Winged Eros" in fact condemned the very behavior Kollontai was accused of promoting—the crude excesses and debased lust she observed during the Civil War era—is beside the point. For our purposes what is important is that the very opposite was imputed to her writings. Once charged, this indictment stuck, reinforced in countless condemnations by Party theorists, Zhenotdel officials, and social activists, in addition to sex educators.[77]

Enlighteners offered a number of explanations for their opposition to Kollontai's ideas. For instance, Glezer claimed that Kollontai's theory posed a serious practical danger to the state, contributing to even higher rates of abortion and abandoned children. Of equal significance was the way such thinking facilitated one's disengagement from society. Dr. Timofeev affirmed the need to "fight against the kind of love that has no other interests," that allows a person to have many lovers at once. Provocatively, Timofeev drew a sharp contrast between this selfish version of love, attributed to Kollontai, and the "correct" interpretation, propounded by Nadezhda Krupskaia. The Kollontia/Krupskaia juxtaposition works on a number of levels, even if Timofeev's aims were more limited: two radically different approaches to sex are embodied by two strikingly different female public figures, with the "good" woman (Krupskaia, Lenin's widow) advocating a healthy balance and the "bad" woman (the unmarried Kollontai) crusading for debauchery. In Krupskaia's view, as represented by Timofeev, "the only form of love permitted is one that does not allow a person to forget one's social responsibilities."[78]

Indeed, despite the disapproval expressed in the *Path to Health* editorial addressed to those peeking behind closed doors or through chinks in the wall, the sex question could by no means be considered a personal or private one. Sexuality had long ago "ceased to be the business of individuals."[79] Because the new society could not be fully achieved until the populace was sexually healthy, the sex question automatically became a social question, a matter of public concern and (medical) intervention.[80] Imagining sex in the Soviet future, Dr. Glezer promised that one day it would again become a private affair, after both the state and the law had withered away. Perhaps unwittingly, Glezer recapitulates the utopian logic of "scientific" Marxism itself, with sexual privacy as the promised reward on the endlessly receding communist horizon. But as long as the sexual problem remained a serious social problem, society would be forced to "regulate" and "normalize" sexual behavior.[81] For their part, medical educators focused their efforts in this realm not so much on surveillance of the private but, rather, on the continued linking of sex with the public—to ensure that, even in this most personal sphere, the interests of the collective were assigned the highest priority. Once readers were exposed to the fundamentals of sex, Dr. Iakobzon promised, they would understand its significance for the individual and for the collective and would come to appreciate why this type of "serious, thoughtful, and scientific" approach was needed to resolve a "question of such paramount importance."[82]

Writers also assured their readers that nowhere else was a solution possible. But this could only occur when the country's economy and structure fully "blossomed with the magnificent flower of socialism."[83] Until that time came, it was necessary to take whatever steps possible to "cure" sexuality. By following specific rules of sexual conduct (laid out in the following chapters), enlighteners would guide the population toward health. Professor Mendel'son predicted that, after receiving educators' scientific explanations of sexuality's "laws," people would fully understand how to behave and what to avoid. "New Russia will not be new until our sexuality is cleansed and refined," declared Dr. Vasilevskii. Yet this was not to imply, he hastened to add, that physicians favored asceticism in sexual matters: "The goal of our revolution is not to set for ourselves strict chastity, a complete denial of sexual joys; the mortification of the flesh once celebrated by Christianity is completely foreign to our epoch . . . [the goal] is, rather, to make sex normal, healthy and pure."[84]

Other physicians made similar protestations.[85] In these assertions they echoed (and sometimes directly quoted) Lenin, who during his conversation with Klara Zetkin repeatedly disputed his austerity:

> Not that I want my criticism to breed asceticism. That never occurred to me. Communism ought to bring with it not asceticism but joy of life and good cheer called forth, among other things, by a life replete with love. However in my opinion the plethora of sex life observable today brings neither joy of life nor cheerfulness, but on the contrary diminishes them. In revolutionary times this is bad, very bad, indeed.[86]

Nonetheless, one gets the sense that Lenin was protesting too much. As Eric Naiman has argued: "Despite such emphatic denials of monastic intentions by Lenin, Bukharin, and others, the condemnations of depravity that inevitably followed these declarations helped create a climate with strong puritanical pressures." Sex educators likewise contributed to this climate, promoting an extremely traditional model of sexual behavior couched in the language of revolution, progress, and science. Dr. Timofeev, for instance, identified Lenin as the ideal "prototype for the person of the future," not only because he was a great revolutionary and tireless social activist but also because he was "an especially sexually modest man" (as well as a splendid skater, scholar, and chess player).[87]

Indeed, their mistrust of physical satisfaction explains the severity of physicians' reactions to Aleksandra Kollontai. In medical writers' estimations, with very few exceptions, healthy sex (defined as the absence of sick and deviant behavior) had little to do with pleasure. Furthermore, for all their concerns about appearing "too sexy," the authors' approach to the sex question and the information they provided was anything but. Enlighteners were quick to heed their own counsel about sexual restraint: there was very little sex in Soviet sex education. In this respect they had a great deal in common with Zalkind, whose twelve "Sexual Commandments" closely followed the content of "legitimate" medical sex advice:

1. Sexual life should not begin too early.

2. Sexual abstinence is essential until marriage, and marriage should occur only when full social and biological maturity has been reached (age twenty to twenty-four).

3. Sexual intercourse should only be the culmination of profound mutual affection and of attachment to the sexual object.

4. The sexual act should only be the final link in a chain of profound and complex experiences uniting lovers.

5. The sexual act should not be repeated often.

6. Sexual partners should not be changed frequently.

7. Love should be monogamous.

8. At every sexual act, the possibility that progeny will result should always be remembered.

9. Sexual selection should occur in accordance with class and revolutionary proletarian selection. Flirtation, courtship, coquetry, and other methods of specifically sexual conquest should not enter into sexual relations.

10. There should be no jealousy.

11. There should be no sexual perversion.

12. In the interests of revolutionary expediency a class has the right to interfere in the sexual life of its members. Sexuality must be subordinated to class interests; it must never interfere with them and must serve them in all respects.

While Zalkind was the target of a significant amount of criticism for his commandments, no such charges were levied against those sex educators who "knew their place," published primarily in health-related venues, and kept their revolutionary enthusiasm at a more subdued pitch.[88]

Although similarly sexless, advice was even vaguer when it focused on acceptable sexual behavior. Starting with two negative measures, Dr. Uspenskii's list of "desirable sexual norms" concluded on a positive, quasi-utopian note:

> Sexual life should not start too early; sexual activity should not be excessive; sexual activity should be worthy of the high form of development reached by humankind. It should not sink to the level of simple satisfaction of animalistic urges but, infused with elements of the highest human emotions, should be supplemented by them, it should be the harmonious combination of spiritual and physical relations, the true source of happiness and cheer. Suffusing human sexual relations with genuine beauty and humanity is one of the most serious tasks facing the new society.[89]

Sexual enlighteners may have avoided the accusation of pornography (by any group other than physicians), but their subject matter suggests another, ultimately insurmountable, complication. Despite physicians' criticism of the excessive attention focused on sexual concerns, their enlightenment work perpetuated, ensured, and indeed relied on such popular interest. When and if sexuality returned to its proper secondary sphere, there would be less call for their expertise and consequently less access to lecture halls, the pages of the popular health journals, and the scant resources of the commissariat. Ironically, their continued authority would appear to hinge on sexuality remaining unhealthy, a conclusion that most assuredly would have troubled these health advocates. By no means should it be understood that these doctors wanted to keep their charges sick and dependent. Rather, even as physicians sought to treat the severe ills that plagued their individual patients, they had a vested interest in maintaining the diagnosis of a sexually sick society.

Whatever their assessment of the obstacles they faced and their chances for success, the fact remains that as late as the end of 1930 Semashko declared, "familial and sexual relations still remain a painful area of our lifestyle."[90] Soon thereafter the Party instituted a very different, far less patient approach to sexuality, one that did away with all references to (and evidence of) illness and abnormality. By ending all public discourse on the matter, the Party not only deprived these medical educators of their leadership role but automatically resolved the sex question, once and for all.

Making Sex

Science, Glands, and the Medical Construction
of Gender Difference and Heterosexuality

In a word, a castrated man is not a man, not in body, not in
character. —A. TIMOFEEV, *V CHEM PROIAVLIAETSIA POLOVAIA*
ZHIZN' MUZHCHINY I ZHENSHCHINY

The famous scientist Virchow said that "all that we worship
in woman she owes to her ovaries." —T. I. IUDIN, *POLOVOE*
VLECHENIE I NENORMAL'NOSTI POLOVOGO POVEDENIIA

• Medical educators used science to assert their authority over sexuality against the competing claims of other
professionals, but science was a double-edged sword. It
could be deliberately abused, or simply misunderstood.
As Dr. Feigin wrote in his 1927 pamphlet *What Is a*
Normal Sex Life, contemporary youths' indulgence in
"intolerable sexual deviance" draws on a surprising
source for legitimacy: "Many people attempt to justify
these abnormal manifestations on the basis of science.
Muddling the most simple scientific facts, they wish to
prove that which in actuality does not correspond to
nature." Less concerned here with depravity per se
than with the youths' justification of these excesses on
the basis of "natural facts," Feigin's intention was to
rescue this territory from such unacceptable and "unscientific" misappropriation.[1]

Yet equally important was the model of medically approved sexual behavior that this pamphlet and the many others like it provided, based (according to its author) on the correct understanding of science and the natural world. Thus after deploring young people's self-serving scientific "muddling," Feigin asked: "What are the norms of a sexual lifestyle in terms of the demands of nature? How should each young person—man or woman— behave, not considering the moral side of the question, but listening only to the 'imperatives of nature,' through which they sometimes want to justify the most unnatural manifestations of sexuality?" To sex educators during the 1920s, the area of science that provided the fullest answers to such questions was endocrinology—and specifically its star attraction, the sex glands.[2]

"The sex glands!" wrote the Leningrad professor P. G. Bakaleinikov breathlessly: "What great secrets are contained in them!" According to the endocrinologist and controversial author A. V. Nemilov: "without normal endocrine secretions there is no health. All that is good in the body and soul of a human depends on these sex hormones. It is precisely these that make a person a person." In an unvarying narrative repeated in countless pamphlets, lectures, and articles, medical educators cited recent developments in endocrinology to advocate abstinence and sublimation, and to warn against the dangers of masturbation and premarital or frequent sex. Dr. Bruk cautioned: "If some evil force were to destroy the sex glands of an entire country's population, this country would perish—and not only because population growth would cease, but also because life would stand still." Bruk's rhetoric is particularly telling: it is not enough to argue for the primacy of the glands; he has to posit a threat to an entire country's glandular reserves by an "evil force." The advocacy of the sex glands' centrality is matched by a keen anxiety about the consequences of ignoring the glands' dictates, impairing their functions, and weakening a nation that is constantly portrayed as embattled. As we shall see, the "evil force" threatening the glands is the set of social processes that blur the boundaries between the genders and lead away from compulsory heterosexuality. The entire program of sexual enlightenment rested on the "proof" provided by the sex glands, leaving two assumptions about sexuality unquestioned: the "naturalness" of both gender difference and heterosexuality.[3]

The notion of scientifically verified sexual difference was central to popular medical education regarding sex. Drawing upon research in the field of endocrinology, and particularly a famous series of gland transplant experiments, writers could prescribe sex-specific behaviors that were justified by the natural differences between men and women. The biological determinism implicit in their analyses of the glands also allowed physicians to define the parameters of normal and abnormal masculinity and femininity. Educators could then pathologize those forms of sexual expression that did not, in their estimation, correspond to these norms. These two functions help explain medical and popular interest in endocrinology during the 1920s, since the science of glands seemed to provide clear-cut, irrefutable evidence of appropriate male and female conduct in this era of social upheaval and political instability.[4] The immediate postrevolutionary years were a time of great insecurity, which was frequently conceived of as a crisis of sexuality and gender. The "glass of water theory," the reputed prevalence of masturbation and prostitution, and an alleged epidemic of impotence seemed to indicate that something was terribly wrong in contemporary life, that the "natural order of things" had been disrupted. Perhaps most alarming to observers and social commentators was the fear that women had stopped behaving like "real" women, and men like "real" men.[5] Research on the endocrine glands seemed to provide conclusive, irrefutable scientific proof that the chaos reigning in Soviet Russia was unnatural. Order would be reestablished, the doctors insisted, but only if people heeded their advice.

Whiny Eunuchs

THE EVIDENCE OF CASTRATION

In the lead issue of the journal *Nature* (*Priroda*) in 1921, the experimental biologist and eugenicist Nikolai Konstantinovich Kol'tsov acquainted readers with the results of a series of experiments that had "rocked the scientific world." Kol'tsov was referring to the "Steinach Operation," first reported by the Viennese physiologist Eugen Steinach in 1920. Steinach claimed to have successfully rejuvenated both animal and human male subjects by tying off the *vas deferens*, the duct that carries sperm away from the testes. As a result, he claimed, gamete production ceased and the sex glands were entirely given over to the increased secretion of hormones, reinvigorating the body by improving blood circulation to the vital organs.[6]

The journal returned to the topic twice more over the next two years with articles by the endocrinologists N. Perna and A. V. Nemilov. Perna's contribution considered the role of the glands in the elaboration of a new scientific worldview. Like Kol'tsov's introduction to Steinach, Nemilov's article traced the experiments on rejuvenation conducted (simultaneously and independently) by the scientist Serge Voronoff, a Russian émigré who directed the Institute of Experimental Surgery at the Collège de France in Paris. Substituting rams and goats for Steinach's guinea pigs and rats, Voronoff's rejuvenation technique employed testicular grafts taken from immature animals of the same species, and in a number of well-publicized human cases, the sex glands of chimpanzees and baboons. Attempts were also made later to rejuvenate women, through the use of x-rays and ovarian simian injections.[7]

Soon other popular scientific journals, newspapers, and even works of fiction fed a growing fascination throughout Russian society with glands; the mixed emotions of awe and horror before the power of the endocrine glands underlay Mikhail Bulgakov's 1925 satire *Heart of a Dog*, whose protagonist, Professor Preobrazhenskii, was widely assumed to be based on Voronoff.[8] It is not difficult to understand the widespread interest in these scientific discoveries. Experiments holding out the promise of a second youth had an obvious appeal in a country whose human and animal populations still suffered such lasting effects of war as famine, disease, and malnutrition.[9] The findings also provided antireligious activists with powerful ammunition to counter belief in god or the existence of the soul.[10]

When sex educators began incorporating information about endocrinological research into their enlightenment endeavors, the focus shifted from rejuvenation to an earlier, equally momentous Steinach experiment first reported in 1912.[11] In this procedure, Steinach successfully transplanted the sex glands of previously castrated rats and guinea pigs from male to female and vice versa. Kol'tsov described the results of this dramatic achievement in his *Nature* article:

> The castrated animals into which the puberty glands of the opposite sex were transplanted reveal surprising features: they begin to develop in the direction of that sex whose glands they possess. Former males, unlike normal castrated males, do not reach the size of a normal male, but remain for their entire lives smaller, like females, and their entire skeleton takes on the appearance of the female skeleton: their organ does not develop, moreover the nipples and mammary glands reach almost the same stage of development as in real females. And psychologically these "feminized males" resemble females even more: they allow males to court them and even suckle the young of others who are placed near them. When I was in Vienna shortly before the war, Steinach showed me a feminized male rat, from whose nipple several drops of milk spurted out upon application of light pressure. On the other hand, "masculinized" females are as large as real males, their skeletons as strong and their chests as broad: their mammary glands are undeveloped, and the clitoris is as developed as the penis.[12]

Kol'tsov presented this experiment as one of several scientific advances leading to Steinach's work on rejuvenation. In sexual enlightenment materials, similar descriptions of the removal and transplanting of the sex glands constituted the central narrative device, the "evidence" upon which later medical advice would be based. Less dramatic perhaps than spurting milk or eyewitness accounts of altered rats, sex education literature nonetheless introduced these experiments in a similarly colorful and evocative manner. Yet for all their vividness, the uniformity in their approach to the subject of the glands, even within the context of the basic similarity common to all sex education texts, is striking. The same, often verbatim, narrative of the importance of the glands appears in one pamphlet after another as if copied from a master original, until the early 1930s when even these references disappear. One likely reason is that few among these doctors were endocrinologists themselves, and a nuanced or sophisticated explanation (or even understanding) of the specialty was unnecessary for their purpose.[13]

This purpose was "to make it clear to [readers] how healthy sex is to be understood" by approaching "the interesting but difficult question of sexual life . . . from the purely scientific point of view."[14] In their formulation the scientific viewpoint began with an introduction to the sex glands and their functions. At the onset of puberty, these glands begin to produce both external and internal secretions: the sperm and egg cells necessary for reproduction and the sex hormones, which enter directly into the blood and become the primary focus of these discussions. Once in the bloodstream, doctors wrote, the hormones have a profoundly invigorating effect upon the body, suffusing it with energy, strength, and vitality.[15] But they cautioned that frequent, deviant, or early sexual activity (before the body reaches sexual maturity, sometime between twenty and twenty-five years of age) overtaxes the glands, leading to premature aging and the threat of impotence or infertility. And infirmity signaled abnormality, as Dr. S. M. Kalmanson reminded his audience at a 1924 lecture on the sex question: "Sex before full development of the sex glands, before the onset of menstruation in women and [development of] mature sperm in men is *not normal*" (original emphasis).[16] Continence represented the best defense against this potential tragedy: "Prolonged abstinence, by accumulating hormones in the blood, ignites it with a joyous blazing of life and helps a person to work, as if powerfully pushing him with a steam engine of internal strength, with the electricity of great energy."[17]

To substantiate this claim and demonstrate the overriding importance of the glands, enlighteners drew upon an experience familiar to countless Russians: the castration of livestock and domestic animals. In *Healthy and Unhealthy Sex Life*, Dr. Donichev used this example to convince a rural adolescent boy of the danger caused to one's glands through abuse—in his case, by masturbation:

> "Do you have a piglet at home, Grigorii?"
>
> "We do," he answered me, surprised.
>
> "And your mother called the horse doctor (*konoval*) for him?"
>
> "She did."
>
> "Why?" I asked him.
>
> "To castrate him, of course."
>
> "And why was it necessary to castrate the pig?"
>
> "So that he would be fat and mild-tempered," he answered me with the same mistrust and surprise.
>
> "And what kind of horse do you have at home?"
>
> "A gelding."
>
> "Why not a stallion?"
>
> "Do you think it's possible to manage with a stallion? He's so wild that it's impossible to get the job done, especially if a mare's around. But a gelding is calm. Although he has less strength, still it's easier to work with him. And he pays no attention to mares."[18]

Other brochures explained the allegedly enervating effects of castration on animals in similar terms: violent, strong, and obstinate animals were made tamer, better tempered, more accommodating.[19] With the shift in temperament came physical changes as well, especially pronounced if the procedure was conducted before sexual maturity. Thus pamphlets related how castration before puberty deprived a stag of his antlers, a bull of his horns, and a rooster of his comb and beautiful plumed tail feathers. Donichev concluded: "A castrated rooster will look like a hen, a castrated bull (that is, an ox) is different from a real bull: he has different horns, a different voice, and a different gait. He is made more like a cow."[20]

From descriptions of castrated animals, the accounts next turned to consider humans who had undergone this procedure for religious, political, or medical reasons, including harem guards, Catholic choirboys, and most frequently, Russia's own *skoptsy*, the religious sect whose members "mutilated themselves, thinking it would please God."[21] Several authors embellished their tales with an illustration (the same in each instance) of one such *skopets*. Like neutered animals, these eunuchs were described as quiet and calm.[22] One booklet painted a particularly bleak portrait of the castrated male:

> Sexual feeling disappears, the growth of the mustache, beard, and other male traits is suspended, the voice becomes high, like a woman's; strength disappears; fat accumulates on the buttocks, hips, and chest, the skin becomes soft and flabby; externally, the man begins to look like a woman. It is not just his external appearance but also his character that changes: such male traits as bravery, energy, and enterprise disappear; instead [we find] sluggishness, callousness, stinginess, depression, and eventually sickness and early aging.[23]

Texts portrayed eunuchs as crafty, malicious, vindictive, lacking in individuality, and mentally deficient. With puffy faces, watery glazed eyes, and pale sallow skin, the physician Sigal labeled them "half-dead." Timofeev concluded: "In a word, castrates are distinguished by those traits that are antithetical to unambiguous masculinity, to a strong and open character."[24]

Texts also described the consequences of "castration," or its functional equivalents, on women:

> Removing a woman's sex glands also has a strong effect on her entire body and character. Sexual attraction disappears, the breasts cease their growth, hair sprouts on the upper lip and on the chin, the voice becomes deeper. In her external appearance and her character she begins to look like a man. Therefore, when a doctor meets strikingly mannish women [*muzhepodobnye zhenshchiny*], the thought always arises: Isn't this a case of undeveloped ovaries, the result of a limited amount of their secretions in the blood?[25]

Deprived of their ovaries, women were seen to develop muscles and to lose their curves and their femininity (*zhenstvennost'*). Doctors noted a similar transformation in women after the onset of menopause. As Glezer put it: "when the glands stop working, [her body starts] withering, followed by aging and then death."[26]

"Thus," concluded Dr. Bruk, "we see how important are each person's sex glands. They 'make' sex; that is, thanks to them, each person feels him/herself to be either a man or a woman and behaves accordingly." Educational materials explained that the role of the glands in the process of "making sex" involves two distinct yet interrelated stages. The first stage, the development of the reproductive organs or primary sex characteristics (like the external secretions of the sex glands), received barely a passing mention in these works (all charges of pornography referred to in Chapter 1 aside). In all the various accounts discussed here, the sex organs are and should be simply functional: once they are working properly, they can be safely ignored. Instead, these doctors are clearly more interested in using sex to talk about gender, appropriating the "discoveries" of endocrinology in order to locate abstract male and female characteristics within the body but outside the sex organs: in the glands and their effects.[27] Thus writers concentrated instead upon the secondary sex characteristics, describing how these traits, which develop as a result of the hormones secreted by the sex glands beginning in puberty, serve to distinguish adult men from women.[28]

Male and female identity, in the eyes of these authors, depended almost entirely upon the secondary sex characteristics. In bodies lacking sex hormones, the physical distinctions separating the sexes would be greatly diminished, producing the manly women, womanly men, and cowlike oxen described above: "intersexual beings," according to several doctors.[29] Yet what is particularly significant in these works is not so much the physical distinctions but the behavioral and psychological differences attributed to males and females. For the glands not only make sex; even more important, they make gender by assuring that men and women "behave accordingly." As defined by educators, secondary sex characteristics include distinctions of "body and spirit" as well as character, demeanor, mental activity, and emotion.[30] They might be "frequently almost indefinable, but nonetheless recognized and felt."[31] One of the primary functions of these assessments, then, is to authoritatively define for readers those indefinable characteristics, to enable them to recognize the distinctions between the sexes and consequently the appropriate conduct for members of each sex.

In their portrayal of eunuchs, enlighteners had already provided a preliminary classification of "normal" male secondary sex characteristics: the castrates they described lacked such masculine traits as bravery, energy, and enterprise. They also distinguished men from women based on the former's purportedly greater logic, objectivity, even-temperedness, and resourcefulness. Doctors depicted men as being more careful, less susceptible to the influence of others, and able to take greater initiative.[32] Among the female secondary sex characteristics noted, intuition and subjectivity replace logic, and feelings in general occupy a much greater role in women's behavior. Dr. Iakobzon deemed women to be so qualitatively distinct from men psychologically and spiritually as to be "of a different order . . . much closer to nature." Denied the purportedly male ability to think abstractly beyond their own individual experience (which, according to Iakobzon, leaves them ill-suited to conduct research), women by contrast are more concerned with their immediate surroundings and practical life tasks. For this reason they excel in "finished products, decorations, individual concrete things." Women are said to possess a better memory, are more perceptive, and read faster.[33]

These inventories of hormonally induced traits make frequent jumps from physical characteristics to the psychological or behavioral, as in this list compiled by Professor T. Iudin:

> All the features of a woman's structure—her round form, her breasts, her wide pelvis, the proportion of fat on her hips, her more passive psyche—all this is the result of the internal secretions of the ovaries; by the same token, the mustache and beard, deep voice, the male body structure, and his mental and psychological activity are the result of the internal secretions of the male sex gland—the testis.[34]

Even invisible differences such as passivity and activity become credibly gender specific when mixed with unmistakable physical particularities like female breasts and male facial hair.

Educators traced these crucial characteristics back to the very first stages of the reproductive process. It is here that sexual difference originated, depending upon whether the sperm's nucleus contains an odd or even number of chromosomes. In one example, the distinctions between men and women are imprinted into the reproductive matter itself:

> Since the egg, unlike the sperm, is unable to move by itself, instead moving thanks to the stimulus of the fibers, its movement is very slow, much slower than the movement of the sperm. The latter is more active and mobile. It is as if the sexual difference between man and woman is visible here: in sexual matters, the former is more active, the latter is more passive. More than a week passes before the egg covers as much distance as the sperm travels in less than two hours.[35]

Not long after fertilization, the primary sex glands appear from which develop the testes in the male embryo and ovaries in the female. At this point the cells of the sex glands begin to produce the hormones that will exert a profound influence upon the future life experiences of these beings: "As soon as [the embryonic sex gland] has formed, the further development of the fetus proceeds according to a strictly predetermined path, differently in the male embryo than in the female."[36]

Following this foreordained course, it is only a matter of time until puberty, when the secondary sex characteristics appear owing to the increased production of hormones by the glands. Yet in the opinion of Professor Mendel'son, the impact of the hormones upon the body is so profound that these differences are discernible even before the onset of sexual maturity:

> Boys are distinguished by their greater agility, activity, naughtiness, bravery, carelessness, negligence in relation to things and responsibilities (for example, the preparation of lessons), yet exhibiting at the same time resourcefulness, comprehensibility, rapid understanding of the essence of the matter. Girls, on the other hand, show greater external control, obedience, cleanliness, and accuracy than boys; they are more industrious but lag behind in the quickness with which they grasp and comprehend ideas. In boys the ability for independent initiative and scope predominates, in girls, exactness and execution.[37]

After puberty, Mendel'son concluded, these traits continue in the same direction, and indeed his list includes characteristics strikingly similar to those others ascribed to adults. Yet regardless of whether educators traced these features back to childhood or tied their appearance to puberty, all stressed the "naturalness" of such manifestations. As readers were repeatedly reminded, such traits only come about when development is normal and healthy: "A person whose sexual development was completely normal expresses all the physical and psychological attributes particular to his sex." Furthermore, the degree of sexual difference or "dimorphism" between men and women connotes more than bodily health. Several medical writers identified it also as a marker of evolutionary progress: the more pronounced the differences between the sexes, the more advanced the race.[38]

Any defect in the glands or impediment to their proper functioning leads to the "intersexual" beings described above. Endocrinologist A. V. Nemilov divided all people into two groups, according to the soundness of their glandular functions. Those whose secretionary capabilities are well developed he labeled especially "feminine" and "masculine." On the other hand, those congenitally burdened with poorly developed sex glands are reminiscent of eunuchs, owing to their weak secretionary activity. In men of this type, facial hair grows sparsely and bones and muscles remain undeveloped. Women suffering from this deficiency possess narrow pelvises, small sagging breasts, and disproportional and unattractive bodies. Feeble, listless, and depressed,

> these are for the most part whiners, lacking faith in life and the desire to fight for one's place in the sun. Individuality in them is poorly defined, sexuality is weak and sometimes completely absent. Such people age rapidly, succumb to all kinds of illnesses, account for a large percentage of cases of suicide and mental illness, and go early to their graves.[39]

Modest Roosters and Tough Hens

THE EVIDENCE OF ANIMAL EXPERIMENTS

To support his assertion concerning the presence of sex distinctions in children, Mendel'son vaguely alluded to the "countless scientific experiments [that] offer a series of interesting conclusions," without, however, providing any additional information about this evidence. The situation was quite different with respect to the literature's claims about postpubescent secondary sex traits. Sex education tracts may have depicted these attributes as self-evident and incontrovertible, but readers were not expected to take their authors' word for it. Here science stepped in to lend a hand and corroborate the physicians' interpretation, providing the purported evidence for what they appropriately referred to as "the dictatorship of sex": the biological basis of physical, intellectual, emotional, and behavioral distinctions between men and women. As Timofeev put it: "Only recently did teachings about the internal secretions excite the entire scientific world and make it possible to penetrate that which earlier was considered secret."[40]

The scientific discovery responsible for uncovering this secret was the sex gland transplant procedure, first performed by Eugen Steinach in 1911, which Kol'tsov so vividly described in *Nature*. Most enlightenment materials introduced the transplant experiment immediately after the subject of castration, to further emphasize the importance of the glands to the body. Occasionally, however, educators passed over the topic of castration entirely in favor of an exclusive focus upon this more dramatic procedure. Several authors cited Steinach's earlier successes with guinea pigs and rats.[41] The majority turned instead (whether out of national pride or the reputed greater clarity of the results) to a similar series of experiments conducted from 1919 to 1922 by the Russian biologist M. M. Zavadovskii on roosters and hens.[42] Zavadovskii's analysis of his findings was repeated in simplified form throughout the 1920s, as in this description by Dr. B. A. Ivanovskii:

> After removing the ovaries, the hen began to grow a rooster's plume, with its bright color and form, spurs, and comb; when the rooster's testicles were removed the bird became smaller; the castrated rooster and hen began to look surprisingly alike.
>
> When a second operation was conducted and the ovaries of the hen were implanted in the castrated rooster, and the testicles of the rooster into the hen, an even more shocking change occurred. The former hens became surprisingly similar to genuine roosters, cried "ku-ku-ri-ku," stamped and shook their wings at the hens, summoned them to eat, fought with the other roosters, etc. The former roosters, on the other hand, were transformed into genuine hens in appearance and character and even began to form eggs, which one could feel in their stomachs, but which they couldn't lay, since they had no way to lay them.

The sacrifices made by this surgically altered poultry are not in vain, however. As Ivanovskii concludes, they now serve as a living testimony to the truth of scientific laws: "These 'former' hens and 'former' roosters even now happily prosper in the Moscow Zoo, and those who find themselves in Moscow ought to drop by there and with their own eyes be convinced of the significance of the sex glands and the power of science."[43]

Many accounts featured a "before and after" illustration of the birds that was first published in Zavadovskii's study (see Figure 2.1). Other pamphlets reproduced the postoperative photographs of Steinach's rats and guinea pigs.[44] Presumably, these images, like those of the *skopets*, were included so that readers unable to visit the Moscow Zoo might also behold the wonders of this scientific revelation.

If anything, the power in such illustrations lay in their ability to document precisely what they could not show. It was suggested above that the intermixing of physical attributes with qualities such as behavior lent credibility to allegations regarding the gender specificity of these "invisible" traits. Similarly, by enabling readers to "see" the animals' (and also the eunuchs') physical transformation, illustrations made it easier to believe the behavioral changes that scientists claimed occurred, as in the following passage from Dr. N. I. Shchukin's *Man and Woman in Sexual Life:*

> Look at figure 1. In the upper left is a normal rooster. Beneath him is the same rooster after his sex glands were removed. He lost his former appearance: his coxcomb, beard-tuft, and ornamentation disappeared. On the lower left is the same rooster after ovaries taken from a hen were grafted under his skin. The ovaries continued to function in such an unusual place and the rooster then resembled a hen. On the right are three drawings of a hen. The one at the top is normal. The next shows a hen after removal of the ovaries. And finally, [we see] the same hen, but with sex glands from a rooster grafted under the skin.
>
> Along with its external appearance, the animal's character and behavior also change.
>
> From all of these experiments it is evident that *the development of secondary sex characteristics depends on the work of the sex glands.* (Original emphasis)

In this example Shchukin's description of what readers were observing also served as evidence for what they could not perceive: the postulated concurrent changes in the animals' character and behavior, and the source of all three processes in the hormones. To reach these conclusions necessitated first accepting that the hen and rooster depicted in the middle and bottom positions of the illustration were indeed one and the same as the "normal" specimens at top. Through a similar jump in logic in the next sentence, such physical evidence also facilitated the extension of these findings to humans. Shchukin continued:

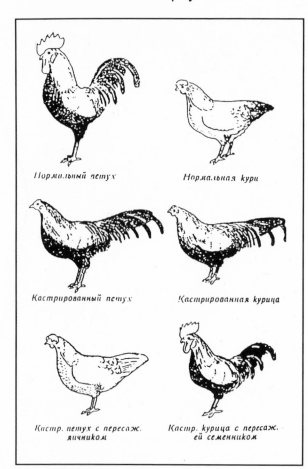

Нормальный петух

Нормальная кури

Кастрированный петух

Кастрированная курица

Кастр. петух с пересаж.
яичником

Кастр. курица с пересаж.
ей семенником

Figure 2.1—M. M. Zavadovskii's Roosters and Hens. Top row from left to right: "Normal rooster" "Normal hen"; middle row: "Castrated rooster" "Castrated hen"; bottom row: "Castrated rooster with transplanted ovary" "Castrated hen with transplanted testis." M. A. Glezer, *Polovaia zhizn'* (Khar'kov: Nauchnaia meditsina, 1929), 35.

These experiments also show that the substance secreted by the male sex glands (testes) is different from the secretions of the *woman's* ovaries, since these substances function differently. In other words, the substance secreted by male glands promotes the development of male secondary characteristics; the secretions of the female glands promote the development of female secondary traits.[45] (Emphasis added)

Shchukin jumps from hens to the ovaries of a woman without so much as a comment. The assumption that hens and women, roosters and men, and more generally, animals and humans, are interchangeable was essential to educators' objectives (and not solely owing to the improbability of performing such experiments on people). As in the writers' analyses of castration, discussion of these experiments shifted freely from animals to humans and back again. In another example, less obvious behavioral characteristics were presented as the natural human equivalents of traits found in Zavadovskii's hens and roosters. After describing the animals' metamorphoses, the educator Dr. I. M. Tkachenko concluded:

> The same [transformation] is observed in humans. The castrated man becomes womanly. He loses the external traits of a man: the beard, mustache, etc. He also changes in spirit. The male mindset, his entire psyche is replaced by the corresponding female type of psyche (he develops femininity [*zhenstvennost'*], along with a love for finery, a preponderance of female interests, the inclination for gossip, garrulity, intrigues, a cunning, crafty mind, etc.).
>
> And, on the contrary, if we remove a woman's ovaries and transplant the material of the male testes, the woman will become a man. She will grow a beard, mustache, develop strong muscles, and the composition of her character, psyche, and "spirit," moreover, will begin to resemble that of the male. She can show bravery, courage, the resourcefulness normally particular to men, etc.[46]

Pamphlets might employ the animal gland transplant procedure as evidence of similar traits in humans, or begin by listing human characteristics that were then confirmed on the basis of these experiments with animals. In each case the evidence was completely self-referential; no outside proof or confirmation was needed. These experiments single-handedly revealed the "truth" about human traits, the authors implied, because animals exist in a natural state; their behavior is pure, untainted by human interference. Thus the manifestation of similar features in humans must be equally natural and therefore normal.

In fact, whereas Steinach was criticized by certain Western scientists for anthropomorphizing his rats and guinea pigs by labeling them "masculine" and "feminine," not one Russian analysis of the gland transplant procedure raised such objections. Moreover, Russian sources went far beyond simply applying these terms to animals. In the introduction to *On the Harm Done by Early Sexual Intercourse*, for instance, Dr. Uspenskii informed his audience, "Animals are divided into *samets* and *samka* ('man' and 'woman')."[47] The rooster with the ovarian grafts in one description of the Zavadovskii experiment was transformed "little by little from a shouting pugnacious fighter and bawler into a modest quiet little hen"; in another description, his loud ku-ku-re-ku became instead a "modest cackle." According to Dr. Bruk, the secondary sex characteristics of humans are similar to those of animals, "because in general a human being is indistinguishable from animals." Such uncritically applied assumptions of interchangeability worked both ways: after concluding his catalogue of human behavioral secondary sex traits, Professor Mendel'son added: "We observe something similar in the psychological structure of male and female animals."[48]

Even Commissar Semashko engaged in anthropomorphism when it suited his purposes, while he condemned others for doing so. In a speech at the Akvarium theater on April 12, 1925, he returned to the argument begun in his January 1 *Izvestiia* editorial. Introducing the subject of sex education, Semashko criticized "the flagrant error made by several comrades" (this time singling out Zalkind, among others) who "crudely applied the biological laws of the animal world to the relationships between humans." Of their theory linking the concept of heat to human sexuality, he remarked: "it follows that we will draw nothing other than laughter—provoking, clearly incorrect, unscientific, and therefore dangerous conclusions."[49]

Semashko accused the writers of ignoring the role of psychology, and especially the unconscious, in the development of the human sex instinct; the idea that the sex instinct's susceptibility to the influence of the unconscious he labeled the "first law of biology on the sex question." The commissar's own exhibition of this "crude biologizing" related to the second law. Explaining that the origin of the sex instinct lay in the sex glands, he then turned to the animal gland transplant experiment to illustrate the glands' other crucial function:

> I will give one illustration of what I said—in *animals* the transplant of female sex glands to the male [*samets*], the male individual, has an influence on the general psychological condition of that individual. The character changes, becomes more feminine, the manners become more feminine, the voice becomes feminine, etc., etc. And conversely, in those cases when we talk about similar transplants of male glands into *women*, this female individual becomes more like a male. Male hair growth appears on the upper lip and chin, her character, voice, and movements get coarser, etc., etc.[50] (Emphasis added)

On the basis of this evidence, Semashko introduced the second biological law: that the differences attracting one sex to the other are not only external but internal.

Given the fundamental Marxist belief in nurture over nature and the prophylactic, environmentalist orientation of Narkomzdrav, such a strictly biologistic interpretation of human behavior is especially significant. Indeed, little attention was devoted in this literature to the possibility that environment caused sexual difference. Even those few authors who, like Bruk, acknowledged the impact of socioeconomic factors on the development of gender difference ultimately championed the dominance of biology over environment:

> Of course, different types of female education, the incorrect upbringing that woman received here before the Revolution and still receives abroad, to a certain extent prevent the correct determination of the character differences separating man and woman. But nonetheless these differences exist and will remain, even if a woman were to receive exactly the same upbringing and education as a man.[51]

Bruk did not consider the possibility that equality of experience would eradicate behavioral differences; his point was, rather, that obstacles to women's education had somehow artificially hindered the natural and proper (but nonetheless distinct) path of female development.

One of the most controversial proponents of the biological basis of sexual difference was the endocrinologist A. V. Nemilov, whose immensely popular treatment of the subject, entitled *The Biological Tragedy of Woman*, sustained several editions over the course of the 1920s. Nemilov claimed to have written these "essays on the physiology of the female organism," as the book is subtitled, in order to promote greater understanding and sympathy for women's biological burden. Ultimately, however, The *Biological Tragedy* was an elaborate scientific justification for women's inequality and intellectual inferiority:

> Nowhere in the world has more been done to make women equal with men than in the USSR, and nowhere is there more progressive legislation on the woman question than here. Yet it is not a secret to anyone that the true position of woman has changed very little since the October Revolution.
>
> And this is not only because we still live in the transitional phase on the path to socialism, but also because the actual implementation of revolutionary principles in this sphere runs up against a very important circumstance, namely, the *biological inequality of the sexes*. . . . [One] can speak about *equality of significance* or *equivalence of potential* . . . , but not about equality in the sense of identical abilities to realize possibilities deep within the body.[52] (Original emphasis)

According to Nemilov, woman's "biological tragedy" stems from the unequal biological responsibilities assigned to her by virtue of her sex. Pregnancy, childbirth, breast-feeding, and menstruation place unavoidable physical and emotional burdens on her, so that "all her life from birth to grave is full of disharmony, which is possible in the best of cases only to shift but not overcome, since outside of sex there is no life." The origin of this "sexual dictatorship" is the endocrine glands, and to emphasize the power that the sex glands hold over women's fate, Nemilov reminded his readers that women's ovaries are unusually large, equal in size to those of a hippopotamus.[53]

In Nemilov's analysis, both men and women suffer from the "biological tragedy of homo sapiens," defined as the endless battle between the brain and the sex glands, the ability to think versus the drive to reproduce. Yet in men this antagonism is brief and quickly inhibited because of the "greater simplicity of [their] sexual functions," enabling them to take full advantage, in the extensive time remaining, of the intellectual, creative, and physical stimuli provided by their hormones. Owing to what he interprets as the greater complexity of women's sexual makeup and the extensive time period during which strenuous demands are made on their sex glands (from first ovulation through pregnancy and into menopause), "this inhibition of the mental center by the sexual center continues, if not always in the same acute form, then at least for a prolonged period of time, occupying a large part of [their] life."[54]

Even such a simple biological process as menstruation had been "scientifically proven" to affect a woman's psyche, decreasing her mental capabilities and powers of concentration. Nemilov supported this claim by citing an experiment conducted on the nervous system of a dog in heat, arguing: "The condition in its biological essence is the same as menstruation in women." Translating these findings "from the language of physiology to the language of daily life," he then offered several examples allegedly demonstrating that menstruation's weakening of women's reflexes interferes with all of their physical and mental functions, and perhaps most significantly given the implications, their professional responsibilities.

> During this time, the tram conductor gives you the wrong ticket and loses count, although she is experienced at her work; a menstruating train conductor moves slowly, gets delayed at stops, and gets lost at the crossroads. The typist's fingers hit the wrong keys on the Remington, she works more slowly than usual, and, no matter how she tries, the text is missing some words and she gets the hyphenation wrong. A dentist can't find the proper drill, the drill bit turns poorly and looks wrong, she can't find the proper phial and instruments, and is convinced that you are in a particular hurry today and won't sit still, etc. At this time, singers lose the sound and strength of their voices, and Dr. Klein is even convinced that an experienced voice therapist, judging by the condition of the throat, will always know whether a woman's blood is flowing or not.

Here Nemilov goes far beyond what was otherwise the typical correlation between animals and humans found throughout sexual enlightenment literature: he uses a gland-based argument comparing menstruating women to dogs in estrus in order to provide a "scientific" answer to an old (and hardly revolutionary) misogynist complaint: why are women so frustrating? Or, given the post-1917 context, why are women *still* so frustrating? As Eric Naiman convincingly argues, the long-standing Russian connection between women and the soul-numbing grind of *byt* was only intensified during the NEP era, when the return of "bourgeois" comforts and luxury was repeatedly embodied by the pampered woman. Nearly all of Nemilov's examples of women's impaired professional functions are problems the typical urban man could be expected to encounter in the course of his day, involving public transportation, secretarial work, and medicine. Nemilov is implicitly engaging in a historical slippage no less egregious than the leap across the canine/human species boundary: the problems of NEP are not the fleeting woes of a transitional period but the age-old aggravations of the menstrual period.[55]

Glands and the Biology of Sexual Attraction

However convincing the various categories of psychological, behavioral, and physical distinctions separating men from women may have been, by far the most persuasive evidence of difference, according to enlightenment literature, lay in the realm of sexuality itself. Here, as biology asserted itself to guarantee the perpetuation of the species, the dictatorship of sex was purportedly at its most visible and incontrovertible. The gender difference that writers detected in the gametes during the act of fertilization continued for the duration of the male and female sexual experiences. It expressed itself, first of all, in the place sexuality occupied in the lives and bodies of men and women. In Dr. Iakobzon's assessment, men are by nature more passionate and sentient than women in sexual matters, but their greater sensitivity is concentrated in the sexual organs; women's less intense sexual feeling is spread throughout the body as well as the psyche. Whereas in men sexuality is directed exclusively toward the goal of intercourse, in women it assumes a far greater role throughout their day-to-day existence. Dr. Mendel'son contrasted men's powerful "demand for the sex act" with the need in women for tender contact, and in a full third of females, with their complete indifference to and even disgust toward intercourse.[56] Such an analysis tries to reconcile what would seem to be a paradox, with women portrayed as both more and less sexual than men and therefore inferior, for both these reasons. Woman's alleged indifference to sexual intercourse becomes connected with the assertion that her entire body (and therefore, her psyche) is governed by a heightened, generalized sensuality. According to this argument, men can conquer and harness their sexuality precisely because it is so localized, goaloriented, and patently visible. Not only can male sexuality, under the guidance of enlightened Soviet medicine, be compartmentalized and put in its proper place (as it were), but it is also reassuringly teleological: the path to male sexual satisfaction is straightforward and simple, an erotic analogy to the path to communism. Women, by contrast, cannot transcend their bodies and their sex, mired as they are in vague, polyvalent sensuality and *byt*.

The one area in which educators observed sexuality to be stronger in women than men is in the desire for children. Several experts claimed that many women consent to sex solely with this goal in mind, and in maternity receive the fulfillment lacking in the sex act itself. Writing in the popular *Woman's Magazine* (*Zhenskii zhurnal*), Dr. Mikulina-Ivanova (one of the few female physicians to write about sexual matters) explained this aspect of sexual difference to her readers:

> Maternity clearly imbues [a woman's] entire life with selflessness, happiness, suffering, and unusually deep feelings, making her act for the satisfaction of this demand. . . . Because of his makeup, man is deprived of these rich experiences and joys. His sex life consists of the constant and varied choice of objects for the satisfaction of sexual need. He has no spirituality in his life, and therefore it is very easy for him to reject all the ethical conditions imposed upon him by paternity and the laws of morality. In the creation of these laws

man always imposes all the requirements on woman, preserving for himself freedom of action. . . . For a contemporary conscious and independent woman none of this is a secret. Therefore she often approaches sex solely with maternity in mind.

While Mikulina-Ivanova may have had the interests of her female audience at heart, her analysis nonetheless reads as a biological justification for male promiscuity; the only compensation she can offer her readers is the promise that "the people of the future," those "chosen by nature," will prove an exception to this pessimistic take on male sexual behavior.[57]

Authors noted men's allegedly greater sexual activity and women's corresponding passivity in the search for a sexual partner as well; like their animal counterparts, men were believed to more aggressively pursue a mate and to initiate intercourse.[58] The reason for this lay in the biology of sexual attraction, and it was in their treatment of this topic that educators elaborated their normative model of sexual behavior. With few exceptions (discussed below) the vast majority of medical enlighteners diagnosed the seemingly omnipotent sex glands as the basis of sexual attraction. Evidence again was provided by reference to castrated animals and eunuchs (in whom sexual feeling was completely absent) and the gland transplant experiments. In a preliminary study cited in several pamphlets, sexual attraction returned to previously castrated animals when the sex glands were regrafted into another area of the body, such as the neck or stomach.[59] The remarkable sexual metamorphoses effected by Steinach and Zavadovskii offered an even more powerful display of the hormones' command over attraction, as "former" female hens and guinea pigs wooed "former" males, who now passively allowed themselves to be courted and pursued.

Some analyses presented attraction as the result of a straightforward physiological process in which the brain, "eroticized" by the glandular hormones, directs the organism to pursue the opposite sex. It is in this specific process, moreover, that Nemilov located the predominant source of woman's natural sexual passivity: "A man suffused with sexual hormones is made energetic to the point of impudence, a woman through eroticized hormones is made weak and passive, to the complete renunciation of her self."[60] Other sources interpreted the biology of attraction somewhat differently. Dr. M. Nestrukh, the author of a much cited popular study on the subject, traced the origin of male sexual attraction to the desire to rid the body of semen accumulated in the sex organs owing to the increased productivity of hormones during puberty. He explained that the accretion of semen asserts pressure on the nerves and the unpleasant sensation of swelling is transmitted to the brain as the body strives to alleviate this discomfort. Without knowing why, the youth seeks out female company and eventually actively pursues intercourse with women to relieve this pressure and swelling. Nestrukh labeled the desire for intercourse with women the second component of male sexual attraction, adding that it was precisely this powerful yearning to escape discomfort that caused men to pursue women so aggressively.[61] This interpretation, even more than Mikulina-Ivanova's analysis, provided a powerful rationale for male sexual promiscuity: If a woman is not interested in sex, a man, compelled by his hormones, will look for satisfaction elsewhere.

Swelling plays an important, though presumably less painful, role in Nestrukh's interpretation of female sexual attraction as well. He located women's experience of this sensation in two distinct processes: during intercourse (referring, presumably, to the swelling of the stimulated clitoris) and menstruation, with the pressure and swelling in the sex organs that accompanies the maturation of eggs in the ovaries. As with males, the desire to alleviate the sensation of swelling through sexual intercourse is the basis of female attraction. And while male sexual attraction is relatively constant, in women it fluctuates, decreasing dramatically during menses.[62]

Glands and Pathology

THE DEVIATION OF HOMOSEXUALITY

Not simply a glandular by-product, the secondary sex traits also reportedly serve to increase attraction and brain stimulation in order to encourage the perpetuation of the species. Indeed, according to Nestrukh, the more pronounced the traits separating male and female (itself an indication of well-functioning glands), the greater the level of sexual attraction between them. But what of the countless individuals who were less than perfect specimens of femininity and masculinity? Was the biology of attraction any different for those denied such spectacular rates of hormonal secretion? Professor Mendel'son described two individuals whom, he reasoned, everyone had encountered at some point in their lives: "a womanly man, with curvaceous body, feminine facial traits, gestures and gait, [and] on the other hand a manly woman, a lean muscular type, with poorly developed mammary glands, a comparatively narrow pelvis, a low voice, and energetic, masculine mannerisms." Yet despite such physical and occasionally behavioral "deviations from the norm," the vast majority turned out to be "completely normal" in sexual matters: "They feel sexual attraction for members of the opposite sex, and are fully capable of having sexual intercourse, reproducing and giving birth like all healthy people."[63]

Others displaying these peculiarities, however, were deemed decidedly "unhealthy," their external aberrations reflecting a far more fundamental pathology:

> Among people with this particular structure one sometimes encounters types that are like the opposite sex, not only externally but in their mental constitution: such thoroughly womanly men love to engage in female handwork, dress in women's clothing, and want to be liked not by women but by men; moreover, they sometimes fall in love with men, seek out male affection, at

the same time feeling complete sexual indifference, often even hatred, for women. Such men are distinguished from women only by the structure of their external sex organs, the majority of which are completely normal.[64]

In this introduction to the topic of homosexuality, same-sex attraction was presented as but one in a series of traits particular to these unhealthy individuals. Thus by focusing as much on deviations in secondary sex characteristics as on deviations in sexual expression, the representation of homosexuality in this literature is consistent with its portrayal of "normal" manhood and womanhood as comprising a wide range of practices and traits not strictly sexual.

For example, according to L. M. Vasilevskii, (male) homosexuals possess a woman's mental constitution and high voice, large breasts, and wide hips. They wear corsets, lipstick, and rouge, dress their hair, expose their neck and throat, and from childhood express a passionate interest in "female" needlework and embroidery. Vasilevskii described lesbians as sometimes having mustaches and beards, a coarse male voice, gait, and pelvic structure. They love to hunt, smoke a pipe, carouse, and embark on dangerous adventures, preferring male clothing and often wearing their hair short.[65]

While the sources generally agreed upon a definition of homosexuality as sexual attraction to members of one's own sex, there was a wide range of opinion over what specifically constituted homosexual sexual practice, and ultimately homosexual identity. The prominent psychiatrist and neurologist V. M. Bekhterev distinguished three types of homosexuality: "complete homosexuality," where there is no attraction to the opposite sex; "incomplete homosexuality," in which there is a predilection for one's own sex; and "indifferent homosexuality," where there is no preference for one sex or the other. Dr. Golomb identified all males who engage in anal sex as "pederasts" (a term that in Russian does not necessarily imply sex with minors) and located homosexuality and lesbianism between fetishism and masochism in his categorization of sexual perversions.[66]

In Vasilevskii's estimation, "the most common male homosexual behavior is '*muzhelozhstvo*,' that is, sexual intercourse through the anus, usually with boys (pederasty)." The author divided "pederasts" into active and passive, depending upon whether they assumed the "male" or "female" role in the sexual act, noting also that their activity might be confined to courting, kissing, hugging, and mutual masturbation. As for lesbianism, Vasilevskii claimed that the "perversion" was frequently encountered among prostitutes or in prisons and was often coerced. Included on his list of specific examples of "lesbian love" were kisses, hugs, mutual masturbation, the stimulation of the sex parts, as well as "even more repulsive methods that there is no need to relate."[67]

Professor V. P. Protopopov distinguished between pederasty, identified as sex between men owing to the absence of women, and homosexuality. Whereas in his analysis pederasts pursue boys or effeminate men, homosexuals are only attracted to masculine men. He explained that intercourse is the pederast's sole interest; there is no psychological element to their behavior, unlike in homosexuals, for whom the sex act is of least and last importance. Moreover, homosexual sexual satisfaction is achieved through a variety of methods (including anal and oral sex, manual stimulation, and kissing), and it is inappropriate to claim predominance for any of these. For this reason, Protopopov concluded: "It makes no sense to talk about active and passive roles, because the most crucial factor is the desire to be loved, to court, etc." Protopopov's conclusions were in turn contradicted by Professor Iudin's "hormonal opposites" theory of sexual attraction, in which "a completely expressed man looks for a completely expressed woman, a feminized man is attracted to a masculinized woman, a homosexual man with a preponderance of female characteristics is attracted more to a man with male characteristics, etc."[68]

Given the lack of consensus on the particularities of same-sex attraction or sexual behavior, how did these authors identify or distinguish homosexuals? Even the external markings of homosexuality were not completely reliable, as Mendel'son himself acknowledged after concluding his list of the traits found in mannish women and womanly men: "Not all men and women with same-sex sexual attraction look like members of the opposite sex: one encounters men with a perfectly correct male appearance." There was little distinction between writers' descriptions of homosexual characteristics and traits and their earlier assessments of the appearance and behavior of eunuchs, and other hormonally deficient men and women. In fact, in at least one physician's analysis, a simple encounter between two individuals of insufficiently expressed sexual type is enough to "summon an explosion of same-sex passion."[69]

Doctors located the origin of these deviated sex traits in the sex glands. The vast majority of sex education materials explained homosexuality as a "biological accident," a congenital defect stemming from the presence of both male and female hormones in the gonads.[70] If, according to this theory, a man possessed more female than male incretory cells, he would be attracted to other men. Similarly, a preponderance of male over female hormones in a woman would result in lesbianism. Once again, the gland transplant experiments provided the evidence for this hormonal interpretation of same-sex attraction, first elaborated by Steinach in 1911. Describing the scientist's artificial creation of "sexual deviation," Vasilevskii concluded:

> Thus the transformation of male to female and female to male was achieved, moreover the behavior of the animals completely changed; the male transformed into a female lost his courage, became meek, cared for the young, fed them and began to arouse sexual attraction in the real males, and the females transformed into males became stronger and braver, pursued the real females, mounted them, etc. Thus the secondary sex characteristics, including the type of sexual attraction, depends solely on the corresponding hormones.

As further confirmation of this theory, Vasilevskii cited another set of experiments in which Steinach grafted both male and female sex glands into a previously castrated male. Depending upon which hormone predominated in this artificial "hermaphrodite," the animal would be attracted either to other males or to females.[71]

The microscope appeared to corroborate Steinach's hypothesis, regardless of whether the glands examined belonged to a male homosexual or to a she-goat who, refusing all male advances, attempted to mate with other females. In each case the fabric of the sex glands, despite the "normalcy" of their external appearance, revealed a combination of male and female hormones.[72] Purportedly even more convincing corroboration of the glandular theory of homosexuality was provided by Steinach's success in "curing" several men who suffered from this affliction. This procedure, first performed by Steinach's colleague the urologist Robert Lichtenstern, involved the removal of the subject's defective testicles and their replacement by a testis taken from a "normal" man:

> The grafted testicle stabilized and just a few days later the character of the sick man changed; he began to flirt with the nurses in the hospital and grew ashamed of his past. Six weeks after the operation he had sex with a woman, a year later married, and from that time on has led a completely normal sex life. All his former, preoperation female secondary sex characteristics disappeared, and the male ones increased. The patient was thirty, and he had first discovered his homosexuality when only fourteen.[73]

The relatively large share of attention devoted to Steinach's experiments and the hormonal understanding of homosexuality in popular sex education literature is all the more noteworthy given that other hypotheses of the origins of same-sex love were seldom cited. The few works that considered alternatives mentioned the theory of homosexuality as a manifestation of congenital psychopathology (Krafft-Ebing, Moll); a result of hereditary syphilis (Tarnovskii); an inborn, intermediate form of sexuality (Hirschfeld, Weininger); or a concatenation of both environmental and hereditary factors (Freud).[74] In contrast, the frequent references to the glandular interpretation may be seen as reflecting the broader general interest in the emerging field of endocrinology, and the remarkable discoveries associated with the endocrine glands discussed at the beginning of this chapter.

Another explanation has to do with the changed policy on homosexuality in the new state. Before the Revolution, anal intercourse among men (*muzhelozhstvo*) was prohibited by Articles 995 and 996 of the Imperial Legal Code; sex among women was not mentioned.[75] Despite a growing popular and literary interest in the subject of homosexuality after the turn of the century, and the increasing support among various segments of Russian educated society (including legal scholars, scientists, and physicians) for a reassessment of this proscription, the law remained on the books until 1917, when it was thrown out along with the rest of the Tsarist Code. The legality of homosexual sex among consenting adults was codified in the first legal code of the RSFSR, the Criminal Code of 1922.[76]

The decriminalization of homosexuality in the 1922 law code should be viewed in the context of the changing attitude in the late Imperial period toward same-sex love as a medical rather than a juridical problem. The impact of European scientific thought on this issue and, in particular, the influence of German-speaking colleagues were influential in Russian professionals' own reformulation. By the late nineteenth century, many Western forensic and medical experts were inclined to view homosexuality as a pathology (either environmentally or hereditarily induced) rather than a crime. Sympathetic Russians also followed with interest the efforts of the German homosexual rights movement—Magnus Hirschfeld's Scientific-Humanitarian Committee in particular—to win decriminalization of male homosexuality.[77]

As justification for their repeated petitions to the Reichstag, Hirschfeld's committee employed an alternate, biological explanation for homosexuality that was gaining currency among Central European physicians at the end of the nineteenth century. (In France, in contrast, the degeneration interpretation of homosexuality remained prevalent among psychiatrists until World War I.)[78] Opposing the view held by orthodox physicians that homosexuality could be acquired (and hence must remain illegal), this alternate interpretation theorized it as the result of a developmental error, leading to a bodily fusion of male and female despite the normalcy of the genitals. Yet not until the publication of Steinach's endocrinology experiments and his elaboration of the hormonal theory of homosexuality on the eve of World War I did Hirschfeld find a plausible causal explanation for this anomaly. Like Kol'tsov, Hirschfeld traveled to Steinach's lab in Vienna to view for himself the feminized and masculinized rats and guinea pigs. Originally skeptical about the possibility of treating this condition, Hirschfeld eventually became a strong supporter of Steinach's corrective surgery method, writing about it in his journal and referring patients for the procedure.[79]

Sexual enlighteners who subscribed to the hormonal theory of homosexuality employed a similar line of thinking:

> [Homosexuality] is not a sign of perversion of taste or character, but a result of a specific illness, a specific irregularity [*nepravilnost'*] in the structure of the system of internal secretions, especially in the structure of the sex gland. From this it follows that homosexuals should not be punished as debauchers but cured as sick people, with the help of an operation. Furthermore, even recently the English poet Oscar Wilde, convicted of same-sex love, paid for this with a long prison sentence, depriving the world of a wonderful poet.[80]

Even though Russian doctors borrowed heavily from German theory, the social and cultural contexts of the debate on homosexuality in the two countries diverged significantly. In Germany the evidence of endocrinology was used by a group of self-identified homosexuals to win support for their own status and way of life. In Imperial Russia there could have been no possibility of a similar community uniting around a homosexual identity to demand civil rights; discussion of same-sex love was restricted to the realms of fiction, the popular press, and the pages of medical and legal journals.

Two other factors should be kept in mind when seeking to explain Soviet physicians' widespread support for a hormonal interpretation of homosexuality in the 1920s. First, the legal sanctioning of consensual homosexual acts in the 1922 Criminal Code occurred before the majority of these authors began publishing. And second, by the time Russians started to write about this topic, the German medical and scientific communities had almost unanimously rejected Steinach's theory, especially his claims about curing homosexuality through glandular transplants.

Specifically, opposition arose to Steinach's contention that histological examination of the testes removed from homosexual subjects revealed cells strikingly similar to those of the ovaries, which he labeled "F-cells." No other scientists were ever able to find F-cells in their testicular specimens. In an extensive review of several studies in 1923, the psychiatrist Kurt Blum concluded that Steinach's glandular explanation of homosexuality could not be confirmed, thereby undercutting Hirschfeld's congenital interpretation of same-sex love. Hirschfeld remained Steinach's only consistent supporter, but eventually even he stopped writing about the theory. By the end of the decade surgeons no longer performed the procedure, and Steinach himself had redirected his professional attention elsewhere.[81]

In Russia in 1923, M. M. Zavadovskii attempted—and failed—to cure a male homosexual by performing Steinach's procedure. A 1928 effort by the psychiatrist Dr. Ia. I Kirov to cure a lesbian using the Steinach method was similarly unsuccessful. When "Efrosiniia" continued to pursue women, Kirov concluded that the failed experiment proved the fallacy of Steinach's ideas. Sexual enlighteners continued to address Steinach's theories favorably even after the publication of Kirov's assessment. Because the article was published in Ukraine's leading scholarly medical publication, at least some of the physicians discussed here should have been familiar with the experiment's failure and Kirov's conclusions.[82]

The often noted lag in the reception of foreign scientific ideas in Russia may have been partly responsible for the strong support that Steinach continued to enjoy among sex educators even at the end of the decade. Nonetheless, I would argue that far more important than the scientific legitimacy of this theory or even the authors' proper understanding of endocrinology was its role in the sexual enlightenment project. The hormonal interpretation of homosexuality served to emphasize the importance of the glands (and hence the need to take care of them), and to pathologize "unmanly" and "unwomanly" behavior. One justification for discussions of homosexuality in educational materials was to confirm the biological "correctness" of heterosexuality, and consequently the appropriate forms of heterosexual sex to be specified by qualified experts. Yet those medical writers who subscribed to a hormonal interpretation of sexual attraction did not consider same-sex love especially dangerous to the general population, since, as a developmental defect, it could not be caught or inherited. Thus, the topic of homosexuality appeared in their analyses of the glands less out of the need to convince readers to refrain from this kind of sex than to emphasize the pathological nature of all forms of unmanliness and unwomanliness and any sort of weakening or transgressing of gender roles. Homosexuality is the one "social pathology" addressed by sexual enlighteners that shifts categories entirely, becoming a biological problem rather than a social one. Since homosexuality, unlike venereal disease, is not defined as communicable, homosexuals become the only "deviants" who cease to be a threat. Despite their incompatibility with strict gender norms, they do not represent a true danger to masculinity and femininity. Gender transgressions were perceived to be a far greater societal threat than sexual ones.

As with the example of the eunuch, the theory of an involuntary, hormonally induced deviation in sexual attraction likewise served to illustrate that normalcy was wholly dependent upon the glands' proper functioning. Thus to ensure sexual and bodily health, readers were advised to avoid behaviors identified as similarly injurious to the glands (such as masturbation and premarital sex) that were *within* their power to control. In the pamphlet *Sexual Knowledge*, for example, Dr. Bakaleinikov concluded his discussion of the hormonal origin of homosexuality by noting:

> If sperm and hormones hold such great significance for the body, doesn't it follow that one should approach sexual literacy with thoughtfulness and great seriousness; doesn't it follow that young people should base their actions on the preservation of highly valuable sexual energy, which gives the most important vital blessing—health? It is easier for a healthy person with a surplus of the sexual juices that comprise an important source of energy to embark on this great path flooded with the light of knowledge.[83]

For Bakaleinikov, to be sexually literate meant to follow the advice of specialists like himself about sexual continence and to redirect this energy toward other goals (a subject we will return to in a later chapter).

Curiously, the rejection of Steinach's theory by Western scientists and physicians was ignored even by the minority of Russian health educators who favored an alternate explanation of homosexuality; there appeared only several vague allusions to a "lack of consensus" on this issue in their writings. The only challenge to the prevailing glandular explanation of homosexuality that received more than a passing mention in sexual enlightenment was that of the noted scientist Vladimir M. Bekhterev. Over the course of the 1920s until his death in 1927 Bekhterev published a number of articles on the topic in both popular health and medical presses and was in turn cited in the works of a handful of other popular medical authors.[84] Bekhterev's environmental interpretation of homosexuality derived from the principles of reflexology, the branch of psychiatry he founded. Dismissing both hormonal and hereditary explanations, he maintained that homosexuality, like heterosexuality, developed as a result of conditional reflexes, in response to childhood environmental influences.[85]

Whatever objections Bekhterev and his adherents may have had to the hormonal interpretation of homosexuality, their contributions to sexual enlightenment, like those of their opponents, were strikingly free of the rancor with which the nerve-gland debate was greeted in other scientific quarters. Naiman has shown that Russian scientists and popular science writers took advantage of a chronological coincidence—that the new field of endocrinology emerged concurrent with the demise of the old regime and the establishment of Soviet power—to portray in revolutionary language the victory of glands (and the science that studied them) over the nerves. Significantly, in his 1922 *Nature* article cited above, endocrinologist N. Perna singled out the work of both Bekhterev and Pavlov on reflexes as examples of the old, nineteenth-century worldview, which had been supplanted by the new, twentieth-century scientific "dictatorship" of the glands.[86]

Few of the sex educators were specialists in either neuropsychiatry or endocrinology, which might explain the relative lack of bitter partisanship among them on this issue. Many writers were able to accommodate elements of both interpretations in their analyses. Dr. Glezer, for instance, distinguished between cases of congenital sexual perversion owing to glandular deficiencies and the far greater number of cases resulting from "nasty habit, imitation, sexual oversaturation and excess." Professor Iudin cautioned that, even if the hormonal explanation of homosexuality were understood to be "correct," it was "by no means [so] in all cases." Conditional reflexes and the educational environment also played a significant role, as did the example of others in jails, hotels, and "certain cultures." In such instances homosexuality was neither a symptom of pathology nor a "biological illness," but rather a "social illness."[87] Dr. Vasilevskii identified one particularly contemptible manifestation of this socially induced disorder:

> It is impossible to deny that particularly refined debauchers often turn to homosexuality. People who are satiated with excesses in normal sex search for new and strong sensations in same-sex relationships, capable of arousing their chilled blood and impotent imagination. In particular, such cases of pederasty are encountered among hedonistic old men, long impotent, who choose defenseless children for their victims, exploiting their need and naiveté.[88]

Certain proponents of the glandular theory also noted several other, often seemingly contradictory, influences in the etiology of same-sex attraction, including mental illness or retardation, feeble-mindedness, progressive paralysis, neuropsychological imbalance, and hereditary degeneration. Just as supporters of the congenital interpretation did not necessarily favor greater tolerance toward homosexuality, neither did proponents of the acquired theory inevitably advocate punitive measures against same-sex love. Having informed his readers that innate homosexuals could be "essentially normal people," and that historically many of the world's most highly gifted artists, actors, and politicians were homosexuals, Dr. Mendel'son nonetheless concluded his article with the observation: "Frequently homosexuality is encountered among degenerates as well: the mentally ill, idiots, and recidivists." Bekhterev, on the other hand, was careful to lay the blame for the "societal evil" of homosexuality on the conditions of one's education, rather than upon homosexuals themselves.[89]

THE DEVIATIONS OF MODERNITY

Although unwilling to entertain the possibility of gender difference as culturally rather than biologically produced, enlighteners nonetheless identified several aspects of current civilization as contributing to the deviation from "natural" gender roles and the laws of attraction. They argued that contemporary culture bombarded the senses with stimuli, dangerously heightening sexual feeling to a degree unknown to either "primitive man" or "savage peoples." Attraction was artificially enhanced by alcohol, spicy food, too much meat, or a sedentary lifestyle. The city, teeming with indecent and unhealthy temptations, represented an especially pernicious influence.[90]

Heading their list as the modern world's most "artificial" creation, and the best indicator of how far culture had strayed from the natural order, was the coquette, who drew upon all tools at her disposal (red lipstick, nail polish, perfume and powder, seductive clothing and jewelry, flirting and feminine charms) to captivate the opposite sex. Professor Sakharov accounted for the development of this phenomenon by explaining that in "primitive" cultures, as well as in the animal world, such physical ornamentation was the province of the males and was used by them to entice and woo the more plain, more modest-looking females. But various economic and social factors, most particularly the rise of capitalism, had radically distorted nature's system of "sexual signalization" by transforming women into parasites of pleasure who competed with one another to attract the wealthiest possible mate. Women of the bourgeoisie and petit-bourgeoisie had become "dressed up doll[s], whose every thought revolved around costumes, fashion, and shining adornments." With the Revolution came the opportunity to remedy the situation. "Only in the current socialistic structure," Sakharov concluded, "built on the foundation of labor and equality between the sexes, is woman emancipated and made again into a person, equal to man and significant not as an amusement but as a comrade."[91]

In the sex educators' pantheon of deviants and social pathologies, the coquette occupies a special place in that, unlike the homosexual, lesbian, prostitute, or syphilitic, she would not be the object of sexological scrutiny without the theoretical framework of Marxism. Clearly not identical to the pathologized nymphomaniac, she is the locus where economic and sexual exploitations meet but without crossing the criminal boundary of prostitution. In addressing this figure, Soviet doctors are broaching a problem raised by radical revolutionary thought, as opposed to the standard, pan-European litany of sociosexual ills. The coquette bears the burden of the Bolshevik disdain for traditional "bourgeois" femininity as the embodiment of *byt*, a hostility that Russian radicalism inherits from both European Marxism and the Russian philosophical tradition.[92] Hence this is one area in which Soviet sexual enlighteners need not look to Western scientific literature for a model, and for which a purely Soviet solution could be expected.

Yet, in the estimation of these authors, the conditions of NEP had seriously undermined whatever remedy the Revolution may have provided. The revival of the market had ushered in the Nepman, whose raison d'être (besides the accumulation of capital) was the pursuit of sensual, inevitably depraved, pleasure. As Dr. Tkachenko elaborated, a "special type of woman-*samka*" soon again appeared in the cities to satisfy these licentious demands, "with her special rotting attributes, methods, flirtations and coquettishness, her garish dress and cosmetics, [looking like] a cheap doll bearing the sign: 'if you don't trick them, you won't make the sale' [*ne obmanesh'—ne prodash'*], and her shameless, open beckoning to the male of the species [*samets*]."[93]

Here is one instance where a comparison between humans and the animal world, through the use of the terms for the female and male of the species (*samka* and *samets*), carried extremely negative connotations. And yet, as these works had previously asserted, in nature males assumed the active role and females the passive in the mating process; the females' "shameless beckoning" of the males that Tkachenko here attributed to animals was in fact precisely what educators found amiss in human interactions. During the mid-1920s the shapely, painted, quasi-prostitute became a pervasive symbol of the ideological taint of NEP through her connection to the pre-Communist past, her status as a commodity, and her overt sexuality.[94] To medical educators writing about the glands, the blatant nature of this woman's sexuality was less troubling than its particularly masculine quality; the coquette upset nature's sexual order through her active pursuit of men. In this respect her "bourgeois" cosmetics, attire, and bearing served as instruments of her predatory transgression.

L. Ia. Iakobzon was the only author who considered the appearance of the coquette to be both natural and logical. In his analysis it was women's biological role to attract men, using everything in their power to do so. Iakobzon cited a Berlin professor who attributed the sharp increase in women's use of cosmetics, sexy clothing, and flesh-colored stockings after World War I to the greater competition for a mate, since "the World War had mowed down a majority of men." Moreover, war survivors also avoided marriage because they suffered from an extremely high incidence of sexual disorders, which Iakobzon related to their worn nerves and to a worsening of social conditions. "These circumstances sometimes compel a new woman, even if she does not require the material support of a man, to go from a defensive stance (even if only fictitious) to a fairly open offensive for a man; here the economic motives of coquetry are replaced with motives of another sort." Distinguishing between coquetry and flirtation (a sexual urge that stops short of intercourse), he concluded:

> I think that coquetry will never disappear; it should retain its place in life. Coquetry, remaining in the boundaries of decency, enters into the behavior of every intelligent woman. The coquettishness a wife directs at a husband prevents him from cooling toward her and thus strengthens monogamy, which is the basis of every cultured society.[95]

Others, however, found the reappearance of such women after the Revolution extremely discomfiting, evidence not of the society's culture but of its pollution by the reviled past. According to Commissar Semashko, the explanation for this contamination lay in the population's psychological unpreparedness for a restructuring of everyday life, which was "lagging behind" the country's economic reconstruction, already underway. To illustrate this point, Semashko cited an observation made by Chernyshevskii, the nineteenth-century radical intellectual, concerning the different requirements for a wife in diverse layers of society. Nobles sought physical evidence of "good blood" such as small hands and feet, an hourglass figure, languishing eyes, frailty, tenderness, and sensitivity. Yet to a peasant such a mate would have been both impractical and unsuitable; he required a robust and healthy wife, capable of arduous physical labor. Thus, every class perceives beauty based on its own conditions of life, labor, and daily experience, and in relation to its class interests. How then should the reemergence of the coquette after the Revolution be understood? Semashko asked his audience:

> In factories, businesses, and villages, haven't you had occasion to observe peasant girls and female workers who tried to look like pure-bloods, like noble girls? Hasn't the red ink in your offices disappeared surprisingly quickly, as it once did in mine, because of its use to color lips? This old-fashioned trick still lives on not only in our offices, but in the factory, in business, in

the village. And female workers and peasants, instead of burning with hate for these former sickly noble girls, imitate them. It would seem that each woman worker and peasant should be morally nauseated by these remnants of the old mode of life, but instead they frequently copy them.[96]

Here the coquette figured as both symptom and cause of the present's contamination by the past; responsibility was shifted away from society (which, according to Semashko's analysis, had previously created the demands for certain kinds of mates) and onto these women themselves. To achieve the psychological preconditions necessary for the successful construction of a new lifestyle required that the old one, here represented as the painted woman, be destroyed. The weapon he proposed for this excision was hatred: "When we ignite this sacred hatred in the breast of each young woman worker, male worker, woman peasant, each laborer of our Union, then we shall see around us a mass of opportunities in order to build a healthy, happy, radiant lifestyle, on the site of the old, putrid, accursed mode of life." In practical terms, Semashko's solution necessitated the inculcation of self-hatred in these women. Other authors, such as Dr. Glezer, agreed:

It is understandable that for a proletarian woman, an equal worker who, like a man, has the right to life and happiness, it is completely indecent to wear lipstick and powder, to get manicures and think only about clothes. . . . She doesn't need to dress up like a coquette to attract a man. She will find a man friend to continue the race and to share in struggle and labor.[97]

Ultimately, the construction of a new mode of life also required men's rejection of this type of woman. Yet in both these analyses, men were absolved of any responsibility in desiring and hence contributing to the reappearance of the coquette after the Revolution. In a 1924 lecture on the sex question later published under the title "Is Femininity Necessary?" the commissar revealed the primary reason behind male exculpation. The lecture began with Semashko's recalling the dozens of notes he received at such venues, all written in a feminine hand and asking the same question:

You talk about equality between the sexes, about lack of force and comradely relations between men and women, you stigmatize every form of artificiality, pomaded and painted woman, as a rude, coarse, sexual provocation. But meanwhile even Komsomol members and Communists cling to precisely these women and run from women-comrades.

In response, he described two extreme types observable among young women, both worthy of condemnation. The first was that remnant of the reviled past, the parasitic aristocratic lady, with her red lips, eye makeup, and hourglass figure. This "looking toward the past" deserved the most severe censure, especially by the women workers and peasants prone to imitate her.[98]

Yet the second extreme type was far worse. This was the "masculine" woman who had "completely lost her feminine traits and transformed herself into a man . . . with disheveled, frequently dirty, hair, a cigarette between her lips (like a man), deliberately gruff manners (like a man), deliberately rude voice (like a man), etc." The mannish woman who had "exterminated all her purely female spiritual qualities" was "incorrect" because "woman at the very least in the present and the near future has her own social function and her special character traits." And to illustrate the biological basis of these feminine traits (and hence the abnormality of the mannish woman), he again turned to Steinach's animal gland transplant experiments. Semashko argued that the dramatic physical and psychological changes experienced by the animals—the "masculinization" of the female specimens and the "feminization" of the male specimens—"demonstrated that the female constitution, designed for the function of giving birth, marks woman with the stamp of femininity, along with the female qualities of tenderness, attention, spirituality, and gentleness." The example of nursing confirmed this conclusion. Whereas men and women could be found in the "treatment" professions of doctor or medic, the "caring" profession of nursing was almost exclusively female. This had come about as a result of natural selection, since caring was a predominantly feminine trait. He then asked:

> Do we need to destroy femininity in the name of sexual equality, displaying its destruction even in its external form: brusque manner, harsh voice, etc.? We don't have to: it's still unclear what type of human being will result in the future. Without a doubt, it will inherit the best aspects of the male and female character. But for now femininity in this sense of the word suits us. . . . That which is best in a woman—and that which will remain regardless of attempts to poison it—needs to be preserved in her. Vulgar equality of the sexes only profanes a correct and good idea.[99]

For this reason, Komsomol and Party members were "instinctively attracted" to "the painted dolls who exaggerated their female traits, overemphasizing them above all else"; the young men could not find this femininity in the mannish "blue stockings," the name, Semashko explained, that had formerly been applied to "masculinized nihilists."[100] Thus ultimately, men's sexual class transgressions were forgivable, since they were only fulfilling their biological role by evincing sexual attraction to the "real" females of the species, that is, those with the proper secondary sex traits.[101] The aberrations of contemporary women had two possible manifestations. The first was the coquette, whose sexual aggression was intrinsically linked to the class contamination of the tsarist past. Yet, as Semashko and the other authors cited in this chapter concluded, the manly woman, transgressing against nature itself, posed the graver threat. Since in the experts' analyses, physical appearance translated into behavior, on the most practical level the "degendering" of women would deprive the country of the traits only they had the ability to fulfill.

Semashko returned to this theme in his *Izvestiia* editorial, criticizing his Party comrades for their ignorance of biology and especially the role of the endocrine glands. In particular he singled out Liadov's thesis that man must overcome the tendency to view woman as a representative of the opposite sex rather than as a comrade. Semashko responded: "That one needs to relate to woman first of all as a comrade—this is the sacred truth, but that you have to destroy in yourself your relationship to another person as to a member of the opposite sex—what is that? The preaching of a monk?"[102] In hedging on the issue of sexual equality by leaving it to be resolved until sometime in the distant future (like communism, or sexual privacy earlier in this chapter), Semashko ignored the full political implications of his biologically based analysis.

In Chapter 1 of this study, I suggested that the paucity of references to Bolshevism in popular medical writings may have stemmed from physicians' attempts to assert their jurisdictive authority over the domain of the sex question. The frequent references to the endocrine glands by Semashko and the other sex educators fulfilled a similar function. Yet with respect to sexual enlighteners' biological reading of gender difference, this explanation is incomplete. The belief in a fundamental difference between the sexes was such an embedded, integral part of the Soviet worldview that even those who subscribed to an environmentalist interpretation of social development would have been incapable of applying this theory to the distinctions between men and women.

Instead, doctors and scientists marshaled all available scientific "evidence" to argue for the primacy of biology in questions of sexual difference: "normal" heterosexual males and females, as well as "defective" homosexuals and lesbians, are the results of overriding biological imperatives and therefore cannot, and should not, be changed by misguided social experimentation, which would "castrate" them just as effectively as the scalpel emasculates the *skopets* and the gelding or virilizes hens and women through ovariectomies. As with their continued support for Steinach's discredited theory to explain homosexuality, sexual enlighteners promoted these ideas even as a growing number of biochemists engaged in endocrinological research had begun to dispute the view of the hormones as "dualistic agents of sex," having discovered the presence of female sex hormones in "normal" male organisms, and vice versa.[103] Men and women, in the understanding of these writers, seemed to belong to related yet distinct species. Were all social obstacles to equal development removed, basic differences between the two would nonetheless inevitably and necessarily remain, as the endocrinologist Nemilov concluded: "We don't know a person, as such, we know only man and woman."[104]

"Nervous People"

Sexual Dysfunction and the Crisis of Nervousness in the 1920s

Nervousness is becoming the social disease of our time.
—DR. L. A. PROZOROV, *SOVETSKAIA MEDITSINA V BOR'BE ZA ZDOROVYE NERVY*

• In the mid-1920s, the medical and popular health press began to devote considerable attention to a phenomenon physicians claimed to be encountering with increasing frequency. Dr. B. Gurvich described one such experience:

> They arrived together, comrades Kh. and N. Both are workers. One is 19, the other 18 years old. First one came in to see me, a pale, thin youth. "What is troubling you?" I asked him the usual question. "For over a year now I've had nocturnal emissions [*polliutsiia*]; it worries me. I didn't know about the existence of the Counseling Center, for a long time I've wanted to see a doctor, but a private one costs a lot of money. I cannot work, I'm upset all the time, I've given up my studies at the factory school, I constantly think about my illness. My comrade is here with me. He has the same problem, and we decided to come to the clinic together for help."

Doctors reported that young men from all walks of life were arriving in alarming numbers at their clinic doors, complaining of a wide variety of debilitating sexual disorders. Like the two workers in the case history above, they were described as shaking, insecure, paralyzed with fear, often threatening to end their lives. According to the venereologist L. Ia. Iakobzon, the number of these cases had reached such "completely inconceivable proportions, [that] if it were possible to conduct an anonymous survey on the sexual abilities of men in the USSR, we would be left with extremely discomfiting conclusions."[1]

Whether actual rates of male sexual dysfunction were on the rise is not the issue here; there is no evidence to confirm or deny that the medical histories discussed in print were cases of "real" patients presenting themselves for treatment. This "epidemic" of male sexual dysfunction is not a matter of epidemiology per se. Its etiology, diagnosis, and treatment were an integral part of the medical discourse of sex, with the Moscow Counseling Center for Sexual Hygiene playing a central role. Originally founded to provide premarital advice and venereal disease screenings, the clinic gradually reinvented itself through the popular press as an authority in the care of sexually dysfunctional men. The impotent man would prove to be particularly disconcerting in the 1920s, embodying the cultural anxieties that haunted Soviet Russia in the age of NEP.

The purported diagnostic and curative success with male sexual dysfunction lay in health writers' ability to exploit the widespread sense of unease and crisis that was pervasive throughout Soviet society during the era. Yet nervousness was not limited to clinic patients. The medical construction of this illness expressed physicians' own anxieties about the male body, the profession's authority over the realm of sexuality, and more generalized fears about the potential impotence of the new state. Equally significant is the doctors' approach to frigidity, which bordered on wholesale neglect. As a sexual dysfunction, frigidity was a poor fit for a model of health that had little use for pleasure. After all, a woman's inability to achieve orgasm did not interfere with procreation, which was the sole acknowledged purpose of sexual intercourse. The female body is also the locus of the physicians' anxieties, but only when it can be characterized as hypersexual rather than understimulated. When frigidity is addressed, it is only within the context of male nervousness.

On January 1, 1925, at the height of NEP, a new periodical appeared in Moscow. Published from 1925 to 1931 by the State Venereological Institute, *Toward a Healthy Lifestyle* (*Za zdorovyi byt*) was "dedicated to questions concerning the fight against venereal diseases and prostitution, the family and marriage, sexual enlightenment and education." The only newspaper in the 1920s devoted exclusively to the sex question, *Toward a Healthy Lifestyle* joined the ranks of growing numbers of "sanitary enlightenment" publications whose aim was the transformation of daily life through a widespread program of health and hygiene propaganda. Its intended audience included not only medical personnel and health educators, but above all the working class. The newspaper's primary goal was to educate workers and to enlist their help in disseminating the correct information about sexual health to their communities. Representing a wide variety of medical specialties on its pages (including venereology, social hygiene, psychiatry, pedology, forensic and sanitary medicine), *Toward a Healthy Lifestyle* illustrates precisely how these members of the medical community conceptualized the sex question: what doctors understood to be its boundaries and content, the origins of contemporary sexual problems, and the methods developed to resolve them.

According to the paper's contributors, popular ignorance was the only obstacle to sexual health; once people received the proper information, all sexual problems would disappear. This orientation was reiterated on page 3 of the first issue, in an announcement publicizing the opening of the Moscow Counseling Center for Sexual Hygiene *(Konsul'tatsiia po polovoi gigiene)*, which offered the public free advice on sex. "The fundamental reason for sexual irregularity lies in the fact that wide segments of the population are very poorly informed about the essence of the sex question, how sexual abnormalities come about, how one should conduct a proper sex life, etc."[2]

Jointly established by the State Venereological Institute and the State Institute of Social Hygiene, the Counseling Center for Sexual Hygiene (also called the Counseling Center for a Healthy Lifestyle) aimed to provide Muscovites with the opportunity to receive information and advice tailored to their own particular sexual experiences. According to the newspaper announcement, the center's founders had two specific segments of the population in mind: first and foremost, they reached out to the young, for whom "new urges, doubts, misgivings demanded . . . [o]pen comradely discussions with a knowledgeable person, timely, genuine, authoritative advice, [which] would render an exceptional service to a young person and prevent many serious emotional experiences." The second group that the doctors hoped to attract was parents. Reminding them of their responsibility in attending to the sexual development of their children at a very early age, the founders again advocated the merits of opportune advice. For both audiences, the focus was on prevention of illness rather than the treatment of preexisting conditions. This emphasis was underscored by the very name given to the clinic: "a healthy lifestyle" linked the mission of this institution to the widespread revolutionary "fight for a new lifestyle," which was aimed at the radical restructuring of all aspects of a person's existence; "sexual hygiene" referred to the rules that were to govern one's sexual behavior, involving such issues as frequency of intercourse, the use of birth control, and the proper sanitary regime during menstruation.

The center was housed in the State Institute of Social Hygiene at number 14 Vozdvizhenka in central Moscow. It opened its doors to the public in November 1925 and received visitors twice weekly, on Monday and Thursday from 6 to 7 in the evening. Soon thereafter the Moscow State Neuro-Psychiatric Dispensary joined as a sponsoring institution.[3]

The clinic operated according to a set procedure: upon arrival at the office, the person seeking advice was greeted by either a venereologist-urologist, a psychoneurologist, or a psychiatrist. To underline the confidential nature of the visit, the physicians, who rotated staffing responsibilities, worked unassisted. The visitor filled out a questionnaire that solicited biographical information and then related his or her question. If the doctor was unable to resolve the issue immediately, the subject was directed to an appropriate medical institution for more specialized care.[4] For this purpose special arrangements were made with, among others, the Department of Therapy at the Bol'shaia Gruzinskaia Walk-in Clinic; obstetrician-gynecologists Professor Rakhmanov and Dr. Lur'e of the State Institute of Obstetrics; the State Venereological Institute; the Neuro-Psychiatric Dispensary; and finally, a consulting lawyer based at the Neuro-Psychiatric Dispensary and the Juridical Counseling Center of the Institute for the Preservation of Maternity and Childhood. Over the next several years, counseling centers based upon the Moscow model opened in many cities throughout the Soviet Union, including Tashkent, Tbilisi, Iaroslavl', Leningrad, Odessa, and Khar'kov.[5]

The staff physicians divided their duties based on their particular specializations: the psychoneurologist and psychiatrist would concentrate on irregularities of early and late sexual development, masturbation, and such sexual "abnormalities" as neuropathic conditions, inorganic impotence, and hypersexuality. The venereologist would focus on birth control, physiological impotence, illnesses of the genitourinary organs, and questions related to marriage. In its organizational charter, the doctors also identified the clinic's presumed clientele and the likely reasons for their visits. Young people would seek advice about the onset of puberty, abnormalities of sexual development, masturbation, neuropathic conditions, and first sexual experiences. The adult population would be interested in questions relating to marriage, the sex education of children, sexual anomalies, sexual neuroses, birth control, and venereal disease. Besides providing the populace with the correct sexual information and concrete advice, the clinic would also serve as a laboratory, furnishing specialists with a convenient pool of subjects. Other goals involved the development of different approaches to the study of individual and societal sexual behavior.[6]

By 1927, physicians associated with the center had gathered enough data to permit the first published analyses of the institution's progress. Their evaluations communicate a great deal about their expectations for the counseling center and about their own professional identity, especially in relation to their colleagues in the West. Every account of the clinic written for a medical audience began with a lengthy discussion of its foreign predecessors, tracing its roots from the founding of the first sex counseling center in the United States in 1895 to its continued extension throughout Europe and especially Germany.[7] After this preliminary historical introduction, the authors turned to the Moscow Counseling Center, presenting it as the Soviet contribution to the growing international movement. As their comments reveal, they fully expected their data to conform to the statistics provided by their European colleagues.

Yet the Russian physicians found themselves faced with a very different portrait of sexual behaviors and concerns. Whereas, according to the studies cited, the largest segment of those visiting the counseling centers in Berlin, Dresden, and Mannheim sought information on sexual hygiene or wished to confirm their health before marriage, the vast majority of those who came to the Moscow Counseling Center were men suffering from sexual dysfunction. In fact, 59.6 percent of this institution's first-year visitors were men, predominantly in their twenties, who complained of impotence, premature ejaculation, nocturnal emissions, or masturbation-related sexual failure. Four times as many men frequented the clinic as women, another point of difference between the Russian and the European clinics, where the gender ratio was more even. Only in terms of age and social origin did the Russian statistics resemble those of their European counterparts; white-collar workers predominated in both, with students following in second place, and "proletarians" a distant third. This comparatively low attendance of workers was attributed by the Russian doctors to the artificial nature of the sample, since advertisements of the clinic's existence had been intentionally restricted to only a few factories and educational institutions. (The doctors never explain why they limited advertisements of the clinic's existence. Presumably it had to do with the fact that, as the first Soviet sex consultation, it was considered to be experimental and that further expansion would depend on its success in handling this initial client base. Doctors also may have feared a larger turnout than they were able to accommodate.)[8]

The authors' interpretation of the data assumed that Russians had yet to attain the higher level of sexual "consciousness" to be found in Europe, where couples visited the clinics for reasons the doctors deemed more "enlightened." Yet this conclusion resulted in part from a flawed comparison: the German clinics to which the Russians referred were the *Eheberatungsstellen* (marriage counseling bureaus), where Germans turned for advice on eugenics and premarital venereal disease testing; in other words, precisely those areas targeted for attention at the Moscow Counseling Center. The low incidence of preexisting conditions in the German statistics can easily be explained by the fact that Germans suffering from sexual dysfunction, rather than utilize the Eheberatungstellen, would have sought treatment at facilities geared specifically toward those problems, an option unavailable to their Russian counterparts given the embryonic state of Soviet medicine. Ironically, by offering advice on birth control and sexual hygiene, the Soviet clinic was far more "progressive" than the German marriage counseling bureaus; in Germany there was a complete separation of functions between these institutions and the birth control and sex advice clinics staffed by sex reformers.[9]

The Russian doctors compared their clinic to the German marriage counseling bureaus because they considered the goals of the two institutions to be the same: prevention of illness rather than treatment of already existing disease. The Counseling Center for Sexual Hygiene had been established as a place where people could take an active role in ensuring their sexual well-being. In the opinion of its founders, attendance would demonstrate the population's commitment to good health through its prophylactic use of the clinic, by embracing the approach to illness that was the cornerstone of Soviet medicine. But the low numbers of women, the rarity of people using the center to assess their health before marriage (originally identified as the most important purpose of the clinic), and especially the disproportionately high incidence of dysfunction, all purportedly demonstrated the Russian population's sexual immaturity and backwardness vis-à-vis the West. Referring to the fact that not one engaged couple had come to the Moscow Counseling Center to seek prenuptial advice (compared to thirty such reported visits at the Berlin bureau during the same time period), the doctors commented: "we see that the idea of a counseling center as such is apparently completely absent among the masses." In the conclusion to the reports written for the medical community, the doctors reiterated their commitment to the principles of prophylaxis, vowing to significantly increase their advertising base and to devote particular attention to promoting the idea of premarital medical consultations.[10]

Special efforts also were made to attract women: a female-only counseling center was opened at the editorial offices of *Woman's Journal* (*Zhenskii zhurnal*), and women's health clinics, which previously had handled issues strictly related to gynecology and maternity, were encouraged to broaden their sphere of competence. The Moscow Counseling Center also expanded the list of services it provided. In 1929 it divided these services into three categories, each of which would be available on a different day. In addition to sex education and hygiene, the center would offer advice on issues relating to marriage and the family, and a lawyer would be present to answer legal questions. Yet despite these attempts to reach women and the continued reiteration of the clinic's prophylactic orientation, the new title given to one of the three subsets, the Division for Sexual Hygiene and the Pathology of Adults, reveals the doctors' recognition that the de facto purpose of the clinic had changed.[11]

The alarmingly high rate of male sexual dysfunction prompted a special response, one that would explicitly target those in danger of succumbing to these maladies. The clinic physicians accomplished this task through a strategy of selective representation and exclusion: to the readers of *Toward a Healthy Lifestyle,* which reported on the clinic in every issue, the counseling center became exclusively devoted to the treatment of sexually dysfunctional men. Other publications presented the client pool rather differently. Whereas the popular *Woman's Journal* and the specialist periodical *Psychohygienic and Neurological Research* (*Psikhogigienicheskie i nevrologicheskie issledovaniia*) stressed the predominance of men and their frequent complaints of impotence, they also listed women's reasons for visiting the clinic.[12] But despite the efforts made by the center to reach women, the message ultimately communicated to the public via *Toward a Healthy Lifestyle* was that female sexuality was relevant only as it concerned men.

In the first report of the center's progress published in *Toward a Healthy Lifestyle*, doctors attributed women's low attendance rate to "false shame" (*lozhnyi styd*). Thereafter, women appeared in discussions strictly as a factor contributing to male dysfunction, such as the disease-infected prostitute to whom the Red Army man erringly turned to prevent nocturnal emissions, or as the beloved wife whose husband feared would abandon him because of his impotence.[13] In analyses written for the medical community, in contrast, the center's doctors were not so much dismissive of female sexuality as simply baffled by it. To explain their low level of clinic attendance, doctors pointed to women's supposed embarrassment, their shaking and indecisive voices, and their constant concern that they be seen by a woman doctor. Yet the authors offered no suggestions as to how they might increase the comfort of their female patients. The clinic physicians also appeared at a loss in regard to female sexual dysfunction (that is, frigidity), acknowledging that "for us, in the sense of giving advice, these were perhaps the most difficult cases."[14]

The first column on the clinic in *Toward a Healthy Lifestyle* referred only generally to the motives behind people's visits: "The reasons for turning to the consultation are the most varied: questions of sexual development, marriage, sexuality, education of children, and various sexual deviations."[15] After that, each subsequent issue's report was devoted exclusively to the problem of male sexual dysfunction. The psychoneurologist Dr. Gurvich acted as the counseling center's newspaper correspondent and described one such case in the next edition. A young man arrived at the clinic, horrified that he was impotent. The doctors learned that his first unsuccessful attempt at intercourse occurred while he was drunk, a condition which, as Gurvich explained to him and to the paper's readers, frequently resulted in sexual failure. This first disappointment resulted in feelings of doubt, which increased every time the man attempted to have sex with his wife and then led to further incidents of impotence. Trying to locate the origins of his problem, the man remembered that at one time he had masturbated. He also remembered reading books about the dangerous ramifications of masturbation and concluded that he was now being made to pay for his old sins. The doctors informed him that previous masturbation does not lead to impotence and pointed out the detrimental influence of alcohol on sexual performance. Gradually the man calmed down, and with his less pessimistic attitude toward his future, his sex life began to return to normal. Gurvich concluded: "We believe that when some sort of sexual complication appears, a man shouldn't immediately panic, decide that he is finished, think about suicide; instead he needs to see a doctor for advice as soon as possible."[16]

In a later issue of *Toward a Healthy Lifestyle*, Gurvich described the appearance at the center of another young man. Excited, shaking all over, he could barely speak from agitation.[17] Recently married and deeply in love with his wife, he reported that his attempt at sex the day before had ended in premature ejaculation. Gurvich quoted him: "'You understand, doctor,' he said desperately, 'if I can't be cured, I'll kill myself. After all, my wife won't stay with me, and if she leaves me, it would be better to die.'" After calming him down, the doctors discovered he had lost his job the morning before, owing to work reductions. Having spent the day appealing to different authorities to prevent the lay-off, he returned home exhausted, "a bundle of nerves" (*iznervichavshiisia*). Gurvich commented: "After his story it became clear to us that here, apparently, was one of those many cases when in circumstances of serious exhaustion or after an extremely unpleasant event the sex act might be unsuccessful. But this, after all, in no way says that a person has developed sexual impotence!" The doctors explained the reasons for his failure and, certain there were no serious problems, sent him back to his wife. They advised him to share this information with her should there be any future such incidents, stating confidently that she would understand him and not think about leaving. Several days later the man returned to the clinic to report that his previous visit had calmed him down so successfully that, no longer afraid, he was able to resume a completely normal sex life.

Subsequent issues of the newspaper focused on other cases, but aside from the specific sexual complaint (nocturnal emission, premature ejaculation, or impotence), they deviated little from this pattern. Indeed, this apparent epidemic of dysfunction seemed to spare no one: among the young men who arrived trembling and terrified at the clinic's doors were Red Army men, workers, students, peasants, and Party members.[18] Each seemed ready to end his life rather than continue to suffer. Yet after one visit to the counseling center, all were miraculously cured. The answer, as conceived by the doctors, lay in the fact that the problem was not really located in their sexual organs; rather, the ailments were all in their heads. Gurvich diagnosed their illness as "sexual dysfunction of a psychological origin," explained as meaning "from thoughts [*ot dumki*], not having the slightest basis in reality."[19]

The clinic doctors' response to their discovery of the psychogenic basis of the widespread sexual dysfunction was twofold. In reports written for the medical community, they recommended that more psychoneurologists become involved in the counseling centers.[20] At the same time that the high incidence of dysfunction warranted a shift from preventive care to the treatment of preexisting conditions, the transfer of attention from the body as the locus of sexual disorder to the head determined which medical specialty would be most needed by the clinic's patients.[21] While the involvement of venereologists in the clinic's work and the advocacy of prevention and hygiene continued, the center's primary orientation became and would remain psychoneurological. Moreover, the physicians' shift of emphasis from the body to the head also reveals that the medical vision of masculinity during this time period was decidedly nongenital. The basis of manhood, according to these sources, lay elsewhere.

The physicians also embarked on a mass campaign of "calming" (*uspokoenie*), which was conducted on the pages of *Toward a Healthy Lifestyle.* Through the repetition of case histories, the doctors hoped to convince their audience that occasional sexual failure did not indicate a real sexual problem: "Many do not know that such setbacks may frequently depend on purely external reasons (exhaustion, unexpected misfortune, inconvenient setting for the sex act, intoxication from alcohol, etc.)." In fact, Gurvich explained, such incidents were normal. In the column (cited above) addressing the problem of nocturnal emissions in two young men, Gurvich wrote:

> Fear and worry were so sincerely expressed on the faces of both youths that I decided to have a detailed conversation with them, in which I tried to make them understand that they did not have any sort of illness. Nocturnal emissions, which each experienced, are a *completely normal* substitution for the sex act in young people who are not yet sexually active, but have already reached sexual maturity. . . . Let us repeat, that if a young man not yet sexually active or a Red Army soldier forced to temporarily interrupt his sex life sometimes has nocturnal emissions, *this is not bad [eto ne plokho].* (Original emphasis)

In a later issue of the paper Gurvich reminded readers that incidents of premature ejaculation after a period of sexual abstinence were nothing to fear and should be treated as something "completely natural." This insistence on the "normalcy" of occasional sexual dysfunction was central to the campaign of "calming" and aimed to bolster the self-confidence of those men shaken by fear of sexual inadequacy and pathology. On yet another occasion, the doctor wrote: "And not knowing all this, they become horrified at the slightest failure and often, thanks to ignorance, lose faith in themselves and their capabilities, out of which may develop 'nervousness' [*nervnost'*]."[22]

Indeed, nervousness was considered to be the real malady afflicting these men. Describing a letter to the counseling center written by a twenty-five-year-old peasant suffering from premature ejaculation, Gurvich concluded: "After his first disappointment there appeared in Comrade A. uncertainty in himself, uncertainty in his sexual strength. . . . an illness developed in Comrade A., but not a sexual illness (his sexual organs, without any doubt, are completely normal); nervousness developed." The doctor was so certain that Comrade A.'s nerves were the real culprit that the genitals no longer even needed to be examined to arrive at this conclusion. This point was reiterated in each column, as the authors confidently concluded that, once the subject had been calmed, enlightened, and sent home, there would be no further problems.

How do we treat [nervousness]? Of course, the greatest victory would be if Comrade A., having read this article, understood that he is not physically ill, believed in his strength and, not fearing failure, began to live an untroubled sex life. If in the beginning there is a setback, then he needs to relate to it calmly, to remember that it will pass, and that the less he pays attention to it, the sooner it will happen. Cases of such cures following an explanatory conversation in our counseling center occur frequently.[23]

The association between nervousness and maleness represented an important shift away from earlier medical notions of nervous illness (and especially hysteria) as the particular domain of women. That the doctors subscribed to and conveyed this idea to their patients was confirmed by the information sheets filled out at the clinic; the question about whether the visitor suffered from nervousness was only included in the section devoted to male sexual experience.[24]

Soviet Nervousness

The focus of the Counseling Center for Sexual Hygiene on nervousness was not an isolated one. In the years after the Revolution and especially during NEP, a vast amount of public attention was devoted to nerves, evoking the image of a society seemingly wracked with and obsessed by psychological disorders. Readers sent anxious letters about their nervous state to advice columns in newspapers, and popular pamphlets counseled on how to detect the symptoms of nervous illness. In the introduction to one such booklet, the psychiatrist L. Rozenshtein wrote: "One can hardly find a different expression that has been so frequently used in such different situations, than the word nerves, nervousness. Rarely, rarely do we meet people who are not nervous or those who don't sometimes feel their nerves."[25] Writers of fiction also drew upon the wide appeal of the topic, as did Mikhail Zoshchenko in "Nervous People," an extremely popular sketch published in the journal *Hippopotamus* in 1925:

Not long ago, a fight took place in our communal apartment. Not just a fight, but an out-and-out battle. On the corner of Glazova and Borova. Of course, they put their hearts into the fight. . . . The main reason is—folks are very nervous [*narod ochen' uzh nervnyi*]. They get upset over mere trifles. They get all hot and bothered. And because of that they fight crudely, as if they were in a fog. As for that, of course, they say that after a civil war people's nerves always get shaken up. Maybe so, but from that theory the veteran Gavrilich's noggin won't heal up any faster.[26]

Such awareness and concern regarding this "nervous age" extended far beyond Soviet Russia. In the last decades of the nineteenth century, doctors' offices across Europe and the United States were increasingly filled with patients suffering from a variety of nervous disorders.[27] In 1869 the New York physician George Miller Beard identified these symptoms as manifestations of a new disease, which he labeled neurasthenia or, literally, nervous exhaustion. According to his analysis, neurasthenia was the result of overtaxing or incorrect usage of one's "nerve force" or nervous energy, most frequently through work. While some forms of nervous energy successfully reinvested the supply of nerve force, others including masturbation, gambling, irresponsible sexual activity, and irresponsible financial activity resulted in a drain, or "dissipation," which in turn led to neurasthenia. The disease could also develop in people exposed to a hectic pace of life who were already sensitive or fragile.[28]

The doctor depicted neurasthenia as a distinctly modern sickness, a symbol and product of the progress of civilization. Yet civilization alone was not enough to produce nervousness:

> The Greeks were certainly civilized, but they were not nervous, and in the Greek language there is no word for that term. . . . The modern differ from the ancient civilizations mainly in these five elements: steam power, the periodical press, the telegraph, the sciences, and the mental activity of women. When civilization, plus these five factors, invades any nation, it must carry nervousness and nervous disease along with it.

Beard was considered highly successful in treating nervous exhaustion through the use of electricity, another symbol of America's progress. But rather than express alarm over the outbreak of "American Nervousness," as he called it, Beard proudly identified it as a sign of the country's superiority: Neurasthenia is "modern, and originally American; and no age, no country, and no form of civilization, not Greece, nor Rome, nor Spain, nor the Netherlands, in the days of their glory, possessed such maladies." The disease's particular national trait was linked to racial, social, and class determinants, as well: it only struck "brain workers" (as opposed to "muscle workers") and only the more "advanced" races (especially Anglo-Saxon) and religious persuasions. Thus nervousness served as a medical confirmation of social status and position; in the opinion of one doctor, the best thing about having it was that you could "move in neurasthenic circles." Beard argued that people from other social or racial groups were susceptible to nervousness only if they were at "stopping places between the strength of the barbarian and the sensitiveness of the highly civilized."[29]

As the neurasthenia diagnosis spread to Continental Europe, the illness became more democratic: it lost its social particularism and its positive status. European physicians also considered neurasthenia a disorder of modernity but challenged the judgment that it was a symbol of progress. In the European context, modern civilization represented an ominous threat to stability rather than the lofty promise contained in Beard's vision.

In the European view, the growing epidemic was induced by the adverse characteristics of modern life: the heated tempo of industrialization, the chaos and temptations of urbanization, and the excessive stimulation of dangerous new ideas, the popular press, and recent inventions. As doctors throughout Europe diagnosed ever-increasing segments of the population (including members of the working class) as neurasthenics, the disease was linked to widespread fears about degeneration and devolution.[30] Physicians were particularly alarmed about the high incidence of hereditary or degenerate neurasthenia, which they believed to be incurable. The Viennese psychiatrist Richard von Krafft-Ebing, for example, concluded that 80 percent of all neurasthenia cases were congenital.[31]

European doctors also added extensively to Beard's five elements, which, combined with civilization, could result in neurasthenia. According to George Drinka, among the possible causes cited were intellectual strain, modern music, the dramas of Strindberg and Ibsen, "nerve poisons" (such as coffee, tea, tobacco, and alcohol), too much fine or exotic food, perfume, sex, luxury, hot baths, also mineral water, unhappy marriages, fear of syphilis, and the dangers associated with masturbation. Susceptibility to neurasthenia was also dependent on the particular life experiences of different segments of the population. In proletarians, the danger of contracting neurasthenia arose from the machines near which they spent their days and the cold cramped quarters where they spent their nights. In men, it came from promotion in the military. In women, it came from childbirth and menstruation. In children the predominant sources were scary stories, fairy tales, and religion. In other words, practically anything associated with modern urban life could lead to the development of the disease.

> Always and everywhere in the sounds of noisy carriages rolling across the pavement, the hiss of locomotion, the cry of street vendors . . . electrical lights . . . not to mention the lack of air . . . one obtains . . . the description of the diverse influences at work during a sojourn in the great cities on those humans predisposed to the development of neurasthenia.[32]

Physicians employed a variety of methods to treat nervousness. Several different types of therapy utilized electricity: faradization (treatment with alternating current), galvanization (with direct current), and franklinization (with static electricity). Neurasthenia was also cured with bed rest and warm milk, hydrotherapy, massage, diet (either fattening or thinning the patient), sea and spa baths, injections of the nervous tissue of healthy young animals, and finally, suggestion and hypnosis. When patients failed to respond to the various methods of treatment, they were pronounced hereditary neurasthenics, which explained their inability to be cured. Doctors identified the vast majority of European neurasthenics as belonging to this category: "The bulk of the patients got slightly better but were never cured . . . [symptoms] shifted and were alleviated but then surfaced all over again."[33]

Cases of neurasthenia were recorded in Imperial Russia as well, and in the wake of the events of 1905 there was a growing tendency to character-ize both the revolutionary movement and repressive governmental policy in terms of psychological disorders.[34] By the 1920s, a dramatic increase in nervous and mental conditions seemed to have taken place: "No matter what group of the population is studied, at the present time everywhere one observes an extreme abundance of nervous and mental illness, devia-tions, dysfunctions, symptoms. . . . surpass[ing] even tuberculosis and other social diseases."[35] Psychiatrists and neurologists found evidence for this claim everywhere. One study conducted by the Neuro-Psychiatric Dis-pensary among spinners at the Krasno-Presnenskaia Tri-Mountain Textile Mill found 46.4 percent of all workers to be nervously ill, 19.7 percent of them with pronounced neurotic symptoms. At the Moscow Textile Fac-tory, 77.7 percent of all those examined (both blue- and white-collar workers) demonstrated nervousness, with 17.7 percent categorized as seri-ously nervous, 22 percent as moderately nervous, and 38 percent as mildly nervous. Similar results were obtained from workers at the Red Labor Fac-tory: only 51.5 percent were considered to have healthy nerves.[36]

Nervousness was not only found in factory workers. A study of teachers diagnosed 50 percent as suffering from mild nervousness, and a further 26 percent from severe forms of the illness. The high incidence of nervous disorders detected among the young was of even greater concern to re-searchers. A 1925 study conducted with over nine thousand school-age children determined that only one-third had healthy nerves. Nor was the Communist Party spared: according to figures cited by A. B. Zalkind, a whopping 80–90 percent of active members suffered from nervous symp-toms.[37] Taken together, these findings suggested to medical writers as well as other social commentators an epidemic of nervous illness that consti-tuted an urgent social problem:

> Although we do not know the exact extent of the dimensions of different levels of nervousness among the entire population and among its subsec-tions, nonetheless we cannot entertain the slightest doubt about the evi-dence of the destruction of neuropsychological health in a significant por-tion of the population. It is natural, therefore, to speak about the nervousness of our time.[38]

Doctors offered a variety of explanations for this upsurge in nervous conditions. Some identified World War I as the main source of the new epidemic and viewed the Soviet cases as part of a Europe-wide phenome-non.[39] However, most Russian physicians writing about nervousness posited a fundamental difference between the outbreaks in the West and those in the Soviet Union and stressed factors endured by only the latter: the two revolutions, the Civil War, the blockades and famine, and the massive epidemics that followed. They attributed primary importance to physical and mental fatigue, a weariness that itself was considered specifically Russian. The result of overtaxing an already shaky nervous system— "exhaustion" (*iznoshennost', utomlenie*), as the extreme form of paralysis-like tiredness was called—occupied a key position in discussions about nervous illness.[40]

Just as the fatigue linked to nervousness was favorably associated in America with privileged minds doing the positive work of furthering civilization, and in Europe with the enervating burdens of a deteriorating modern world, so in Russia exhaustion was deemed emblematic of the Soviet condition and the particular circumstances of the post-1917 experience. According to one specialist, V. V. Dekhterev: "War, Revolution and the never-before-seen-in-the-world tempo of rebuilding all social forms of labor and daily life of the peoples of the USSR demanded from the population a colossal stress on the nervous system, deeply exhausted it, and increased the likelihood of its becoming injured." Zalkind linked nervous exhaustion to a whole host of possible causes:

> Unregulated, disorganized work, foul living conditions, disordered and completely insufficient food, the absence of rational rest, qualitatively disrupted and quantitatively restricted sleep, the shift from arduous mental scientific work to active social work, a disordered sex life—more and more new blows unceasingly fall upon the overdriven nervous system.[41]

Poor hygiene and sanitation, overcrowded and underheated housing and schools, and indeed the dislocations and relocations associated with life in the 1920s were also identified as contributing to the inordinately high incidence of neurasthenia in Soviet Russia. Nervous exhaustion could follow alcoholism; debilitating illnesses such as typhus, malaria, and influenza; or a congenital predisposition to weak nerves. Like their European colleagues, many Russian doctors wrote about a hereditary tendency to nervous exhaustion, similarly identifying those features of modern existence responsible for its manifestation into a full-blown illness.[42] Analyses also linked the emergence of the condition to severe psychological or moral shock or an extremely unpleasant emotional experience. One psychiatrist developed the diagnosis of "acquired invalidism" (*nazhitaia invalidnost'*) to define the most severe form of neurasthenia.[43] Sufferers of this extreme variety of nervous exhaustion were purported to become old before their time; apathetic, unable to work or relate to their surroundings, they were completely lost to society.

Like their American counterparts, many Soviet doctors were especially concerned with the pathologies of mental laborers, but with one important difference. Of chief interest to them were the young proletarian students and Party activists who appeared to be particularly susceptible to exhaustion, and hence nervousness:

> And so to the surprise of medicine, which usually has no clients from the proletarian sphere, proletarian students get for themselves before their Party card and their professional card a "psychocard" [*psikhbilet*] . . . these neuropathic dysfunctions never befell the proletariat before in such a quantity and quality. But since we have before us an entire class generation of the Revolution . . . this statistic becomes extremely alarming.[44]

In the eyes of Soviet physicians, young people were engaging in too much intellectual work without sufficient breaks, or without a proper rest period between their mental pursuits and their extensive social (*obshchestvennye*) responsibilities. Another factor identified by specialists that would become controversial over the course of the decade was the mental exhaustion experienced by proletarians and peasants who made the transition from manual to mental labor, including those who had been promoted to Party organizational posts and the vast number enrolled in institutions of higher learning. Doctors also singled out Red Army soldiers and Party activists who had conducted arduous and prolonged work at the front during the Revolution and Civil War as being especially susceptible to the most severe form of neurasthenia, acquired invalidism.[45] To combat this alarming phenomenon, psychiatrists promoted "mental hygiene." Originating in the United States in 1908, this international movement conformed to the general principles of Soviet medicine by promoting the prophylaxis of nervous and psychological illnesses and raising the standards of care for those already suffering from such disorders.[46] In Soviet Russia, the prevention of exhaustion constituted one of mental hygiene's primary objectives. Specialists advised a more rational approach to determine how to spend one's time. They advocated a choice of career in accordance with personal abilities, inclinations, and temperament; frequent breaks during intellectual work; and proper exercise and rest.

Other symptoms of neurasthenia identified by physicians included shaking and irritability, excitability, insomnia and troubled sleep, severe headaches, dizziness, eye and ear irritation, back and chest pain, heart palpitations, irregular heartbeat, stomach upset, frequent mood swings, memory loss, inability to concentrate or to work, complete apathy and lack of will, the tendency toward obsessive and compulsive behavior, paranoia, and hypochondria.[47] Diagnosed neurasthenics were predominantly young and suffered from feelings of insecurity, uncertainty, and low self-confidence; as in Gurvich's columns, the phrase used most frequently to describe them in the popular health press is "uncertainty in oneself, in one's abilities" (*neuverennost' v sebe, v svoei sile*). Soviet medical writings portrayed neurasthenics as completely dissatisfied with their lives, with no chance for future happiness.

Evidence of such psychological despair was everywhere, and Russian society as a whole seemed to reflect many of the individual neurasthenic's most serious symptoms, in particular a pervasive sense of insecurity and hopelessness. However exhausted the country had been during the revolutions and Civil War, the introduction of NEP in 1921 with its promise of economic respite for private producers and traders brought no relief to its "shattered nerves." For some, this insecurity appeared to come primarily from the material difficulties associated with life at the time. For others, it manifested itself as a crisis of identity, as various segments throughout society questioned their own status, purpose, and fate as well as those of the nation. In the aftermath of the Kronstadt Rebellion and the Workers' Opposition, for instance, some Party members began to doubt the loyalty of the working class and hence their own role as its leader. Others were unable to make the transition from an oppositional to a ruling party or mourned the shift from revolutionary fighter to peacetime bureaucrat. The suppression of Kronstadt and the subsequent "retreat" of NEP proved a similar source of distress to many intellectuals and supporters of the Revolution, leading to mass resignations from the Party and the Komsomol, and anxious discussions about the country's future among the population as a whole.[48]

For medical authors and other social commentators, one of the most disturbing manifestations of this malaise was the wave of suicides reported to be ravaging the country's youth.[49] Suicidal tendencies played an important role in the symptomology of male sexual disorders, as well, and physicians considered sexual dysfunction a similarly conclusive indicator of mental instability among Russia's young men. Doctors maintained that the fear of sexual impotence frequently prompted suicide attempts, a connection "corroborated" by the following review of a book on impotence in a popular health journal: "Sexual impotence in men is a source of wretched suffering. How strongly it influences the psyche can be judged by the fact that many kill themselves because of it."[50] This relationship between suicide and sexual dysfunction was also communicated through Gurvich's columns in *Toward a Healthy Lifestyle*. Each man who arrived at the clinic was described as shaking and pale, unable to work, completely lacking in self-esteem, and threatening to end his life.[51]

If low self-confidence and a neurasthenic malaise appeared to be particular national traits in Russia in the 1920s, in the estimation of several medical authors male sexual disorders represented a related badge of Soviet uniqueness. Commenting on the high incidence of male sexual dysfunction throughout Europe and Russia before and especially during World War I, the venereologist-urologist L. Ia. Iakobzon concluded:

> the result of [the war] was the appearance of many tens if not hundreds of thousands of cases of sexual dysfunction among the war's participants, and sometimes also in those who remained in the rear. All of this was in the

West, all this was here among us. But in the Union . . . we endured two revolutions and, importantly, years of famine, years of ruin accompanied by hunger, unemployment, epidemics, etc. All of these are factors that could not but have a great influence on the nervous system and the psyche. As a result, naturally, here in the Union sexual dysfunctions should be widespread and, moreover, should be encountered at a relatively young age.[52]

Iakobzon directed two clinics for the treatment of sexual disorders in Leningrad, and in his opinion what made the Soviet situation unique was the diverse social and class composition of the cases, a fact corroborated by the visitors to the Counseling Center for Sexual Hygiene. The doctor contrasted his patient sample of Red Army soldiers, semiliterate young peasants, workers, students, and intellectuals to that of a Berlin physician, who contended that the majority of impotents hailed from the "cultured classes." The first reason for the discrepancy, Iakobzon argued, stemmed from the fact that in Europe people of modest means lacked the resources to visit private clinics. Yet in Russia, it was not just a question of greater accessibility to medical care. The arduous conditions of life in the Soviet Union were responsible for this particular manifestation of nervousness as well: "Here people become exhausted quicker than in the West. There is much proof for this assertion. Truly here people get exhausted faster and our intelligentsia rarely lives to an old age. In the West it is not rare for professors to live to seventy or eighty, but here I hardly know of any elderly representatives of science."[53]

Impotence and the "Nasty Habit"

Among the variety of factors identified by physicians as contributing to the epidemic of nervousness and male sexual dysfunction in revolutionary Russia, most were considered beyond the immediate control of either the patient or the medical profession. Indeed, the basic premise of the campaign of "calming" was to help men come to terms with the conditions of labor and life that society, for the time being, was unable to change. One exception to this sense of powerlessness, over which doctors believed that they (and the sufferers themselves) could exercise some influence, was masturbation; and a great deal of attention in the popular health press was devoted to curbing this sexual practice. In the opinion of some medical writers, excessive masturbation could lead to exhaustion of the nervous system, resulting in nervousness.[54] Others diagnosed impotence as the result of a masturbation-induced form of hypochondria known as "onanophobia."

Former masturbators, under the influence of antiquated notions about the supposed unusual danger of their "secret vice" and their "sin of youth," very frequently develop real obsessive fear of the possibility, or, more accurately, the imagined consequences, of masturbation. This masturbatory hypochondria, or "onanophobia," linked usually with self-reproach and self-flagellation, controls the life of the onanist; it, in the view of many specialists, is more dangerous than masturbation itself.[55]

Insecure young men were seen as particularly susceptible to the misinformation spread by parents, comrades, cheap boulevard literature, and even some ill-informed health workers regarding the supposed horrors associated with the act.[56] It was referred to as the most dangerous form of deviant sexuality, and it was assumed to lead eventually to impotence, progressive paralysis, idiotism, tabes, and ultimately insanity. The path from onanophobia to impotence was relatively direct:

It appears to the sick man that sexual energy, activity, and the normal sex act are completely impossible for him. And for him sexual passivity, uncertainty in this regard, becomes a general sense of uncertainty in all areas of his life. A person already poisoned by the thought that he ruined himself through masturbation, suffering in addition a neurasthenic condition and living with tortured thoughts of uncertainty, finds that his spontaneous automatic processes are destroyed by his psychological condition. He is sure in advance that he has lost his sexual abilities, and when circumstances are such that he should display them he indeed turns out to be impotent.[57]

Such expressions of alarm about the consequences of self-stimulation were prevalent throughout medical advice literature. One such arena was the question-and-answer page in *Hygiene and Health of the Worker and Peasant Family*, in which queries about onanism and its consequences occupied a disproportionate amount of space. Although the journal omitted the questions themselves, the answers nonetheless indicate the correspondents' troubled state of mind. Letter writers attributed all kinds of illnesses and problems to the practice: blue rings under the eyes, inability to do math, tumors and nose bleeds, tuberculosis, cold hands, hair loss, anemia, and venereal disease.[58]

Disputing such claims, the column's doctors emphasized that nerves were the real source of the masturbation-related conditions afflicting such correspondents as "Slav-ii":

You are overworked with an excessive load, your nervous system is shattered, and therefore you don't have the strength to cope with your nasty habit. Turn to one of the clinics for nervous illnesses or to one of the provincial health centers with a specialist for nervous conditions. Besides that, study carefully Associate Professor Mendel'son's brochures, *Onanism and the Fight against It* and *The Nervous System and Sexual Life*.[59]

While it was repeatedly asserted that nervousness was the true illness afflicting the correspondents, the relationship between neurasthenia and masturbation was also frequently mentioned. Readers were informed, on the one hand, that prolonged and frequent masturbation could lead to neurasthenia, and on the other, that nervousness deprived one of the willpower to break the so-called "nasty habit."[60]

The advice offered also suggests that many medical professionals contributed to this atmosphere of anxiety through their numerous and confusing references to the relationships between self-stimulation, degeneration, and heredity. Both the journal's question-and-answer columns and a number of other writings that appeared in its pages and in the popular press reported that onanism could be a sign of tainted heredity: "it needs to be said that onanophobia to a great extent, just like persistent, excessive masturbation, is observed only in hereditarily burdened people. Thus immoderate masturbation is an already existing defect, an innate deficiency of the nervous system."[61] Healthy adults, in other words, did not indulge; those who continued to do so after reaching the age of sexual maturity were demonstrating their hereditary weakness. As with neurasthenia, a young man who masturbated might conclude on the basis of this expert medical opinion that he was doomed, unable to stop the practice or escape the far greater psychological or neurological illnesses that awaited him and his descendants.

Other doctors, including those connected with the Counseling Center for Sexual Hygiene, played down the role of heredity and disputed the debilitating impact of self-stimulation. According to Dr. Iakobzon, only 11 percent of all cases of sexual dysfunction were connected with masturbation, and in only a few of those cases was masturbation itself responsible for the dysfunction. Dr. Khaletskii claimed that 95 percent of the population engaged in onanism in any historical era, and that the only ones to fall ill as a result were those "who represent incorrectly all the horrors with which masturbation is supposed to be associated. . . . [T]hose who never heard about the dangers of masturbation do not become ill from it."[62] Ultimately, the wisdom of both messages is questionable: "normal" or "aberrant," the male masturbator was prone to nervous disorder as a result either of the act itself or of fear about its nonexistent pernicious effects. The presumed result of such a conclusion—on what was believed to be an already nervous population—is even greater anxiety.

Panic, Production, and the Treatment of Impotence

Onanism was assumed to be widespread among Soviet men but its consequences were unclear. Far more troubling was the problem of impotence. It was precisely the "normalcy" of the men experiencing sexual dysfunction and the universality of their complaint across social groups and classes that made the apparent epidemic so threatening. Fear was not based on population policy; the question of the men's inability to reproduce was raised by neither the patients nor the doctors who wrote about them.[63] The danger posed by these men was linked not to reproduction but to production: "those suffering from sexual impotence usually become unhappy and lose their joy of life, succumbing to the most somber thoughts, even to thoughts of suicide. They consider themselves unfit and unnecessary members of society, and withdraw from their transformation into useful workers."[64] In the estimation of medical specialists, young men in the prime of life who should have guaranteed the country's future instead posed a grave danger to its survival. The very fate of the Revolution seemed in jeopardy as ever-increasing numbers of men became incapacitated, suicidal, and unable to engage in the labor that defined the new state's identity.

In his chapter on "Revolutionary Anorexia," Naiman examines the role of the female body as an ideological symbol during NEP. He argues that the most powerful marker of female sexuality was menstruation (which was considered a sign of the disruption of capitalism) and that the idealized female body was one that had been purged of all fat, incapable of menses, and hence completely desexualized.[65] The male body also functioned as a site for the expression of social and political anxieties during the 1920s, with the poles of idealization and danger reversed. The threat of a healthy (menstruating) female and the reassurance of an anorexic woman who has stopped bleeding had a parallel in the nervous impotent youth and his self-assured productive counterpart. On the symbolic level, there could not have been a greater contrast between the pervasive iconographic image of the strapping young proletarian, hammer raised, triumphantly building socialism and the shaking, exhausted, suicidal men who crowded the doctors' offices. In the context of discussions on nervousness and impotence, masculinity was defined as the ability to engage in productive labor. Thus anxiety about male dysfunction represented broader concerns with the potency, viability, and destiny of the workers' state.

The pages of the medical press portrayed a generation of men suffering severe psychological distress, desperately in need of assistance, both for their own sake and to serve the needs of their country. Less severe a response than suicide to the despair of the times and the dashed hopes of the Revolution, the discourse of sexual dysfunction provided men with an acceptable vehicle to express dissatisfaction with NEP Russia and the demands placed on them by contemporary society. If young men responded to their social and political powerlessness by becoming sexually impotent, the role of the medical profession was to help men to accept, or at the very least to live with, the features of life that they also were powerless to change. In his brochure *Sex and Neurasthenia*, Dr. Khaletskii advised his readers: "Be encouraged! Begin to look people directly in the eye, since there's nothing wrong with you. Your uncertainty in yourself will lead to your becoming truly powerless." Should further advice be necessary, he urged his readers to seek out the help of a doctor. These popular health texts were unanimous in their estimation of the role of the physician in treatment.[66] In their evaluation, the doctor's power of suggestion was so forceful that often the act of consultation was enough to initiate the healing process:

> All cases of purely psychological sexual impotence respond to treatment, but demand at times great patience from the sick person and also from the doctor. In a majority of cases success is achieved through skillful psychological influence on the patient: psychological treatment here consists of calming [*uspokoenie*] the sick person by explaining the incorrectness of his thoughts and feelings in order to return to him a sense of trust in his (never really lost) sexual strength and to train him to divert attention away from his own organ.[67]

Writers were not concerned with establishing a precise relationship between various symptoms of nervous illness or a fixed sequence of the sexual dysfunction's progression; low self-confidence might lead to nervousness, resulting in impotence, or occasions of sexual failure could induce nervousness and hence feelings of insecurity and thoughts of suicide. The physicians' primary imperative was to calm the sufferers who populated their clinics and comprised their readership. Once placated, the men would become capable of listening to the medical explanations of their conditions and, already half-cured, be able to resume their labor and other obligations. The most crucial advice given by the doctors of the Counseling Center for Sexual Hygiene was the exhortation "not to give in to panic," a warning that ran like a mantra through its newspaper column in *Toward a Healthy Lifestyle*.

> We consider that the case of comrade A. is one of the many incidents when an accidental failure results in uncertainty in oneself, hesitation during sexual intercourse. This insecurity is due to the tendency to "panic," to thoughts of incurability, etc. A great portion of these cases has no serious foundation. They are completely curable and frequently after the first conversation with a doctor such sick people begin to feel completely validated [*polnotsennymi*].[68]

Significantly, physicians themselves could have been responsible for contributing to the atmosphere of panic. It is likely that some exploited this panic for financial gain, cashing in on the widespread concern with nerves and impotence by publishing advice literature or advertising disreputable miracle cures. Even such a well-respected publication as *Hygiene and Health* arguably transgressed the blurry line between responsible advice and blatant self-promotion by regularly advertising Mendel'son's numerous publications on its medical advice pages (instances may be found in almost every issue, which leads to the assumption that Mendel'son himself was the journal's advice columnist). Leaving aside questions of such journalistic or medical improprieties, the harsh tone taken by the advice column and the frequency with which it diagnosed its letter writers as nervously ill also presumably contributed to the sense of crisis.

Conversely, this might also explain the prevalence in Russia of the term "nervousness" (*nervnost'*) instead of its Greek counterpart (*nevrasteniia*). If in the West there was the tendency to elevate the condition of nervousness into the full-blown disease of neurasthenia, in Soviet Russia the instinct appears to have been the opposite. While many Russian doctors wrote about neurasthenia, the word is rarely used by those dealing specifically with sexual dysfunction, and never in the writings of the Counseling Center for Sexual Hygiene. The treatment of nervousness was remarkably disembodied, with no reference to any particular organs or explanations about the inner workings of the nervous system. In contrast to the enlighteners who never let their lack of endocrinological expertise prevent them from discussing the intricacies of glandular secretions, Soviet psychiatrists and psychoneurologists chose to steer clear of medical terminology reflecting their particular specialty. The physicians' choice of language should be seen as part of their method of calming; using the term *nervousness* as opposed to *neurasthenia* removed from the condition the stigma of a "real" illness and normalized it, making it less alarming, more temporary, and more curable. A second related motivation for avoiding the term *neurasthenia* might have been its association with degeneration and heredity. By labeling impotent men nervous, as opposed to neurasthenic, doctors shielded them from anxiety about their tainted lineage.

The proclivity to panic, to transform a social problem into a full-blown crisis, was a widely observed feature of life in the 1920s.[69] Discontent over such social ills as mass unemployment and child abandonment generated anxious and seemingly endless discussions in which the word panic appeared repeatedly, casting doubt upon the very fate of the Revolution. Young men figured prominently in these debates, which questioned their fitness as standard-bearers of the future socialist paradise and centered frequently on the problems of suicide and sexual depravity.[70] In a lecture on the sex question delivered in early 1926, Commissar Semashko addressed the topic of panic in relationship to the supposed sexual turpitude of the young:

> We have in this sphere a panic, and even several of our well-known comrades feed this panic. . . . We will never allow anyone to declare, as if every one of our *komsomolki* and *komsomoltsy*, every student in a worker school was the personification of depravity . . . [that sexual activity among the young has declined in recent years] needs to be considered before giving in to panicked shrieks about the wave of depravity that has swept over our youth.

N. Shvarts, a physician writing in *Toward a Healthy Lifestyle* in 1929, echoed Semashko's sentiments:

> Now we hear everywhere our youth being censored, that they are dissolute, rude, depraved. . . . [T]he depravity of our youth is a bugaboo, with which social opinion frightens itself and others. . . . [O]ur youth is far from those horrors that are attributed to it, and it would be a good thing if public opinion rid itself of that delusion.[71]

The themes raised in these passages—the branding of young people as sexual libertines, the intentional exploitation of a climate of fear, the condemnation of certain "opinion makers"—had first been elaborated by Semashko in the 1925 *Izvestiia* editorial cited above.[72] In the commissar's estimation, it was precisely works like those by Liadov and Zalkind that incited panic among the population; these writers argued that sexuality had become unnatural and identified the sexual depravity of Russia's youth as the most alarming evidence of the separation of sex from nature. Both Semashko and Shvarts suggested that such condemnations would only increase the level of nervousness in young people and hence the cases of impotence that doctors were striving to forestall. At issue was a fundamentally different approach to the idea of sexuality. Whereas these other "social thinkers" condemned sexual activity per se as a sign of immorality, Semashko and other physicians acknowledged the validity of male sexuality, provided it be contained within their fairly restrictive interpretation of normal practice. Moreover, in tracing the source of male sexual dysfunction to the head (nervousness) as opposed to the body (a biological or physiological disorder), doctors offered these men a way out of their sexual problems. Young men could easily be cured of sexual disorders by heeding the physicians' advice, whereas in the estimation of their Party comrades they appeared doomed.

The sentiments expressed by medical authors speak to the conflict with Party ideologues over issues of jurisdiction (see Chapter 1). The contested domain was not simply the sex question itself but authority over the population with which it was most closely associated, in this case young men. In part the doctors and ideologues disagreed over method; the medical approach to sexual problems stressed education rather than the flat-out condemnations and prohibitions characteristic of Party pronouncements on the subject. This is not to suggest, however, that physicians were in any way less concerned with control than were the Party moralists. Like the health writers who exploited fears about masturbation, the numerous references to suicide, exhaustion, and nerves in the counseling center's columns demonstrate that these doctors were not above making use of the widespread interest in these issues and anxieties about the young to increase their own authority, even as they criticized others for doing so. In the same way, their campaign of calming through continual reference to the epidemic of sexual dysfunction no doubt contributed to the atmos-phere of panic surrounding those it sought to reassure. Physicians tried to combat sexual problems through education rather than coercion, yet they readily exploited the general alarm over an illness that would be cured by the very fact of relying on them and their expertise for treatment.

Frigidity, Medical Silence, and the Politics of the Female Orgasm

In view of the vast attention focused upon male sexual disorders, the lack of medical and public interest in similar problems among women is conspicuous. Was the fact that frigidity failed to receive even a fraction of the attention shown to male dysfunction due solely to "false shame," the embarrassment believed to prevent women from seeking out help, as was suggested in *Toward a Healthy Lifestyle*? Or were women actually sexually healthier than men? Doctors themselves admitted that this was not the case. Citing "a majority of specialists," *Hygiene and Health* reported in re-sponse to a reader's question that frigidity was widespread among women, affecting 50 percent of the female population.[73]

Yet despite the health journal's apparent acceptance of this high figure and its reference to a group of presumed experts in the field of frigidity, most doctors who wrote on issues of sexuality for the general public simply avoided the subject. The counseling center reports in *Toward a Healthy Lifestyle* mentioned frigidity only in relation to its effect on the sexual abilities of men. Other publications followed its lead in their discussions of the center's work, as for instance in an account that appeared in a 1928 issue of *Hygiene and Health*. Even though the chronicle began by stating how many men and women had visited the clinic, the rest of it was devoted to the different sexual complaints of the male patients. The article concluded by reiterating the impor-tance of such an institution, since people lacked the most fundamen-tal information about sex, and suggested that it advertise its existence more widely so that all those who needed it could receive help. Since the report excluded women completely, it evidently was aimed at a male audience.[74]

The dearth of attention to female sexual problems in newspapers and journals extended to popular pamphlet literature on the sex question. One representative example was a brochure on the relationship between the nervous system and sexuality by the prolific A. Mendel'son, who was also an editor of *Hygiene and Health*. Despite the considerable attention shown in the pamphlet to male impotence and its relationship to neuras-thenia, frigidity was never mentioned. An associate professor of neuropathology, Mendel'son introduced the topic of female sexuality by stating: "The connection between the female sexual apparatus and the nervous system is especially close and complicated; therefore the sex life of a woman contributes to the origin of many neuropsychological conditions."[75] Yet he devoted only a scant three pages out of thirty-one to describe those factors of a woman's life that, according to him, most frequently led to nervous illness—menstruation, pregnancy, abortion, childbirth, and menopause.

The lack of medical interest in frigidity was so pervasive that Iakobzon, one of the only doctors who wrote about the problem, was prompted to argue for its relevance:

> Doctors frequently hear the question: do we need to fight against frigidity in women? I think that we do. I completely share the point of view of the renowned Viennese psychiatrist and psychologist, Professor Freud, that orgasm is a wonderful reward of nature to living things for the fact that they reproduce. Nature entrusted to women all the difficulties of maternity; woman therefore has no less right to satisfaction in sex than does man.[76]

Yet those few authors who, like Iakobzon, acknowledged and addressed the topic of frigidity still treated male and female sexual disorders differently. Even in dysfunction, men were accorded a sense of agency that was denied women. To be cured of their impotence men were urged to take the active step of dealing directly with doctors, either personally or through a medium such as the counseling center column in *Toward a Healthy Lifestyle*. Women, on the other hand, were completely dependent upon others to combat their frigidity; either the problem was seen as physical, and thus correctable through surgical intervention, or it was believed to be the fault of the woman's sexual partner. In either case, her sexual satisfaction was entirely in the hands and under the control of others.[77]

In those cases not diagnosed as physical, the fault lay with the husband, who even here in the realm of the female orgasm became the focal point of medical attention. In specialists' estimation, a man's sexual behavior in marriage was crucial to the sexual well-being of his mate, especially during the first days of matrimony. Therefore, he should refrain from overeagerness on the honeymoon and be especially careful not to force himself on his bride, at the risk of irrevocably turning her against the sexual act. "Many men don't know that the female sexual appetite in normal conditions is weaker than in men; they also forget that excitement comes from courting them."[78] A far greater problem was men's lack of sexual skill and especially the tendency to ejaculate prematurely, as the venereologist and urologist R. M. Fronshtein concluded:

Premature ejaculation of semen influences the man above all psychologically. Physical satisfaction usually is received fully. This, however, severely influences the woman, since as a result of the shortness of the act she is usually
denied physical satisfaction. A significant number of illnesses in the female
sexual sphere and a significant number of nervous illnesses in women have a
close and direct link to men's premature ejaculation during the sexual act.[79]

In Iakobzon's analysis, even masturbation—to which a woman "not
rarely" turned "to reach orgasm and prevent the painful feeling of dissatisfaction" after her partner's premature ejaculation—could best be treated
by "strengthening the sexual abilities of her husband." There was never a
question of addressing women directly regarding the mechanics of sexual
satisfaction. If medical writers like Iakobzon considered a woman's orgasm
at all, it was as the responsibility and province of her man: "Sexual frigidity may arise in a woman in marriage in connection with the weak sexual
abilities of her husband. . . . Therefore I tell a woman that the reason for
her sexual dissatisfaction is the sexual dysfunction of her husband and
that I need to treat him."[80]

Despite women's lack of agency in bringing about her own or her husband's sexual pleasure, her ability to achieve orgasm could still be considered responsible for the success of the marriage:

> Frigidity in woman can have a social significance: it can have a dangerous ef-
> fect on the husband, since there are men who can only perform the act on
> the condition that it bring pleasure to the wife. This can cause frequent dis-
> agreements and fights between the spouses and even infidelity by the hus-
> band; in other words, the wife's frigidity can undermine the harmony of the
> marriage and threaten its survival. . . . On the other hand, the woman's sex-
> ual dissatisfaction can lead her to look for new sexual relationships in which
> she could experience orgasm.[81]

In several of the cases of dysfunction described by the counseling center's
physicians, the patient's sense of accountability for (and inadequacy
about) his partner's sexual pleasure was seen as the decisive factor in the
etiology of his nervousness.[82] Both Iakobzon and Fronshtein predicted
that the husband's inability to bring his wife to orgasm as a result of his own
sexual dysfunction might also become the source of a nervous disorder in
her, most likely in the form of hysteria or neurasthenia. Although according
to Iakobzon such cases of mental illness among women were rare, he maintained that nonetheless they "need to be cured."[83] Yet, as with his support for
women's right to have an orgasm (during intercourse), Iakobzon remained
silent about how this objective should be accomplished.

With frigidity and female nervous disorders dependent upon the presence of previous sexual dysfunction in men, doctors could rationalize
their neglect of women in the treatment of nervousness (and sexual dys-

function, for that matter); once men were healed of their sexual disorders, women would necessarily also be sexually fulfilled and mentally healthy. A number of other factors explain the lack of medical interest and popular fora devoted to the psychosexual problems of women. Of primary importance was the inherent link between women and reproduction. To be "normal" in terms of sexual behavior for a woman meant to be reproductive, and of course frigidity did not prevent pregnancy.

Because nervous illness did not impinge upon a woman's ability to conceive, there was very little interest expressed in the popular medical press in the mental health of "normal" women as sexual beings. In fact, the mental health of sexually active women received attention only when women ceased to be "normal" by engaging in "abnormal" or "deviant" and nonreproductive sex, as prostitutes or lesbians. Of great significance in this regard is the contribution of B. Gurvich, the Moscow clinic's columnist in *Toward a Healthy Lifestyle,* to the 1926 collection *Soviet Medicine in the Fight for Healthy Nerves.* The only article in the volume to address the problem of female sexuality and its relationship to nervous illness, Gurvich's chapter examined the psychopathology of prostitutes.[84] Health writers may have blamed "false shame" for women's lack of initiative in seeking out advice on sexual matters, but the impression conveyed to both men and women in newspapers, pamphlets, and journals was that the female experience per se was unimportant, at best dependent upon the actions of men. By neglecting "normal" women's sexuality, physicians contributed to and reinforced the idea of women's experience as particular, nongeneralizable, and therefore not a matter of public concern or interest.

The authors' inability or unwillingness to address frigidity, though jarring when compared to the advice and practices of the sex reform movement in Europe, is remarkably consistent with the dominant features of the ideology of sexual enlightenment. Given that physical pleasure was not even an acceptable category for the new discourse of Soviet sexuality, the inability to achieve orgasm could only be a problem if it got in the way of production and reproduction. As defined by the doctors, the male orgasm was essential to both while the female orgasm was almost an afterthought. For women, the real climax of sexual activity was supposed to come nine months after the act, with the birth of the all-important child. Indeed, a woman's inability to achieve orgasm can be conceived of as a problem only indirectly: presumably, a man's ejaculation can be qualified as premature solely if his climax occurs before he can satisfy his partner. Once again, however, the negative consequences are defined largely in terms of the man's mental health, since his perceived sexual failure results in the pernicious syndrome of nervousness. Ironically, this dogged insistence on the lack of female agency only increases the burden on the already fragile male: thanks to the masculine ethos of postrevolutionary Russia, frigidity is transformed from "female trouble" into yet another nervous ailment afflicting Soviet men.

four

Envisioning Health

The Politics of Gender in Sexual Enlightenment Posters

• In a 1922 article that appeared in the journal *Social Hygiene*, A. V. Mol'kov, the director of the State Institute of Social Hygiene and a prominent health educator, summarized the fundamental principles of Soviet medicine with the axiom "The health of workers is the task of workers themselves." This slogan, which would become ubiquitous during the 1920s, was meant to "[exhort] the masses to self-reliance," an independence that would be possible only after they had attained sanitary literacy (*sangramota*). Yet the obstacles to such an achievement were colossal, owing to the scarcity of doctors, the widespread suspicion of "modern" medicine, and the general illiteracy of large segments of the population. The years of war, revolution, and domestic strife had touched off a series of epidemics that ravaged both the civilian population and the soldiers at the front. Typhus, cholera, scurvy, smallpox, venereal disease, malaria, and famine were rampant, and the situation continued to deteriorate throughout the Civil War.[1]

Such was the atmosphere in which sanitary enlightenment originated under the new regime. Like political agitprop, which was employed at this time to galvanize the masses in defense of the Revolution against internal and external adversaries, this program of health education developed rapidly during the first years of Soviet power in order to battle the country's other enemies: disease, sickness, and by extension that which physicians considered their root cause, the Russian population's ignorance (*nevezhestvo*) of even the most basic principles of hygiene. Information on health issues was deemed vital not only to combat already existing illnesses and prevent the further spread of disease, but also to ensure the continuing health of the population that would build the new society.

Given the dangers and taboos associated with sexuality, the guidance of medical experts was considered particularly crucial in helping workers reach health independence in that area of life. Before they could be expected to take their well-being into their own hands, workers needed to know what "health" signified in this context. Implicit in this process of sanitary enlightenment, then, was the proviso that the populace must learn to think about health in the same way that doctors did. Educators had at their disposal an entire arsenal of enlightenment techniques to convey their ideas. Among these methods, posters were an ideal means for spreading information among the population, especially in light of the particular circumstances of medical practice after the Revolution. Perhaps most significantly, the visual representation of health allowed the medical profession to battle sanitary illiteracy long before viewers might become literate.

Since a healthy populace was deemed essential for the successful realization of Communism, physical health was never far removed from political well-being. Not only did illness and poor hygiene endanger the working masses; there were also categories of people (disease carriers, the morally suspect) whose actions or very existence seemed to threaten the health of the regime. In displaying rules to govern how people ate, bathed, worked, relaxed, and reproduced, sanitary enlightenment posters specified the types of health conduct that Narkomzdrav desired from the population.[2] Conversely, posters also illustrated behaviors—and, by extension, people—condemned for being "unhealthy." To explore these issues, we shall interpret a large body of posters that deal with the subject of sexual enlightenment.

Two principal objectives underlie this discussion of the commissariat's visual depiction of the sex question. The first goal concerns the meaning of "health" within medical sex education and the "fight for a new lifestyle," a campaign in which matters of fitness and well-being played a considerable role. Historical analyses of the demands made on Russian society during the 1920s often emphasize the population's ideological, Party, and labor obligations.[3] The medicalization of sexuality involved the removal of sex from the private realm by defining it as a public medical problem necessitating expert intervention, regulation, and education. Sexuality's new status as a legitimate public concern and the social mission to transform this area of daily life after the Revolution make it possible to talk explicitly about sexual behavior in terms of collective responsibilities and membership in the new body politic. Thus sexual enlightenment posters put a premium on the representation of both inclusion and exclusion as the "friends of health" and its enemies. Within the sphere of sexual health, gender played a crucial role in the process of creating responsible "new people" and enemies of the forces of progress. Thus the second objective is to examine how posters utilized and drew upon images of gender difference, and especially ideas about the feminine, to envision health, and sexual health in particular. Gender shaped the requirements for health and "normal" sexuality as presented in these posters and was deployed in the definitions of wellness, illness, and lifestyle (*byt*).

In making claims about who or what was healthy, sanitary enlightenment posters simultaneously created an audience to whom these ideas were supposed to appeal. Given the tasks of sanitary enlightenment, the kinds of spectators—those independently thinking, healthy workers—"invented" by the posters merit serious consideration. I do not pretend to analyze how viewers understood them or whether these images influenced popular perceptions and behavior. Furthermore, there is room for speculation about the audiences at which sex enlightenment materials were aimed, but no singular "message" or intention on the part of those who designed them is assumed.[4] At issue are the social, political, and cultural conditions that shaped the way these works were produced as well as "read." For our purposes, the crucial concerns are the content of the posters themselves and the context that framed and gave them meaning: life, and specifically medical life, during the 1920s.

The History and Agenda of Sanitary Enlightenment

Popular health education was not new to Russia in 1918. Many socially committed district council (*zemstvo*) doctors had attempted to spread sanitary information among "the people" in the second half of the nineteenth century as part of their commitment to "make Russia healthy" (*ozdorovlenie Rossii*).[5] Physicians engaged in popular education encountered mistrust among local populations and district council officials. Animosity reached a point of crisis during the cholera epidemic of 1892–1893 when health workers from outside the local communities, who were trying to treat the disease, were chased out of town, beaten, and murdered by angry mobs. Recognizing the dire need for rudimentary knowledge about health, in part to prevent future epidemics as well as to secure the safety of doctors themselves, the Commission for Popular Hygiene Education was established at the Fifth Congress of the Pirogov Society of Russian Physicians in 1893.[6] Located in Moscow, the commission acted as a clearinghouse of medical education by collecting, reviewing, and compiling educational materials to be used by doctors throughout the empire. However, the scope of hygiene instruction remained limited because of the continued suspicion of the censors and the regime, especially after physicians' widespread support for political reform in 1905. It declined still further during World War I, when medical energy was directed into other channels.

Sanitary enlightenment was truly a product of the October Revolution, despite important continuities in personnel over the divide of 1917.[7] Indeed, state authorities deemed sanitary measures, hygiene, and health education crucial to the Revolution's primary mission to transform daily life. Thus Lenin highlighted the connection in a famous statement to the Seventh Congress of Soviets in 1919. Referring to the lice that carry the typhus virus, he remarked: "Either socialism will defeat the louse, or the louse will defeat socialism."[8]

This commitment was also embodied in the structure and mandate of the new Commissariat of Public Health. Narkomzdrav considered education an essential component in its prophylactic approach to health, which stressed the elimination of conditions contributing to disease over the treatment of preexisting illnesses. Soon after the founding of the commissariat, the Department of Sanitary Enlightenment was established in the sanitary-epidemiological section. Under the leadership of venereologist N. S. Isaev and sanitary doctor I. D. Strashun, the office oversaw the establishment of regional affiliates throughout the country and the training of doctors in sanitary enlightenment methodology. In 1928 one particularly active bureau, the Moscow Health Department's Division of Sanitary Enlightenment, achieved independent status as the Institute of Sanitary Culture. These various enlightenment organizations convened congresses, designed museum exhibitions and posters, published scholarly journals as well as lecture outlines and teaching aids, and disseminated a wide range of popular educational materials.[9]

In fact, a Russian living in the 1920s would have been hard-pressed to avoid exposure to health education of one form or another. Sanitary enlightenment houses were established in most cities and lectures were conducted in factories and schools. Peasants and workers not only were exposed to sanitary posters and newspapers but also saw sanitary plays, agitational trials, movies, magic lantern shows, and traveling health exhibits. They served on the sanitary committees of their places of employment or residence and subscribed to the vast number of popular-scientific publications that flourished throughout the decade.[10] The new status and role of health education after the Revolution was reflected in its name change; before 1917, health education was referred to as "the dissemination of hygienic knowledge" (*rasprostranenie gigienicheskikh znanii*).[11] In contrast, the term *sanitary enlightenment* implied a fundamental shift away from merely imparting factual information about hygiene to shaping an entire worldview through the prism of health and the principles of science. It was considered (by public health physicians, at least) to be a branch of, and on par with, the general political enlightenment that was a cornerstone of the new regime.[12]

The year 1921 marked a reorientation in sanitary enlightenment tactics and objectives. Health education shifted from its "defensive" role of fighting the famine and epidemics of the Civil War period to an "offensive" one, as it developed the campaign to "make labor and lifestyle healthy" (*ozdorovlenie truda i byta*). Yet, although this program dates from 1921, before 1924 the activities of regional enlightenment bureaus were rather limited, owing to the budgetary constraints of NEP, which forced institutions to fend for themselves financially.[13] According to Strashun, health educators witnessed the "extinction of sanitary enlightenment" during these years (1921–1923), since only the largest and best-provided of cities had the resources to allocate money for the production of informational materials. By the mid- to late 1920s, when local budgets had become relatively stabilized, the kinds of posters presented in this chapter would have been visible throughout the country.[14]

The crusade to make labor and lifestyle healthy reflected the basic emphases of Soviet medicine: prevention and training to independently manage one's own physical and psychological well-being. "Consciousness," that marker of political maturity, figured prominently here as well, since a healthy worker was automatically a conscious one. Indeed, in the concepts of sanitary literacy and consciousness we witness the formulation of dual sets of obligations pertaining to matters of health. The responsibilities of the state toward the health of its citizens were defined in three of the founding principles of Narkomzdrav, which called for universal, free, and qualified medical assistance. Through sanitary enlightenment the conditions and terms of this transaction for the population—and the behaviors expected in exchange for this care—were spelled out. Good health was as much a communal as an individual commitment. The mandatory universal enrollment in the drive to make labor and lifestyle healthy involved deputizing each member of the new society to monitor the progress toward health of every other member. To be healthy meant ensuring that those around you adhered to the same program of health conduct.[15]

Health consciousness also relied on the ability to recognize the dangers and impediments obstructing the path to good health. In the words of one sanitary enlightenment specialist, I. M. Katsenelenbogen: "If you know your enemy well, and you know from which side he's preparing to attack you, then it is easier; it is obvious, not only how to defend yourself, but how to defeat him." Working according to the maxim "by example, not by mandate" (*ne nakazom, a pokazom*), posters represented an especially appropriate method for reaching the public and identifying its enemies and its allies. Images could be produced inexpensively and could penetrate areas of the country that for years to come would not have their own doctors or sanitary personnel. Especially in the first half of the decade, when such was most often the case, the health posters that hung in ZAGS (marriage and birth registry) offices, dormitories, worker and student clubs, parks, cafeterias, reading huts, and railway stations were potentially the only continual contact people had with Soviet medicine (see Figure 4.1).[16]

Figure 4.1—Moscow Health Department Sanitary Enlightenment Portable Exhibit, Central Park of Culture and Rest, mid-1920s. Installations such as this might have addressed a variety of health-related topics or focused entirely on one theme, such as the sex question. Photo no. 15065, Poster and Photograph Collection (NITs "Meditsinskii muzei" RAMN).

Sanitary enlightenment posters arrived on the scene soon after the appearance of revolutionary political posters, in the second half of 1918. Health posters utilized the forms of visual representation that would be familiar to Russians from the *lubok* (the peasant broadsheet), the icon, and the political poster, which guaranteed that their audience would already know how to "read" them. Previous exposure to political posters as well as icons helped prepare one to look at images of health through a similar moral framework, through the repetition of immediately decipherable images and simplistic dichotomies.[17] The goal was to ensure comprehensibility, irrespective of whether a person was literate or took the time to read the minimal accompanying text. As Kanevskii put it: "The very first glance at a poster should peak our interest and in this short time perform its task—'conquer.' If on the contrary the material treated in the poster cannot fully communicate its contents in a few seconds and thus become fixed in our consciousness, then it is not suitable." The viewer's reaction was likewise supposed to be instantaneous; posters were meant to influence "quickly, sharply, like a lightning bolt."[18]

Representing Health

An antisyphilis poster dating from the early 1920s, "Syphilis is curable" (Figure 4.2) clearly follows the representational tradition of the religious icon, depicting a distinctly Soviet vision of heaven and hell, the trinity, and the Virgin Mary and child (the Red Army man's presence and clothing date this picture to either during or immediately after the Civil War). To help viewers identify the poster's moral dichotomy, there is an overt spatial separation of good from bad, underlined by the very different use of crosses. The red cross, that icon of modern healing, is vividly contrasted with the religious cross, which literally crushes those who refuse to take their health into their own hands. The illustration thus predicts what will happen to people who put their faith in religion as opposed to science. Yet these buried figures are not enemies; neither the disease nor the person(s) responsible for its transmission are pictured. Instead they are victims, both of the illness itself and of their own ignorance—an ignorance that explains why people would not treat syphilis, as well as why they would continue to look to religion for their salvation.

Despite the absence of enemies, the image is not lacking in heroes. At the center stands Soviet medicine, represented by a male doctor in a white coat, wearing glasses (as usual) to connote intelligence and perspicacity. Completing the trinity, to the doctor's right and left are two figures immediately recognizable to viewers: the male proletarian and the Red Army soldier. These two, who look to the doctor in the middle, are actively engaged in the fight to make everyday life healthy. Indeed, the worker literally takes his health into his own hands by clasping the physician's hand. Suggested in this healing touch, the touch of reason and science, are several of the conditions for consciousness: recognition of medical authority, affirmation of self-discipline, and a commitment to watch over the health of the entire community. The woman on the right, not much larger in size than the children on the left, is the passive recipient of health, which will be fought for by the active cooperation of the triumvirate in the middle. While the woman is included in the paradise featured at the top (perhaps because of her status as mother), her downturned head reinforces her subordinate standing and her lack of consciousness, since she, like the children, does not visually acknowledge the authority of Soviet medicine.

What is perhaps most striking about this picture is the extent to which it is desexualized, in view of the subject matter. As the images make clear (the man's clothing and clean-shaven face, the woman's bare head), the poster was designed to engage an urban audience. Yet syphilis in the cities was considered a sexually transmitted disease, whereas the supposedly nonsexual variety found among the peasantry was believed to be spread through the sharing of common dishes and utensils, close quarters, and poor hygiene.[19] This poster is not concerned with the prevention of sexual diseases, however. Instead it invokes the by now familiar, revolutionary,

Figure 4.2—"Syphilis is curable / In the very beginning of the disease syphilis is cured quickly / Neglected syphilis is cured slowly, through long and careful treatment / The consequences of untreated syphilis: madness, paralysis, deformity, stillborn children, idiot children."

and heroic images of the worker and soldier in order to encourage viewers to seek treatment for preexisting conditions.

Compared to the increasingly formulaic health posters produced only a few years later, "Syphilis is curable" is remarkable for its ambiguities. Is the mother looking at her nursing baby, reading the explanation about long and accurate treatment, or is she glancing (and is it sympathetically? or disapprovingly?) at the syphilitic mother and her mentally retarded children? Are the healthy literate boys on the upper left, one of whom also motions to the message about treatment below him, depicted for the same reason as the healthy mother? Does the physician also gesture to the notice, or at the fate awaiting those who refuse his expertise? In any case, the characters' downward gazes and pointed fingers serve to stress the huge distance separating those on top, in the brightly lit world of health and knowledge, from those imprisoned at the bottom.

One of the striking features of sanitary enlightenment posters in general is that, other than the few explicitly targeting females and focused on women's health, they are peopled primarily by men. The male image becomes both normative and neutral: his health needs and problems can stand for anyone's. Women, on the other hand, can represent only women's particular health issues. This assumption of a male subject is made more obvious by the kinds of illustrations in which women—or specific parts of them—predominate. One such example, entitled "What every woman should know," shows three vivid renderings of a woman's torso, from breasts to right above the knees.[20] The first is a frontal depiction of the female reproductive organs, followed by two side views of the uterus, one gravid, with full-term fetus, and the second postdelivery. Representing women's bodies to an assumed female audience (because pictures like these appeared only in such "women-only" spaces as gynecological clinics), the poster portrays their sex-specific responsibility of "knowing" and implies that female health is necessarily associated with reproduction.

According to Elizabeth Waters, the predominance of the men in (political) posters can be explained by the fact that the October Revolution was largely a male event and was perceived as such by those who designed and commissioned its symbols.[21] Waters's reasoning holds true for health posters as well. Sanitary enlightenment illustrated health as a male event and, consequently, naturalized maleness. The reason for this lies in the way knowledge, and especially consciousness, is gendered within these images. Men were considered more conscious, eager, and capable of making their lives healthy, so posters (other than those expressly designated for female viewers) were either implicitly or explicitly coded to appeal to men. Men's education took precedence; once properly informed, they would in theory pass the new knowledge on to women.

Women occupy a distinctly marginal position in "Illness is easier to prevent than to treat" (Figure 4.3), which also depicts health through spatial relationships. Far more men are shown, and they are also clearly the subject.

Figure 4.3—"Illness is easier to prevent than to treat / If you want to be healthy, follow these rules / Sun, air and water are the best friends of health / For any illness, see a doctor!" Author compiler Dr. G. Ia. Bruk, artists A. Sachkov and V. Mikhailov (Moscow: Narkomzdrav RSFSR, 1927). Print run: 10,000.

Although not specifically concerned with the theme of sex education, this poster conveys a sense of the more general representation of the healthy lifestyle campaign. Reminding viewers of the importance of prevention, it portrays the rules of personal hygiene that would guarantee wellness.

The enemy remains hidden, while the doctor, though not physically present, still makes an appearance, reminding those independently managing their health of his authority, should prevention fail. The center of the composition depicts the "friends of health," enclosed within the sun of enlightenment, which illuminates the different ways knowledge of health is used and daily life experienced. While the first poster equates women and children as passive recipients of knowledge to be passed on by more enlightened men, in this poster male children are part of the same collective as male adults, and the same beneficiaries of the rewards of good health. Engaged in cleaning and washing, women's labor makes health possible. Sun, air, and water may enable women to perform household chores, but only men are invited to enjoy their benefits. While the sun illuminates how women should behave, its rays also trap them within these scenes of domesticity; as the title suggests, if women desire to be healthy, they must remain safely within the boundaries of this realm.

In "Physical culture is the implement of class struggle" (Figure 4.4), the woman shown in the bottom left corner is no longer a passive recipient of

Figure 4.4—"Physical culture is the implement of class struggle. / What bourgeois sport is good for: / Training fascists / Individualism, professionalism, and record-breaking / What Soviet physical culture is good for: / Training the Red fighting man / Collectivism, "massism" and making the [working] class healthy / Physical culture is an amusement for the bourgeoisie / a necessity for the proletariat" (Moscow: Moszdravotdel, 1927). Print run: 7,000.

the health fought for by men or the provider for the good health of men. She now represents a direct danger to male health and a symbolic political threat as well. The physical culture movement of the 1920s (see Chapter 5), a major component of the "fight for a healthy lifestyle," specifically addressed young people and especially young men. One of the primary motives of interesting youth in physical culture was to keep them from engaging in such dangerous, noncollective behaviors as masturbation and premarital sex. Thus the ornamental woman in the bottom left corner functions as the sexualized symbol of the individualism that is represented by Otto the weight lifter, in sharp contrast with the communal ideal depicted at right.

What does it mean that women have no place in the Soviet world featured on the right? They are not a part of the collective, the proletariat, or the class. Whereas women were excluded in Figure 4.3 from enjoying the rewards of individual health prevention, here they escape the burdens shouldered by those who protect the health of their country. Able to keep the dandy from his tennis match, the woman might prove just as capable of distracting a young man from the important work of defending his homeland or revolution, a threat underlined by her association with the bourgeoisie and, even more significant, fascism. Given the sexual abstinence orientation of the physical culture movement, the antisex subtext of this illustration becomes clear. In the visual language of these posters, the depiction of Soviet society as an all-male world suggests not so much the exclusion of real women from the *fizkul'tura* movement or from the working class but more the symbolism of woman *as* sexuality.[22] Having sublimated their sexual energy through exercise, the men have no need for that particular amusement, or for the consequent threat to collectivism represented by this woman.

If the young, conscious male proletarian characterizes the ideal of masculinity and health to which all men should aspire, symbolic representations of women in health posters are primarily negative. Two of the most vivid threats to the health of men during the era are illustrated by female images: the prostitute in the city, and the old woman folk healer (*babka* or *znakharka*) in the countryside. These two dangerous women are pictured in Figure 4.5, which was also intended for use as a board game. At the center, an industrial worker (face flushed either from the heat of the machinery or as a sign of his poor health) grips the lever that will determine his fate—an idea reiterated by the now familiar slogan about health independence within the left-hand gear.

The rules and object of the game are as follows. Players (up to six) begin at Square 1, which proclaims: "Making labor and lifestyle healthy is the foundation of victory over social diseases." The first to make a complete circle (indeed, a revolution) and return to this point wins. Displayed in the spaces along the way are both good health behaviors and those that lead to illness. A player landing on a square with a red circle, signaling a

Figure 4.5—"Board game: Toward a Healthy Lifestyle." In left wheel: "Making labor and lifestyle healthy is the task of workers themselves." In right wheel: "Through making labor and lifestyle healthy to the victory over social diseases." Compilers K. Lapin and A. Berliand (Rostov na Donu: Narkomzdrav, late 1920s).

bad health choice, must move to the square indicated by the other number in the box, where the correct practice is illustrated or could be learned (at a medical clinic, for instance).

Square 34 shows a smiling woman in red, tapping a man on the shoulder in front of a beer hall. The red in the woman's cheeks is from rouge, not the arduous work of the proletarian or a signal of bad health. And yet, returning to Square 12, we learn that her attractive exterior is misleading, as well as threatening. This space features a microscope allowing viewers to "see," through technology, the spirochete that causes syphilis. Square 12 in turn directs players back to Square 3, which contains a venereal-disease clinic and hence reveals the ultimate significance of the woman's touch. Just as in the preceding poster, the man here is presented as the innocent actor in this transaction, easily corrupted by the prostitute's predatory sexuality. The connection established between the transmission of syphilis and the sexually dangerous woman is strikingly different from earlier, pre-NEP approaches to the disease in visual propaganda, as in Figure 4.2. In that poster, ignorance was blamed for preventing sufferers from seeking treatment. After the introduction of NEP, a more identifiable agent, and enemy, was needed. At that time a dramatic

shift in the depiction of sexually transmitted diseases occurred: the prostitute, widely drawn upon to personify this hated policy, assumed the
role of the easily identifiable human transmitter, becoming the most
prevalent visual image of the source of venereal disease in sex-education
posters.[23] In Square 37 we find the same man, perhaps after his encounter with the woman in red, turning for help to the folk healer.
Square 27 discloses the consequence of this meeting, depicting a cross-
covered graveyard as its only possible outcome and linking religion with
a death caused by ignorance (as in Figure 4.2).[24]

That the game is about the experience of, requirements for, and dangers to
men's health is underlined by the worker in the center and the overwhelming presence of males; the masculine orientation is apparent even if one ig-
nores the text or if the viewer is illiterate. Other than the two dangerous females, women appear only sweeping room interiors (Squares 6, 28), with
backs turned (Square 8), or in silhouette, accompanying a groom to the marriage bureau (Square 19). The industrial setting, frequent inclusion of male
proletarians, and scenes of women engaged in domestic tasks serve to under-
score another important feature of the way these illustrations represent the
health campaign. While offering positive images of men both at work and in
everyday life, the posters' portrayal of women at remunerated labor is decidedly negative, as either sex worker or folk healer. As unwanted remnants of a
reviled and unhealthy past, both occupations had to be eliminated before the
new society could be made healthy. The dichotomy between positive male
and negative female occupations accentuates the relationship between female
health and the realm of private life, and the apparent dependence of male
health on the restriction of women to this sphere.

The game also depicts two other social diseases threatening the well-
being of our worker: tuberculosis and alcoholism. Alcohol is represented
metonymically, through the presence of a bottle (Squares 22, 31, 32) or by
association with the prostitute standing in front of a bar. The link between
prostitution and alcohol consumption—that is, the view that drinking led
men to prostitutes—is developed in the next image (Figure 4.6). While in
the game-board poster, women who do not pose a threat to men's health
are turned away from viewers, here only the prostitutes gaze directly at the
spectator. The face of the man in the top picture is hidden by shadow; those
in the circle at center are in profile, looking at the prostitutes across a table
littered with bottles. As Sander Gilman has written in his analysis of nineteenth-century representations of syphilis in anatomy books: "The infected
male is anonymous, faceless, for he is the incidental victim of the female's infection."[25] In contrast, the knowing and direct glances of the women are
paired with the graphic depiction of the disease for which they are responsible. A microscope is no longer needed to see the evidence of the prostitute's
sexual pathology although the inclusion of the pie chart, with its hard data,
underscores the "scientificity" and legitimacy of these graphic drawings.

The presentation of the genitals in the primary stage of syphilis is consistent with the formula for depicting sexual organs as evidence throughout

sex education materials during this time period. Healthy genitals are never shown; biological functions and the internal structure of the organs are presented in cross sections or in diagram form. Showing the genitals covered with sores and papules may aid viewers in recognizing the presence of venereal disease and thus encourage them to get help, but it also functions as a scare tactic, to warn men in the most vivid way possible to avoid bars, drinking, and the company of prostitutes.

In some posters, text and drawing seem to carry conflicting messages. "Let us step up the fight against prostitution" (Figure 4.7) exhorts viewers to join the heroic, larger-than-life proletarian in "helping" such women, regardless of whether they desire this assistance. The text and background image refer to the "official" explanation for prostitution, then seen as a consequence of the mass unemployment, labor shortages, and exploitation associated with NEP. For these socioeconomic reasons Narkomzdrav held that the prostitute could not be considered responsible for her actions. "A fight against prostitution, not against the prostitute" (*Bor'ba s*

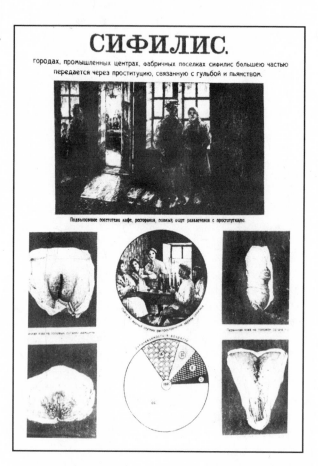

Figure 4.6—"Syphilis. In cities, industrial centers, and factory settlements, syphilis is primarily transmitted through prostitution, connected to carousing and drunkenness. Drunken visitors to cafes, restaurants and bars look for entertainment with prostitutes. Drunkenness is the loyal traveling companion of the spread of the syphilis infection" (Penzensk: Penzensk gubzdravotdel, 1923). Print run: 3,000.

Figure 4.7—"Let us step up the fight against prostitution—the shameful legacy of capitalism / Let us help girls and women get qualifications [for work] / Let us expand the building of boarding houses and workshops for the unemployed, clinics and venereal dispensaries / Let us strike at debauchers!"

prostitutsiei, ne s prostitutkoi) was the primary slogan of the medical campaign against the phenomenon during NEP.[26] The poster illustrates the state's commitment to assist these women by providing hostels for the homeless, treatment in venereal clinics, and placement in the special institutions combining these two functions—the labor clinic—where inhabitants learned an industrial trade and received an education.[27]

The foreground image, however, is far less generous or sympathetic. While the behavior of both the man and the woman qualifies them as debauchers, the man, with a shocked look on his face, is treated as an ill-behaved naive child, snatched safely away from the seductive woman who is the sole object of the worker's wrathful gaze. Pointed toward the institutions that have been built to help her, the woman stands defiantly, hand on hip. While her clothing and cigarette mark her as a prostitute (or a "Nepwoman," with whom she is symbolically associated through her attire, overt sexuality, and association with money), she is also linked with the capitalist past and is thus doubly unwelcome.[28]

In the visual language of these posters, touch plays a role of considerable importance, vividly conveying ideas about authority, control, and agency.[29] Figure 4.2 displays the healing, knowing touch of the physician, who confers both health and the correct knowledge onto the proletarian.

Figure 4.8—"Syphilis is one of the most common reasons for diseases of the brain and spinal cord / Beware of syphilis!" Artists M. S. Legedinskii and A. T. Naishtat, edited by L. M. Rozenshtein, S. N. Volkonskaia, and F. Iu. Berman (Moscow, 1930).

The loss of control as the body succumbs to disease and the corrupting knowledge associated with deviant sexuality is embodied in the contagious touch of the prostitute, depicted in Figure 4.6. In Figure 4.7 we encounter a third kind of touch. The arm that prevents the man from becoming the prostitute's latest victim by snatching him back into a safe sunlit industrial world represents the intervention of the state and its partner, conscious (male) society. While the poster concludes by promising to strike at all debauchers, it is significant that the worker does not touch the prostitute because of her potential for contamination.

Over the course of the 1920s, the iconography of the prostitute—her attire, carriage, and proximity to the beer hall—recurred so frequently in health posters that eventually she would have become instantly recognizable to spectators. In Figure 4.8 as with the board game, therefore, a visual shortcut is possible; the word *prostitute* is no longer necessary in order to identify her occupation. Including both left-hand and right-hand scenes leaves no doubt as to which figure is the victim of syphilis and which its agent. The poster progresses from the assumption that the prostitute is the one carrying the disease to the representation of her as the disease: she embodies the syphilis that should be avoided at all costs. Thus the exhortation to "Beware of syphilis" also admonishes those who viewed the poster to beware of this woman.

Figure 4.6 presents viewers with a graphic illustration of the genitals in the first stage of syphilis. "Beware of syphilis" (Figure 4.8) depicts the end result of the disease, a fate worse than death itself perhaps: syphilis of the brain and the spinal cord. In representing the experience of syphilis in one of its most advanced forms, the poster portrays the suffering of the entire man (as opposed to just the penis) resulting from contact with the prostitute.

Equated with disease in "Beware of syphilis," the prostitute in Figure 4.9 is equated with all women. By engaging in casual sex all women become figurative prostitutes, since the danger posed to men's health by sexual contact with them is the same. Like the women in the other posters, this woman is well fed, smoking a cigarette, with one hand provocatively on her hip. In this case, her illness—in the form of a pink sore on her upper lip—is visible to the audience, if not to the man, and the moment of contagion is foreshadowed by the touch of their cigarettes and the passing of the flame. Another equally crucial marker of the danger this woman poses and shares with the others is the very fact of her being outside, on the boulevard, in the dark.

Our attention thus far has focused primarily on the masculine orientation of these compositions—the use of male subjects and the appeal to male viewers. Yet, obviously, women also saw the images, which conveyed information relevant to them as well. Posters urged men to fight actively in order to attain and maintain good health. The message imparted to urban women as well as men was that to a great extent women's health depended upon the space they occupied, and consequently their behavior

Figure 4.9—"Casual sex: the main source of the spread of venereal disease" (Moscow: Narkomzdrav RSFSR). Print run: 10,000.

within that space. At the same time as men were cautioned about the kinds of women and behaviors to avoid on the boulevard, women were warned to avoid the boulevard itself. In these posters only prostitutes, or women who should be identified as prostitutes, ventured out into public at night. To preserve their reputation and hence their health, women were instructed never to stray far from home. Yet the danger was not just a question of transgressing acceptable boundaries but also a question of appearing in those locations alone. A single woman on the street at night became automatically suspect.[30]

"Article 150" (Figure 4.10), which followed Figure 4.9 in a Narkomzdrav series on venereal disease, introduces the second victim of the illness, and the third symbolic feminine image in sexual enlightenment. Having contracted syphilis from the prostitute, the same man now passes it to his innocent and trusting spouse. The presence of the disease is unknown to the woman, who sees only the romance reflected by the silhouette, but viewers witness his evil intent, portrayed by his horrible face and contaminating hand. The man's recognition of his contagion is underlined by the reference to article 150 of the Criminal Code, which held a person criminally liable, if aware of the condition, for spreading venereal disease or for exposing another to the risk of infection.[31] Unable to snatch the man away before he is contaminated by the prostitute, now the hand that reaches for him is the punishing arm of the law.

Viewed on its own, Figure 4.10 presents man as the source of danger and corruption. Yet it should be kept in mind that "Article 150" was part of a series of posters meant to be shown together. Thus even in illustrations that focused on male culpability, the prostitute as the origin of sexually transmitted venereal disease was a constant point of reference. Nonetheless, such severe representations of men as monstrous and knowingly evil were the exception in sex education. Far more frequently, as in Figure 4.11, images expressed the idea that venereal disease was contracted by men out of ignorance and susceptibility to the twin seductions of dangerous sexuality and alcohol.

In this antigonorrhea poster (Figure 4.11), which directly addresses a male viewer, extramarital sex and venereal disease are explicitly equated with prostitution, a contention supported by the scientific data in the bar graphs and statistics, even though, according to an article written two years earlier by Commissar Semashko, statistics could also be used to present a very different scenario:

> whether for good or for bad, we now wage the fight against venereal disease through the propaganda of abstinence, humane rather than animalistic relations to woman, etc. Everywhere we indicate the safety of abstinence and the danger of promiscuous sexual intercourse. As a result, fear of becoming sick plays a considerable role as a restraining factor against depravity. In part this explains the fact that despite the existence of NEP's dens of vice, the rate of

Figure 4.10—"Article 150 severely punishes those who infect someone with venereal disease" (Moscow: Narkomzdrav RSFSR). Print run: 10,000.

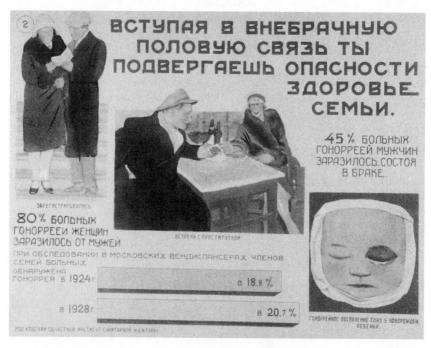

Figure 4.11—"By entering into an extramarital sexual relationship you endanger the health of your family" (Moscow: Institute of Sanitary Culture).

infection from prostitutes is held to low proportions. According to the statistics of Drs. Loginov and Belen'kii . . . among sick Red Army personnel of the Tomsk garrison only 4.9 percent were infected by prostitutes.[32]

If, as Semashko contended, the spread of infection by prostitutes was so statistically insignificant, how is the prevalence of this image in sexual enlightenment to be understood? Possible clues may be found in Figure 4.11, in which the unsuspecting wife and the diseased prostitute (accompanied by the ubiquitous cigarette and bottles of alcohol) are presented as negative images of each other. The women are dressed in almost identical clothing; only the hats are slightly different, and the colors of the coats and their fur trim have been reversed. The man is dressed identically in both drawings, suggesting a short lapse of time between the two scenes.

The depiction of these two women as functional opposites reinforces their sexual and moral difference. In sex education posters, only two options of sexual behavior are made available to women. A woman can either opt for the passive sexuality of the wife or, as initiator or active participant, be marked as a prostitute whose sexual deviance is linked to disease and the market. She is either the innocent victim of disease resulting from sex initiated by a man or a contagious and predatory actor. In a revealing explanation of the sources of gonorrhea, the venereologists Bychkov and Isaev wrote: "Gonorrhea among men is spread primarily through sexual intercourse with prostitutes and casual acquaintances; at the same time the majority of women are infected by their husbands."[33]

Because of their active role in sexual encounters, prostitutes are not considered "real" women, those who passively "are infected," who endure both sex and contagion. Similarly, "normal" female sexuality inevitably leads to reproduction, and the positive portrayal of women as sexual participants is restricted to those compositions that also contain or refer to healthy offspring. This link between reproduction and a more passive female sexuality is reinforced by showing the prostitute as the sole example of women engaged in nonprocreative sex. As these images suggest, the pathology represented by the prostitute derives as much from her engagement in recreational sex as from her capacity to spread disease. Yet it is solely in relation to the prostitute that the practice of nonreproductive sex is acknowledged. Sex education enforces a vision of compulsory heterosexuality, where the single possible form of infidelity involves a man cheating on his wife, the lone potential source of contagion to a man is a dangerous woman, and the only way a disease might pass from one woman to another is through an adulterous husband.

The presentation of the two alternatives of female sexuality provides a behavioral blueprint for both male and female spectators. While male behavior is held responsible for introducing venereal disease into the family, eradicating the illness itself ultimately depends upon the conduct of women; the only way to prevent the spread of disease is to ensure that women choose the second sexual option. In these illustrations, sexually aggressive women—as prostitutes—inevitably deprive themselves of the rewards of family and motherhood; women's reputation and fate require that they remain sexually passive. Depicting women as either innocents or sexual aggressors also provides men with a simplistic formula to help them make sexual and life choices: a man's health and ultimately the health of his family depends upon the sexual behavior (and implied morality) of the partner he chooses. Yet significantly, his right to make that choice, to be a sexual agent and sexually active, is never questioned.

Whereas previous posters reflected primarily an urban milieu, "The paths of sexuality" (Figure 4.12) also embraces the context of the country-side. It exhibits the three alternatives of sexual behavior available to the worker/peasant, pictured in the upper left corner.[34] He can either progress immediately from healthy work, through general and sanitary enlighten-ment, to ZAGS, thus achieving a healthy marriage, a happy family, and vi-able descendants. Or, if he makes the first mistake by becoming entangled with a prostitute (note the bottle of vodka in his back pocket), he can then visit a doctor, be treated and enlightened, and eventually arrive at the marriage registration bureau to find his waiting bride.

Yet should our worker/peasant choose the crooked path, however, his fate takes a dramatic turn for the worse. Treatment by a *babka* will eventu-ally lead to infertility, unhealthy offspring, stillborn children, or the syphilitic's last stop before death, the psychiatric hospital. Because "The paths of sexuality" portrays the experience of village life, several examples of nonsexual syphilis are also included: spreading and/or contracting the disease by eating from a common bowl, sharing tools at work, and kissing religious artifacts such as icons and the cross.

In the sharply gendered world of these posters, with their separate spheres and distinct sexual roles, the experience of illness is also por-trayed differently for men and women. Representative of men's suffering is the syphilitic in Figure 4.12, remarkably similar to the one featured in Figure 4.8: his sickness is depicted as an end in itself, a tragedy on its own terms (reinforced by the drawing of the diseased penis). Women's illness, on the other hand, is always linked to maternity, either by the in-ability to conceive or by the presence of congenitally ill children. The emotional appeal is directed instead at the sickness of the child (as in Figure 4.11) and especially the degeneration of the family. A single woman, as symbolic or actual prostitute, is never shown suffering from venereal disease, just passing it to men.

The image of woman as mother surrounded by healthy children is ac-companied in this illustration by a second positive maternal female figure, the nurse or medical assistant to the doctor. Just as the healing touch of the physician at center is opposed to the corrupting touch of the priest, the nurse or midwife serves as a counterpoint to the negative image of the

Figure 4.12—"The paths of sexuality / The straight path goes toward health / The crooked paths lead to illnesses."

folk healer. More frequently, however, enlightenment visuals contrast the female folk healer and the male doctor; the nurse or female medical assistant never appears independently, as does the male physician, to characterize Soviet medicine. In Figure 4.13, for example, the doctor steps in to bar the folk healer's access to the sick man, his arm shielding the patient from a form of physical contact that would be as harmful as the contagious touch of the prostitute.

Depicting folk healing as female and modern health care (represented by the authoritative figure in white) as male posits a dichotomy between the two in terms that would be immediately understandable to viewers, who may not grasp the difference between the jars and herbs of the *babka* and the pills and vials of the doctor. Similarly, the medication or therapies used to treat disease are never shown independently of the physician. Since only he knows how to use them, it is his personal authority that symbolizes the power of Narkomzdrav and modern healing.

Figure 4.13—"Only a physician can diagnose an illness and determine the proper treatment" (Moscow: Narkomzdrav RSFSR). Print run: 10,000.

The female medical assistant, lacking this command of knowledge and hence the power it confers, cannot represent Soviet medicine in the same way.

In visual materials designed for an urban audience, the dichotomy between positive and negative female images was expressed sexually. Owing to the understanding of prostitution as an urban problem and entrenched assumptions about female peasant sexual innocence (and the consequent nonsexual nature of syphilis in the countryside), enlightenment posters aimed at rural viewers presented the requirements for female health and morality in predominantly nonsexual terms, and this was the case even when addressing such sex-related issues as pregnancy and childbirth. The constellation of rural feminine behavioral models is pictured in Figure 4.14, one of a series of mothercraft aids produced by Okhmatmlad. The folk healer and the doctor's female assistant represent the negative and positive health care choices of the peasant woman, whose physical well-being and status as mother depend upon her selection. To aid viewers with their choice, the picture contrasts the most unhygienic features of peasant life with the comfort and hygiene of the hospital. Animals roam the room; the table is covered with crumbs of food and dirty dishes. The icon over the bed confirms the woman's ignorance and thus her reasons for turning to the *babka*, who stares down at the tightly swaddled child with contempt. In the sanitary scene on the right, doctor, nurse, and patient smile as the unencumbered baby is washed in fresh water. The new mother, barely mussed from her delivery, is a model of peaceful satisfaction, in sharp contrast to the unkempt and suffering woman at the left.

In another poster from this series (Figure 4.15), the dangers associated with the folk healer are indicated by the numerous religious icons, the unlucky black cat, and most vividly, her spitting in the child's face. The old woman's black head covering is opposed to the sterile white cap and gown of the nurse at right, whose status is confirmed by her literacy, use of the modern scale, and the recording of scientific data. While this nurse or medical assistant occupies a visible position of authority (further emphasized by the visual contrast between her and the barefoot peasant women in the background), the doctor sign on the door clearly indicates her subordinate position in the medical hierarchy.

Perhaps the most interesting aspect of the right-hand frame is the change in the way the mother is wearing her head scarf. This transformation symbolically raises her status from an unenlightened peasant, whose kerchief is tied under her chin, into a conscious worker, who wears her scarf knotted at the nape of the neck. By rejecting the folk healer and embracing the modern clinic, the new mother is entitled to this badge of consciousness, which also enhances her resemblance to the medical assistant entrusted with her baby's care.

10. РОДИ В БОЛЬНИЦЕ,

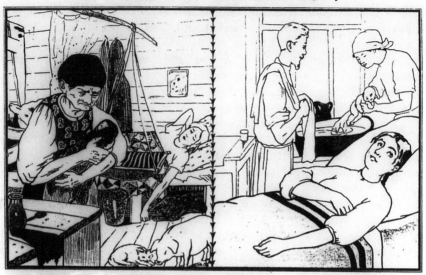

БАБКА КАЛЕЧИТ ТВОЕ ЗДОРОВЬЕ.

Figure 4.14—"Give birth in a hospital / The folk healer ruins your health" (Moscow: Moszdravotdel). Print run: 20,000.

18. НЕ ХОДИ   НЕСИ РЕБЕНКА
К БАБКАМ   В КОНСУЛЬТАЦИЮ

Figure 4.15—"Don't go to the folk healer / Bring your child to the clinic" (Moscow: Moszdravotdel). Print run: 20,000.

Figure 4.16—Moscow Venereal Disease Clinic, mid-1920s. Photo no. 11721, Poster and Photograph Collection (NITs "Meditsinskii muzei" RAMN).

The distinction between the enlightened woman worker and the ignorant peasant is further developed in a Moscow Health Department poster that addresses the provision of the 1926 Law Code mandating paternal child support for illegitimate children.[35] Captioned "Don't abandon your child. Go after the father for child support," the image depicts a distraught peasant woman (kerchief tied under her chin) in the act of depositing her baby on a doorstep.[36] She is comforted by a woman with head scarf in the "enlightened" position, who in the second frame points her, now protectively clutching her newborn, toward the relevant articles in the Criminal Code posted conveniently on a nearby wall. The contrast between the two women hints at the conflict between city and country, and especially the opposition of the peasantry to the new family code. It is the responsibility of the worker—who might represent the newly conscious mother, a Zhenotdel activist, or perhaps the social welfare commitment of the state—to educate the woman who, as a peasant, does not know that the legislation is for her own good.

Yet it is only the presence of the unenlightened peasant that lends the proletarian her authority. Women never appear alone; they are always accompanied by another woman, a man, or children.[37] In fact, the nearest approximation of a single woman in these posters is the drawing featuring a female torso and exposed uterus described above. The male form can stand alone to represent a single man, a class, or an entire society, whereas the female image lacks this ability. Women's meaning is constituted in relation to the other details and figures that accompany them in each drawing: they may represent a behavior or disease to be avoided, or a population in need of education and direction.[38]

Sex education illustrations communicate the limits that were placed on woman's requirements for healthy citizenship, and consequently on her participation in civil society. Woman's health depended upon her observance of boundaries by remaining in her proper place and sphere; her well-being was ensured by staying off the boulevard, near her home and children, and ceding the central role of healer to men. By embracing Soviet medicine and rejecting folk remedies and the *babka*, a peasant woman could become enlightened and be symbolically awarded the status of the proletarian woman. Yet women could never transcend their fundamental difference from men, a difference confirmed and sanctioned by the seemingly objective, rational principles of science and medicine.

Enlighteners believed that they were in the midst of a health emergency. Men were sought out first in visual materials because in this crisis atmosphere it was assumed they were both more conscious and more committed to making the country healthy. In thinking about the types of behaviors being advocated to both women and men, it is important to keep in mind the principal role posters played in constituting reality. By the mid-1920s, women's participation in the public sphere was a fact. One of the ways doctors appealed to men was by representing a world in which men's status was central and unthreatened, in which good health meant the exclusion of women from the boulevards and public spaces and the removal from society of illness, now coded as female.

The final image (Figure 4.16) is a photograph taken at a Moscow venereological clinic during the mid-1920s. In its formulaic composition it is remarkably similar to the posters already featured. The photo vividly depicts Soviet medicine as hierarchy; the male physicians, spatially separated by the table from the others, stare authoritatively at the X-ray in front of them. The women, perhaps nurses or assistants, are out of visual distance from the X-ray, and their subordinate position is reaffirmed by their proximity to the child. Two of the women examine the child, which, though not requiring the expertise needed to decipher an X-ray, connotes education and a professionalism that is nonetheless a direct extension of their maternal nature, emphasized by their gentle touch. Yet behind them stand two other women, gazing directly at the camera (and the viewer), the barest hint of a smile on their faces. What function do these flirting women serve in the photograph?

Even as doctors commissioned and designed sanitary enlightenment materials during the 1920s, the composition of Soviet medicine was gradually changing, as increasing numbers of women entered the profession. Perhaps images such as this photograph and the other posters featured here served as a palliative to physicians as well? By placing male doctors at the center of Soviet medicine, and hinting at the potentially disruptive and irrepressible nature of female sexuality, these images reinforced the unchallengeable authority of men in matters of Soviet health.[39]

Conserving Soviet Power

Thermodynamics and the Sins of Youth

It is clear that in questions of sexuality we need to be governed by the demands of hygiene that stand guard over the health of the individual, as well as by the interests of the entire society, of the state, of that enormous collective that can only develop correctly if the sex life of its members is normal, and corresponds to its interests. —DR. B. SIGAL, "POLO-VAIA ZHIZN' NASHEI MOLODEZHI"

• The twenty-five-year-old Savel'ev entreated Dr. Donichev, whose expert advice had already cured him of impotence allegedly owing to years of sexual excess and dissipation: "I understand now why I became weak, and now you could say I feel healthy. Medicine cured me. Only I am afraid of making other mistakes. Doctor, tell me how I should live from now on. Tell me about the correct kind of sex life." By way of answering Savel'ev's plea in *Healthy and Unhealthy Sex Life*, the doctor first reminded him of his obligations to society. Paraphrasing Lenin, Donichev explained: "In love two people participate, and a third life comes into being. This involves a societal interest and there arises a debt to the collective." Consequently, one's sexual behavior should be governed not by a desire for satisfaction but, rather, by the condition that no harm befall others as a result of this pleasure. After all, Donichev continued, a person should always bear in mind that in both life and work one does not live solely for oneself. It is especially important that this be remembered by "the members of the one working family, the citizens of the Soviet republic. Each of us bears our share of labor in our economy and each of us has our responsibilities to society. Sexuality therefore should not only give us satisfaction, but place responsibilities on us." In the doctor's estimation, two fundamental obligations govern sexual behavior. First, one must preserve one's health and the health of one's sexual partner, since only strong healthy people are able to succeed in building the country. Second, one must produce and raise healthy children, who will be able to continue their elders' work in the creation of this new world.[1]

These two principles—the maintenance of one's own sexual health and the reproduction of healthy offspring—constituted the basis of an entire subgenre of sexual enlightenment known as sexual hygiene. Sexual hygiene referred to the various rules and prescriptions governing all aspects of an individual's sexuality beginning with the first manifestations of sexual development in puberty and ending at the close of one's reproductive years—rules that, if observed, would guarantee an individual's sexual health. Since one's health was inextricably entwined with the future well-being of the state, a significant share of these regulations aimed to improve the quality of coming generations through the advocacy of both positive and negative eugenics. Making sex healthy depended in part upon eliminating prostitution and venereal diseases, combating exhaustion and nervousness, and maintaining prescribed gender roles for men and women. Yet the elimination of deviant practices and bad health habits was but half the battle. Only through the active disciplining of one's own body—a commitment benefiting one's collective, class, and country—would the sexual *ozdorovlenie* of Russia be achieved.

Purged of a wide range of negative behaviors, the medical vision of "normal" sexuality entailed participating in a series of eugenic measures, including abstinence outside of and before marriage, the sublimation of sexual desire through physical culture and civic work, premarital disease screening, the correct choice of marital partner, and the rejection of abortion in favor of reproduction or the far less desirable alternative of birth control. Physicians' idealized model of appropriate sexual conduct was comprised of two figures—the disciplined youth and the reproductively fit adult. This interpretation of sexual "normalcy" (or its synonym, sexual "health") had far-reaching consequences both for the field of sexual enlightenment and for the enlighteners themselves.

Sexual Discipline and the Bodily Economy

At first glance, the enlightenment approach to adolescent and young adult sexuality is puzzling. In terms of positive eugenic goals, the disciplined youth has a clear appeal both to a society obsessed with mobilization and to a profession whose struggle for jurisdiction over the sex question rests so strongly on the promotion of a policy of restraint. On the other hand, the problems that allegedly arise when young people fail to curb their sexual desires cannot compare to the social ills already discussed, both in terms of the apparent harm done to others and the public anxiety they caused: one can safely assume that the average Soviet citizen could see syphilis and prostitution as clear and present dangers to the general well-being, whereas masturbation and early marriage, however troubling, would rank much lower on the scale of woes pervading revolutionary society. True, "onanophobia" was a concern, and under some circumstances masturbation would even be defined as "contagious." But here again, it can be difficult to understand how autoeroticism, early marriage, and premarital sex could be so demonized in a country that had explicitly renounced all religious traditions and objections. Superficially, the inclusion of such phenomena in the enlighteners' repertoire of sociosexual pathologies makes little sense.

The problem with these "negative" manifestations of teenage and young adult sexuality lies not with the acts themselves but with the educators' view of sexuality's relation to the life of the individual, and especially to society. Their objections can be understood in terms of the metaphors they employed when they cast premarital sexuality as aberrant and harmful. The doctors did not invent these metaphors, but this was not the only imagery available to them at the time. The demonization of premarital and extramarital sexual activity of all kinds is the logical result of their manifest preoccupation with energy and their implicit acceptance of the bodily economy as a virtually closed system.

The closed bodily economy is an idea that, while never made explicit, underlies much of the antipathy to sexuality found in late nineteenth-century Russian religious philosophy and philosophically inflected literature. Nikolai Fyodorov's hugely influential *Philosophy of the Common Cause* (*Filosofiia obshchego dela*), published posthumously in 1906, is most famous for arguing that humankind must band together to achieve the scientific resurrection of the dead (an idea that reverberated with Bolshevik dreamers for years after the Revolution).[2] It was equally noteworthy for the corollary that this miracle could be achieved only if humanity overcame the distractions posed by sexuality and reproduction. Even in Fyodorov's thoroughly religious worldview, the opposition to sex is not a question of morality and theology, but rather one of limited resources: the body's energy is not entirely renewable, nor are our attentions inexhaustible. Lev Tolstoy, who was familiar with Fyodorov's as-yet-unpublished work, uses a similar approach to the bodily economy to make a moral argument against sex and marriage in his 1889 *Kreutzer Sonata*. Tolstoy's concern is not with the dissipation of energy but rather with excess: sexuality becomes an increasingly demanding presence in the individual's life because of the improper and immoderate intake of energy in all its forms, including tobacco, rich and spicy foods, and erotically stimulating music exacerbated by inactivity.[3]

Behind Fyodorov's and Tolstoy's thought is a common nineteenth-century approach to energy that views it in all its forms as fundamentally identical and therefore fungible. Metaphors of energy were important weapons in the discursive arsenal of crusaders against degeneration, dissolution, and debauchery. In his 1873 *Sex in Education: A Fair Chance for the Girls*, Edward H. Clarke cites a vast medical literature warning that the increased demands placed on women's brains by higher education are often detrimental to their reproductive and psychological health (the body can be expected to do only so much), an assessment echoed the following year by Henry Maudsley:

> The energy of a human body being a definite and not inexhaustible quantity, can it bear, without injury, an excessive mental drain as well as the natural physical strain. . . . Or, will the profit of one be to the detriment of the other? It is a familiar experience that a day of hard physical work renders a man incapable of hard mental work; his available energy has been exhausted. Nor does it matter greatly by what channel the energy be expended; if it be used in one way it is not available for use in another. When Nature spends in one direction, she must economize in another direction.[4]

A similar reasoning buttressed the crusade for sexual continence, positing that men had a limited supply of semen (a "spermatic economy"), which, if wasted, led not just to reproductive disaster but to physical and mental exhaustion and dissolution. The most notorious attempt to implement sexual continence was in the Owenite communes in New England, where intercourse was allowed but ejaculation all but prohibited.[5]

Even if the moral climate of revolutionary Russia was decidedly different from its late tsarist predecessor, the new regime's obsessive concern with energy—where it came from, how it might be channeled and harnessed—betrays a consistency between pre- and postrevolutionary approaches to the bodily economy. Now all the country's power must be harnessed for the building of socialism: if energy is to be spent, it must be part of a rational plan for bringing progress and enlightenment to the entire nation (as is the case with the massive "electrification" campaign of the 1920s), rather than squandered for selfish, individual reasons.[6] Energy was sexuality's most valuable commodity, a potent antidote to the exhaustion that seemed to be debilitating contemporary life. Consequently, Soviet medical discourse embraced two related objectives: to condemn the wasting of sexual energy that characterized the recent past and to promote its potential as a natural elixir with wide-ranging benefits for the country's welfare. Sex education literature was permeated with the language of waste and energy. Through the presentation of two alternative directions of sexual energy, educators thus defined the boundaries of sexual behavior.

Energy was negative if it had been misdirected or misused: sexuality was purportedly at its most deviant when the young squandered their supply on carnal satisfaction, which inevitably resulted in their withdrawal from societal engagement.[7] Frequent associations were made between this negative deployment and the contention that sexuality had lost its proper place or function. Thus (echoing Tolstoy) the energy of the bourgeoisie had become occupied solely with love, wine, and fatty food, and (for those engaged in casual sex) preventing pregnancy.[8] Pointing to castrates as the most extreme example of the energy-less body, writers nonetheless emphasized the consequences of energy depletion for those yet capable of sexual activity—and hence safely within the medical sphere of sexual authority. Dr. Rozenblium commented: "Sexual energy has such significance for a human being that its irrational wasting quickly exhausts the organism, making it decrepit, sluggish, good for nothing." Moreover, the sexual enlightenment emphasis on waste—of semen, hormonal secretions, or nervous health—and the varieties of impotence that inevitably followed echoed a far broader concern with energy and its absence; in a state whose origin was marked by war, famine, disease, and social upheaval, the material and ideological significance of energy in the construction of the new society cannot be overestimated.[9]

The definition of energy offered by Dr. Timofeev in his pamphlet *Where to Direct the Sexual Energy of Youth* (*Kuda dolzhna napravliat'sia polovaia energiia molodezhi*) further emphasizes this connection of the sexual to the societal. Explaining that in Greek the word for "energy" signifies "work capability" or "capacity for action," Timofeev nonetheless preferred to convey its meaning through examples evocative of popular, production-oriented themes:

> The clearest examples of the manifestation of energy are in things that produce work: a river that flows, an automobile that moves, a tractor that plows the earth, a lathe that produces a rotary movement. Such energy can be kinetic or potential—hidden, as in coal, which has the ability to produce heat. There are a variety of energy forms: steam, electricity, water, machines, and general forms—the energy of motion and heat. All are part of nature and justify the definition [of potential energy] as the capacity for action. A human being, as a part of nature, is wholly subordinated to its laws. Therefore in humans, too, energy is the organism's capacity for action.

The definition of sexual energy follows from this characterization. Since the boundaries of sexuality encompass the primary and secondary sex traits as well as the sex act itself, this force, originating in the endocrine glands, is far more comprehensive than the specific power needed for intercourse.[10]

The importance and influence educators attributed to sexual energy required that it be husbanded, expressed erotically only under the proper conditions in marital couplings for reproductive purposes, with a clear and essential social function. Otherwise, the one appropriate outlet is sublimation, which purportedly reclaims these precious resources for the needs of the state and society. The sexual enlightenment approach to sublimation was the polar opposite of the better-known Freudian schema of sublimation and repression. If Freud's implicit model was the steam engine (trapped energy threatens to blow up the entire mechanism), the enlighteners posited a "bodily machine" whose primary problem was shortage rather than excess, always threatening to run out of steam just when its owners need it most.

The Deviations of Underage Sex and Sexual Excess

One of the most important regulations that educators sought to impress upon readers concerned the appropriate age at which one could safely begin sexual activity. In their view, sex life should commence only with true sexual maturity. While the recommended age varied slightly, most writers fixed this period at between twenty and twenty-two for women, and twenty-three and twenty-five for men. Only those who had reached this age were thought to possess the consciousness to control their instincts and bear the physical and social responsibilities for their actions.[11]

Not heeding these age recommendations promised disastrous consequences. Dr. Vasilevskii warned that "attraction that has been awakened too early is impatient and unrestrained, getting satisfied anyhow and anywhere, and this whole realm is filled with danger, dirtiness, and deformity." The sex glands figured prominently in explanations of sexual normalcy once again. Authors cautioned that sexual activity before full maturity causes the glands to become exhausted and overburdened, depriving the growing body of the hormones necessary to ensure normal physical and mental development. To make the case clearer Dr. Protoklitov turned to the principles of animal husbandry:

> Why does a good, understanding owner not harness a horse until the proper time, not burden it with excessive weight, although the horse would have enough strength to bear this burden? The owner does this because he knows that if a young horse takes up heavy work prematurely, it will become worn out and ultimately grow weak. It is necessary to give a horse enough time to develop, get strong, and only then can it assume arduous toil without danger to its system. Human sex organs also demand a very careful approach. If they are forced to work prematurely, if they are stimulated it will lead to the weakening and the exhaustion of the system, and destroy a person's health.[12]

In addition to obstructing normal development, the premature depletion of the body's supply of sex hormones might result in anemia, mental sluggishness, neurasthenia, or premature aging; a weakening of one's muscles, productivity, memory, and creativity; and the inevitable diminishing of one's sexual abilities; in other words, and almost certainly not coincidentally, precisely those symptoms the literature characterized as plaguing Soviet society's "nervous people."[13] The broader social ramifications of this deviation were also emphasized: by interfering with the development of mental and moral capabilities, early sex was also held responsible for damaging one's social worth and hence societal commitment. Only one writer, the same Dr. Rozenblium, argued the issue from the point of view of sexual satisfaction, maintaining: "People who have yet to attain full maturity do not derive from the sex act all those sensations that constitute the joy of healthy sexual intercourse. Their experiences are frequently strained and for the most part are significantly weaker than they expected." Rozenblium observed that "healthy, fit, established people get the most satisfaction from the sex act. And we know that men reach this point from twenty-four to twenty-seven, and women from twenty-one to twenty-three."[14]

Female readers were offered an additional incentive to postpone their sexual initiation: "The more slowly sexual development takes place, the more magnificent will be its blossoming; a woman . . . remains young, beautiful, attractive, and productive much longer."[15] Indeed, the promise of youth and beauty for women who behave themselves sexually is held out as a reward throughout this body of advice literature; it is not clear whether educators found the more general (and gender-neutral) purported benefits to be insufficient inducements for females or they considered such appeals to feminine vanity particularly successful.

If normal sexual feeling arose only after the body reached full maturity, how did physicians explain these unnatural, early manifestations? Despite several references in their analyses of the sex glands to the few, rare cases of extremely premature sexual development stemming from hormonal deficiencies (young boys with full beards, for example, or girls of seven or eight menstruating), medical authors placed the blame for the premature onset of puberty and subsequent early appearance of sexual feeling (as with the subject of sexual attraction) squarely on the external environment: "Abnormal conditions of life create abnormalities in the sphere of sex."[16] Again such culprits as the modern city, racy books, vulgar conversations and anecdotes, the cinema and theater, erotic pictures, parties with dancing and "courting," drinking and gambling, and the corrupting influence of comrades facilitated a premature sexual awakening and ultimately led one's thoughts to the sex act itself. How and where young people spent their leisure time also had great significance, and writers did not consider the various state- and Party-sponsored youth and worker clubs that sprang up during the 1920s immune to such temptations.[17]

The deleterious conditions of contemporary *byt*—the oppressive closeness of peasant and worker housing, the sharing of beds by boys and girls or children and adults, intercourse in the presence of children—were deemed especially conducive to the stirring of premature sexual interest. In Glezer's estimation, sexual awakening occurred even earlier in the countryside, owing in part to rural youths' proximity to nature. Consequently all possible steps were to be taken to shield the young from such pernicious influences.[18]

Several possible manifestations of such premature sexual interest—all highly undesirable from the perspectives of personal and collective sexual hygiene—were predicted, especially casual sex or sexual excess, early marriage, and masturbation (again, the mixed message of "onanism"). While these deviations were considered harmful to the developing nervous and endocrine systems, the dangerous elements of each behavior—its particular constellation of bodily and social consequences—were nonetheless distinct. According to Lass, among the 40 percent of youths under the age of seventeen who identified themselves as sexually active, only 11 percent were involved in long-term relationships. Of those questioned, 14 percent had their first sexual experiences with prostitutes (in this instance, "youth" is obviously limited to males). Dr. Lass noted that this figure was probably low, given the difficulty in calculating the number of women engaged in "hidden" (part-time) prostitution. Hence he concluded that prostitutes, women working as prostitutes for supplemental income, and other female acquaintances of "dubious character" were the usual partners in such casual sexual encounters. Furthermore, Lass claimed that 25 percent of student youth suffered from venereal diseases as a result of such interactions. Another author emphasized that it was the frequency of venereal infection resulting from these encounters, not the fact that they were short-term, that made casual sex so "frightening."[19]

For women, a group that in this literature was necessarily distinct from the "prostitutes" implicated above, a particular set of health complications was attributed to casual sex. One article on female sexuality claimed that the risk of venereal infection from this behavior was even higher for women, since men tended to be more thoughtless toward a chance sexual partner than a wife (perhaps reinforcing the medical perception of women engaged in casual liaisons as pseudo-prostitutes and hence not worthy of the caution shown to spouses). In addition to the venereal disease and bodily exhaustion that also endangered men, an additional complication purportedly threatened women, namely, the specter of unwanted pregnancy, which haunted unmarried females during each act of intercourse and would eventually lead to the development of nervous disorders. An unplanned pregnancy was burden enough for someone who was married; as a consequence of a casual sexual relationship it became a true misfortune, prompting women to go to great and hazardous lengths to rid themselves of the fetus. The writer also emphasized the eugenic consequences of such interactions: "A woman entering a casual sexual relationship does not always know who impregnated her. In these conditions she runs the risk of bringing into the world a child with an unfavorable hereditary predisposition."[20]

The literature warned that young people who engaged in casual physical interactions would not possess sufficient restraint and willpower to keep from succumbing to sexual excess. In these accounts excess accelerated the depletion of the body's sex hormone supply, which, like bodily energy in general, was assumed to be limited and not subject to renewal through eating and resting.[21] Furthermore, once the body grew accustomed to such excess, it demanded ever-greater amounts and varieties of stimulation and sought them out in "wine, smoking, and sometimes even narcotics." While this trinity of vices recalls prerevolutionary and religious objections to debauchery, it also highlights the enlighteners' concern with the role of alcohol in sexual dissipation. Alcohol was blamed for facilitating a young man's first fall into the arms of a prostitute, overpowering his instinctive sense of shame at purchasing the "feminine caress." And because "a young person in a drunken state chooses his casual girlfriend indifferently," contracting a venereal infection in these circumstances became almost unavoidable.[22] Alcohol was also seen as contributing to a woman's sexual promiscuity, by clouding her judgment and interfering with her ability to recognize the potential risks of such behavior. According to Vasilevskii, frequent drunkenness was "well known" to be the first stimulus pushing girls into prostitution.[23]

Finally, sexual excess was held to be responsible for indirectly contributing to several other, even more sinister, carnal deviations. Rozenblium maintained that men suffering from impotence as a result of sexual immoderacy (as opposed to the "psychological" type seen in Chapter 3) eventually turned to perversions in order to achieve arousal:

> Oral and anal sex, sex with children, etc., all these deviations are provoked predominantly by the dissatisfaction of men who are sexually weak, who do not get a healthy, joyful feeling from normal intercourse. . . . This group of sick sexual perversions also includes such dangerous tendencies as the urge to torture and even kill the person with whom one is having sexual intercourse.[24]

The writer excluded those behaviors originating in an illness or congenital aberration (an apparent reference to the glandular interpretation of homosexuality), adding, somewhat curiously, that such practices were encountered predominantly in the children of alcoholics. A rare exception in this body of literature, such specific reference to particular forms of "depravity" served as a scare tactic to keep people from excess and simultaneously implied that such information is (or should be) equally uninteresting to readers.

Deviance and the Solitary Sin

Educators justified their lack of attention to other types of perversions by explaining that the relative rarity of such acts did not warrant further emphasis. Physicians who wrote about sex were careful to avoid the charge of titillating their audience. Overtly politicized subjects or stories ripped from the headlines were similarly ignored. Indeed, what makes the purported dangerousness of the behaviors discussed here so striking is the very banality of these acts, especially when compared to the kind of serious sex crimes that figured prominently in the popular press, such as the Chubarov Alley gang rape of 1926. Concerns about hooliganism among the young and the sexual depravity said to accompany it generated widespread media attention during these years, as well as countless lectures addressed to Komsomol members, students, and young workers.[25]

Yet for all the notice shown to the subjects in these different venues, there is no place in sex education literature for a consideration of serious sexual crimes, or even for a discussion of hooliganism. The only writer who mentions hooliganism is a peasant youth bent on politicizing sexuality, not a medical author. In part this was a matter of specialization; sex crimes were the domain of forensic doctors, not the venereologists and social hygienists who were composing most of the enlightenment materials. At the same time there seems to have been a concerted effort made to avoid the sort of issues and hence populations over whom physicians would have to share their authority, whether with Party members, lawyers, or the police. Moreover, hooliganism could not be (or was not) understood in terms of the bodily economy, which was so important to the medical approach to premarital sexual deviance. In other words, a large epistemological and behavioral gap separated those defined as sexually unhealthy or deviant by sex educators and those given similar labels by other kinds of experts.

Thus whatever their reasons for avoiding other anomalies, according to sexual enlighteners the most "dangerous sin" of sexuality was masturbation, to which the early awakening of sexual feeling was said to lead almost inevitably. While medical attitudes toward the long-term effects of this "incorrect form of sexual satisfaction," as Vasilevskii put it, may have varied considerably, doctors nonetheless agreed in their estimation of its deleterious effects on the young body, its pervasiveness, and finally its status as a sexual abnormality. Because the masturbatory act precluded conception, Dr. Uzhanskii labeled it "from the point of view of biology and also for society and the state an act against nature, that is, an anomaly, an abnormality, an illness." Dr. Iakobzon, to explain his reasons for writing a pamphlet on the subject, declared: "Masturbation is an evil; one must fight against evil. To successfully fight against the enemy, one needs to know the enemy."[26]

At first glance, the tone of this medical advice and the level of danger ascribed to masturbation might seem to contradict the tactics of some of the very same doctors who entertained the topic in their campaign against nervousness: their discussion of masturbation seems calculated to incite anxiety rather than assuage it. The difference can be attributed in part to the temporal relevance of the transgressions: past offenses (if truly in the past) were readily forgiven. Continued into the present, such behavior had implications too wide-reaching to be treated so lightly, since present engagement in the political and civic life of the country was the goal of sex advice directed at the youth. Ultimately, however, these two tactics were part of the same process: getting young people to better discipline their bodies and control their behavior.

Accounts reinforced and substantiated claims about the prevalence of this vice by invoking the language of statistics and the various surveys on sexual behavior conducted among students and the young. Several quoted neuropathologist Oskar Berger's famous conclusion that "out of a hundred young people, ninety-nine masturbate from time to time and the hundredth, the so-called sinless one, is hiding the truth."[27] According to Dr. Rozenblium, 80–90 percent of all men masturbated at some point in their lives; the numbers for women, while slightly lower, were still substantial. Citing "many researchers," Vasilevskii assigned an even higher figure (90–95 percent) and declared that the pervasiveness of onanism was "most horrendous."[28] One unavoidable conclusion of such studies was the democratic nature of this vice. If, as Engelstein has shown, some medical experts before the Revolution persisted in seeing masturbation as the province of the upper classes or of urban dwellers, by the 1920s they seemed to share the assessment that all layers of society were equally infected with this abnormality.[29]

A unique archival source would seem to corroborate this medical conclusion. This is a letter written in 1929 by one Alfei Ivanovich Ziatiushkov, a rural Komsomol member from the Vologda village of Kubensk. Found in the papers of the social hygienist and sex expert G. A. Batkis, it offers a rare perspective on the sex question "from below." It is easy to see why Batkis retained the letter and why other sexual enlighteners would have appreciated it. The young, educated, politically active Ziatiushkov was a model correspondent, telling sex educators everything they wanted to hear. He confirmed their worst fears about the dissoluteness of contemporary youth and corroborated their claims about the prevalence and causes of masturbation. Yet at the same time, Alfei provided a shining example of the redemptive power of education: through reading medical pamphlets he had cured himself of his own addiction to the "nasty habit."

Alfei began his letter, addressed to "Dear comrades!" by citing two brochures, Bekhterev's *The Significance of Sexual Attraction for the Organism's Vitality* (*Znachenie polovogo vlecheniia v zhiznedeiatel'nosti organizma*) and Fronshtein's *Masturbation* (*Onanizm*) from the Narkomzdrav series "Questions of Sexual Life" (*"Voprosy polovoi zhizni"*), which he credited with making possible his personal victory over masturbation, and which, in his opinion, when properly distributed would help contemporary youth resolve the sex problem.[30] These texts are cited extensively throughout the letter, and Alfei's analysis is clearly structured by, and at times taken directly from, these brochures.

Alfei identified himself as a student, which allowed him to speak with authority about the sexual behavior of the young, and his testimony provided cause for both encouragement and alarm. He reported, on the one hand, that increasing numbers of students were refraining from sexual intercourse, especially in comparison to the period between the Revolution and 1924. Overshadowing this positive development, on the other hand, was the fact that masturbation remained extremely "well developed": "As one of the students from the second level [*stupeni*] I am sure that the majority of them do not know how to correctly resolve the sex question. Therefore, on the basis of my observations and conversations, I am certain and convinced that the majority of students from the fourth and fifth forms of (our) second level are infected with masturbation." The causes of this infection, in Alfei's estimation, included the following:

> The external reasons mentioned in the books above, such as a "depraved environment"; poor living conditions; coarse undergarments rubbing against the sex organs; malnutrition, which redirects sublimation toward deep mental activity; "men's frequent conversations about the sex question," as mentioned in Bekhterev's book, and, consequently, their mutual influence on each other; lack of physical activity; as the books indicated, reading deviant literature (as I would call it), and a series of other factors.

Alfei identified ignorance as another factor contributing to the popularity of this vice. To illustrate the current lack of understanding regarding the sex question, he offered the "confession" (and the name) of one rural youth, Anatolii Ziatiushkov, who must have been a relative: "I try to release more (of this raw material), because it is harmful," wrote Anatolii, as quoted in Alfei's report.

The recitation of his own case history (appropriately enough for a tale of masturbation, it begins with "Observing myself") enhanced Alfei's claims and his credentials as an authority on rural student sexuality. He related that his experience with masturbation began at the age of seventeen, under the influence of his comrades ("I need to try, at least once"). But matters did not stop there, and by eighteen Alfei was completely under the influence of his illness, replicating, in his opinion, Professor Fronshtein's description of habitual masturbation by engaging twice daily in "stimulation, erotomania, and ejaculation." Courting beautiful girls intensified and exacerbated his condition, as he now added "mixed masturbation" (the use of fantasy) to his onanistic repertoire.[31] The development of a self-diagnosed disorder of the nervous system after learning about the dangers of masturbation from medical workers and popular literature fur-

ther confirmed for Alfei the accuracy of Fronshtein's analysis. Having repli-
cated the symptoms of onanophobia, which such medical texts attributed to
the nervously ill (his afflictions included chronic headaches and various
pains, problems in school, and a growing sense of dissatisfaction with
himself and his life), he was likewise cured by their preferred method of
treatment: the act of reading these medical works and hence placing his
confidence in the authority of legitimate medicine.

> But now, after reading these books, I feel completely different. I set for myself
> the task of conquering masturbation, which I have accomplished, and of not
> having sexual intercourse with a woman until the appropriate age for mar-
> riage (25). In less than a month I even overcame the nervous disorder, inten-
> sified my intellectual activity (I am preparing for VUZ [college]) and even in-
> creased my participation in civic work.

The "victorious supremacy" of masturbation among pubescent boys
and girls was attributed in texts like the ones Alfei cited to the chronological gap that separated the premature appearance of sexual feeling from the
much later age of true sexual, and hence social, maturity. Other interpretations explained onanism as a result of the interplay between this factor
and the subject's weak will. Again, as with premature development in general, physicians took care to emphasize the social causes of this sexual abnormality. Dr. Glezer, for instance, blamed the colossal prevalence of masturbation among rural youth, and especially shepherds (who had a lot of
free time on their hands), on the conditions of country life and in particular on the behavior of adults, who allegedly masturbated openly in the
presence of children. Nor were city youths immune to such influences:
Glezer claimed that artel masters were equally guilty of engaging in and
teaching this vice to their apprentices. Inertia along with the other stimulants available to adolescents also led youth to the "nasty habit."[32] Others
who turned to onanism, including both teenagers and adults, were
prompted by the fear of satisfying their desires "naturally."[33] Males sought
to avoid prostitutes and the hazards of infection, and females the consequences of losing their virginity. According to Dr. Shpak: "Many, many
girls buy their chastity at a high price, the price of replacing it with abnormal satisfaction, masturbation."[34]

Yet, writers cautioned, people would be sorely mistaken to conclude on
the basis of masturbation's prevalence that the act was normal, unavoidable,
or less risky than other forms of sexual expression. As one hypothetical
reader confronted Dr. Iakobzon: "You contradict yourself: you say that
masturbation is an evil, and at the same time that almost every person
masturbated at some point in his/her life. That means it is normal. Why
fight against it?" That self-stimulation robbed the body of the hormones
necessary for proper development was not the only reason educators offered to explain its "dangerousness." Of particular concern was the ease

with which one could indulge in this practice. As a result of onanism's ever-present availability, it easily became habitual, with dire individual and societal consequences. Dr. Lass wrote that when the autoerotic act was repeated frequently, there was a continuous need for newer and more acute stimulants, which in turn strengthened the desire for repetition, leading some to masturbate several times a day. The psychological consequences of such addiction were particularly ruinous: constantly aware of doing something "sinful," the masturbator nonetheless was unable to fight the powerful urge, since his willpower weakened as the habit became stronger. Kicking the onanistic habit proved extremely difficult, statistically speaking, as well; according to Lass's findings, only 70 percent of habitual masturbators were able to do so and even 8 percent of those who married continued to indulge.[35]

Publications attributed to continued and intense masturbation a number of maladies and conditions, portrayed as the "natural" consequence of the system's losing its "best juices." There were thus strong similarities between medical assessments of habitual masturbators' physical appearance and the way authors described other hormonally deprived subjects, such as eunuchs: the faces of chronic onanists became pale and anemic, their eyes dull, their expression apathetic and lifeless, and their movements lazy.[36] Another drastic result attributed to such "immoderate wasting of the sexual reserve" by men was impotence, in any one of its possible incarnations: incomplete erection, premature ejaculation, low or zero sperm count, and consequently, infertility.[37] Women who had prematurely exhausted their glands through self-satisfaction allegedly had many more difficulties with pregnancy or suffered from the vaguer, but equally alarming, "loss of psychological sexual traits specific to women."[38]

As with the subject of masturbation-related neurasthenia, a few isolated medical voices sought to play down, or at least limit, the risks associated with this act. Dr. Uspenskii, for instance, argued that the principal danger lay in excess, whether it be in masturbation or in intercourse. Another pamphlet, addressed to teenage girls, was even more emphatic: while acknowledging that onanism was an illness, and not without harm to the body, it concluded: "You can't go crazy from masturbation and it never leads to serious illnesses; all such talk on the subject is invention."[39] Such efforts at diminishing anxieties, however, proved the exception.

Soviet sexual enlightenment literature on masturbation followed in a long tradition of European popular medical texts on the subject, dating back to the publication of the anonymous *Onania* in the early 1700s. Indeed, virtually every one of the causes and consequences of self-stimulation identified by the educators in this chapter thus far could be found in the assessments of both their tsarist predecessors and their foreign colleagues.[40]

The topic of onanism also raised issues unique to the Soviet context, playing into fears and concerns particular to the postrevolutionary experience. In this regard the vehemence of the medical antimasturbation crusade is not altogether surprising, given the Soviet discomfort with the very idea of pleasure; after all, what else is masturbation but the most self-affirming act of sensual gratification? On another level, Soviet medical writings on masturbation spoke to the practical, physical need of the state for strong bodies, a concern expressed in their analysis of male impotence. One author warned that the practice leads to "a decline in energy and a weakening of the will now, precisely when we need people with strong wills and great energy for the immense construction facing our youth."[41]

More fundamentally, however, onanism appeared to represent a uniquely dangerous form of sexual expression. In one important sense, because of its antagonism to the collectivist ideals of the new state, auto-eroticism posed a graver threat than impotence, or even intercourse, regardless of whatever excesses or forms of deviance might attend that act. Physicians explained that as the "solitary vice" became habitual, the virus of solitude would gradually infect every other aspect of the masturbator's existence. In the language of these pamphlets, onanists become introverts who "strive for solitude," "avoid contact with others," "love to be alone," and "go deep into their own internal world."[42]

While similar charges were leveled against masturbation by medical writers in a variety of historical and national settings, such behavior became ideologically seditious in Soviet Russia. Far more threatening than any mere physical incapacitation, this withdrawal would eventually become total; and, as these writers implied, political alienation would ultimately follow such physical and psychological distancing. With all thoughts concentrated on his own sexual organ, according to Dr. Vasilevskii, the masturbator's circle of interests becomes increasingly narrow: "To satisfy his passion unimpeded, he separates himself from his comrades and generally from society, becomes reclusive, inactive, and morbidly pensive. As a result he inevitably falls behind in mental development, and feelings of community [*obshchestvennost'*] and comradeship die away in him." In another pamphlet, Dr. Tsukker charted the progression from sexual indulgence to societal subversion in even more explicitly political terms:

> This type of youth or girl begins to avoid comrades, becomes quiet, secretive, pale, stops being interested in social questions; even close comrades no longer interest him. And so from the moment that he begins to masturbate he becomes a ballast for the collective: at the same time as he does damage to his own system, he becomes an outsider to society.

Tsukker explained that previously the problem of masturbation was considered solely from the perspectives of morality or the potential danger to the individual organism. But health concerns now embraced the social as well as the physical body.[43]

The antisocial nature of masturbation was manifested in a second, seemingly contradictory, phenomenon that elicited even greater anxiety:

onanistic infection. The medical opinion that this vice (and hence the behavior it inspired) was contagious profoundly increased its potential social danger. Some writers pointed to the influence of verbal suggestion, as in the advice of comrades "more experienced in the matter of satisfying their sexual demands" who recommended this act as a way to "get satisfaction, experience strong sexual sensations" without running the risk of venereal infection.[44] Others focused on instances of physical indoctrination: "The shame experienced at first [with masturbation] weakens with time and the child not only stops hiding his nasty habit from comrades, but strives to draw them into it."[45] Nor did educators limit this behavior to children; recall Glezer's artel masters and shepherds. By performing the solitary vice in public, and inculcating others to do the same, the onanist stood the concept of collectivity on its head. As Thomas Laqueur notes, "while all other sex was social," masturbation when not done alone "was social in all the wrong ways." Indeed, as a result of masturbation the collective was irrevocably damaged, deprived of valuable members through self-imposed isolation or through distortion when its members became too collectively oriented: doing in a group what had previously been done in private.[46]

In eerily suggestive tones, given the larger battles then being fought in the country's collectivization campaign, Alfei also bears testimony to the perils of masturbatory contagion. Here, apparently, was one realm in which the collective ideal went a bit too far:

> I am a peasant by birth, am often at home, and therefore I am very familiar with the varieties of our youth's diversions and lifestyle. On weekdays the guys are busy with work responsibilities, but the evenings are for idleness— they hang out [*na posidelkakh*] doing nothing. Naturally, the sexual dominant prevails in their brains, finding its release in masturbation. This is aggravated even further by the idleness of church holidays and by dressing in coarse canvas underwear, and also by young people's conversations on ribald sexual themes. For instance, I was a witness to such an incident in the village of Dulovo in Verkhne-Vologodskoi volost, Vologodskoi district and province, where I myself am from. During one of the summer (church) holidays, the youth (older and medium-age kids) gathered outside of the village near a haystack and, after a conversation about the sex question, replete with foul language, everybody masturbated, in front of one another. What an instructive example for the younger generation!

One wonders what Alfei was doing while this debauchery was taking place. Did he stand there and watch? Run away? Intervene? Join in? Perhaps he held himself back from this collective activity to protest the damage done to the "true" collective ideal that this group seemingly (and actively) perverted. Whatever his personal role in the events described, Alfei also condemned the culprits for their influence as negative role models. It seems that the *smena*, the younger generation on whose destiny and prospects so much of society's hopes were pinned, was no less susceptible to this habit: "Is masturbation among the younger generation gradually being overcome? No, it is not. Listening to the depraved conversations of older kids and seeing their masturbatory acts, the younger kids imitate them and begin to masturbate themselves."[47]

In its abrupt leaps from the personal to the political, from the solitary to the collective, Alfei's letter recapitulates the tortured logic that allowed sexual enlighteners to portray masturbation as both an antisocial, individualist pathology and a decidedly social ill that could be discussed alongside prostitution and venereal disease. Masturbation weakened the collective as both a centripetal and a centrifugal force, both encouraging young boys to explore their own desires in relative privacy and also becoming a group activity that spread antisocial narcissism through social interaction.

The Deviation of Early Marriage

So what alternatives to masturbation and sexual excess were available to young people? Early marriage—a monogamous long-term commitment, begun before the age of marital maturity—was considered equally unacceptable. Introducing this topic in an article for *Hygiene and Health*, Professor Mendel'son described two clinical cases that summarized the dimensions of this particular sexual problem, which he claimed was encountered "more and more frequently" in recent years:

> Not long ago, someone who at first glance seemed to be an adolescent of fourteen came to me due to hysterical fits. It turned out, however, that she was seventeen, in her second common-law marriage, and had even undergone a D&C [*vyskablivanie matki*] for abortion. Last year I had to treat a twenty-year-old student for melancholia, a widower with two small children, who had begun his "normal" sex life at fifteen.

In addition to the psychological damage, educators enumerated a variety of other physical and social consequences of such early unions.[48] In the first place, people at this age were just too undisciplined to refrain from overdoing it. Dr. Rozenblium explained: "That which in casual sexual intercourse is simply harmful, in marriage can be downright fatal." It was assumed (perhaps unrealistically, given the dire housing situation) that married couples would have more opportunities for, and no moral proscriptions against, sexual encounters. As a result the loss of internal secretions would occur even faster. Again Rozenblium alone warned of the consequences of early marriage for sexual pleasure, linking the exhaustion of the sexual apparatus with the threat of future sexual dissatisfaction rather than simply impotence.[49] He identified such physical dissatisfaction, as well as the changes in personal interests and ideas that come with age, as important factors contributing to the dissolution of these relationships.

For Dr. Zalutskaia, "evidence" of the harm caused by early marriage was provided by the example of females in Central Asia, transformed into old women by the age of thirty as a consequence of early unions. Premature marriage could also, it appears, prove fatal. Zalutskaia cited a paper presented at the Paris Academy of Sciences claiming that the death rate of women who wed between the ages of fifteen and twenty was seven times higher than among those who married after twenty; many more men married between eighteen and twenty reportedly died than did bachelors of the same age group.[50]

Both pregnancy and its interruption were represented as damaging to a young woman's health. Not only would the experiences of gestation and especially labor become considerably more difficult and painful owing to the body's immaturity, but the growing fetus and, later, the nursing infant would take from the mother the nutrients necessary to complete her own development, leaving her anemic and exhausted.[51] Sexual enlightenment depicted the termination of a pregnancy as particularly traumatic for the young female body even if the operation was conducted in sanitary conditions by a trained physician. Dr. Mendel'son cited "new research" proving that abortion in young females caused extreme cases of reverse development, in which the sex organs atrophied and the hormonal secretions of the uterus ceased, resulting in irreversible infertility. Consistently, others emphasized the inevitable premature fading of beauty and youth resulting from abortion at such a young age.[52]

In view of sex educators' long-term goals, they also emphasized the impact of early marriages on the offspring of such unions. Doctors maintained that not only were the sperm and ova of immature individuals of inferior quality but the young mother's body also could not provide enough nourishment to the growing fetus. As a consequence such children frequently died; those who survived were depicted as weak, frail, puny, and sick.[53]

The peasant correspondent Alfei also offered alarming confirmation of the prevalence of this abnormality, pointing to several political consequences of far greater immediacy than the long-term dangers associated with eugenics:

> As a result of drunkenness and hooliganism, premature sexual intercourse can also be observed in the village, necessitating early marriage and compelling young couples to tear themselves away from the necessary task of fighting for collectivization, for the improvement of the economy, drawing them onto the path of individualism and *razdel* [division of the household], not to mention small-scale peasant farming.

Razdel refers to the division of multiple family households in Russian peasant society, in which younger male members, together with their wives and children, were provided with a portion of the family's property in order to establish their own household. As a reliable, collective-minded Komsomol member, Alfei would have deplored both the *razdel* and the small peasant holding as smacking of egotism and selfishness. Clearly, he had learned his political as well as his sexual lessons. In this sexual denunciation, he is cooperative enough to provide names and addresses of some of the culprits:

> An example: the village Dulova, Nikolai Alfeiovich Ziatiushkov (twenty-one yrs.) married only because of the pregnancy of his girlfriend, from the village Doru, who gave birth one month after the wedding. Now these "young people" are obtaining a portion of the household [*razdel*]. As a consequence of hooliganism (the inability to have a good time [*guliat'*]), the majority get married when they are between nineteen and twenty-one years of age: Pegorov, Alek., Iakunichev, Val., etc.[54]

What did Alfei expect from doctors: a sexual health campaign waged parallel to the one for collectivization? One wonders what Batkis and the other educators would have made of this overt politicization of the sex question, since nowhere in this body of literature do we find such vituperative attacks or such linking of the sexual with the political. Medical writers, after all, sought to persuade gently, not frighten their readers through public shaming or the sort of personal condemnations that had far-reaching implications in the political climate.

The Solution of Abstinence

Given the dire consequences attendant on each and every manifestation of youthful sexuality, what was this overly stimulated, sexually precocious segment of the population to do? How could their prematurely sparked libidinal interest and passions be kept in check until that time when they could be used more responsibly and less dangerously? For Alfei, the answer lay in education. He drew a direct causal link between scientific ignorance in matters of sex and engagement in masturbation and premature intercourse, culminating in inactivity, hooliganism, and apathy toward "the improvement of agriculture." He concluded: "I think that the distribution of this literature in the countryside—the series of brochures entitled "Questions of Sexual Life"—should become the immediate task of every cultured peasant, every Komsomol and Party member, every cultured person."[55]

While sanitary enlighteners undoubtedly shared Alfei's faith in the transformative power of (approved) scientific literature, they also had a more specific, unequivocal solution in mind: "Young people, in the interests of their own health and the health of their offspring, [should choose] the path of abstinence until full sexual maturity."[56] Educators saw in premarital continence half the solution to Russia's sex question (see the next chapter for eugenic marriage, the other half). Abstinence was identified as the only foolproof way to prevent disease, pregnancy, and the premature depletion of glandular secretions. The benefits also extended far beyond such prophylactic considerations. Whether rehabilitating those already sexually active or anticipating and heading off sexual discoveries, the most valuable contribution of abstinence lay in its power to discipline the body. And in sexual enlightenment a disciplined body automatically became a socialized body, since the practice of abstaining indicated and encouraged a commitment to personal health, the health of society, and the revolutionary project of the new state.

At the heart of this crusade for abstinence was the doctors' concern with energy and its deployment. Yet prior to exploring the uses of pent-up sexual energy, it was necessary for educators to refute long-held beliefs about its harmfulness. According to (uneducated) popular wisdom, continence caused pimples and increased the incidence of nocturnal emissions.[57] More seriously, it was feared that the body would poison itself if the products of the sex glands were not released regularly, or that it would lead to any one of several nervous-related conditions and illnesses.

Responding to such concerns, each discussion of abstinence in sexual enlightenment materials, however brief, contained a version of the refrain: "Abstinence is not only not harmful, but useful." As Donichev advised one of his young patients: "Humans don't ever suffer from any kind of dangerous complications from abstinence. We doctors don't know of a single illness that might arise from sexual abstinence." Dr. Nikulin concurred, asserting that the idea of continence being dangerous was not only scientifically unfounded, but also contradicted "biological truth."[58] The only exception to this pronouncement concerned the "hereditarily nervous," for whom abstaining would prove too taxing on the system; they were advised to marry early rather than substitute casual sex or the use of prostitutes.[59] Writers repeatedly invoked the authority of science and scientific experts to support this assertion: scientists "concluded," "studied," "acknowledged," and "proved" that continence was both safe and beneficial.[60] Evidently, the perception of it as dangerous was not restricted to the lay public: an article on the safety of abstinence written by the eminent professor of venereology R. M. Fronshtein and published in the medical journal *Vrachebnoe delo* suggests that this belief persisted as late as the mid-1920s in a segment of the medical world as well.[61]

Educators saw the advantages of abstinence extending far beyond such physical, bodily concerns as the prevention of venereal disease or unfavorable pregnancies and into the realm of the sociopolitical. Summarizing the general improvement that abstinence promised to society, Dr. Golomb wrote: "The value of sexual abstinence . . . is not restricted to the boundaries of individuality. The benefits of this form of life extend to the family, society, and the state." Moving beyond the health of the individual to that of the community also assisted physicians in dispelling a second misconception about continence: its reputation as a bourgeois practice. We have already examined the phenomenon of certain young people, particularly students and Komsomol members, who in the days after 1917 branded as bourgeois any manifestation of sexual restraint. When linked to the eugenic needs of society and the state, abstinence more easily shed its association with such excoriated notions of individual morality. Thus, for instance, Dr. Rozenblium argued: "There is nothing bourgeois [*meshchanskii*] in the demand for sexual abstinence. [It] is a condition for health and for an energetic community. Society and the state demand sexual abstinence from the young." Such a commitment to continence appeared to be possible only in the USSR, after the demise of capitalism and the hypocritical bourgeois sexual order that accompanied it.[62]

If the final emphasis in the advocacy of abstinence rested upon the idea of communal benefits and obligations, the potential that this practice held for the individual was also crucial to authors' arguments. In the struggle to abstain (and educators acknowledged that it was often a struggle), the human will was strengthened and tempered. Just as a strong will (the reward of sexual restraint) had political significance in that it helped forge the new person required by Soviet society, so too did a weak will (the source of sexual excess). As much is demonstrated in the following reference by Rozenblium to an incident in Russia's recent past: "Well-known facts show that almost all Russian agent provocateurs who turned in revolutionaries to the tsarist police were notable for their sexual depravity. Their weakness of will was the result of this, leading them to such base occupations as provocation."[63]

Aside from this political subtext, discussions of the will in relation to abstinence frequently had a clear gender subtext as well. Most medical writings on the topic assumed a male subject and listed benefits similarly specific to men, among which those deemed lacking in Russia's population of the nervous and impotent were conspicuous.[64] The purported gains of abstinence to the male reflected educators' assumptions about the greater difficulty of this practice for men. Because male sexuality was perceived as more powerful and harder to control, abstinence for young men involved a conscious, active struggle. Young women, on the other hand, "easily" did without. The only exception to this rule were those who became artificially stimulated through reading erotic novels. In the estimation of Professor Mendel'son: "Such depraved girls are only half virgins, since in their mind they have already lost their virginal purity."[65]

Sexual enlightenment offered extensive advice that promised to make the transition to and practice of abstinence easier. With suggestions about what to eat, wear, and read, and about how and in what company to spend one's time, writers posited a totally regimented existence whose observation promised to discipline both the physical and ultimately the social body. Taken together, these behavioral suggestions constituted what one author referred to as an individual's "moral self-education," based upon self-abnegation, the steeling of one's organism, and the choice of the correct path in life, in which a strong sense of willpower and the sincere desire to order one's sexuality played a prominent role.[66] Educators repeatedly emphasized the need to establish a regular daily routine in which the correct schedule of rest, sleep, and work was assiduously accounted for and maintained. It was recommended that abstainers sleep with their hands over the covers (to prevent unconscious self-stimulation) on a cold, hard mattress under a light blanket, since a warm and especially soft bed was held responsible for most night-time erections. Upon awakening, it was necessary to get up immediately, in order to avoid the laziness, sexual fantasies, and arousal to which those who spent excess time in bed were disposed.[67]

Doctors counseled readers to begin each day with a special hygiene regimen, a cold bath, and physical exercise, and to avoid at all costs a sedentary lifestyle. Tight clothing and underwear were to be shunned as facilitating sexual arousal. Abstainers were cautioned to refrain from excess in food (especially meat) as well as stimulants of every kind, including spices, caffeine, and alcohol, which was considered particularly dangerous to those fighting against masturbation.[68]

As for other sensory stimulants, readers were warned against "erotic literature, unseemly anecdotes, and pornographic pictures." Dr. Lass suggested that young people stay away from all forms of popular entertainment promoting "love for all that is unnatural" and instead attend informative film and theater presentations depicting nature, ethnographic studies, or the country's technical achievements. Finally, confirming the male-oriented perspective of much of this abstinence advice, several authors specified that a particular type of individual be shunned. As Mendel'son put it: "Avoid the society of frivolous or dissolute women, who, partly out of unconscious coquetry, partly out of conscious calculation, arouse in men an increased sexual desire (on the contrary, the society of pure women, with serious intellectual faculties, encourages a modest life)."[69]

Of course there were limits to the benefits of abstinence, whether as health practice or disciplinary technique, and educators noted that refraining from sex after reaching full maturity not only was "silly" but, more important, contradicted the laws of nature. Setting the age of thirty as the absolute upper boundary for both men and women, writers nonetheless disagreed as to the consequences of later continence. Dr. Lemberg alone argued that refraining from sex had no physical or emotional repercussions. The claim that older bachelors became egotistical and eccentric owing to abstinence he characterized as naive; that abstaining women became "old maids" he labeled "a product of the bourgeois way of life." He concluded: "Happily, this type of woman has disappeared in our day. Women educated for socially useful labor on equal terms with men will always find their place."[70]

Others saw more dangers in abstaining after full sexual maturity. In the few references to later continence in men, the negative consequences were localized in the sexual realm. Thus a man who remained abstinent after thirty faced sexual weakness or full impotence, although his general neuropsychiatric health would remain unaffected. This paucity of references may have stemmed from the medical belief that such discussions were unnecessary (concern lay with restraining male sexual behavior rather than the opposite). In keeping with the assumption that sex played a relatively larger role in women's lives, writers emphasized the more generalized disorders wrought by prolonged virginity on the female personality and body: continence reportedly caused women to become bitter, callous, stingy, hypochondriacal, suspicious, and exasperated. "Denied the joys of love," such women directed their maternal instinct toward domestic pets instead. Moreover, the natural nervous "release valve" provided to males in nocturnal emissions was unavailable to them: "having a destructive effect on the nervous system, it cannot prevent the withering that characterizes old maids."[71]

Physical Culture and the Redemption of Sublimation

Abstinence was said to provide another valuable benefit, one that linked the preservation of the physical body with the transformation of the body politic. In explanation, sexual enlighteners returned to the subject of energy and the enormous, though fixed, amount of unstorable energy produced by the sex glands. Earlier it was believed this energy must necessarily find its release in sexual intercourse. Yet the examples of castration and rejuvenation seemed to disprove this, since hormonal energy was utilized by the body for a wide variety of processes and functions that were not strictly sexual. "After all," remarked Dr. Uspenskii, "one type of energy can be transformed easily into another: thermal energy is transformed into kinetic energy, making the steam engine possible. Electric energy is transformed into light energy, and we have electric lighting." Thus energy that might be rapidly squandered on sexual pleasure could also be altered. Ultimately it was a matter of channeling the force into the proper and appropriate direction, as illustrated by Dr. Bruk in yet another production-oriented metaphor:

Any power can be useful or harmful depending on how it is used. The Dnepr rapids were dangerous. They interrupted navigation on a major river, destroying rafts and barges. But these same rapids, put into locks, become very useful. They provide inexpensive electric energy (power) [that revives] an enormous area, and the locks make the Dnepr navigable to its mouth. It is the same with sexual power; it can cause harm, can even be the cause of venereal infection or suicide. But this same sexual power, expended on something else, can be very useful.[72]

And the name for this transfer of energy from "less valuable paths" to the "more valuable"? Readers were informed that "science" labeled this process "sublimation." In sexual enlightenment, Freud's concept was itself converted into a distinctly Soviet phenomenon. In psychoanalytic theory it is the force of the sex instinct that is diverted into the higher realms of intellectual and creative activity, or put to use in the pursuit of other socially valued endeavors. In the Russian medical recasting, the ever-important hormones displaced the libido as the source of this usable energy. Thus the ultimate goal in educational discussions of abstinence was to persuade readers to redirect the hormonally produced energy saved from sexual dissipation into more productive channels. Timofeev explained to his readers that, when an object is electrically charged, whatever excess is produced will be released externally.[73] The same occurs with a body's energy, produced by the hormones of the sex glands: its excess "electricity" must somehow be discharged. The question, then, was what use could and would be made of this power source?

Shifting sublimation from the psyche to the realm of the physical enabled educators to complete their idealized vision of the body, one that practiced simultaneous self-control, self-denial, and social engagement. In Soviet sublimation, it was the last category that held the greatest promise. Whereas reproduction was presented as the sexual, corporeal obligation of an adult to the new society, for younger readers this function was assumed by abstinence; through sublimation, their commitment to the revolutionary project would be ensured.

But how were adolescent and young adult men and women supposed to redirect this potential sexual energy, which threatened to drive them toward illicit forms of release? As much energy as possible was supposed to be devoted to socially useful activities, but the doctors readily admitted that public works alone would not shield youth from depravity. Given medical authors' concerns about the debauched nature of NEP, the need for a more *reactive* method of energy redirection was particularly urgent. Thus sexual enlightenment devoted considerable attention to promoting a more physical surrogate for revolutionary sublimation, one with manifold benefits to the individual as well as the collective and state: physical culture.[74]

First publicized in the 1820s and widely advocated throughout Europe and the United States in the late nineteenth and early twentieth centuries, physical culture was an approach to exercise that stressed the harmonious development of mind and body through physical conditioning and observance of the rules of hygiene, preferably in conjunction with the curative natural resources of sun, air, and water. As manifested in Russia after the Revolution, this approach to exercise foregrounded a hostility to "Western"-style spectator sports and "record-breaking" (and, occasionally, competition). It also demonstrated an explicit link to social and political engagement. Physical culture received a great deal of attention in sexual enlightenment because of its purported contribution to regulating the body and thus helping to make sex healthy.[75]

Advocates of *fizkul'tura* claimed that it waged the battle against disordered sexuality on a number of different levels. Movement increased the blood's circulation to the muscles and skin and thus prevented its stagnating (*zastoi*) in the pelvis. Diagnosed as a consequence of inactivity, this concentration of blood in the region of the sex organs was held responsible for drastically increasing sexual feeling. By sublimating one's energy through physical exertion, *fizkul'turniki* (practitioners of physical culture) were easily distracted from sexual thoughts and preoccupations. According to Dr. Vasilevskii: "That unhealthy, artificial demand for sexual excitement that tortures young people and saps their strength, leading them either to masturbation, to casual and base sexual ties, or, finally, to prostitution—has no power over the gymnast or sportsman: for him, it almost does not exist." *Fizkul'tura* was particularly valued for its role in combating onanism; Commissar Semashko considered it the only way to cure this vice.[76]

Sanitary enlightenment literature attributed many other physical, psychological, and social benefits to *fizkul'tura*. It asserted that physical exercise improved one's memory and strengthened the bones as well as the respiratory, muscular, and nervous systems, the last being particularly crucial for the fight against nervous complaints. Precisely because the dangers of infection by vestiges of the old lifestyle persisted, young people were believed at risk even after they had been incorporated into the collective. If stuffy rooms, parties, dancing, and even sometimes committees and meetings were thought to lead to collective sexual depravity, *fizkul'tura*, on the other hand, ensured the right kind of collective. Educators saw in it a natural defense against the pernicious influence of alcohol and bars, tobacco-filled rooms, card-playing, prostitutes, venereal disease, and the wrong sort of comrades.[77]

Thanks to physical culture, Soviet youth were now free to enjoy the full creative benefits of revolutionary sublimation, both individually and collectively. If the sexual enlightenment literature is to be believed, such benefits were manifold. History provided writers with many examples confirming the accuracy of the sublimation hypothesis. Such "best representatives of humanity" as Newton, Kant, da Vinci, and Beethoven all applied their sexual energy to "the highest forms of creativity" rather than to its more direct function.[78] Nor were such benefits limited to individuals: according to Dr. Ivanovskii, the great cultural achievements of ancient Greece and the Renaissance were due to the accumulation of sexual energy, just as its squandering in sexual depravity and licentiousness explained the fall of ancient Rome.[79]

Texts referred to the work of "researchers" (including "the famous Darwin") to argue that love—or alternately, "competition for the female"—represented the basis for this flowing of (evidently male, heterosexual) creativity: "The medieval singers, troubadours, and poets who contributed so much to music, singing, and poetry—all this was born out of a burst of love for members of the opposite sex."[80] Yet such creative production required this love to remain unfulfilled; as soon as the sexual energy was spent, creativity disappeared. Citing as evidence an example dear to the Russian heart, authors referred to the case of Pushkin, who supposedly produced his best work during periods when he was forced to abstain. Just as sexual attraction might be diverted into the higher realm of creation, the pressure of physical and mental exertion served to quench sexual desire; readers learned that another famous Russian writer, Maksim Gor'kii, was little troubled by sexual attraction, having been forced to work assiduously to overcome the poverty and deprivations of his working-class childhood.[81]

Nor were the benefits accruing to libidinal redirection restricted to the ranks of literary and artistic giants. Sublimation, unlike creative genius, was a most democratically apportioned gift, since each and every individual who abstained from sexual activity possessed the same opportunity to reap the rewards of this energy windfall. Accordingly, sexual enlightenment literature emphasized sublimation's various potential uses and advantages. Of crucial importance for those who had not heeded the call to abstinence in time was sublimation's purported power of redemption. This process was deemed capable of mending the bodily (and spiritual) damage inflicted by sexual excess, early sex, and masturbation. Having summarized the potential consequences of such glandular self-abuse, Dr. Rozenblium nonetheless admonished readers against exaggerating these hazards, since the damage could be "cured" through the redirection of energy. Alluding to the various experimental efforts at battling age, Dr. Ivanovskii maintained that only through sublimation, as opposed to artificial measures, could "true rejuvenation" be attained.[82]

However vague writers were as to whether this process was conscious or subconscious, sacrificing personal gratification raised "a person's social value." The act was transformed automatically into a form of social engagement. Sublimation functioned both as evidence of a commitment to society and the means to achieve this, since the denial of individual bodily pleasure enabled abstainers to contribute even more energy, strength, and attention to the needs and welfare of communal bodies.[83]

The era of capitalism provided countless examples supporting the claims made for sublimation's social value. That people who utilized their energy for mental or physical labor suffered the pangs of sexual attraction less than "idle people" explained for Dr. Karov why the proletariat experienced the sex question less acutely than did the bourgeoisie. Living wholly at the expense of others, these "good-for-nothings" allegedly devoted their entire existence to the satisfaction of their personal desires. Karov acknowledged that sometimes even workers engaged in sexual excess, pursuing pleasure to escape capitalism's harsh realities of exploitation and the burdensome conditions of life. Dr. Bruk offered an even more sinister explanation: capitalists in fact encouraged the proletariat's sexual debauchery as a way to deflect its interest from social questions and its own oppression.[84]

Happily, the arrival of the dictatorship of the proletariat had changed all that by gradually rechanneling the energy of the working class onto the path of socialist construction. Viewing the redirection of sexual energy toward social action as a common feature of great cataclysmic upheavals, authors nonetheless identified Russia's own experience in the Revolution as the most positive example of the power of sublimation.[85]

In many accounts Gel'man's 1922 sex survey provided the statistical confirmation of this claim. Asked what effect the Revolution and Civil War had on their libido, 53 percent of the male and 21 percent of the female students in a sample of 1,552 respondents at the Sverdlov Communist Academy claimed that they had experienced a weakening of sexual feeling during this period. Commissar Semashko attributed these findings to the fact that "under the conditions of revolutionary and civil struggle, each youth, grasping the colossal, universal importance of these questions, instinctively sought the release of his energy precisely in the realm of political action." Only one source, Dr. Bruk, cited the impact of hunger, and in particular the famine of 1921–1922, as a factor contributing to this purportedly lowered libido.[86]

A negative argument about a revolution's potential for sublimation was also made through references to the earlier, unsuccessful Revolution of 1905 and in particular the period of reaction that followed. Writers described how the disillusionment resulting from the suppression of the Revolution led to widespread displays of depravity, especially among the intelligentsia and the young. Because the energy that had accumulated during the revolutionary events had not found a useful application, the populace's "coarsest primitive instincts" prevailed, finding expression in "leagues of love" and "Athenian nights." Pornography in all forms of art flourished, attracting a mass following.[87] Here sex is posited not as political, but as antipolitical: in a remarkable reversal of the Freudian insistence on the primacy of eros, sexual dissipation is the result of social and political frustration.

As the events of 1917 and the Civil War receded into the past, it became less likely that educators' targeted audience had experienced "revolutionary" sublimation themselves. Therefore, in addition to the invocation of the Revolution as a mobilizing tactic, writers offered other motivations for sublimation, more immediately relevant to contemporary youth's own experience. Sexual energy might be put to work serving the current needs of the nation, and humanity; in the political fight for the future communist society, in such organizations as the Komsomol; in raising the country's cultural level; or in the production of valuable works in the realms of science, art, technology, and physical labor. With more of the youth's attention devoted to such important social matters, sex would return to its secondary, "natural" position. Dr. Bruk declared: "Not all the time in the world for love and an hour for work, but the other way around: all the time in the world for work and an hour for love."[88]

What if these various prescriptions to control the sexual drive of youth failed to achieve their goal? Most writers did not even entertain such a possibility, adamant as they were that the strategies of sublimation outlined above would guarantee the desired behaviors. In one of the rare instances where these disciplinary techniques were acknowledged as not always being successful, the youths in question received scant sympathy. Writing about "The Truth about Young People's Sexuality" in *Path to Health*, Dr. Lifshits published in full the "most poignant," "most difficult" of the many letters received at the periodical. The writers were four young men, all members of the working class, from eighteen to twenty years of age. The correspondents represented themselves as—and according to the qualities outlined in this chapter, appear to be—model youths: all, after eight hours of work, attended night school, studying mathematics, physics, the social sciences, and drawing. Each engaged in civic work, two of the four were Komsomol members, and all fulfilled various union, factory, and Komsomol obligations. A few also found time for physical culture, in particular basketball, rowing, and light athletics. They also tried to read whenever possible, and it is clear from their letter that the four were quite familiar with the sex advice offered to the members of their generation; having enumerated the activities comprising their very full days, they concluded, "It would appear that all our sexual energy should be transformed into mental energy."[89]

The much desired transformation, however, failed to occur, and each observed that a great deal of sexual energy remained, "demanding its natural application." Having discussed their predicament, the youths came up with three possible solutions, each ultimately unacceptable: sex with a female acquaintance; sex with a prostitute; or masturbation. They deemed the first option inappropriate for ethical reasons (having sex and then breaking off the relationship), because they had neither the time to pursue nor the opportunity to meet such acquaintances, and because such an interaction might end in child support (that is, pregnancy), the demands of which were well beyond their financial means. The youths considered prostitution to be equally objectionable, not only out of ethical concerns, but because they feared venereal infection and did not have the money to pay for sex. And finally, masturbation was ruled out because of its damaging effect on the body.

The workers' first entreaty for "authoritative, comradely, and concrete advice" was directed to the Moscow Counseling Center for Sexual Hygiene, but it remained unanswered. Afraid that their appeal to the health journal would similarly be ignored, they were even more fearful of receiving "a formal, soulless letter, where you will recommend the same old *fizkul'tura,* increased intellectual work (which we already have), and (in our view) similar primitive tools of the sexual moralist." The youths concluded their letter with the following plea: "Put yourself in our position and give us a concrete solution to get out of this sexual dead-end. A transformation of sexual energy into intellectual energy in the future is out of the question. Beyond this—we have nowhere to go."

It seems unlikely that the four would have found much satisfaction in Dr. Lifshits' response. He began by reminding them that there was indeed a ready solution to their dilemma—the path of discipline—and quoted Lenin's statement that "discipline, even in love, is not slavery." Why, he asked, did they expect that one's every demand would be immediately satisfied? "Patience, comrades," he cautioned. "The cult of desire is foreign to the proletariat, bourgeois through and through." Their participation in physical culture and academics was commendable, but what of their will, their intelligence? All this comes at a price: "We have denied ourselves much and continue to deny ourselves. A little self-denial in one's sexual life does not rank among the most difficult kinds of restrictions." Lifshits was not simply chastising the youths for making much of their seemingly unimportant personal discomfort. Representing sacrifice as the loftiest quality of the proletariat, he also implied that any manifestation or acknowledgment of desire by young people—even the desire to be free of desire—was a gesture hostile to working-class interests, in and of itself a counterrevolutionary act.

But if the workers found their situation to be truly "unendurable," Lifshits was able to propose an alternate solution. If they had indeed come of sexual age prematurely, why, he queried, did they not consider a fourth sexual option, and the most natural one at that: marriage? "For some reason this has never entered your heads." He scolded the writers for automatically assuming that sex would lead to child support, reminding them that men might voluntarily take responsibility for the consequences of pregnancy. (Most likely for different reasons, such as purported harmfulness versus discomfort or inconvenience, neither Lifshits nor the correspondents considered birth control as an alternative to either child support or pregnancy.) Lifshits ended the article with the following severe pronouncement: "Or maybe you don't like this. In that case don't complain and don't reproach us for too 'general and formal' an answer."

That the option of marriage had never entered the youths' heads suggests how conscientiously they had followed the enlightenment literature designated for their age group. Yet in advocating marriage, Lifshits made it clear that it was a solution of last resort, recommended to those unsympathetic individuals lacking the willpower (or perhaps the political commitment) to hold out until a more appropriate, and advisable age. Ideally, the new Soviet marriage required that young people wait until they had reached the necessary level of physical, emotional, and political maturity, at which point the laws of eugenics would govern their next set of responsibilities.

Doctors without Boudoirs

Hygiene, Eugenics, and the Sexless Socialist Family

Socialist society's new person should be born from a eugenic marriage.—P. ROKITSKII, "EVGENIKA I BRAK"

Answering the Sex Question

The lead article in *Path to Health's* special 1926 issue on sexuality was a front page editorial entitled, appropriately, "The Sex Question." The title appears just as suitable for the illustration accompanying the piece (Figure 6.1). The image is a visual depiction of the "sex question," successfully resolved, as a tableau of contented revolutionary domesticity. The mother and father, clearly adults, have taken all the necessary precautions to produce a healthy child and have been richly rewarded for their efforts. The home is a model of domestic proletarian comfort: the table is laden with food, the samovar steams cheerily, books line the shelf. Yet even in this most private realm of life, the proper balance has been struck between the personal sphere and social engagement. Under the watchful gaze of Lenin, the father prepares a military toy for his son while the mother reads the Party newspaper.

This illustration represents the culminating, idealized model of Soviet sexuality, the finished product of sexual enlightenment. Yet where is the sex in this pictorial sex question? Used to produce healthy offspring

61 (47714x)(05) „1926-] Пролетарии всех стран, соединяйтесь

ЗДОРОВЬЕ ТРУДЯЩИХСЯ · ДЕЛО САМИХ ТРУДЯЩИХСЯ

ПУТЬ К ЗДОРОВЬЮ

ЕЖЕМЕСЯЧНЫЙ ЖУРНАЛ

№ 7-8 ГОД ИЗДАНИЯ ВТОРОЙ № 7-8

ПОЛОВОЙ ВОПРОС

РЕДАКЦIЯ

Figure 6.1—"The sex question" (*Put' k zdorov'iu* 7–8 [1926]: 1). Departing from its regular practice, *Path to Health* devoted an entire issue to a single topic: the sex question. The editorial accompanying this cover illustration promised that sexual literacy would transform daily life and relations between the sexes, resulting in the "new family."

for the socialist future, in this visual rendition sex has served its true purpose and is no longer necessary, as if sex, rather than the family, is what has withered away. In looking at this illustration one is reminded of Lifshits's assertion to the young worker correspondents: desire is foreign to the proletariat. From the stern faces of the mother, father, and especially Lenin, we learn that sex is serious business. The scene is devoid of pleasure; happiness is expressed solely by the presexual boy. The mother and father's lack of physical intimacy is underlined by the space between them, equal but separate (not to mention different) in their different spheres. With sex out of the way, the couple is free to get on with more important tasks such as raising the family and building the country. It is this sexless-sex model that would exert itself with ever greater tenacity in the 1930s.

The denial of pleasure—even to responsible adults, acting within the confines of heterosexual monogamy—represents one of the most striking aspects of Soviet sexual enlightenment. We have discussed the vast amount of attention focused on the problem of male impotence and the almost complete silence on the topic of female frigidity during the 1920s. It is significant that, for the medical authorities who addressed this crisis of dysfunction, men's fitness for production provoked the greatest concern; their sexual satisfaction, like that of women, barely merits mention. Although the medical approach to impotence took for granted that men had certain sexual needs, this was still a far cry from celebrating a husband's right to enjoy himself to the fullest (even with his lawfully wedded wife).

Such neglect of the legitimacy of sexual fulfillment represents a radical departure from the marital advice being offered by Soviet physicians' counterparts throughout the rest of Europe during the same period. To combat the rising divorce rate and the declining birthrate, and to redress the losses associated with World War I, European sex reformers were advocating the companionate marriage, whose linchpin was the sexually satisfied wife. The future of the family, and indeed society, rested upon women's readily accepting their duties as mothers and caregivers. To ensure this goal, marriage manuals alerted men to the importance of their spouses' achieving orgasm, and their responsibility in making it happen; instructions were provided. Marriage could not be healthy if both partners were not sexually fulfilled.[1]

It is important to reiterate here that, with this prime exception, the content of sex advice within Russia and Europe was surprisingly consistent during the 1920s. Nor can there be a question of coincidence regarding the similarity of the other areas of popular instruction: Soviet doctors read their foreign counterparts' publications, printed a number of them in translation, and attended the same international conferences. Likewise, many of those European sex reformers who advocated companionate marriages were Soviet enthusiasts, and some even visited the Soviet Union to observe the revolutionary experiment firsthand.[2] Yet any reference to pleasure as the key to a healthy marriage was deliberately omitted in Soviet sexual enlightenment.

Given the long streak of asceticism in Russian culture, perhaps such an-
hedonia is not surprising: sources as dissimilar as the Russian Orthodox
Church and the nineteenth-century radical intelligentsia evinced a strong
discomfort with physical bliss. After the Revolution, the Bolshevik desig-
nation of pleasure as a telltale mark of capitalist perversion and, most immediately, the gluttonous excesses associated with NEP only added to this
atmosphere of mistrust. Lenin's sacrifice of the joys of listening to
Beethoven and playing chess—described by him as too distracting from
the cause—comes to mind here as well.[3]

Still, how are we to explain this antipathy to pleasure in the one place
where, in principle, it might be acceptable to have it? Furthermore, if sexual fulfillment was not going to motivate (or reward) husbands and wives,
what would? The motivations of the medical authors themselves are key
here. Even though the marriage manual is the most important forum for
this sort of information in Europe and the United States, it is not what
these doctors want to be writing. As with other sex-related topics addressed above (such as the family code or sex crimes, for instance) educators may have been simply reluctant to interfere in areas that they had
determined to be beyond their mandate. Perhaps physicians were con-
strained by their own association of sexuality with disease. In any event,
the very notion of pleasure seems to offend the sensibilities of many of
these authors. We are frequently left with the feeling that sex itself—not
merely its perceived aberrations—was somehow suspect.

Both sex reformers and sexual enlighteners viewed parenthood as the
purpose of marriage, but here the similarity ends. While advocates of the
companionate marriage looked to it as a guarantor of a healthy birthrate
and a source of social stability, they also saw a harmonious union—with
fulfilling sex at the core—as its own reward. For Soviet writers, compatibility was important but only as the means to a greater end; the couple itself
was ultimately of little consequence. Thus in countless Soviet enlightenment publications, the key quality in a successful marriage is health, not
harmony, and ultimately the health of the couple's future children. Physicians used popular eugenics to promote their positive model of adult sexuality. Defining the reproduction of healthy children as the ultimate and
paramount goal of adult sexual normalcy left little room for pleasure, especially once the aim had been achieved. Men and women would then be
free to leave such sexual concerns behind, to better devote themselves to
the needs of the collective and society.

Marital Hygiene

With mind and body tempered through abstinence and physical culture, having avoided the pitfalls of self-stimulation and early sex, young
Russians would eventually reach adulthood. Yet sexual maturity in no way
conferred the right to unbridled freedom and breadth in sexual expres-

sion; adult sexuality would be equally disciplined and rule bound, if not more so, because its stakes were so much higher. Accordingly, the emphasis in enlightenment materials directed at this age cohort shifted to what this sexuality should look like, how to regulate it properly, and the boundaries within which it should be contained.

If adolescent sexuality was classified as healthy and normal only when it had been sublimated out of existence, adult sexuality achieved this status solely within the confines of wedlock. Dr. Uspenskii maintained: "Normal sex only takes place in marriage; without it one can't talk about normal sex."[4] This assumption, perhaps more than any other, determined and structured the parameters of advice. In countless pamphlets and lectures, the sections on healthy or normal sex focused entirely on marital hygiene, the rules and regulations governing conjugal intercourse. Limiting the confines of sexuality in such an easily discernible way greatly simplified the educators' tasks. More important, in marking every alternative to marital sex as abnormal, it served as a crucial step toward the imposition of the sexless-sex model described above.

Authors' advocacy of marital hygiene did not represent a blanket endorsement of any marriage as the solution to adult sexual requirements and demands. It was not the institution per se that would guarantee that sex be healthy and normal, but rather the kind of marriage that was possible only within Soviet society: a marriage between equals, founded upon the ideals of mutual affection, respect, and ultimately responsibility. Like their legal counterparts, physicians envisioned adult relationships as a partnership between equals, but they lent no support to promoting the withering away of the family. Motivated first and foremost by concerns about health, medical authors favored the term "marriage" to describe their ideal relationship, and the practice of official registration as the best way to ensure the well-being of the union's offspring. Responding to the charge that marriage would damage Soviet society by turning the proletariat into the bourgeoisie, Dr. Lass categorically stated that marriage in no way contradicted the ideals of socialism and communism. After all, Marx himself was a family man. Lass cited the Bolshevik theorist Emil'ian Iaroslavskii's condemnation of the false, "Philistine" idea that marriage demeans the human spirit, a charge that Iaroslavskii specifically levied against Alexandra Kollontai: "If even very conscious comrades refer to Karl Marx as a Philistine for his fidelity to his wife, then it is not surprising that we encounter comrades who think that the love of 'worker bees' is the communist ideal of family life." Objecting to unions based on narrow economic interests, Lass offered an alternative model for the ideal Soviet marriage:

> A marriage of comrades is a completely different matter, the basis of which is not only the feeling of attachment and physical attraction, but a profound commonality of internal interests, a mutual striving toward definitive ideals. Such a marriage transforms the personal into the social, individual love into its highest form—love for society, for the collective that is dear to it in ideological terms, and raises a person above the petit bourgeoisie and Philistinism.[5]

Others emphasized the economic conditions that were to distinguish Soviet marriage from the variety found in capitalist societies, and the social programs that would make these new unions possible. Opportunities for educational and professional advancement would equally prepare both partners for the responsibilities of marriage, and the rational organization of communal cafeterias, laundries, and nurseries would liberate women from "domestic slavery." With all of everyday life thus restructured, wives would be free to join their husbands in the work of building the country.[6]

Despite the variations in their interpretations of the ideal conjugal union, all these medical writers shared the association of marriage with reproduction. For the vast majority, marital sex without procreation was just as harmful and abnormal as extramarital sex. Readers were repeatedly reminded that reproduction was, after all, the biological purpose of intercourse. As Dr. Bernatskii explained it, childless marriages contradicted the laws of nature; any childless family that at first glance looked happy in actuality only appeared to be so, having deprived itself of full satisfaction. Clearly, this form of fulfillment was rated far higher than the more physical variety. Identifying sexual attraction as the basis of marriage, Bernatskii also emphasized that this feeling existed as a type of incentive, to facilitate the reproduction of offspring. Others seemed loath to allow pleasure any role in conjugal relations; Dr. Mamutov defined sexuality as "the continuation of the race—and that's it!" Dr. Timofeev, offering a similar interpretation, added disapprovingly: "But people look at it as a source of satisfaction."[7]

A minority of educators, however, did make the point that conjugal sex was in and of itself a positive thing—provided that intercourse correspond to all of their hygiene specifications. Paraphrasing Lenin's famous dictum about the norms of sex desired by the new society, Dr. Vasilevskii declared: "The goal of the Revolution is not chastity but normal, healthy, and pure sex." Sex for its own sake may have the right to exist, he continued, but not as in the animal world of the *samka* and *samets*. Yet even the few works expressing a positive attitude toward sex stressed the physiological and neurological benefits of intercourse rather than the simple fact that it felt good.[8]

Notably, most of these texts focused upon the particular benefits of martial sex for women, an emphasis reflecting the dual assumptions about gender that colored so much of this advice: whereas men, being automatically more interested in sex, needed no convincing of its benefits, such was not the case for women, whether for reasons of fear, previous bad experiences, or a disinterested, "naturally" lower libido. Thus Dr. Lur'e described the positive influences of marital sex (and, in particular, semen) on a woman's health. Citing the "definitive conclusions" reached by (again unidentified) scientists, Lur'e informed his readers that sperm deposited in the vagina was absorbed by, and positively influenced, the female organism, helping to explain why menstruation became less painful and more regular after marriage. He also noted that intercourse helped the body reach its final stage of development: the growth of hair on the pubis and an increase in the size of breasts and hips were somehow connected to being sexually active.[9]

In addition to targeting their audience (married adults) and reminding them of their primary function, physicians also provided more specific information on the particulars of normal sex, rules that they claimed would make people happy and useful members of society. Like the other areas of sexuality covered in this literature, marital hygiene advice was framed negatively. Thus readers were cautioned first of all not to have intercourse too often. The normal sex act was supposed to result in a pleasant sensation of tiredness and relaxation, leaving the body feeling physically and mentally healthy and refreshed on the following day. Symptoms suggesting that one had expended too much sexual energy included irritability, headaches, fatigue, moodiness, or lowered work productivity. Dr. Berman provided an extensive list of the potential consequences of overindulgence in married adults: anemia, muscular weakness, a decrease in intellectual faculties, hypochondria, melancholia, digestive complaints, heart and vascular system ailments, and of course the various potential sexual disorders.[10]

As for the appropriate frequency, sources maintained it was impossible to generalize, since this would vary from person to person, depending upon factors such as diet, race, age, and physical condition. Readers were advised to be attentive to their own sense of well-being: feeling neither too tired nor too excited between sexual encounters, and certain that one's work performance was not adversely affected.[11] Yet, as Dr. Feigin cautioned, because sometimes even one's personal sense of wellness did not correctly reflect the body's true condition, it was safer to obey the conclusions of science, which recommended two to three times weekly for healthy adults, and one to two for somewhat weaker individuals.[12] While having sex more often might have no visible effect on younger people, such immoderacy was said to lead certain older subjects to neurasthenia, or even to death from stroke. In any event, intercourse should never take place twice (or more) on the same day, although certain allowances for excess were made during one's honeymoon, provided that sex not be accompanied by artificial stimulants. It was emphasized that arousal should happen "naturally," that is, without the aid of alcohol, pornography, or sexual fantasy. In what seems a clear-cut example of the kind of scare-tactic advice that would lead to even greater performance anxiety, Dr. Mendel'son warned that erections achieved by way of such stimuli might lead to impotence.[13]

People seeking specific information about the mechanics of the sex act would have been sorely disappointed. Only one writer, Dr. Dembskaia, mentioned a particular sexual position, instructing her female readers that "intercourse should take place in the horizontal position with the man on top, since that way the [woman's] muscle groups can better relax." Dembskaia further stipulated that sex take place at night, directly before going to sleep. Citing favorably an unnamed "ancient" tome on sexual advice, Dr. Uspenskii specified that sex should not take place while standing, sitting, in or after a bath, on an empty stomach, or directly after a meal and should never be followed by any sort of strenuous physical activity.[14] A handful of other authors provided pieces of advice that implied that sex was supposed to be pleasurable, without imparting any additional information as to how this enjoyment might be had (or indeed what that pleasure would entail). It was maintained, for instance, that intercourse should "begin and end normally," and that the normal sex act was based on a form of satisfaction that could not be achieved through casual sex.[15]

Couples were advised to abstain if either partner was not in the mood, was under the influence of alcohol, or felt tired, angry, afraid, or sick. Expressing an extreme functionalist position, Dr. Mikulina-Ivanova (like Dr. Dembskaia, a woman doctor writing for a specifically female audience) argued that intercourse should cease when a woman reaches menopause, since at that time eggs are no longer produced and therefore pregnancy is impossible. To deal with the heightened level of sexual arousal often experienced by menopausal women, Mikulina-Ivanova recommended medical intervention, presumably hysterectomy or ovariotomy.[16]

Physicians unanimously and categorically opposed sex during menstruation, insisting that intercourse was then dangerous to both women and men, not to mention "undesirable and unappealing."[17] They portrayed the uterus during this time as a "wound" that could become easily infected by germs carried in the semen.[18] Describing menstruating women as "weaker" or "not well," authors urged husbands not to burden their spouses with sexual demands and to take special care of them for the duration of their menses.[19] Not that any "humane" man would make such demands in the first place; sources noted that husbands "in more or less cultured circles" readily agreed to such temporary abstinence.[20]

Men were also urged "not to bother their wives" during pregnancy, since sex during this time was "unnatural."[21] Pointing to the example of female animals, who did not allow sexual access once they were impregnated, Dr. Burlakov remarked: "Unfortunately, man is not particularly inclined to consider the woman when he seeks to satisfy his sexual arousal, and this is something that must be considered." Recognizing that prohibiting sex for the full nine months was an unrealistic demand, enlighteners therefore specified particular periods when sexual activity should be avoided. Mikulina-Ivanova claimed that women developed a deep aversion to sex once they were pregnant but nonetheless conceded that sex might continue until the second half of the pregnancy, after which time it amounted to teaching the fetus prostitution. She also contended that sex during pregnancy would ultimately have a negative impact on the child's future intellectual abilities.[22] Others counseled abstinence during the first and last trimester, during the first month and a half and last two months of pregnancy, or during the days each month when the pregnant woman would normally menstruate, and they cautioned that even during safe periods sex be limited to once or twice a week. Again Dembskaia offered the only practical suggestions about sexual positions, writing that if a pregnant women experienced pain or discomfort during sex, she might try intercourse lying sideways or on top of her partner.[23]

Birth Control and Abortion

Of all the forms of "unnatural" sex adults were cautioned to avoid, intercourse that made use of contraception presented the biggest challenge to educators. On the one hand, birth control was considered unhealthy, either because the method itself was deemed unsafe or because it interfered with the body's "natural" functions. Several physicians categorically rejected all forms of birth control as harmful and "as unnatural as masturbation," attributing to their employ such complications as sexual dysfunction, inflammation of the sex organs or uterus, migraines, nervous disorders, and endometriosis.[24] On the other hand, it was widely understood that access to contraception forestalled the even greater risks to individual health associated with abortion, which had been legalized in 1920.[25] Characterized by this contingent as a "compromise of contemporary life," and a "sad necessity," it was still far preferable to abortion and hence the "lesser of two evils."[26] Approval of birth control as an agent of liberation, enabling people (and especially women) to enjoy sex for its own sake, was entirely absent from medical writings. This is yet another point of distinction between Soviet sex enlighteners and European sex reformers (many of whom were also socialists or, at least, socialist-leaning), for among the latter support for contraceptives was widespread.

Birth control advocates dismissed the objections raised by certain opponents about degeneration and a declining birthrate, arguing that Russia rejected such thinking because of its fundamental commitment to population quality over quantity. Not surprisingly, however, given the intended audience of this literature, both sides focused their arguments on the individual body. For birth control supporters, safeguarding the woman's well-being, both physical and otherwise, took priority. Access to contraception was considered necessary if a woman suffered from severe exhaustion or some other form of illness, or in cases of extreme need, a far too common occurrence during the unstable years of NEP. Enlighteners also pointed out that by destroying a woman's health, frequent births did no favor to her other children, who could be left motherless.[27]

The view of so many professionals that contraception was dangerous prompted them to offer very different kinds of advice. Dr. Donichev counseled his male interlocutor not to consider it until his family was at the point of poverty or overcrowding, at which time he might appeal to a physician for concrete suggestions. If it was felt that pregnancy must be avoided, Donichev suggested that the couple refrain from intercourse before and after menstruation, while acknowledging, however, the unreliability of this practice. Mikulina-Ivanova recommended that a husband and wife alternate months in which each was responsible for protection. Others ranked the available methods in degrees of safety and reliability or simply counseled couples and especially women to reproduce.[28]

Authors listed several ideal requirements for birth control: it should be reliable, safe, easy and convenient to use, and inexpensive. As no form of contraception (with the exception of abstinence) met all of these criteria, accounts proceeded to weigh the relative benefits and disadvantages of each available method, classified into several distinct categories: physiological, mechanical, chemical, surgical, and biological. Following such extensive reviews, people were advised to stick with the least harmful and most reliable of the available choices, which, for the vast majority of authors, were condoms for men and diaphragms or caps for women.[29] Yet, individual preferences notwithstanding, all sanitary enlighteners recommended consulting a physician before selecting any device.

They also repeatedly stressed that reproduction remained sex's true function. Witing in *Path to Health*, Dr. Fedotova asked rhetorically which was better, abortion or birth control: "We will be compelled to answer: best of all is to have the baby." A series of illustrations underscored this point, showing fetuses, plump healthy newborns, and their mothers in scenes at a maternity clinic. Indeed, the journal was straightforward about its use of these images. As a box in the left-hand corner explained: "The article discusses birth control, but the drawings that accompany it continue to refer to pregnancy. Once again we tell the reader that birth control methods are a sad necessity, but pregnancy is the normal manifestation of an organism's life."[30] The crying and smiling infants featured on the same page as a piece on abortion and infertility served a similar purpose.[31] Ostensibly a supplement to the small box at center, which lists the things that keep a baby quiet (clean dry diapers, breast milk until six months, well-ventilated rooms, and so on), the babies' provided an obvious visual reminder of the consequences of abortion.

As in their preference for birth control over abortion, health educators considered medical termination the lesser of two evils when compared to its back-alley alternative. Disdainful of the hypocrisy of prerevolutionary Russia and the capitalist West, where women who did not perish from botched operations were subject to the same criminal penalties as their abortionists, health educators applauded the Soviet government for legalizing the procedure in order to restrict its performance to doctors working in a hospital setting.[32] By doing so, the state acted "to tear women out of the hands of the folk healer" and at the very least ensure her survival.[33] The conclusion that five years of legal abortion "had not led to widespread depravity" justified writers' support for this approach, as did the dramatic decrease in termination-related fatalities, complications, and illnesses, despite a slight annual increase in the number of operations performed.[34]

In addition to concerns about women's health, the sexual enlightenment approach to abortion was dictated by its assessment of the phenomenon as primarily a socioeconomic problem, best battled through the improvement of the country's economy.[35] Explanations thus emphasized the social factors compelling termination, chief among which was financial need, followed by illness, poor living conditions, the burdens of house-work and child care coupled with employment outside the home, and the demands of social and political work. Acknowledging the far more selfish reasons motivating certain women to end their pregnancies (pursuit of pleasure, worries about their figure, and so on), accounts nonetheless maintained that such occurrences in contemporary Russia were the exception, promising that, as the economy improved and the range of social services available to women expanded, abortions would begin to disappear of their own accord.[36]

In the meantime, in cases where an abortion was sought for social as opposed to medical reasons, the writing team of doctors L. A. and L. M. Vasilevskii maintained that a physician "has the right and even the responsibility" to try and talk the woman out of the operation. While some writers in pursuit of this goal emphasized woman's civic maternal duty, many more focused attention on the seemingly endless risks associated with the procedure. Methods of persuasion varied. Reminding his audience that women resorted to abortion only under duress, out of financial need, Dr. Gens cited with disapproval an article entitled "Abortion Kills Women." He urged educators not to upset them: "Tell women of the dangers," he concluded, "but don't frighten them." Such advice often went unheeded, however, with most authors favoring some variety of scare tactics. Consequently, a great deal of attention in this literature was devoted to the physical hazards of the operation. According to Professor Khanzhinskii, the best that a woman could hope for was continued illnesses of the reproductive organs; the worst was the grave, which carried away no small percentage of women seeking to terminate their pregnancies.[37] For Dr. Al'tgauzen, the operation and its aftermath were reminiscent of a train wreck:

> Imagine that you are traveling on a fast train, and the train suddenly stops. One car hits another, falls apart, many people are injured. The train is destroyed. A very similar thing happens with abortion. The entire body is prepared for pregnancy, and suddenly the embryo is torn out, everything stops, is injured.[38]

Possible complications, the likelihood of which purportedly increased with each additional abortion, included circulatory disorders, infection, anemia, blood poisoning, chronic inflammation of the uterine walls, severe pain, nervous disorders, cessation of menses or a sharp increase in blood loss, lifelong invalidism, exhaustion, enfeeblement, loss of work capability, premature old age, and death. Women who had undergone terminations were deemed "irritable, impatient, impossible to be around." Professor Lichkus held abortion-related complications responsible for forcing the husband to go outside the marriage for sexual satisfaction, the inevitable result of which was the introduction of venereal disease into the family. Others focused on the financial burden of such a debilitating illness. Dr. Shpak estimated the number of workdays lost in the Soviet Union per annum as a result of "successful" abortions, without complications, to be five million; when the cost of women's labor as mothers and managers of the household was included, the figure rose to ten times that much.[39]

Educators acknowledged that these consequences depended on a great many factors, which included the method used, the experience of the person conducting the operation, and the conditions in which it took place. Yet even when performed in sterile conditions by a qualified (medical) specialist, an abortion reportedly posed serious health risks. Working blindly "in the depths of the uterus," the surgeon was forced to rely on the sensation of the instruments alone. In such circumstances it was impossible to know whether the uterus had been punctured or the abdominal organs injured. If this information was not sufficiently persuasive, the point was made more forcefully through illustrations, such as one depicting an intestine that had been pulled into the uterus and drawn out through the cervix as a result of the physician accidentally puncturing the uterine wall.[40]

Whatever the dangers associated with medical abortions, they multiplied when the procedure was attempted by the woman herself or performed by the reviled folk healer, who induced miscarriage by having the woman ingest quinine, Spanish fly, or gunpowder, or by using nails, spinning spindles, goose feathers, wooden sticks, or knitting needles. It was claimed that hundreds of thousands of women died from such back-alley abortions and many more were left invalids. According to one statistic, 50 percent of women treated in hospitals were there as a result of complications from such procedures.[41]

Abortion was held responsible for producing eugenically inferior offspring in future pregnancies, or for preventing conception altogether. The threat of resulting infertility made it a matter of particular urgency to keep first-time pregnant women from having the procedure. Dr. Al'tgauzen and his collaborators instructed such women to give birth no matter what, regardless of their financial situation. For them no reason justified ending a first pregnancy, "even if [a woman] says that her husband has left her, or has nothing to feed her children: that is only self-persuasion."[42] It was alleged that the development of the female body was fully completed only after pregnancy, labor, and breast feeding. By interfering with these processes, abortion ensured that physical and spiritual development would be incomplete and one-sided. The sex organs in particular would remain unformed, making miscarriages in future pregnancies far more likely and deliveries far more difficult. A particularly visible physical consequence of this break in development was premature aging; science, according to Dr. Shpak, had established that each termination makes a woman look two to three years older. Spiritual shortcomings were equally evident. He cautioned: "Women who do not have children might be talented scientists, artists, writers, social or political activists, but they will never possess that softness, attractiveness, and 'femininity' that is observed in women who were at least once mothers."[43]

Conversely, women who gave birth were deemed not only more feminine but healthier. Physicians asserted that pregnancy was good for a
woman's health (and character), a natural form of rejuvenation that increased her life expectancy beyond that of men and childless women.[44]
The long list of complications associated with abortion had no equivalent
here. More than just a guarantee of well-being and beauty, maternity constituted a woman's "social duty" and an emblem of her normalcy. Yet the
specific, quantitative requirements of this "civic deed" varied from writer
to writer. Dr. Karov declared that the "guarantee of a woman's health, the
strength of the family, and the might of the state" require a woman in a
"normal family" to give birth every three to four years. Others counseled a
two- or three-year pause between pregnancies. Dr. Feigin fixed the norm at
four children, satisfied that this number best fulfilled parental instincts
and guaranteed population growth without exhausting the mother. Still
others warned that frequent births were as difficult on the female organism as frequent abortions and advised women to stop at two and terminate any subsequent pregnancies.[45]

However, just because maternity was identified as woman's social function
did not imply that motherhood should be an all-encompassing occupation:

> But, of course, we do not advise a woman to devote her entire life to mater-
> nity, drawing her away from work, from the surrounding environment. . . .
> There needs to be a middle ground. Labor, creativity, and society are the best
> things in the life of each person, and for a woman maternity needs to be
> added to that list.

Yet just what this "middle ground" entailed would become far less open to
interpretation over the next several years. In 1934, women were informed
that industrialization had done away with the social conditions making
abortion necessary. Now that their sole rationale for rejecting motherhood
was eliminated, women were left with few alternatives but to follow doctors' advice in becoming more "feminine," "healthy," and "normal."[46]

Popular Eugenics, Soviet Style

By far the most important regulations associated with marital hygiene
were ones that should have been followed long before a couple was married and ready to reproduce. These were the prescriptions governing marital choice (*brachnyi vybor*), the factors that would help determine the suitability of one's future spouse. Mendel'son even provided a convenient
compatibility checklist:

> (1) Ascertain whether your own health permits you to marry—both in your
> own interests, and in the interests of your wife (or husband).

(2) Inquire whether or not your future wife (or husband) is personally healthy, whether there is evidence of unfavorable heredity (are the parents of the marriage candidate healthy?); whether your future wife can give birth without risk to her health.

(3) Consider whether your future husband (or wife) is suitable in terms of character, political convictions, etc.[47]

Ultimately, writers considered health to be by far the most crucial stipulation governing marriage suitability. A flyer produced by the State Venereological Institute began: "Comrades! You are entering marriage and beginning your family life. Think about the following: health is a person's highest blessing. It is the foundation of both personal and familial happiness. Are you healthy, comrade?"[48]

Yet it was not only one's personal health or the impact of bad health on one's future spouse that was at issue. Because sexual enlightenment assumed reproduction to be the ultimate goal of sexual relations and marriage, health was neither solely nor primarily one's own; it belonged instead to one's offspring and ultimately to the society of the future. To convey this point and to justify the state's involvement in the enforcement of personal responsibility, writers introduced the topic of eugenics.

Mark Adams and Loren Graham have demonstrated in their work on scientific eugenics in the 1920s that a significant segment of the Russian academic community developed a strong professional interest in questions of human heredity and genetics.[49] Yet despite a commonality of particular interests and the participation of at least two prominent members of the scientific establishment in sexual enlightenment (notably, the psychiatrists P. I. Liublinskii, who coedited the *Russian Eugenics Journal* (*Russkii evgenicheskii zhurnal*) and T. I. Iudin, whom Adams described as "one of the society's most active and prolific members"), the vision of eugenics promoted by sex educators was strikingly different from its various academic incarnations. Scientific eugenics became caught up in the debates between heredity and environment that would assume ever greater importance throughout the decade. Adams, for instance, has described the desire for immediate action and frustration with the theory of the immutability of the gene pool that prompted many Marxist eugenicists to reject Mendelian genetics and turn instead to Lamarckism as the basis for a socialist eugenics.[50]

Graham focuses on the growing hostility toward the concepts of eugenics, heredity, and genetics beyond the scientific establishment among Marxist theorists and the radical student population in particular. According to their critics, eugenicists overemphasized biology at the expense of socioeconomic factors in development. Although many Marxist scientists and theorists rejected Lamarckism as "scientifically baseless," support for it continued to grow among the lay public, as did the identification of genetics as a "bourgeois science." The strong ties that existed between Russian eugenicists and their Western counterparts—such as participation in international congresses and societies, and reviews and translations of foreign scholarship in their publications—only confirmed this accusation.[51]

In responding to these charges, Russian eugenicists fought an uphill battle. For instance, the Bureau of Eugenics in the Academy of Sciences gradually abandoned its research on eugenics and human heredity and turned instead to the study of plant and animal genetics.[52] Ultimately, however, no approach was successful in legitimizing the discipline. The movement ended suddenly in 1930, with the disbanding of the Russian Eugenics Society, the closing of its journal, and the dissolution of other eugenics organizations throughout the country. Several of the movement's leaders lost their academic positions or had their departments or institutes disbanded. Serving as the "death certificate" for Russian eugenics was the entry in the *Great Soviet Encyclopedia* (*Bol'shaia sovetskaia entsiklopediia*), written, significantly, by the Bolshevik social hygienist and sexologist G. A. Batkis. He condemned eugenics as a "bourgeois doctrine" and described its leaders' ideas as "fascist" and guilty of "Menshevizing idealism."[53]

Even though sexual enlightenment would suffer a similar fate by being abruptly terminated in 1931, during the 1920s the brand of eugenics it popularized entirely escaped the attacks, criticism, and conflicts plaguing its academic counterpart. As with their appropriation of ideas from the scientific disciplines of endocrinology and psychoneurology, health educators' advocacy of what is here referred to as popular eugenics easily accommodated what might have been seen as contradictory influences: in this case, the impact of both nature and nurture on the development of healthy offspring. To explain Narkomzdrav's simultaneous (financial and institutional) support for both "hereditarian eugenics" and "environmentalist" social hygiene, Adams points out that the commissariat's "character was shaped by the many enterprises that came under its aegis; . . . [it] came into being as a professional network encompassing divergent agendas."[54]

Yet sexual enlightenment's incorporation of hereditarian and environmental factors in its representation of eugenics owed less to the wide variety of specialties it embraced than to its very understanding of eugenics. The Marxist belief in the ability to change one's environment and destiny and the desire for immediate tangible results that fueled support for Lamarckism were not an issue for sex educators. Rather, the goals of eugenics harmonized completely with their two fundamental objectives: the prevention of disease and the overall improvement of the population's health.[55] In restricting their interest and attention to measures whose impact on the body was never in doubt, physicians could provide advice with immediate benefits for the here and now at the same time as they looked toward the long-term improvement of future generations.[56] This "watered-down" version of eugenics permeated sexual enlightenment literature, regardless of whether writers employed the word itself.

Defined by medical authors as the science of improving the human species, eugenics would "place under its control those desiring to create a family and their future descendants and show them the proper way to avoid mistakes." Of primary concern were heritable traits, yet writers were also careful to emphasize the influence of the environment on development. To make sexual relations healthier and guarantee the reproduction of eugenically fit offspring required that enlightenment advice seek to shape behavior affecting both of these factors.[57]

A minority of sex educators presented their practical advice in terms of options both negative (preventing the "unfit" from reproducing) and positive (encouraging reproduction among the fit). Of the various negative alternatives, P. Rokitskii favored the regulation of marriage as preferable to the more radical solution of surgical intervention (as in sterilization, for example). At the same time he expressed the hope that in the future the improvement of the human race would be pursued by increasing the propagation of society's best specimens, rather than simply curtailing the reproduction of its worst.[58]

For his part, Dr. Rozenblium favored a form of positive eugenics over the various preventive strategies followed abroad; he focused in particular on the negative eugenic policies practiced in the United States, which included forced institutionalization, castration, and sterilization. Yet he also argued that the kinds of positive eugenic measures pursued by Catherine the Great (who reportedly isolated healthy soldiers in special settlements to propagate superior offspring) or the Japanese (who, he claimed, paired Japanese widows with tall Koreans to yield taller soldiers after the Russo-Japanese war) were equally unworkable. "Only a free, voluntary choice can produce not only a healthy but also an intelligent and capable person." The task of eugenics was "to influence this choice."[59]

Given their assessment of the urgency of their task and the limitations of the medium, doctors had to convince their audience as quickly and directly as possible of the potential dangers they posed to their spouses and, more important, to their offspring. Therefore, discussions of positive and negative eugenic options notwithstanding, most considerations of eugenics in the sexual enlightenment field were limited to publicizing a law requiring couples to discuss their health before registering their marriage; advocacy of premarital medical checkups; and the identification of particular diseases that writers claimed interfered with one's "right to marry" (*pravo na brak*). The presence of these illnesses dictated either postponing matrimony until proper treatment or prohibiting it altogether. Primary among this group were the four "most serious and destructive" of the "social diseases": syphilis, gonorrhea, tuberculosis, and alcoholism, all of which were depicted as causing irrevocable harm to one's eugenic health.[60] A similar threat was posed by the presence or history of certain mental illnesses or such heritable conditions as hemophilia, epilepsy, congenital mental retardation, color blindness, night-blindness, and deaf-muteness.[61] People with cataracts or with malformed, weak, or diseased hearts or livers were likewise cautioned not to reproduce, as were those suffering from malaria and diabetes, whose purportedly weak and sickly offspring would be especially susceptible to infectious childhood diseases such as diphtheria, scarlet fever, and measles. Enlighteners also regarded as impediments to matrimony those biological or physical disorders interfering with conception such as undeveloped sexual and reproductive organs (especially in women) and sexual dysfunction (especially in men), although it was pointed out that these conditions did not necessarily preclude matrimony, as long as one's partner was made aware of them beforehand and still agreed to the union.[62] Dr. Bernatskii favorably cited the list of factors preventing marriage developed by a German doctor who recommended wedlock be avoided if the intended had not been breast-fed, had a family history of tuberculosis or mental "abnormalities," was a child of alcoholics, or had bad teeth. From the perspective of science, Bernatskii claimed, such stipulations were "rational and substantiated."[63]

And what of those unfortunate individuals whom medicine has determined "unfit" to marry and reproduce? For some physicians, birth control was the answer. Professor Iudin suggested that people who were hereditarily unsuitable, though themselves healthy, be permitted to marry if provided with contraception. Sterilization presented a more broadly discussed option. Within sexual enlightenment, as in scientific eugenics, there was a variety of opinion regarding sterilization, although it was never championed widely in either community. Nonetheless, whereas consideration of the procedure by the vast majority of academic eugenicists had ceased by 1925, its advocacy in sex education continued for several more years.[64]

Eugenics and the Law

"Marital consciousness" was a question not only of good health but also of law. Included in the Soviet family code of 1926 was the stipulation that couples who intended to marry inform one another about their personal health. Article 132 of the Code of Laws on Marriage, the Family, and Guardianship required those seeking to register a marriage officially at ZAGS to present written documentation confirming this exchange of information and made special mention of the need to alert one's future spouse to the presence of venereal disease, mental illness, and tuberculosis. The presence of disease did not preclude marriage; it was the conscious concealment of one's illness that was held criminally actionable. The code prohibited marriage before the age of eighteen (article 5), to the mentally ill or "feeble-minded" (article 6b), and between close relatives (article 6v).[65]

Even as sexual enlighteners publicized the exchange of information decree, they expressed strong dissatisfaction with the measure, which they considered "eugenically insufficient." After all, they reasoned, people believing themselves fully healthy might unknowingly carry and pass a debilitating hereditary illness to their offspring. There were also practical factors militating against the success of this policy, as a 1929 article on the law made clear: according to Dr. L. Gurvich of the State Institute of Social Hygiene, ZAGS employees were so overworked that during the registration procedure they neglected to read this provision, which was required of them by article 133 of the family code.[66]

As early as 1919, certain members of the medical profession had supported an alternative method to deal with the problem of hereditary illnesses. This was mandatory premarital medical screening and certification, and throughout the 1920s the issue was widely debated on the pages of the medical press and at conferences and professional gatherings.[67] A 1925 letter to the editor of the health commissariat's official publication, *Narkomzdrav Bulletin (Biulleten' Narkomzdrava)*, offers a fairly representative example of the rationale behind support for mandatory certification. Comrade Romanov, a health worker from the city of Shchigrov, wrote to describe the local health organization's attempts to publicize the idea of certification as a prophylactic measure. Romanov favorably assessed the half-year experiment, which provided information on the illnesses precluding marriage, and claimed that the population "clearly and correctly" understood the intentions behind the measure. He now turned to Narkomzdrav, requesting direction from the center, assistance in coordinating regional systematic work in this sphere, and information about the legal status of such certification.[68]

Following this letter was the commissariat's official position on this issue, written by V. M. Bronner. His explication closely paralleled the decisions reached at the first and second All-Union Congresses for the Fight against Venereal Disease.[69] According to Bronner, the commissariat opposed mandatory certification, with the intention of prohibiting marriage to VD sufferers, for several reasons. He argued that this measure would fail to produce the desired results because a couple's sexual relationship usually preceded the official registration of marriage. He also feared that the introduction of this law would lead people to choose cohabitation without registration.[70] Bronner pointed to the difficulty of determining the presence of both syphilis and gonorrhea during certain stages in their evolution, even by a highly qualified and experienced specialist using serological and bacteriological testing. At best, an expert could only confirm that at the moment of examination no evidence of disease was visible. These considerations led Narkomzdrav to conclude that while medical certification was in principle "desirable," it was nevertheless entirely "premature." The article also summarized the extraordinary practical obstacles to the implementation of universal mandatory certification: the country sorely lacked medical workers with the requisite level of expertise and the laboratories necessary for research and testing, not to mention the organizational and supervisory personnel required to ensure that healthy people did not stand in for disease sufferers during the examination.[71]

Other educators adopted similar positions, expressing dissatisfaction with the policy of mutual disclosure even as they explained it, and at the same time promoting the idea of voluntary premarital medical visits. "The family is too important a union," opined Dr. Lifshits, "for capriciousness and chance to play with the health of parents and children." Therefore, couples were advised to "exchange a medical certificate of health before they exchange wedding rings."[72]

Illustrations presented readers with vivid displays of both the desired response and the inevitable consequences of not heeding medical advice. Figure 6.2, for instance, offers a fairly typical depiction of the iconography of healthy and unhealthy marriage decisions. Having put their trust in medicine, the couple on the left is amply rewarded. Indeed, the bottom left-hand scene bears a striking resemblance to the domestic idyll shown in "The sex question" (Figure 6.1). In addition to the two healthy children, the couple's reproductive health is emphasized by the blooming flowers on the windowsill and the centerpiece bowl of fruit. This time Mother entertains the child while Father connects with the goings-on beyond the room through reading a newspaper. While the pair at left are also sexually separated (through physical distance and averted glances), it is a separation of completion, not failure, unlike the isolation of the right-hand couple. Either out of ignorance or perhaps because of an uncontrollable libido, this somber pair foolishly rushed into matrimony. Their punishment is a life of barrenness and poverty, marked by their vacant expressions, the empty chair, stark walls, and a solitary half-loaf of bread.

Common to the opponents of mandatory certification was the conviction that education rather than punitive measures was the best way to prevent the spread of venereal disease in one's family. They reasoned that only through enlightenment would people come to accept their responsibilities toward their future families and toward society and seek out medical consent to marry if they had ever suffered from infection in the past. But to ensure that people did not hide the fact of earlier illness from their physicians, such interactions necessarily had to remain voluntary. Once attained, this "health consciousness" would eventually lead people to confirm their well-being before the commencement of any sexual relationship rather than solely before the registration of an official marriage.[73]

If the attainment of health consciousness was an insufficient incentive, authors appealed to other virtues as well. One pamphlet aimed at teenage girls and young women asserted that premarital checkups were the trend among the more cultured segments of society. This kind of argument could be applied to Western countries as well, demonstrating once again the flexibility of the genre's anti-Western rhetoric. Focusing on the financial

Figure 6.2—"Before you go to ZAGS visit a doctor. / The doctor will cure you / if you have gonorrhea / with timely treatment, you will be able to have children / otherwise you might not have children." Poster and Photograph Collection (NITs "Meditsinskii muzei" RAMN).

burden posed to society by the sick offspring of such unhealthy marriages, several accounts claimed that such interference by the state to safeguard society's interests occurred, as Feigin put it, in almost "all cultured countries."[74] Favorable descriptions followed of the mandatory examination policies and marriage restrictions that were under consideration or had been adopted in countries like Sweden, Norway, and Denmark, as well as in several German and American states. Evidence from Russia's own past served a similar purpose; thus readers learned that Russia also shared in this tradition, having passed a 1722 law supported by Peter the Great forbidding marriage to the mentally retarded.[75]

Others couched their arguments in terms of values and goals particular to the revolutionary state. For Dr. Rozenblium, the goal of healthy marriage was not just individual happiness but the well-being of the entire society, though he noted that he had in mind only "the society of workers." Mikulina-Ivanova focused on the long-term communal benefits of this educational initiative:

> It is essential that each young man and woman know that the person who does not possess this certification is sick, harmful to society. Thus in twenty or thirty years we will reach the point when a person lacking this document will not find a partner of the opposite sex, not even a sick one. Everyone will have the desire to be cured.[76]

The medical profession's support for an educational approach that stressed voluntarism did not prevent calls by individual sanitary enlighteners for the introduction of tougher measures. Mikulina-Ivanova described the law on mutual disclosure as a social hygienic rather than a truly eugenic measure, since the decision to marry was left to the couple and the presence of mental illness was the only medical condition prohibiting registration. Claiming that all eugenic organizations considered the current practice unsatisfactory, she supported the Russian Eugenics Society's call for the introduction of mandatory medical examinations, as well as their proposed additions to the current law. The society recommended that marrying couples be allowed to register only after their second visit to ZAGS (after intensive eugenic propaganda and medical examinations); that physicians be excused from doctor-patient confidentiality restrictions if they discovered that a prospective spouse had a venereal disease; and that marriage between two people with intellectual defects be forbidden. The author offered several additional amendments: that the presence of syphilis or gonorrhea in an infectious stage preclude marriage, and that such unions be considered invalid if a person's spouse turned out to be mentally ill or suffering from venereal infection.[77]

Ultimately, however, even Mikulina-Ivanova acknowledged that such legal measures would prove ineffective unless accompanied by widespread sanitary propaganda. Thus she labeled the exchange of information statute a first step in the process of "medical and eugenic control over marriage," to be followed by mandatory examination when the population had acquired a sufficient level of culture. She also called for the widespread extension of marriage consultation bureaus on the model of the Moscow Counseling Center for Sexual Hygiene. The writer appealed for greater financial support for the clinic, which she claimed was barely functioning: lacking sufficient finances, it was forced to operate in a borrowed office, where its two doctors each worked an hour a week "out of love for science and humanity."[78]

Throughout their treatment of eugenics, sanitary enlighteners repeatedly stressed that heredity, like health, was ultimately a matter of state. To protect society against unhealthy marriages and to guarantee the well-being of its future inhabitants warranted whatever intervention the country (and its self-appointed representatives) found necessary.[79] Yet as the objections raised in discussions about the feasibility of compulsory testing indicate, the government ultimately had little power to enforce any such interventionist measures. Nor did the medical profession necessarily or consistently favor such an approach, since a policy of education over coercion on sexual matters was deemed both more practical as well as more philosophically appropriate. And despite physicians' efforts to safeguard their jurisdiction over the sex question from that of competing institutions and to convince their audience to look to them alone as authorities in such concerns, what for them constituted this area of jurisdiction was limited.

This ambivalent attitude toward (forcible) intervention is also evident in the way that the medical profession made use of the relevant articles of law. Indeed, on issues ranging from forced treatment to privacy and consent, doctors overwhelmingly defended voluntarism, even if such an orientation was motivated by a public health, rather than a civil rights, agenda. Their approach is clearest when examining these issues in relation to venereal disease, by all accounts the illness that posed the greatest danger to the medical model of a healthy, eugenically sound marriage.

In dealing with individuals discovered to have a venereal disease, only as a last resort did doctors turn to forced testing and treatment, a power confirmed in a special resolution by the Central Executive Committee of the All-Russian Congress of Soviets (VTsIK) and the Council of People's Commissars (*Sovnarkom*) from January 1927.[80] According to the text of this decree, public health organizations had the right to forcibly examine and treat a person suspected of having a venereal disease in an infectious stage if this individual refused to go along with these procedures voluntarily. Yet a number of safeguards were built into the resolution. Only those whose sickness was detected during a routine medical examination (this category included pregnant women discovered to have syphilis in any stage) or who lived, worked, or studied in conditions that would put others at risk of infection could be compelled to undergo such forcible testing and treatment. Furthermore, only the relevant health institutions (venereal clinics or dispensaries, sanitary inspectorates, or Okhmatmlad units) had the right to order such measures.[81] And as the instructions that accompanied the resolution made clear, these institutions were to try all available means to convince the individual in question to agree voluntarily to such testing and treatment.

The emphasis on voluntary acquiescence was prompted by concerns for therapeutic success and for public health. Because so many people stopped treatment or turned to a private doctor or less reputable source for care, or assumed themselves "cured" when initial symptoms disappeared, it was of primary importance that they complete their course of therapy, and this would only happen if the attending doctors and clinic could maintain their trust. For similar reasons, physicians were extremely protective of the sufferer's privacy. Narkomzdrav supported the principle of doctor-patient confidentiality, as it related both to patients' identities (and specific reasons for treatment) and to sharing information on their condition with employers or family, including spouses.[82] Even as they attempted to change the population's conception of venereal disease from something shameful to a curable condition, physicians were acutely aware of the often dire consequences faced by sufferers—from being ostracized by family and friends to losing their housing and jobs if their illness was discovered, irrespective of whether it was in an infectious stage.

Thus once a person ventured into a clinic, the staff's primary motive was to keep him or her coming for treatment. While the clinicians endeavored to convince the patient to share knowledge of the condition with spouses and to have immediate family members tested (through the extensive sanitary enlightenment work that was to accompany their sessions), ultimately it was up to the individual to provide written consent for such contact to be established. As with more general issues of privacy, physicians were prompted by the fear that if pushed, the patient would discontinue therapy and hence put the family at greater risk. An exception to this protocol was made only for the spouse of someone in a contagious stage of the infection, with proof of current cohabitation, who arrived at the clinic in person to ask whether the partner was undergoing treatment.[83] Given these constraints, ultimately what protection remained to others was the right to prosecute after the fact according to the Criminal Code's articles 150 and 192 (which specified the penalties for violating public health and safety laws at the local level).[84] This was, no doubt, of little consolation if an infected baby was born blind or stillborn, or if one's fertility was affected.

The Conjugal Bed and the Sickbed

Along with the debates over compulsory and voluntary eugenic measures, the question of doctor-patient confidentiality highlights a deep-seated ambivalence about the metaphorical entry of doctors into their patients' bedrooms. If Russian physicians rescued practical eugenics by subsuming it into the categories of public health and disease control, they

were being not only expedient but remarkably consistent. The goal of promoting sexual health could be achieved only by combating sexual disease.
The further the patient was from deviance, the less interested (and com-
fortable) the doctors were in dealing with actual sexual practice. Sex educators were highly preoccupied with asserting and retrenching their disciplinary authority over sexual matters, but by no means did this translate
into an Orwellian voyeur watching over the marital bed. The doctors did
not want to be in the bedroom at all, at least not (to borrow from the
common Russian proverb) as "uninvited guests." Far preferable for them
was to be present only as a surrogate, as the internalized voice of reason
acquired through successful sexual enlightenment. Their goal was fundamentally Foucauldian: they wanted disciplinary control over the sex question in order to teach the population to discipline itself.

Here we should recall the drawing with which this chapter began: the
happy healthy family sitting at the table as a visual representation of "The
sex question" (Figure 6.1). For the sexual enlightenment doctors, as for
the model family in the picture, sex is instrumentalized entirely for its
outcome, whose anerotic image overshadows the act itself (much as Lenin
watches over the father and son). In a peculiar "great leap forward," the
rendering skips over sex entirely. While it is doubtful that even the most
loyal Soviet citizens thought about domestic bliss while in the throes of
sexual passion, this illustration does seem to represent the physicians'
own form of self-discipline: in writing about sex, they always had their
eyes on this particular prize.

The image in "The sex question" replaces the bedroom with the family
room, suggesting that sexual privacy may not be entirely postponed until
the distant future after all. (While it is true that housing shortages meant
families had to squeeze several generations into one room, my point remains the same: the room is shown as a space for the family, rather than
for intimacy.) The doctors only want to be in their patients' bedrooms
long enough to make sure married couples are having healthy sex, where-
upon they can retreat. Eugenics, marital hygiene, and birth control are all
about setting the proper scene for sex, rather than sex itself. As long as the
husband and wife are not having sex too frequently, enjoying it too
much, or abusing birth control, they can safely be left alone (again, we recall that sexual enlighteners had no interest in writing marriage manuals).
The healthy child is the evidence of healthy sex. When the sexual partners are disease-ridden, or ignorant of proper hygiene, then the physicians
are on the scene. Just as the public health posters showed only diseased
genitalia (see Chapter 4), the medical educators define their role only in
terms of the avoidance of unhealthy sex. The conjugal bed fell within
their purview when it was also a sickbed. Otherwise, the happy couple
who took the doctors' rational advice reaped an all-too-rare reward: safe
from depravity, venereal disease, and the vagaries of heredity, they could
finally be left alone.

Conclusion

Unfortunately, a vast majority of people and specifically adults who have already reached full maturity still show much more attention to sexual feelings than is desirable from the perspective of society. And [this], doubtless, will continue until socialism provides people with newer, more useful and more agreeable sensations. —A. TIMOFEEV, *V CHEM PROIAVLI-AETSIA POLOVAIA ZHIZN'*

Toward the end of his entry on "The Sex Question," published in the first edition of the *Great Medical Encyclopedia* (*Bol'shaia meditsinskaia entsiklopediia*) after several pages spent enumerating the extent of the sexual mess in which Western countries found themselves, Dr. Z. Gurevich finally turned to the contemporary situation in the Soviet Union:

> In the USSR the sex question, as it is understood in capitalist countries, does not exist. Neither is there the heightened attention, unhealthy curiosity and at the same time sanctimonious attitude, so characteristic of the relationship to this question in capitalist countries. The USSR is the only country in the world that has basically solved the problems that, in bourgeois society, lead to the never-ending and unresolvable sex question.[1]

Reading this postmortem, one is left to ponder the implications of this stance for the public discourse on sexuality in the subsequent decades of Soviet history. As anyone who traveled in the Soviet Union in its final

years can attest, the official sexless-sex model would have enormous staying power. Ironically, for once, it was the female code of behavior that
would become normative: sexuality is best if missing. The same trajectory
ties the neglect of any real consideration or acknowledgment of female sexuality in the 1920s to the infamous declaration by a middle-aged Russian
woman that "we have no sex [*u nas seksa net*]" during a Soviet-American
talk show event in 1987.[2] Except that now this understanding of absent
sexuality applied to everyone.

Setting aside the ideological content of Gurevich's encyclopedia entry,
its announcement of the sex question's demise was largely accurate. By
the end of 1931, sexual enlightenment was no more: the flood of articles,
brochures, and lectures had ceased, almost overnight. That public discussions of sexuality, no matter how "unsexy," would disappear is not in itself surprising, given what is known about the Cultural Revolution, the
"Great Break," and the policies associated with the consolidation of "Stalinism." Yet in contrast to many other areas of life and the history of particular ideas, individuals, or institutions, there was neither decree from
above nor newspaper denunciation to explain or announce the end of sex
education. Ironically, the same factors that prevented the elaboration of a
single educational methodology (which the establishment of a scientific
center for sex education was intended to rectify) may help explain why
sex educators continued in their work for as long as they did, since for
many other seemingly "suspect" topics or endeavors, the end came considerably sooner. Sexual enlightenment was very much an interdiscipli-
nary enterprise, conducted simultaneously by individual physicians, public health journals, and a number of different institutes; its very lack of
cohesion or coordination may account for its durability.

After extensive searching, I did find a handful of sex enlightenment
materials (including a few articles and pamphlets, and at least one poster)
dating from the mid-1930s. Their very publication supports the argument
that the Great Break was not quite as definitive as has been assumed.
Nonetheless, the fact that their appearance was preceded by more than
two years of total silence on the subject after the surplus of the 1920s is
suggestive. Since a number of these pieces favorably discuss birth control
and the availability of legal abortion, perhaps these writings allowed
physicians to register their disapproval of the coming ban on the procedure, already widely discussed by 1934. Whether this was a last gasp of
support for sex education in a changed climate or something else entirely
is difficult to say without further information. Also noteworthy in this regard is the fact that almost all of the sex education articles published in
the public health journal *Hygiene and Health* in 1935 were written by the
same authors (Mendel'son, Lur'e, and Iakobzon) whose work appeared regularly in the periodical's pages in the 1920s.[3]

In contrast, less puzzling is the 1934 publication of the popular pamphlet "Venereal Diseases and the Struggle against Them" (*Venericheskie*

bolezni i bor'ba s nimi) by N. A. Torsuev, the future director of the soon-to-be-renamed Bronner State Venereological Institute.[4] In part Torsuev bases his claim of vastly diminished rates of venereal infection (in comparison with the purportedly astronomical rates in the West) on the nearly complete "liquidation" of the few remaining sources of prostitution in the USSR. (The publication does, however, also applaud the availability of legal abortion.) Sexually transmitted disease is no longer presented as a large-scale social problem with serious ramifications for the Soviet state, but rather as an ever shrinking aberration. Despite Torsuev's discussion of the various venereal infections and instructions on personal disease prophylaxis, this information is not situated within the broader discussion of sexuality that characterized all popular pamphlets from the 1920s. No longer tethered to the previous decade's ideological debates about sex, isolated publications such as this one are not part of, and do not form, the discourse of the sex question.

In part, sex education suffered from the changes taking place throughout the medical and scientific communities during the Cultural Revolution. As Adams and Graham point out regarding the demise of eugenics, no discipline linking the biological to the social or extending the laws of biology to humans "survived the Great Break intact." Adams describes the introduction of a new pejorative word in Russian, *biologizirovat'*, meaning "to biologize," which was "understood as one of the several sins collectively referred to during the period as 'Menshevizing idealism'." Graham explains, "it was far better to recognize the nonreductive and qualitatively distinct nature of man."[5] Eugenicists were not the only ones guilty of "biologizing" by applying the laws of animals to human behavior, or vice versa. Although Semashko himself criticized Zalkind and others for this type of transgression, neither he nor the other sexual enlighteners were above doing the same when it suited their purposes.

The "new biosocial fields that had grown up with such vigor in the previous decade, [and now] broken apart, dissolved, or renamed" included those most closely associated with sexual enlightenment: social hygiene and social venereology.[6] Like eugenics, a victim of the attacks on foreign specialists and sciences, social hygiene met its end in 1930, the same year Semashko was removed as commissar of Narkomzdrav. At the end of that year, the State Institute of Social Hygiene was reorganized as the Institute of the Organization of Health Care and Hygiene, its top priorities now practical health care and the organization of medical facilities. Despite this significant shift, the newly named institute sponsored the 1931 meeting of sex educators and was designated as the site for the ill-fated scientific bureau. In 1934 this institute was eliminated as well, along with thirty-seven other research facilities devoted to public health (Solomon notes that the teaching of social hygiene in medical schools continued for several years longer).[7]

As Susan Solomon points out, the social hygienists most closely associated with the discipline's development fared better than many of their counterparts in other fields attacked during the Cultural Revolution. Among them were several doctors active in sex education. A. V. Mol'kov, who had hosted the 1931 sex educators' organizational meeting, taught at Moscow Medical Institute Number One and remained the director of the new institute until 1934, when he assumed this same post at the Institute of Hygiene at Khar'kov Institute Number One. Until his death in 1965, G. A. Batkis taught at Moscow Medical Institute Number Two, heading the department of health care organization. He also "took refuge during the hard years" (1934–1938) at two different departments of sanitary statistics, first at the Erisman Institute and then at Narkomzdrav SSSR.[8] N. A. Semashko chaired the department of health care organization at Khar'kov Institute Number One and also taught at Moscow Medical Institute Number Two, while continuing to write about the history of Soviet medicine for both domestic and foreign consumption. No one could have been more surprised by the former commissar's survival than Semashko himself, who destroyed most of his personal papers and kept a packed bag by his apartment door in case he was arrested in the middle of the night.[9]

Venereology was also affected severely by the changing political climate. The January 1931 issue of *Venereology and Dermatology* published its first "self-criticism" *(samokritika),* admitting, among other mistakes, the following:

> The journal did not fight actively enough for the realization of Lenin's principle of the party position *(partiinost')* in science, did not fight actively enough with all the deviations from the party line, with hostile theories, with apolitical tendencies in science, etc. . . .
>   [T]he journal did not sufficiently ensure that printed work utilized the methodology of dialectical materialism.[10]

In the same issue the social venereology section disappeared, and a new one, "The Construction of Health Protection, Social Pathology, and Prophylaxis of Skin and Venereal Diseases" *(Stroitel'stvo zdravookhraneniia, sotsial'naia patologiia i profilaktika kozhnykh i venericheskikh bolezne i),* was added. The institute's Division of Social Venereology was likewise renamed the Division of Social Pathology and the Prophylaxis of Skin and Venereal Diseases *(Otdel sotsial'noi patologii i profilaktiki kozhnykh i venericheskikh boleznei),* further signaling the discipline's shift in attitude toward such "social anomalies" (in the new terminology) as prostitution.

On April 8, 1931, the director of the State Venereological Institute, Professor N. S. Efron, was "relieved of his post at his own request" and made assistant director of the Division of Scientific Instruction. He was temporarily replaced by Dr. I. S. Kokanin, who served until V. M. Bronner assumed this position in 1932. Yet Bronner's career was also threatened during this period, as a direct result of his leadership role in social venereology.[11]

The fate of social venereology was underscored in an entry dated July 8, 1931, in the institute's register of directives, a document that is the closest approximation to the archival "smoking gun." Section 10 of Decree 71 recorded that, effective immediately, Dr. M. S. Barash was to be removed from his post as director of sanitary enlightenment for the social venereology division and transferred to the employ of Narkomzdrav for "failing to correct, and distorting, the class line in his work." One of Barash's professional duties had been as Bronner's assistant editor of the division's enlightenment newspaper, *Toward a Healthy Lifestyle*. The paper suffered a similar fate, mandated in the following section of the decree, which stipulated that its "next edition be temporarily suspended, since past issues contained politically harmful directions in many places and articles." (The newspaper never resumed publication.) The final section of the decree concerned Bronner himself, who as director of the social venereology division was to be informed of the following:

> In the work of the department as a whole there are a number of shortcomings in the implementation of the class position in science and medicine. Therefore, I suggest that you correct these intolerable mistakes as quickly as possible and in the future pursue a decisive course in the Bolshevik leadership of your department, and of the colleagues under your supervision, and in doing so guarantee the fulfillment of the party line both in theory and in practice.[12]

Such specific allusions to sexual enlightenment did not recur in any of the published articles of denunciation or self-criticism. Yet allegations and confessions of an overemphasis on "social pathology" at the expense of publicizing "achievements in the struggle against venereal disease in light of the successes of socialist construction" speak volumes.[13] By early 1932, the approach to the struggle against venereal disease had been dramatically altered. The 1930s fight against venereal disease was to be aimed primarily at the new construction sites (such as Magnitogorsk); "not one case of venereal disease" (at the project settlements) was the new battle cry. When social venereology as a subfield of the discipline ceased to exist, so too did all discussions of the population's sexual behavior. Amazingly, the issue of sex dropped completely out of the institute's journal, which focused instead upon statistics, diagnosis, medication and treatment, and medical training. After what was clearly a sufficient amount of self-criticism and censure (he was accused, among other failings, of "lack of party-mindedness *[bespartiinost']*, opportunism, and rotten liberalism"), in 1932 Bronner assumed the directorship of the institute.[14] Yet he avoided the subject of sexuality, devoting the remainder of his career (and his life) to questions of medical education.

In a letter written in 1935 to the new commissar Grigorii Naumovich Kaminskii, Dr. Ia. I. Zdravomyslov (curiously, the same Zdravomyslov that Semashko singled out for the scientific ignorance that characterized his work), uses Kaminskii's speech at the Seventeenth Party Congress as an excuse to attack Bronner's reputation. Responding to the commissar's presentation, entitled "Improving Quality Must Be at the Center of All Our Work," Zdravomyslov urges him to attend to the "functionalism and deception" evident within the Health Commissariat itself. As an example he pointed out that, thanks to the commissar's address, Bronner (in whose honor the State Venereological Institute had been named) had been awarded the title of Honored Scientist for his contributions to Soviet medicine.[15] Zdravomyslov continued:

> But is everything all right on the venereal front, and shouldn't Professor Bronner, as the person in charge of this front, be held responsible for the collapse that has occurred rather than given high honors? He approached the resolution of the tasks of venereology not with a Soviet directive, but solely through personal initiative, creating a monument to his own name.

One wonders how frequently such personal animosities and jealousies were behind the denunciations that terminated the careers and lives of so many people in the purges. In any case, the letter suggests an awareness that all was not well in the fight against venereal disease and that the search had begun for scapegoats on which to blame this state of affairs. Bronner was arrested on October 23, 1937, and shot soon afterward.[16]

*M*any of the ideas advanced in sexual enlightenment were also discredited during the Cultural Revolution. Although physical culture, for instance, remained a central tenet of sexual enlightenment until its demise, by the end of the decade a more "practical" alternative had gained ascendancy. It was resolved that physical education should focus specifically on preparing young people for production work and military service. At the Sixteenth Party Congress in 1930, Stalin called for the younger generation to be trained to defend the country from attacks by its enemies; and in 1931, on the initiative of the Komsomol, the physical education program "Prepare for Labor and the Defense of the USSR" (*GTO: Gotov k trudu i oborone SSSR*) was initiated.[17]

By 1930 diagnoses such as "nervousness" and "exhaustion" were impolitic, if not downright "counterrevolutionary." In a 1930 article in *Revolution and Culture (Revoliutsiia i kul'tura)*, V. Vnukov denounced the "specialists" who in the quiet of their university centers and meetings "stealthily" concluded "as if purely medically, neutrally," that the newly trained cadres (hailing from the peasantry or proletariat) were not qualified to carry out their duties. According to Vnukov, the specialists found these young people exhausted from too rapid a promotion; unaccustomed to intellectual work, they soon became "stupid" and were thus completely unsuited for this type of life. He asserted that nothing could be farther from the truth; exhaustion was solely the result of poorly organized work.[18]

Similar charges were made the following year in the *Journal of Neuropathology and Psychiatry (Zhurnal nevropatologii i psikhiatrii)*, only this time the names of several of the guilty specialists were included. The article's author, N. I. Propper, first singled out mental hygiene as "a powerful weapon of control over the masses in the hands of the bourgeoisie" and then condemned those of his colleagues who refused to criticize this American invention. The bulk of his attack, however, was aimed at Professor Gannushkin's theory of acquired invalidism and the many studies conducted during the 1920s that had "proved" the prevalence of nervous illnesses, the harm of such a fast pace of social construction, and the inability of workers and peasants to perform "brain work." Referring to research by Professor Emdin and Dr. Ol'shanskii on neuroses among leading Party workers of the Northern Caucasus, Propper asked:

> How can one remain silent and not characterize the following as harmful? It is sufficient to cite just two figures: 80 percent of active party members suffer from "irritability" and 80 percent suffer from illnesses of the "cardiovascular system." This means that if you talk to a leading party worker, you should know that you are speaking to someone who is nervously ill.[19]

Propper also denounced a similar project by Professor Dekhterev, which had found a high percentage of neurasthenia among a group of worker and peasant students who had completed worker schools (*rabfaki*) and were attending Moscow Medical Institute Number One at the time of the survey. Propper termed such accusations "particularly false and harmful," since these very students had performed outstandingly in their courses; moreover, they "almost never visited the school medical clinic," a fact the author could personally confirm as an assistant in the same clinic where Dekhterev also worked.[20]

As Martin Miller relates, the field of psychoneurology suffered also because of its association with psychoanalysis and Freud. While the Freudian emphasis on sexuality had been criticized throughout the 1920s, even by many supporters of psychoanalysis, by the end of the decade there was no one willing to publicly defend the discipline. At the 1930 Congress on Human Behavior, which pronounced the demise of psychoanalysis, one of the chief attackers was A. B. Zalkind, the author of the Twelve Commandments and the psychiatrist Semashko had condemned for writing incorrectly on the sex question. Once a supporter of Freud's ideas himself, Zalkind now declared psychoanalysis to be bourgeois, anti-Soviet, anti-collectivist, and racist. Not surprisingly, his about-face did not save him, and soon after the conference ended he himself was attacked for his earlier support of "Freudism." Zalkind died in 1936, though whether of natural causes or by his own hand is still a matter of debate.[21]

$\mathcal{T}$he state's priorities shifted when it embarked on its program of mass industrialization. Epidemics of nervousness and venereal disease called into question the country's ability to fulfill the Five-Year Plan and tarnished the image of the happy, healthy population building socialism. Pointing to the "family discord and disintegration, and disordered sexuality, [which], unfortunately, remain a dark spot in our everyday life," Commissar Semashko acknowledged in late 1930 that it would be unrealistic to expect significant progress in this area. I have argued that such declarations of sexual illness were an integral part of sexual enlightenment, continuously justifying physicians' authority over the sex question. Semashko accompanied this small acknowledgment of defeat with the familiar reassurance: "There's no need to panic," since Soviet "youths are far more moral than their prerevolutionary counterparts." Unfortunately for Semashko, the evidence cited is the same source he had drawn upon repeatedly throughout the decade, the Gel'man survey of 1922, which begged the question of what effect, if any, sex education had had upon sexual behavior in the interim.[22]

Any explanation for the demise of sexual enlightenment must also be sought in sexual enlightenment itself, in its content and its advocates. Reflecting on the preconditions for the successful resolution of the sex question, Dr. Timofeev cited the elimination of all capitalistic remnants associated with NEP, the strengthening of production, and the battle for a socialist lifestyle. Working from this solid basis, he proposed a strategy for making sex healthy that involved a two-pronged attack: the battle "against whatever facilitates an increase in sexual demands, and the creation of sensations and feelings that will replace sexual feelings." Semashko similarly had more than once explained the sexual debauchery following the failed 1905 Revolution by the fact that young people and other "sensitive types" had been deprived of useful channels for the redirection of their sexual energy.[23]

The heady pace of the Five-Year Plans seemed to be just what the doctors ordered. In a sense, the state took on the function of the endocrine glands. (Not coincidentally, this assumption of state control occurred at the same time that the glandular explanation for homosexuality fell from favor.)[24] It solved the problem of sexual attraction through legal measures and mandatory sublimation by way of rapid industrialization and the collectivization of agriculture. Excluding the small amount of sexual energy (and secretions) needed for reproduction, the remainder would be redirected toward state building and the collective. No longer considered a social problem to be corrected through education, whatever inappropriate sexual behaviors persisted would be treated through prohibitions, as in the recriminalization of prostitution in the early 1930s and of sodomy in 1934.[25]

Especially revealing of this shift in approach is the 1937 case of the "Chernskaia Hooligan Party," in which a group of teenage boys were accused of forming a "counterrevolutionary organization" that, in addition to terrorizing the other students, met twice weekly in the school bathroom, where they engaged in sexual acts and parodied Soviet power through the insignia and rules invented for their group.[26] If we recall how overzealous the peasant correspondent Alfei's denunciation of the village masturbators appears (see Chapter 5), even in the context of the brutal collectivization campaign, by the mid-1930s the conflation of sexual and political deviance no longer seems so out of place. Alfei's disgust was politically motivated in as much as the local youths favored the wrong kind of leisure activity and collective experience and were either unable or unwilling to be enlightened and transformed—all aspects of the ideological struggle for a new lifestyle of the 1920s. By the 1930s, the unspecified sex acts that took place in the school bathroom, whether mutual or not, had become explicitly political; the sexual deviant is by nature a political criminal, and it is no surprise that a political criminal would also be a sexual deviant.

In 1936 abortion was likewise prohibited, access to divorce greatly restricted, and contraception made all but unavailable—measures signaling a far more interventionist role on the part of the state in its effort to enact a pronatalist agenda.[27] As Dan Healey has noted, one of the manifestations of this "socialist compulsory heterosexuality" was that "family life became the subject of prescriptive scrutiny, where before Bolshevik leaders had said little about the internal dynamics and psychology of the husband-wife relationship."[28] This newfound attention entailed a major departure from the "hands-off" approach to the married couple in sexual enlightenment, but an approach nonetheless equally unconcerned with the pair's sexual satisfaction as the basis of its marital harmony.[29] If anything, conjugal pleasures of the flesh were even more out of place in the 1930s. Indeed, the fact that "many people [didn't] give a damn about the family, looking on marriage as a means to satisfy their own personal whims," was used to justify the new restrictions on divorce.[30] The wife's fulfillment would come instead from her vaunted status as mother (preferably of several children), homemaker, and/or (unpaid) social activist, the attractive and beautifying role model promoted in the *obshche-stvennitsa* movement.[31] For men, physical fulfillment could have decidedly negative connotations, as a series of tougher child-support laws and other measures enforcing paternal obligations ensured that they pay for their moment of pleasure.[32]

In part, responsibility for the fate of sex education lies in the commissariat's success at silencing all competing voices. Concluding his 1927 *Izvestiia* editorial, "Ignorance and Pornography," Semashko wrote:

> It is necessary to place a decisive end to this flow of corruption. The publishing world should raise a loud voice of protest and warning against it. *Glavlit* should concentrate its attention not on preserving the innocence of theatergoers, but on this systematic and rude corruption of the young by the printed and spoken word.[33]

By the end of the decade, he got his wish. Private publishing on the sex question decreased dramatically during 1929 and had completely disappeared by 1930. The private publishers and doctors who had threatened Narkomzdrav's authority were closed down and forced out of business during the First Five-Year Plan. Narkomzdrav maintained its hegemony over publications on sex until late 1931, when these also vanished, not to reappear until the end of World War II.[34] Ironically, the same criteria traditionally identified as the basis for medical professionalization—the centralization and unification of physicians—eventually contributed to doctors' loss of authority. The possibility of continuing to publish in alternative locations was sacrificed with the victory of their own publishing house, a press now closely controlled by the dictates of the Party, which no longer tolerated discussion on these issues; nor did it tolerate claims for a higher language of science separate from overt references to the Party.

Ironically, while there can be no disputing that the sexual enlightenment movement's abrupt elimination was caused by state fiat, the fifty-year moratorium on the sex question that began in the 1930s was also a bureaucratically inverted form of physician-assisted suicide. By aligning the purpose of sexuality so closely with the needs of the state, doctors and enlighteners had provided the country's leadership with handy discursive tools with which to dismantle the disciplinary edifice they had tried so hard to create. The advice literature produced in the 1920s invoked sex only to negate it, dwelling in detail on disease and distress, defining healthy sex almost entirely in terms of absence and restraint. Semashko's declaration in the 1920s that the sex question is "sick" inadvertently summed up the contradictions of an entire movement's attempt to build disciplinary authority over an unhealthy phenomenon whose successful treatment would obviate the need for the specialists who define it. The High Stalinist 1930s abounded in metaphors of surgical intervention to save the body politic from harmful infection, while the sex question itself had become a disease, transmitted not by prostitutes or wayward youth but by public health professionals themselves. Like the hapless peasants and workers from the 1920s VD posters, sexual enlighteners had entered into a dangerous liaison with an untrustworthy partner. And the consequences proved fatal.

Abbreviations List

GARF—State Archive of the Russian Federation

GISG—State Institute of Social Hygiene

GMAM—Moscow State Municipal Archive

GMI—State Medical Publishing House

GVI—State Venereological Institute

Komsomol—Young Communist League

KOTiB—Committee for Making Labor and Lifestyle Healthy

Narkompros—People's Commissariat of Enlightenment

Narkomzdrav—People's Commissariat of Public Health

NEP—New Economic Policy

Sovnarkom—Council of People's Commissars

TsGA—Central State Archive

VTsIK—Central Executive Committee of the All-Russian
Congress of Soviets

Zhenotdel—Women's Section of the Communist Party

Notes

Introduction

1. Laura Engelstein, *The Keys to Happiness: Sex and the Search for Modernity in Fin-de-Siècle Russia* (Ithaca: Cornell University Press, 1992). Other aspects of the sex question are discussed in Evgenii Bershtein, "Tragediia pola: dve zametki o russkom veiningerianstve," *Novoe literaturnoe obozrenie* 1.65 (2004): 208–28; Evgenii Bershtein, "Psychopathia sexualis v Rossii nachala veka: politika i zhanr," in *Eros and Pornography in Russian Culture*, ed. M. Levitt and A. Toporkov (Moscow: Ladomir, 1999), 414–41.

2. Richard Stites, *The Women's Liberation Movement in Russia: Feminism, Nihilism, and Bolshevism, 1860–1930* (Princeton, N.J.: Princeton University Press, 1978), ch. 9; Barbara Evans Clements, "The Effects of the Civil War on Women and Family Relations," in *Party, State, and Society in the Russian Civil War: Explorations in Social History*, ed. Diane P. Koenker, William G. Rosenberg, and Ronald Grigor Suny (Bloomington: Indiana University Press, 1989), 105–27. The quotation is from N. A. Semashko, *Puti sovetskoi fizkul'tury* (Moscow: Izd. vysshego soveta fizkul'tury, 1926), 57. In Russian, *bol'noi* means both "painful" and "sick." (Unless noted otherwise, all translations from the original language are my own.)

3. The definitive study is Eric Naiman, *Sex in Public: The Incarnation of Early Soviet Ideology* (Princeton, N.J.: Princeton University Press, 1997). See also Katerina Clark, *Petersburg: Crucible of Cultural Revolution* (Cambridge: Harvard University Press, 1995), 210–11.

4. David L. Hoffmann, *Stalinist Values: The Cultural Norms of Soviet Modernity, 1917–1941* (Ithaca: Cornell University Press, 2003), ch. 3; Dan Healey, *Homosexual Desire in Revolutionary Russia* (Chicago: University of Chicago, 2001), chs. 7–8; N. B. Lebina and M. V. Shkarovskii, *Prostitutsiia v Peterburge* (Moscow: Progress-Akademiia, 1994), 154–61.

5. The term was first used by Nicholas Timasheff in *The Great Retreat: The Growth and Decline of Communism in Russia* (New York: Dutton, 1946).

6. Catriona Kelly, *Refining Russia: Advice Literature, Polite Culture, and Gender from Catherine to Yeltsin* (Oxford: Oxford University Press, 2001), xliv, 243–44, 282 (quote); Hoffmann, *Stalinist Values*, 5–7 (quotations, 5–6); Clark, *Petersburg*, Introduction.

7. Anne E. Gorsuch, *Youth in Revolutionary Russia: Enthusiasts, Bohemians, Delinquents* (Bloomington: Indiana University Press, 2000); Elizabeth A. Wood, *The Baba and the Comrade: Gender and Politics in Revolutionary Russia* (Bloomington: Indiana University Press, 1997). Quotation is from Ia. I. Kaminskii, *Polovaia zhizn' i fizicheskaia kul'tura* (Odessa: Svetoch, 1927), 13.

8. Wilhelm Reich, *The Sexual Revolution: Toward a Self-Governing Character Structure*, trans. Theodore P. Wolfe (New York: Orgone Institute Press, 1945); Timasheff, *The Great Retreat.*

9. Richard Stites, *Revolutionary Dreams: Utopian Vision and Experimental Life in the Russian Revolution* (New York: Oxford University Press, 1989); William B. Husband, *"Godless Communists": Atheism and Society in Soviet Russia, 1917–1932* (DeKalb: Northern Illinois University Press, 2000), ch. 3; Michael David-Fox, *Revolution of the Mind: Higher Learning among the Bolsheviks, 1918–1929* (Ithaca: Cornell University Press, 1997), 101–17; Tricia Ann Starks, "The Body Soviet: Health, Hygiene, and the Path to a New Life in the Soviet Union in the 1920s" (PhD diss., Ohio State University, 2000).

10. David L. Hoffmann and Yanni Kotsonis, eds., *Russian Modernity: Politics, Knowledge, Practices* (New York: St. Martin's Press, 2000), esp. the introduction and conclusion; Hoffmann, *Stalinist Values*, 18; Michel Foucault, *The History of Sexuality,* vol. 1, *An Introduction,* trans. Robert Hurley (New York: Pantheon, 1978).

11. Laura Engelstein, "Combined Underdevelopment: Discipline and the Law in Imperial and Soviet Russia," *American Historical Review* 98.2 (1993): 338–53 (344).

12. The two positions are delineated in Wendy Z. Goldman, *Women, the State, and Revolution: Soviet Family Policy and Social Life, 1917–1936* (Cambridge and New York: Cambridge University Press, 1993), 1–58. See also Stites, *Women's Liberation Movement,* 376–79; Healey, *Homosexual Desire,* 133–34.

13. D. Rossiiskii, "Istoriia meditsinskogo obrazovaniia v dorevoliutsionnoi Rossii," *Bol'shaia meditsinskaia entsiklopediia,* 1 izd. (Moscow: Sovetskaia entsiklopediia, 1936), 17: 661.

14. "V. M. Bronner," in *Vrachi-bol'sheviki: stroiteli sovetskogo zdravookhraneniia,* ed. E. I. Lotovaia and B. D. Petrov (Moscow: Meditsina, 1970), 241–51; Z. Tikhonova, *Narodnyi komissar zdorov'ie (o N. A. Semashko)* (Moscow: Gos. izd. politicheskoi literatury, 1960).

15. Allan M. Brandt, *No Magic Bullet: A Social History of Venereal Disease in the United States since 1880* (New York and Oxford: Oxford University Press, 1987), 22; Benjamin Nathans, *Beyond the Pale: The Jewish Encounter with Late Imperial Russia* (Berkeley and Los Angeles: University of California Press, 2002).

16. "Chto kazhdy dolzhen znat' o polovoi zhizni" (Khar'kov: Kosmos, 1927). The price for the entire set of eleven brochures was three rubles and twelve kopecks.

17. For some of the countless examples of questionable credentials and information in European and American sex advice, see Robert Darby, "Circumcision as a Preventive of Masturbation: A Review of the Historiography," *Journal of Social History* 36 (Spring 2003): 737–58; Roy Porter and Lesley Hall, *The Facts of Life: The Creation of Sexual Knowledge in Britain, 1650–1950* (New Haven and London: Yale University Press, 1995).

18. Sex advice in Europe and North America was also highly gendered, relying on different stratagems to advance a binary model of sexual behavior. Thomas Laqueur, *Making Sex: Body and Gender from the Greeks to Freud* (Cambridge: Harvard University Press, 1990); Lucy Bland and Laura Doan, eds., *Sexology in Culture: Labelling Bodies and Desires* (Chicago: University of Chicago Press, 1998), and *Sexology Uncensored: The Documents of Sexual Science* (Chicago: University of Chicago Press, 1998).

19. Hoffmann, *Stalinist Values,* 10, 16–17 (quote), 45.

20. The connection between the USSR and Germany was particularly strong in the medical fields most closely involved with sexuality, especially social venereology and social hygiene, which both had their origins in Germany. Susan Gross Solomon provides several examples of Soviet-German medical and scientific cooperation in

"The Soviet Legalization of Abortion in German Medical Discourse: A Study of the Use of Selective Perceptions in Cross-Cultural Scientific Relations," *Social Studies of Science* 22.3 (1992): 455–87. European and American sex reformers' support for the Soviet Union is discussed by Atina Grossmann, *Reforming Sex: The German Movement for Birth Control and Abortion Reform, 1920–1950* (New York: Oxford University Press, 1995), 15, 20, 38, 52, 121; and Julie L. Thomas, "International Intercourse: Establishing a Global Discourse on Birth Control, 1914–1939" (PhD diss., Indiana University, in progress), ch. 4.

21. Kelly, *Refining Russia,* xxiii.

22. Among the medical organizations concerned with children's sexuality during the 1920s are the State Institute of Social Hygiene, the State Institute for the Protection of Children's and Adolescents' Health, and the Moscow Institute of Sanitary Culture. GARF, f. A482, op. 1, dd. 256, 543, 335, 118; f. A579, op. 1, dd. 861, 869; f. 9636, op. 1, dd. 39, 50.

23. Healey, *Homosexual Desire,* ch. 6; Cassandra Marie Cavanaugh, "Backwardness and Biology: Medicine and Power in Russian and Soviet Central Asia, 1868–1934" (PhD diss., Columbia University, 2001); Gregory J. Massell, *The Surrogate Proletariat: Moslem Women and Revolutionary Strategies in Soviet Central Asia, 1919–1929* (Princeton, N.J.: Princeton University Press, 1974); Paula A. Michaels, *Curative Powers: Medicine and Empire in Stalin's Central Asia* (Pittsburgh, Pa.: University of Pittsburgh Press, 2003).

1—Disciplining the Sex Question in Revolutionary Russia

1. Quotations from Klara Zetkin, *My Recollections of Lenin* (Moscow: Foreign Languages Publishing House, 1956), 58. Unlike the German example singled out by Lenin, references to Freud's theories are relatively rare in Soviet sexual enlightenment for adults. His ideas are given more attention in discussions of early childhood sexuality and sex education for children. On the reception to Freud in Soviet Russia, see Martin A. Miller, *Freud and the Bolsheviks: Psychoanalysis in Imperial Russia and the Soviet Union* (New Haven: Yale University Press, 1998); Aleksander Etkind, *Eros nevozmozhnogo: istoriia psikhoanaliza v Rossii* (Moscow: Gnozis, 1994).

2. Zetkin, *My Recollections of Lenin,* 61, 63–64, 66.

3. Private publishing houses were legalized in a Sovnarkom decree from December 12, 1921. Alan Ball, *Russia's Last Capitalists: The Nepmen, 1921–1929* (Berkeley and Los Angeles: University of California Press, 1987), 21, 146–48; Jeffrey Brooks, "The Breakdown in Production and Distribution of Printed Material, 1917–1927," in *Bolshevik Culture: Experiment and Order in the Russian Revolution,* ed. Abbott Gleason, Peter Kenez, and Richard Stites (Bloomington: Indiana University Press, 1985), 151–74.

4. Susan Gross Solomon examines Commissar Semashko's own multiple agendas in "Social Hygiene and Soviet Public Health, 1921–1930," in *Health and Society in Revolutionary Russia,* ed. Susan Gross Solomon and John F. Hutchinson (Bloomington: Indiana University Press, 1990), 175–99.

5. For a fuller discussion of doctors as social experts, see Kenneth M. Pinnow, "Cutting and Counting: Forensic Medicine as a Science of Society in Bolshevik Russia, 1920–1929," in Hoffmann and Kotsonis, *Russian Modernity,* 115–37.

6. John F. Hutchinson, *Politics and Public Health in Revolutionary Russia, 1890–1918* (Baltimore: Johns Hopkins University, 1990); Neil B. Weissman, "Origins of Soviet Health Administration: Narkomzdrav, 1918–1928," in Solomon and Hutchinson, *Health and Society,* 97–120.

7. Engelstein interprets this increase in attention as a response to student unrest beginning in 1899. Engelstein, *Keys to Happiness,* 226, 232.

8. *Trudy Vysochaishe razreshennogo s"ezda po obsuzhdeniiu mer protiv sifilisa v Rossii* (St. Petersburg, 1897); Engelstein, *Keys to Happiness,* ch. 5, also p. 200; V. M. Bronner, "Iazyk faktov," *Venerologiia i dermatologiia* 10 (1927): 895–96.

9. Dr. I. M. Malyshev and Professor A. I. Liants, from GARF, f. A482, op. 19, d. 38, ll. 66–71 (66, 67, 67, 71). Women in prerevolutionary Russia identified as prostitutes were compelled to submit to regular medical examination to ensure that they were free of disease. Laurie Bernstein, *Sonia's Daughters: Prostitutes and Their Regulation in Imperial Russia* (Berkeley and Los Angeles: University of California Press, 1995).

10. GARF, f. A482, op. 19, d. 38, ll. 69, 71.

11. Ibid., op. 19, d. 24, ll. 80, 81; op. 1, d. 27, ll. 1, 15–17; op. 1, d. 46, ll. 9–10, 17, 22.

12. Ibid., op. 19, d. 1, l. 28; op. 1, d. 46, l. 92.

13. This transformation is described by the USSR's representative to the 1928 meeting of the World League for Sex Reform in Copenhagen. Archive of the Semashko Institute of Social Hygiene, Economics, and the Administration of Public Health, f. Semashko, op. 6, d. 1, l. 257.

14. GARF, f. A482, op. 1, d. 46, l. 66; d. 42, l. 51; d. 46, ll. 163, 124.

15. Engelstein, *Keys to Happiness,* 249.

16. GARF, f. A482, op. 1, d. 46, l. 124.

17. Ibid., l. 125ob; op. 19, d. 1, ll. 71–72ob.

18. Ibid., op. 19, d. 1, ll. 72–72ob.

19. Ibid., op. 1, d. 46, l. 125ob; D. N. Zhbankov, "O polovoi zhizni uchashchikhsia zhenshchin," *Vrachebnoe delo* 10–12 (1922): 225–34. Several of these surveys are cited in Sheila Fitzpatrick, "Sex and Revolution: An Examination of Literary and Statistical Data on the Mores of Soviet Students in the 1920s," *Journal of Modern History* (June 1978): 252–78; and Susan Gross Solomon, "Innocence and Sexuality in Soviet Medical Discourse," in *Women in Russia and the Ukraine,* ed. Rosalind Marsh (Cambridge: Cambridge University Press, 1994), 121–30.

20. V. M. Bronner, "Polozhenie i perspektivy bor'by s venericheskimi boleznimi v Respublike," in *Raspredelenie zaniatii i tezisy dokladov Vserossiiskogo s"ezda po bor'be s venericheskimi bolezniami* (Moscow, 1923), 11.

21. GARF, f. A482, op. 19, d. 20, ll. 2, 48 (quote); op. 1, d. 46, ll. 160, 163.

22. Ibid., op. 19, d. 38, l. 203; op. 1, d. 297, l. 47.

23. Founded in 1922 as the State Venereological Institute, in 1926 the GVI's name was changed to the Bronner State Venereological Institute in gratitude for V. M. Bronner's dedication to the fight against venereal disease. In the early 1930s the name was changed again, to the Bronner Combined State Dermatological and Venereological Institute. In 1937, after Bronner was arrested, it was renamed the SSSR Ministry of Health Central Dermato-Venereological Institute. Still functioning, its present name is the Scientific-Research Central Dermatological and Venereological Institute.

24. "Ot redaktsii," *Venerologiia i dermatologiia* 1 (1924): 3; Frances L. Bernstein, "Prostitutes and Proletarians: The Labor Clinic as Revolutionary Laboratory in the 1920s," in *The Human Tradition in Modern Russia,* ed. William Husband (Wilmington, Del.: Scholarly Resources, 2000), 113–28. Unless otherwise noted, the photographs and posters reproduced in this book are from the collection of the "Medical Museum" Scientific Research Center of the Russian Academy of Medical Sciences, Moscow (NITs Meditsinskii muzei RAMN).

25. A. Kushelevskii, "Venerologicheskii dispanser i rabochaia otvetstvennost'," *Voprosy zdravookhraneniia* 3–4 (1929): 64–68. In 1927, Bronner was appointed to head Narkomzdrav's Division of Social Diseases. From 1932 until his arrest in 1937, he was also the director of the State Venereological Institute.

26. GARF, f. A482, op. 1, d. 520, ll. 115ob, 116; ibid., d. 601, l. 301; Solomon, "Social Hygiene," 181–85.

27. Semashko Institute, f. Semashko, op. 6, d. 1, ll. 228–57.

28. GARF, f. A482, op. 1, d. 601, ll. 308, 309, 308ob.

29. Ibid., d. 46, ll. 126, 145, 152, 169.

30. Bronner, "Polozhenie i perspektivy," 11.

31. A detailed analysis of this and later family codes is provided by Goldman in *Women, the State, and Revolution*. Prerevolutionary legal codes on the family are discussed in William G. Wagner, *Marriage, Property, and Law in Imperial Russia* (Oxford: Clarendon Press, 1994).

32. Goldman, *Women, the State, and Revolution*, 51, 3.

33. Prof. V. P. Osipov, "Dr. L. Ia. Iakobzon, *Polovoe bessilie*," *Kniga i revoliutstiia* 3–4 (1920): 76.

34. The following description is taken from I. D. Strashun, "Sanitarnoe prosveshchenie v dele bor'by s venericheskimi bolezniami (Zadachi i metody)," in *Raspredelenie zaniatii*, 35–36.

35. Ibid., 36. Agitational trials were mock courtroom scenes staged widely during the 1920s to educate the populace on a variety of social, cultural, and political norms. Within the realm of public health, there developed an entire subgenre known as sanitary trials (*sansudy*) to address such topics as the fight against prostitution, alcoholism, and folk healing. Elizabeth A. Wood, *Performing Justice: Agitation Trials in Revolutionary Russia* (Ithaca and New York: Cornell University Press, 2005).

36. N. L. Rossiianskii, "Vrachebnaia etika i venericheskie bolezni," in *Raspredelenie zaniatii*, 42.

37. "Vserossiiskii s"ezd po bor'be s venericheskimi bolezniami," *Biulleten' Narkomzdrava* 16 (1923): 12, 13.

38. "Protokol zasedaniia plenuma organizatsionnogo biuro po sozyvu vsesoiuznogo s"ezda po bor'be s venericheskimi bolezniami," *Venerologiia i dermatologiia* 1 (1925): 90–91.

39. His presentation was later reprinted in the GISG's journal; see G. A. Batkis, "Soderzhanie i metody vneshkol'noi raboty po polovomu prosveshcheniiu," *Sotsial'naia gigiena* 6 (1925): 146–48. Batkis further develops these ideas in "Polovoe vospitanie i prosveshchenie v usloviiakh sovetskogo stroia," *Venerologiia i dermatologiia* 6 (1925): 193.

40. Ibid., 147.

41. Ibid., 148.

42. "Rezoliutsiia po voprosu o seksual'nom vospitanii," in *Rezoliutsii i Postanovleniia 2-go Vsesoiuznogo s"ezda po bor'be s venerizmom* (Khar'kov: Narkomzdrav USSR, 1925), 5.

43. GMAM, f. 2194, op. 1, d. 160, l. 1; N. Ivanova, "Seksual'naia pedagogika," *Zhenskii zhurnal* 6 (1930): 15; D. I. Lass, "Pervaia Moskovskaia konferentsiia po seksual'noi pedagogike," *Vrachebnoe delo* 4 (1930): 313–14. On the debate over the location of the 1931 congress, see Norman Hare, ed., *World League for Sexual Reform: Proceedings of the Third Congress* (London: Ken Paul, Trench, Trubner, 1930), 583–84.

44. GMAM, f. 2194, op. 1, d. 160, ll. 1ob, 3.

45. Igor S. Kon, *The Sexual Revolution in Russia* (New York: Free Press, 1995), 75.

46. N. A. Semashko, "Kak ne nado pisat' o polovom voprose," *Izvestiia*, January 1, 1925, 5.

47. Ibid. The article the commissar is referring to is A. B. Zalkind, "Polovoi vopros s kommunisticheskoi tochki zreniia," *Na putiakh k novoi shkole* 6 (1924): 47–57, reprinted later that year in *Polovoi vopros*, ed. S. M. Kalmanson (Moscow and Leningrad: Molodaia gvardiia, 1924).

48. See Naiman, *Sex in Public*, ch. 6, for a more detailed discussion of Zalkind's and Liadov's analyses of sexuality.

49. Semashko, "Kak ne nado pisat'," 5.

50. N. A. Semashko, "Nevezhestvo i pornografiia pod maskoi prosveshcheniia, nauki i literatury," *Izvestiia*, April 8, 1927, 3. All quotations in the following discussion of Semashko's ideas come from this article.

51. Cited in Semashko, "Nevezhestvo i pornografiia."

52. I. G. Gel'man, *Polovaia zhizn' sovremennoi molodezhi. Opyt sotsial'no-biologicheskogo obsledovaniia* (Moscow and Petrograd: Gos. izd., 1923), 145–49.

53. Ibid., 107–8. Drs. Z. A. Gurevich and F. I. Grosser also warned against the dangers of popular literature, which "introduces people to deviations, how to masturbate, etc." *Voprosy polovoi zhizni* (Kiev: Gos. izd. USSR, 1929), 212. N. A. Semashko, "Voprosy polovogo vospitaniia," in *Polovoi vopros*, ed. Em. Iaroslavskii (Moscow: Izd. GIZh, 1925), 22, and "Na putiakh k novomu bytu," *Gigiena i zdorov'e rabochei i krest'ianskoi sem'i* 22 (1930): 3. Compare the illustrations in this series to those found in *Polovoi vopros v svete nauchnogo znaniia*, ed. Prof. V. F. Zelenin (Moscow and Leningrad: Gos. izd., 1926). Published by the State Publishing Company, this collection also contains an article written by Semashko.

54. GARF, f. A482, op. 1, d. 601, l. 58.

55. Ibid., d. 602, ll. 500–507, 609, 623. As has been suggested above, little in fact separated the various publications in terms of content. Thus while the Okhmatmlad list focused more exclusively on female sexuality and assumed a female readership, its treatment of topics covered differed little from similar brochures published in any of the other lists. GARF, f. A482, op. 1, d. 640, ch. 3, ll. 534, 543, 545–49.

56. Dr. B. Sigal, "Ozdorovite svoi polovoi byt," *Gigiena i zdorov'e* 15 (1929): 13.

57. S.P., "Chto chitat' po polovomu voprosu," *Put' k zdorov'iu* 7–8 (1926): 33; Dr. Ia. F. Zil'berg, "Chto chitat' po polovomu voprosu," *Za novyi byt* 23–24 (1928): 24.

58. Dr. Ia. F. Zil'berg, "Chto chitat' po polovomu voprosu," 24 (Nestrukh); S.P., "Chto chitat' po polovomu voprosu," 33–34 (Okinchits, Bremener); Dr. Ia. F. Zil'berg, "Chto chitat' po polovomu voprosu: Nepravil'nosti polovoi zhizni," *Za novyi byt* 7–8 (1929): 24 (Iakobzon, Fronshtein).

59. "Bibliografiia. Chto chitat' po polovomu voprosu," *Gigiena i zdorov'e* 18 (1927): 16.

60. Dr. B. A. Ivanovskii, *Polovaia zhizn' i fizkul'tura* (Moscow and Leningrad: Gos. izd., 1928), 4; Dr. G. Rozenblium, *Kakoe znachenie imeet brak dlia zdorov'ia liudei* (Khar'kov: Kosmos, 1926), 50.

61. Dr. B. S. Sigal, *Polovoi vopros* (Moscow and Leningrad: Molodaia gvardiia, 1925), 6.

62. Dr. Ia. I. Zdravomyslov, *Voprosy polovoi zhizni* (Leningrad: P. P. Soikin, 1926), 5.

63. "Polovoi vopros," *Put' k zdorov'iu* 7–8 (1926): 1.

64. Dr. L. Mandels, "Ozdorovlenie polovogo byta," *Gigiena i zdorov'e* 2 (1927): 10.

65. Dr. L. M. Vasilevskii, *Polovoe zdorov'e* (Moscow: Izd. G. F. Mirimanova, 1925), 8; Dr. M. A. Glezer, *Polovaia zhizn'* (Khar'kov: Nauchnaia meditsina, 1929), 58.

66. Dr. N. Donichev, *Zdorovaia i nezdorovaia polovaia zhizn'* (Moscow and Leningrad: Gos. izd., 1930), 26, 86–87.

67. N. A. Semashko, *Novyi byt i polovoi vopros* (Moscow and Leningrad: Gos. izd., 1926), 28.

68. Dr. Ia. D. Golomb, *Polovoe vozderzhanie (za i protiv)* (Odessa: Svetoch, 1927), 13; Dr. D. I. Lass, *Zdorovaia polovaia zhizn'* (Moscow: GMI, 1929), 5; A. Uspenskii, *Polovaia zhizn' i ee otkloneniia* (Khar'kov: Kosmos, 1926), 5 (quote).

69. Glezer, *Polovaia zhizn'*, 53; Uspenskii, *Polovaia zhizn'*, 98; Dr. M. Lemberg, *Chto neobkhodimo znat' o polovom voprose* (Leningrad: Priboi, 1925), 34; Dr. A. N. Karov, *Chto dolzhny znat' muzhchina i zhenshchina vstupaiushchie v brak* (Odessa: Svetoch, 1927), 14–15.

70. Sigal, *Polovoi vopros*, 51; Dr. L. V. Pisareva, "O polovoi probleme v sviazi s vyiavleniem novogo byta u komsomol'skoi i rabochei molodezhi," *Programma zaniatii 2-go vsesoiuznogo s"ezda po bor'be s venerizmom* (Khar'kov: Narkomzdrav USSR, 1925), 14.

71. Dr. F. Iu. Berman, "Garmoniia polovoi zhizni," in *Teoriia i praktika sanitarnogo prosveshcheniia*, ed. S. N. Volkonskaia and F. Iu. Berman (Moscow: Izd. Moszdravotdela, 1926), issue 4 (1926), p. 77.

72. Glezer, *Polovaia zhizn'*, 55. Richard Stites discusses this behavior and the anxiety it provoked in *Women's Liberation Movement*, 358–62, 379–83. See also Peter Konecny, *Builders and Deserters: Students, State, and Community in Leningrad, 1917–1941* (Montreal and Ithaca: McGill-Queens University Press, 1999).

73. Rozenblium, *Kakoe znachenie imeet*, 24.

74. Zetkin, *My Recollections of Lenin*, 64–65. The theory posited that intercourse, like thirst, was a simple physiological need that should be satisfied accordingly.

75. Kollontai left the country in 1923 as part of a diplomatic mission to Norway, a posting widely seen as a response to her involvement in the Workers' Opposition. Her status as a "Bolshevik feminist" has been challenged by Eric Naiman, who sees her writings as consistent with prevailing Party discourse advocating the desexing of women and expressing a "relentless repugnance toward female physiology." Naiman, *Sex in Public*, ch. 6.

76. A. Kollontai, "Dorogu krylatomu erosu," *Molodaia gvardiia* 3 (1923): 111–24, and *Liubov' pchel trudovykh* (Moscow and Petrograd, 1923). A detailed analysis of these works and their misinterpretation by contemporary critics and subsequent historians can be found in Stites, *Women's Liberation Movement*, ch. 11.

77. Lemberg, *Chto neobkhodimo znat'*, 34; D. I. Lass, *Sovremennoe studenchestvo. Byt, polovaia zhizn'* (Moscow and Leningrad: Molodaia gvardiia, 1928), 8. Semashko also joined in the criticism: Kollontai was the third comrade cited in his 1925 *Izvestiia* editorial, which also briefly censured her "Make Way for Winged Eros" for its "biological ignorance." Semashko, "Kak ne nado pisat'," 5. The commissar repeated and expanded his critique in several additional articles, including "O biologicheskom podkhode k postanovke polovogo vospitaniia," *Zvezda* 5 (1924): 151.

78. Glezer, *Polovaia zhizn'*, 56–57; Dr. A. Timofeev, *Kuda dolzhna napravliat'sia polovaia energiia molodezhi* (Khar'kov: Kosmos, 1927), 30–31. A longtime advocate of women's issues, Nadezhda Krupskaia was very involved in education policy and propaganda work during this time period. Robert H. McNeal, *Bride of the Revolution* (Ann Arbor: University of Michigan Press, 1972); and Stites, *Women's Liberation Movement*, 239–43, 325–26.

79. Kaminskii, *Polovaia zhizn'*, 24.

80. Dr. G. Ia. Bruk, *Chto takoe polovoe vlechenie* (Moscow and Leningrad: Gos. izd., 1929), 92; Dr. A. K. Platovskii, *Polovaia zhizn' sovremennogo studenchestva* (Rostov na Donu, 1926), 4.

81. Glezer, *Polovaia zhizn'*, 38, 53, 62.

82. L. Iakobzon, "Polovaia zhizn' cheloveka," *Gigiena i zdorov'e* 18 (1929): 11.

83. Gurevich and Grosser, *Voprosy polovoi zhizni*, 209.

84. Professor A. Mendel'son, "Polovaia zhizn' cheloveka," *Gigiena i zdorov'e* 5 (1923): 6; Vasilevskii, *Polovoe zdorov'e*, 4, 21.

85. Dr. O. Feigin, *Chto takoe normal'naia polovaia zhizn'* (Leningrad: Izd. avtora, 1927), 30; Berman, "Garmoniia polovoi zhizni," 85; Efimov, "Na puti k novoi sem'e," 2; Uspenskii, *Polovaia zhizn'*, 99.

86. Lenin from Zetkin, *My Recollections of Lenin*, 65. Lenin denies his "monastic asceticism" three times in three pages.

87. Naiman, *Sex in Public*, 131; Timofeev, *Kuda dolzhna napravliat'sia*, 50.

88. Dr. A. B. Zalkind, *Polovoi vopros v usloviiakh sovetskoi obshchestvennosti* (Leningrad: Gosudarstvennoe izdatel'stvo, 1926), 47–49. Writing in a *Pravda* editorial, Nikolai Bukharin called the commandments "nonsense and philistine scum, which want to climb into all pockets." Cited in Kon, *Sexual Revolution*, 58, 300n11.

89. Uspenskii, *Polovaia zhizn'*, 100–101.

90. Semashko, "Na putiakh k novomu bytu," 3.

2—Making Sex

1. Feigin, *Chto takoe normal'naia*, 3. Most likely Feigin had in mind such controversial arguments as the "glass of water" theory.

2. Ibid.

3. Prof. P. G. Bakaleinikov, *Polovoe znanie* (Leningrad: Izd. avtora, 1927), 10; Prof. A. V. Nemilov, *Biologicheskaia tragediia zhenshchin* (Leningrad: Seiatel', 1927), 16; Bruk, *Chto takoe polovoe vlechenie*, 75.

4. For alternate analyses of the endocrine glands, abstinence, and rejuvenation, see Naiman, *Sex in Public*, ch. 3; Mikhail Zolotonosov, "Masturbanizatsiia. 'Erogennye zony' sovetskoi kul'tury 1920–1930-kh godov," *Novoe literaturnoe obozrenie* 11 (1991): 93–99.

5. On similar anxieties in France at the end of World War I, see Mary-Louise Roberts, *Civilization without Sexes: Reconstructing Gender in Postwar France, 1917–1927* (Chicago: University of Chicago, 1994).

6. Prof. N. K. Kol'tsov, "Opyty Shteinakha po omolozheniiu organizma," *Priroda* 1–3 (1921): 3–26; Eugen Steinach, *Verjüngung durch experimentelle Neubelebung der alternden Pubertätsdrüse* (Berlin: Springer, 1920). For Steinach's life and scientific work, see Chandak Sengoopta, "Glandular Politics: Experimental Biology, Clinical Medicine, and Homosexual Emancipation in Fin-de-Siècle Central Europe," *Isis* 89 (1998): 445–73; Eugen Steinach, *Sex and Life: Forty Years of Biological and Medical Experiments* (New York: Viking, 1940).

7. Prof. N. Perna, "Znachenie organov vnutrennei sekretsii," *Priroda* 8–9 (1922): 9–18; A. Nemilov, "O peresadke semennykh zhelez u mlekopitaiushchikh i cheloveka," *Priroda* 7–12 (1923): 77–84; Serge A. Voronoff, *Rejuvenation by Grafting*, trans. Fred F. Imianitoff (New York: Adelphi, 1925 [1924]).

8. M. A. Bulgakov, *Sobranie sochinenii v piati tomakh* (Moscow: Khudozhestvennaia literatura, 1989), 2:129–40; Zolotonosov, "Masturbanizatsiia," 96.

9. A number of popular works on rejuvenation point to the impact of the war to argue for the widespread adoption of this procedure in Russia, especially with respect to livestock. V. S. Muralevich, *Chto takoe starost' i omolozhenie* (Moscow: Moskovskii rabochii, 1923); M. Gremiatskii, *Chto takoe omolozhenie* (Moscow and Leningrad: Gos. izd., 1930), 54–55.

10. The journal *Bezbozhnik* published a series of antireligious pamphlets that incorporated the subject of endocrinology, including B. M. Zavadovskii, *Estestvoznanie i religiia* (Moscow: Bezbozhnik, 1925); Ts. Perel'muter, *Nauka i religiia o zhizni chelovecheskogo tela* (n.p.: Bezbozhnik, 1927).

11. E. Steinach, "Willkürliche Umwandlung von Säugetier-Männchen in Tiere mit ausgeprägt weiblichen Geschlechtscharakteren und weiblicher Psyche," *Pflügers Archiv für die gesammte Physiologie* 144 (1912): 71–108.

12. Kol'tsov, "Opyty Shteinakha," 6–7.

13. Dr. O. Feigin incorrectly attributed the Voronoff rejuvenation technique to Steinach in *Polovoe sozrevanie i polovoe vospitanie* (Leningrad: Izd. avtora, 1927), 11. Semashko criticized Dr. Lass for confusing the endocrine glands with the salivary glands. See "Nevezhestvo i pornografiia," 3.

14. Lass, *Zdorovaia polovaia zhizn'*, 8; Bakaleinikov, *Polovoe znanie*, 3.

15. Feigin, *Polovoe sozrevanie*, 7–10; Dr. N. I. Shchukin, *Muzhchina i zhenshchina v polovoi zhizni* (Moscow and Leningrad: Gos. izd., 1928), 19–20; Zdravomyslov, *Voprosy polovoi zhizni*, 48; Dr. B. S. Sigal, *Polovaia zhizn' rabochei molodezhi* (Moscow and Leningrad: Molodaia gvardia, 1926), 22; Dr. L. M. Vasilevskii, *K zdorovomu polovomu bytu* (Moscow: Zdorovaia Moskva, 1926), 4.

16. For early sexual activity, see Vasilevskii, *K zdorovomu*, 20–22; Dr. L. M. Vasilevskii, *Polovye izvrashcheniia* (Moscow: Novaia Moskva, 1924), 35. Dr. S. M. Kalmanson, "Iz doklada vracha S. M. Kalmansona na dispute po polovomu voprosu v Kommunisticheskom universitete trudiashchikhsia vostoka, 20/V 1924 g.," in Kalmanson, *Polovoi vopros*, 4.

17. Bakaleinikov, *Polovoe znanie*, 4.

18. Donichev, *Zdorovaia i nezdorovaia*, 8–9.

19. Dr. N. Shvarts, "Biologicheskii ocherk," in Kalmanson, *Polovoi vopros*, 34; L. A. and L. M. Vasilevskie, "Polovaia zhizn' cheloveka," in ibid., 55.

20. Donichev, *Zdorovaia i nezdorovaia*, 11.

21. Shchukin, *Muzhchina i zhenshchina*, 21. See also F. Berman, *Sputnik sanlektora: Konspekt lektsii* (Krasnodar: Izd. sanprosveta IX Kubarmii, 1921), 22, 196; L. I. Faingol'd, *Polovoe sozrevanie cheloveka* (Odessa: Svetoch, 1927), 8. For the *skoptsy*, see Laura Engelstein, *Castration and the Heavenly Kingdom: A Russian Folktale* (Ithaca: Cornell University Press, 1999); Aleksandr Etkind, *Khlyst: Sekty, Literatura i Revoliutsiia* (Moscow: Novoe Literaturnoe Obozrenie, 1998); Claudio Sergio Ingerflom, *La secte russe des castrates* (Paris: Les Belles Lettres, 1996).

22. Donichev, *Zdorovaia i nezdorovaia*, 18; Shchukin, *Muzhchina i zhenshchina*, 22; Sigal, *Polovoi vopros*, 18.

23. Ivanovskii, *Polovaia zhizn'*, 11–12.

24. Sigal, *Polovaia zhizn' rabochei molodezhi*, 20; Timofeev, *Kuda dolzhna napravliat'sia*, 19–20.

25. Ivanovskii, *Polovaia zhizn'*, 12.

26. Dr. A. Uspenskii, *O vrede rannikh polovykh snoshenii* (Khar'kov: Kosmos, 1927), 12; Dr. K. P. Veselovskaia, *Pedologicheskie osnovy polovogo vospitaniia* (Moscow, 1928), 16. Glezer, *Polovaia zhizn*, 33.

27. Bruk, *Chto takoe polovoe vlechenie*, 74. In their popularization of developments in endocrinology to argue for sex-specific behaviors, Soviet enlighteners followed in the footsteps of their Western counterparts' slightly earlier efforts. Nelly Oudshoorn traces the history of sex endocrinology and the way new thinking about the sex hormones was incorporated into medical notions of masculinity and femininity in the early twentieth century in Europe, in *Beyond the Natural Body: An Archeology of Sex Hormones* (London and New York: Routledge, 1994), ch. 1.

28. Prof. A. Mendel'son, "Polovye razlichiia v svete sovremennoi nauki," *Gigiena i zdorov'e* 10.17 (1924): 10; Shchukin, *Muzhchina i zhenshchina*, 19.

29. Dr. Ia. D. Golomb, *Polovaia zhizn' normal'naia i nenormal'naia* (Odessa: Svetoch, 1926), 11; Prof. M. Nestrukh, *Polovoe vlechenie v prirode* (Moscow: Novaia Moskva, 1924), 91.

30. Ia. S. Shapiro, *Polovoe vospitanie detei v sem'e* (Moscow: Izd. Narkomzdrava RSFSR, 1928), 5.

31. Dr. L. Ia. Iakobzon, *Voprosy pola* (Moscow and Leningrad: GMI, 1929), 55.

32. Golomb, *Polovaia zhizn'*, 11; G. P. Sakharov, "Vnutrenniaia sekretsiia i omolozhenie," in *Biosotsial'naia priroda polovoi zhizni cheloveka*, ed. N. P. Iordanskii (Moscow: Prometei, 1930), 66.

33. Prof. A. Mendel'son, *Nervnaia sistema i polovaia zhizn'* (Leningrad: Leningradskaia pravda, 1929), 8; Iakobzon, *Voprosy pola*, 60–61.

34. T. I. Iudin, *Polovoe vlechenie i nenormal'nosti polovogo povedeniia* (Moscow: Izd. Narkomzdrava RSFSR, 1928), 17.

35. Dr. M. A. Aroni, *Kak voznikaet i razvivaetsia chelovecheskii zarodysh. Obshchedostupnoe izlozhenie v sviazi s gigienoi beremennosti* (Khar'kov: Kosmos, 1926), 11. Such gendered anthropomorphism is by no means limited to the period in question. See Emily Martin, "The Egg and the Sperm: How Science Has Constructed a Romance Based on Stereotypical Male-Female Roles," *Signs: Journal of Women in Culture and Society* 16.3 (1991): 485–501.

36. Mendel'son, "Polovye razlichiia," 10.17 (1924): 10.

37. Ibid., 11.18 (1924), 13.

38. Berman, *Sputnik sanlektora*, 196; also Iakobzon, *Voprosy pola*, 58.

39. Nemilov, *Biologicheskaia tragediia*, 33.

40. Mendel'son, "Polovye razlichiia," 11.18 (1924): 14; Kaminskii, *Polovaia*

zhizn', 13; A. Timofeev, *V chem proiavliaetsia polovaia zhizn' muzhchiny i zhenshchiny* (Khar'kov: Kosmos, 1926), 11.

41. Dr. V. A. Khachatrian, *Polovye otkloneniia i polovoe vospitanie. Onanizm i bor'ba s nim* (Tbilisi, 1929), 10–11; G. P. Sakharov, "Proizvol'noe izmenenie pola u zhivotnykh," in Iordanskii, *Biosotsial'naia priroda*, 63; B. I. Slovtsov, E. S. London, and I. I. Kryzhanskii, "Omolozhenie i izmenenie pola," in *Novoe v voprosakh pola*, ed. L. V. Blumenau et al. (Leningrad: Obrazovanie, 1924), 45.

42. M. M. Zavadovskii, *Pol i razvitie ego priznakov* (Moscow: Gos. izd., 1922), and *Pol zhivotnykh i ego prevrashchenie (mekhanika razvitiia pola)* in *Izbrannye Trudy* (Moscow: Agropromizdat, 1990), originally published in 1923.

43. Ivanovskii, *Polovaiai zhizn'*, 13–14. Other works that describe both experiments include Veselovskaia, *Pedologicheskie osnovy*, 16–18; Prof. P. Sorokhtin, *Obshchie osnovy polovogo vospitaniia dlia pedologov, vrachei i pedagogov* (Moscow: Prometei, 1930), 7–9; Timofeev, *Kuda dolzhna napravliat'sia*, 24–25.

44. For Zavadovskii's study, see Glezer, *Polovaia zhizn'*, 35. For Steinach's, see Addendum, Kalmanson, *Polovoi vopros*.

45. Shchukin, *Muzhchina i zhenshchina*, 24.

46. I. M. Tkachenko, *O polovom voprose* (Kiev, 1926), 37–38.

47. Alexander Lipschütz, *The Internal Secretions of the Sex Glands: The Problem of the "Puberty Gland"* (Cambridge: W. Heffer, 1924), 298, 365, as cited in Sengoopta, "Glandular Politics," n. 49; Uspenskii, *O vrede*, 4 (*samets* and *samka* are the generic words for the male and female of animal species).

48. Bakaleinikov, *Polovoe znanie*, 5; Khachatrian, *Polovye otkloneniia*, 11; Bruk, *Chto takoe polovoe vlechenie*, 61; Mendel'son, "Polovye razlichiia," 11.18 (1924): 14.

49. Semashko, "Voprosy polovogo vospitaniia," 17, 18.

50. Ibid., 19.

51. Bruk, *Chto takoe polovoe vlechenie*, 64–65.

52. Nemilov, *Biologicheskaia tragediia*, 47–49.

53. Ibid., 54, 64.

54. Ibid., 17, 93, 93.

55. Ibid., 88–89; Naiman, *Sex in Public*, 225; Eric Naiman, "Historectomies: The Metaphysics of Reproduction in a Utopian Age," in *Sexuality and the Body in Russian Culture*, ed. Jane T. Costlow, Stephanie Sandler, Judith Vowles (Stanford: Stanford University Press, 1993), 270.

56. L. Ia. Iakobzon, "Polovaia kholodnost' zhenshchiny," *Gigiena i zdorov'e* 6 (1927): 2; Mendel'son, *Nervnaia sistema*, 13.

57. Dr. N. Mikulina-Ivanova, "Polovaia zhizn' zhenshchiny," *Zhenskii zhurnal* 7 (1926): 17.

58. Sakharov, "Vnutrenniaia sekretsiia i omolozhenie," 66; Golomb, *Polovoe vozderzhanie*, 16.

59. Faingol'd, *Polovoe sozrevanie*, 8; Kaminskii, *Polovaia zhizn'*, 12; Shapiro, *Polovoe vospitanie*, 6.

60. Bruk, *Chto takoe polovoe vlechenie*, 45; Nemilov, *Biologicheskaia tragediia*, 92.

61. Nestrukh, *Polovoe vlechenie*, 101–2.

62. Ibid., 104, 107.

63. Prof. A. Mendel'son, "Polovye izvrashcheniia v svete sovremennoi nauki," *Gigiena i zdorov'e* 23.30 (1924): 3–4.

64. Ibid., 4.

65. Vasilevskii, *Polovye izvrashcheniia*, 37–38.

66. V. M. Bekhterev, "O polovom izvrashchenii, kak osoboi ustanovke polovykh refleksov," in *Polovoi vopros v shkole i v zhizni*, ed. I. S. Simonov (Leningrad: Brokgauz Efron, 1927), 166; Golomb, *Polovaia zhizn'*, 25. The complete list of sexual perversions includes fetishism, homosexuality, pederasty, lesbianism, sadism and masochism, sodomy, erotomania, and nymphomania.

67. Vasilevskii, *Polovye izvrashcheniia*, 38, 39.

68. V. P. Protopopov, "Sovremennoe sostoianie voprosa o sushchnosti i proiskhozhdenii gomoseksualizma," *Nauchnaia meditsina* 10 (1922): 56; Iudin, *Polovoe vlechenie*, 21–22.

69. Mendel'son, "Polovye izvrashcheniia," 23.30 (1924): 4; Lemberg, *Chto neobkhodimo znat'*, 10.

70. Bakaleinikov, *Polovoe znanie*, 16; Glezer, *Polovaia zhizn'*, 32–33; Golomb, *Polovaia zhizn'*, 29–30; Mendel'son, "Polovye razlichiia," 11.18 (1924): 14; Slovtsov et al., "Omolozhenie," 48.

71. Vasilevskii, *Polovye izvrashcheniia*, 42–44. Steinach's results are published in "Pubetätsdrüsen und Zwitterbildung," *Archiv für Entwicheklungsmechanik* 42 (1917): 307–32.

72. Vasilevskii, *Polovye izvrashcheniia*, 44; Iudin, *Polovoe vlechenie*, 21.

73. Vasilevskii, *Polovye izvrashcheniia*, 44–45. Every Russian account of this procedure neglects to mention that the woman with whom the subject had sex six weeks after the operation (and on many other occasions) was a prostitute, or that the primary reason for the removal of the man's testicles was tuberculosis; both factors were discussed in German sources. European reports of this procedure can be found in Sengoopta, "Glandular Politics," 467. Russian descriptions include Slovtsov et al., "Omolozhenie," 48; Nestrukh, *Polovoe vlechenie*, 96; Protopopov, "Sovremennoe sostoianie," 61; Golomb, *Polovaia zhizn'*, 28, 30; Iudin, *Polovoe vlechenie*, 21.

74. Berman, *Sputnik sanlektora*, 210; Golomb, *Polovoe vozderzhanie*, 9–10; Professor P. I. Liublinskii, *Prestupleniia v oblasti polovykh otkloneniiakh* (Moscow and Leningrad: Izd. I. D. Frenkel', 1925), 124–26; Bekhterev, "O polovom izvrashchenii," 173; V. M. Bekhterev, "Polovaia deiatel'nost' s tochki zreniia refleksologii," in Zelenin, *Polovoi vopros v svete nauchnogo znaniia*, 147.

75. Liublinskii, *Prestupleniia*, ch. 5; Healey, *Homosexual Desire*, ch. 4; Engelstein, *Keys to Happiness*; Laura Engelstein, "Soviet Policy toward Male Homosexuality: Its Origins and Historical Roots," in *Gay Men and the Sexual History of the Political Left*, ed. Gert Hekma, Harry Oosterhuis, and James D. Steakley (New York: Harrington Park Press, 1995), 155–78.

76. Prof. A. A. Zhizhilenko, *Polovye prestupleniia (St. 166–71 Ugolovnogo Kodeksa)* (Moscow: Izd. Pravo i Zhizn', 1924), 12–16, 19–25. Only Azerbaijan and Georgia among the other republics included antisodomy statutes in their first criminal codes. By the late 1920s prohibitions against a variety of (male) homosexual practices were added to the codes of the Central Asian republics. Healey, *Homosexual Desire*, 158–62.

77. Engelstein, *Keys to Happiness*, 155–64, 228–29; Jeffrey Weeks, *Coming Out: Homosexual Politics in Britain from the Nineteenth Century to the Present* (London and New York: Quartet Books, 1977), ch. 2; Dan Healey, "A Social History of Homosexuality in Soviet Russia, 1917–1934" (MA thesis, University of London, 1991), 5. On the Scientific-Humanitarian Committee, see Sengoopta, "Glandular Politics"; Harry Oosterhuis, "Homosexual Emancipation in Germany before 1933: Two Traditions," *Journal of Homosexuality* 22.1–2 (1992): 1–27.

78. Robert A. Nye, "The History of Sexuality in Context: National Sexological Traditions," *Science in Context* 4 (1991): 398.

79. Sengoopta, "Glandular Politics," 465, 468.

80. Vasilevskii, *Polovye izvrashcheniia*, 46.

81. Sengoopta, "Glandular Politics," 468–69.

82. M. M. Zavadovskii, "Issledovanie semennika gomoseksualista," *Trudy po dinamike razvitiia (Prodolzhenie "Trudov laboratorii eksperim. biologii Mosk. Zooparka")* 6 (1931): 65–70; Dr. Ia. I. Kirov, "K voprosu o geterotransplantsii pri gomoseksualizme," *Vrachebnoe delo* 20 (1928): 1587–90; Healey, *Homosexual Desire*, 149–50, 173–74.

83. Bakaleinikov, *Polovoe znanie*, 16.

84. Sex educators who supported the Bekhterev interpretation of homosexuality include Sorokhtin, *Obshchie osnovy,* 21–22, 27; Khachatrian, *Polovye otkloneniia,* 50–51; Shapiro, *Polovoe vospitanie,* 29–30.

85. See V. M. Bekhterev, *Obshchie osnovy refleksologii cheloveka* (Leningrad: Gosudarstvennoe izd., 1926); V. M. Bekhterev, "Ob izvrashchenii i uklonenii polovogo vlecheniia," in Simonov, *Polovoi vopros,* 293–325; Bekhterev, "O polovom izvrashchenii"; V. M. Bekhterev, *Znachenie polovogo vlecheniia v zhiznedeiatel'nosti organizma* (Moscow: Narkomzdrav RSFSR, 1928). This biosocial explanation for homosexuality received far greater consideration and support in the specialist (especially psychiatric) literature. Healey, *Homosexual Desire,* esp. ch. 5.

86. Naiman, *Sex in Public,* 143–44; Perna, "Znachenie organov vnutrennei sekretsii," 10–11. The history of Soviet endocrinology is discussed in D. M. Rossiiskii, *Ocherk istorii razvitiia endokrinologii v Rossii* (Moscow, 1926); N. A. Shereshevskii, "Ocherk istorii endokrinologii v SSSR," *Problemy endokrinologii* 4 (1937): 452–58.

87. Glezer, *Polovaia zhizn',* 32–33; Iudin, *Polovoe vlechenie,* 22, 26; Mendel'son, "Polovye izvrashcheniia," 5.

88. Vasilevskii, *Polovye izvrashcheniia,* 46–47.

89. Golomb, *Polovaia zhizn',* 25; Vasilevskii, *Polovye izvrashcheniia,* 40; Mendel'son, "Polovye izvrashcheniia," 24 (1924): 5; Bekhterev, "O polovom izvrashchenii," 180. For this reason, Bekhterev strongly advocated children's coeducation, which was widely supported by sex educators as the surest method of prevention.

90. Lemberg, *Chto neobkhodimo znat',* 4–5; Uspenskii, *Polovaia zhizn',* 26; Mandels, "Ozdorovlenie polovogo byta," 10.

91. G. P. Sakharov, "Chelovecheskii polovoi dimorfizm," in Iordanskii, *Biosotsial'naia priroda,* 73. See also Glezer, *Polovaia zhizn',* 36; Golomb, *Polovaia zhizn',* 10.

92. On the Russian philosophical sources of the Bolshevik hostility to both traditional femininity and *byt,* see Naiman, "Historectomies."

93. Tkachenko, *O polovom voprose,* 17–18.

94. Eric Naiman explores the Party discourse surrounding the well-fed "Nep-woman" as a symbol of the ideological distortions of NEP and the idealization of her anorectic, desexed War Communist opposite. Naiman, *Sex in Public,* ch. 6. In an alternate reading, Spencer Golub describes the "grim, mannish, plain, and armed 'Amazonka'" as the Bolshevik's characterization of the "new woman." *The Recurrence of Fate: Theatre and Memory in Twentieth-Century Russia* (Iowa City: University of Iowa Press, 1994), ch. 7.

95. Iakobzon, *Voprosy pola,* 83, 70, 87, 50, 53.

96. Semashko, *Novyi byt i polovoi vopros,* 30–32.

97. Ibid., 32; Glezer, *Polovaia zhizn',* 36.

98. N. A. Semashko, "Nuzhna li 'zhenstvennost'?" *Molodaia gvardiia* 6 (1924): 205–6.

99. Ibid., 206.

100. Ibid. On similar concerns to those expressed by Semashko within the Komsomol, see Anne Gorsuch, "Flappers and Foxtrotters: Soviet Youth in the 'Roaring Twenties,'" *Carl Beck Papers in Russian and East European Studies* 1102 (March 1994): 18, and "'A Woman Is Not a Man': The Culture of Gender and Generation in Soviet Russia, 1921–1928," *Slavic Review* 55.3 (Fall 1996): 658–60.

101. Others may not have agreed: a significant amount of propaganda was directed at soldiers, [male] Komsomol, and Party members who married outside their class. Mark von Hagen, *Soldiers in the Proletarian Dictatorship* (Ithaca: Cornell University Press, 1990), 192–94.

102. Semashko, "Kak ne nado pisat'," 5.

103. According to Oudshoorn, the first such challenge appeared as early as 1921. *Beyond the Natural Body,* 25–27.

104. Nemilov, *Biologicheskaia tragediia,* 39.

3—"Nervous People"

1. Dr. B. Gurvich, "O polliutsiiakh," *Za zdorovyi byt* 6 (1929): 2; L. Ia. Iakobzon, *Polovaia kholodnost' zhenshchiny dlia vrachei i studentov* (Leningrad: Prakticheskaia med-itsina, 1927), 68. Similar factors are cited to explain the publication of a special text-book to familiarize doctors and medical students with the widespread problem: Professor B. N. Khol'stov, *Funktsional'nye rasstroistva muzhskogo polovogo apparata i funktsional'nye rasstroistva mochevykh organov nervnogo proiskhozhdeniia* (Leningrad: Prakticheskaia meditsina, 1926), Introduction.

2. "Konsul'tatsiia po polovoi gigiene," *Za zdorovyi byt* 1 (1925): 3.

3. According to several later accounts that attributed the opening of the clinic to November, the January 15 opening day advertised in the first issue of *Za zdorovyi byt* remained only on paper. By 1929 the Institute of Social Hygiene (and consultation) had moved to 1 Sadovaia-Kudrinskaia. Irina Sirotkina discusses the history of the Moscow State Neuropsychiatric Dispensary in *Diagnosing Literary Genius: A Cultural History of Psychiatry in Russia, 1880–1930* (Baltimore and London: Johns Hopkins University Press, 2002), 157–58.

4. GARF, f. A579, op. 1, d. 841, l. 50. In 1926, the clinic was staffed by Dr. Shishov, a venereologist-urologist; Dr. Gurvich, a psychoneurologist; and Dr. Brukhanskii, a psychiatrist.

5. "K otkrytiiu konsul'tatsii po voprosam nervno-psikhicheskogo zdorov'ia i polovoi zhizni," *Gigiena i zdorov'e rabochei sem'i* 9 (1925): 9 (Leningrad); Liberman, "Molodezh' i polovoe zdorov'e (K rabote konsul'tatsii po polovoi gigiene)," *Za zdorovyi byt* 6 (1929): 2 (Iaroslavl'); S. Monikh, "Konsultatsiia po polovym i brachnym voprosam," *Za zdorovyi byt* 9 (1930): 4 (Tbilisi); N. I. Chuchelov, "Opyt raboty konsul'-tatsii po polovoi gigiene v Tashkente," *Sovetskii vrach* 2 (1930): 76–78 (Tashkent); M. I. Cherkes, "K voprosu ob organizatsii i metodike raboty sanitarno-prosvetitel'nykh kabinetov pri vendispanserakh i konsul'tatsii po voprosam polovoi zhizni i polovoi gigieny pri rabochikh klubakh," *Vrachebnoe delo* 3–4 (1931): 170–74 (Khar'kov).

6. GARF, f. A579, op. 1, d. 841, ll. 51–52, 58–59.

7. B. R. Gurvich and L. E. Zalutskii, "Opyt konsul'tatsii po polovoi gigiene," *Venerologiia i dermatologiia* 2 (1928): 574–75, and "Opyt postroeniia polovoi konsul'-tatsii," *Sotsial'naia gigiena* 7 (1928): 136–37.

8. B. R. Gurvich and L. E. Zalutskii, "Opyt konsul'tatsii po polovoi gigiene" (hereafter referred to as "Opyt konsul'tatsii") in *Psikhogigienicheskie i nevrologicheskie issledovaniia*, ed. L. M. Rozenshtein (Moscow: Narkomzdrav, 1928), 232. This statement is as close as the doctors ever came to an analysis of the reasons that more workers (the group that was supposed to be targeted) did not utilize the consultation. The high incidence of impotence is corroborated by a 1927 sex survey cited by Fitzpatrick in "Sex and Revolution," 266.

9. The *Eheberatungstellen* and these other clinics in Germany are analyzed in Grossmann, *Reforming Sex*; Cornelie Usborne, *The Politics of the Body in Weimar Germany* (London: Macmillan, 1992).

10. Gurvich and Zalutskii, "Opyt konsul'tatsii," 236 (quote); L. S. Gurvich, "O rabote konsul'tatsii po ozdorovleniiu byta," *Vestnik sovremennoi meditsiny* 10 (1929): 584.

11. GARF, f. A579, op. 1, d. 417, l. 1; "O rabote konsul'tatsii po ozdorovleniiu byta," *Zhenskii zhurnal* 9 (1929): 22; Dr. Zalutskii, "Ozdorovlenie byta," *Zhenskii zhur-nal* 11 (1930): 21. On the efforts to combine sexual with women's consultations, see A. Rakhmanov, "Konsul'tatsiia dlia zhenshchin," *Biulleten' Narkomzdrava* 9 (1926): 3–9; A. Iu. Lur'e, Z. I. Baisheva, and E. S. Kushnirskaia, "Opyt raboty polovoi konsul'-tatsii pri ZAGSE," *Zhurnal po izucheniiu rannego detskogo vozrasta* 3–4 (1930): 295–306; A. Iu. Lur'e, "Polovaia konsul'tatsiia," *Za zdorovyi byt* 10 (1930): 1; GARF, f. A579, op. 1., d. 841, l. 48.

12. Zalutskii, "Ozdorovlenie byta," 21; Gurvich and Zalutskii, "Opyt konsul'tatsii," 237–38.

13. B. Gurvich, "O polliutsiiakh," 2; B. Gurvich, "Polovaia slabost' muzhchin (Iz konsul'tatsii po polovoi gigiene)," *Za zdorovyi byt* 4 (1928): 2.

14. Gurvich and Zalutskii, "Opyt konsul'tatsii," 232–33, 238 (quote). This is particularly significant, since Dr. B. Gurvich was a woman. The implications of a woman doctor treating men for sexual impotence are never addressed in any of the sources.

15. "K ozdorovleniiu byta," *Za zdorovyi byt* 1 (1928): 2. The article is signed: Consultation for Sexual Hygiene at the State Institute of Social Hygiene.

16. B. Gurvich, "K ozdorovleniiu byta (Iz konsul'tatsii po polovoi gigiene) II," *Za zdorovyi byt* 2 (1928): 2.

17. B. Gurvich, "Polovaia slabost' muzhchin," 2.

18. Thus, although white-collar workers predominated in the statistical medical accounts cited above, the cases described in *Toward a Healthy Lifestyle* presented a far more diverse composition. See GARF, f. A579, op. 1, d. 841, ll. 40–42ob; B. Gurvich, "O polliutsiiakh"; B. Gurvich, "Eshche o polovoi slabosti muzhchin (Iz konsul'tatsii po polovoi gigiene)," *Za zdorovyi byt* 6 (1929): 2; B. Gurvich, "Po povodu pisem o polovykh rasstroistvakh," *Za zdorovyi byt* 9 (1930): 2.

19. B. Gurvich, "Polovaia slabost'."

20. Gurvich and Zalutskii, "Opyt konsul'tatsii," 239.

21. Iakobzon reported in 1926 that only 27 percent of cases of sexual dysfunction were due to venereal disease. *Voprosy pola,* 131.

22. B. Gurvich, "Polovaia slabost'"; B. Gurvich, "O polliutsiiakh"; B. Gurvich, "Eshche o polovoi slabosti muzhchin"; B. Gurvich, "Polovaia slabost'."

23. B. Gurvich, "Po povodu pisem," 2.

24. GARF, f. A579, op. 1, d. 841, l. 48ob. On hysteria as a female illness, see Elaine Showalter, *The Female Malady: Women, Madness, and English Culture, 1830–1980* (New York: Pantheon, 1985); Mark S. Micale, *Approaching Hysteria: Disease and Its Interpretations* (Princeton, N.J.: Princeton University Press, 1994).

25. L. M. Rozenshtein, *Nervnost' i bor'ba s nei* (Moscow: Izd. Narkomzdrava, 1928), 3.

26. Mikhail Zoshchenko, "Nervous People," *Nervous People and Other Satires,* trans. Maria Gordon and Hugh McLean (London: Victor Gollancz, 1963), 124. Other examples of popular fiction from the 1920s dealing with nerves and nervousness include Mikhail Bulgakov, "Sobach'e serdtse," in *Sobranie sochinenii v piati tomakh* (Moscow: Khudozhestvennaia literatura, 1989) 2: 129–40; Lev Gumilevskii, *Sobachii pereulok* (1927; Riga: Gramatu draugs, 1928); and the satires of Il'f and Petrov.

27. George Frederick Drinka, M.D., *The Birth of Neurosis: Myth, Malady, and the Victorians* (New York: Simon and Schuster, 1984).

28. George Miller Beard, "Neurasthenia, or Nervous Exhaustion," *Boston Medical and Surgical Journal* 3 (1869): 217; Tom Lutz, *American Nervousness, 1903: An Anecdotal History* (Ithaca and New York: Cornell University Press, 1991), 3–4.

29. George Miller Beard, *American Nervousness: Its Causes and Consequences* (New York: G. P. Putnam's Sons, 1881), vii–viii, cited in Lutz, *Nervousness,* 4, 6. "One doctor" cited in ibid., 6.

30. Anson Rabinbach, *The Human Motor: Energy, Fatigue, and the Origins of Modernity* (New York: Basic Books, 1990), esp. ch. 6; Drinka, *Birth of Neurosis,* ch. 9, esp. 212–13.

31. Drinka, *Birth of Neurosis,* 217.

32. Dr. Fernand Levillain, a follower of Charcot, and the author of *La Neurasthenie: Maladie de Beard* (Paris: A. Maloine, 1891), cited in ibid., 219.

33. Ibid., 230.

34. Engelstein, *Keys to Happiness,* ch. 7; Julie Brown, "Revolution and Psychosis: The Mixing of Science and Politics in Russian Psychiatric Medicine, 1905–1913," *Russian Review* 46.3 (1987): 283–302.

35. L. A. Prozorov, "Organizatsiia nevro-psikhiatricheskoi pomoshchi v usloviiakh nastoiashchego vremeni, v chastnosti, psikhpomoshchi sel'skomu naseleniiu," in *Sovetskaia meditsina v bor'be za zdorovye nervy. Trudy 1 Vsesoiuznogo soveshchaniia po psikhiatrii i nevrologii i gosudarstvennogo nevro-psikhiatricheskogo dispansera,* ed. A. I. Miskinov, L. A. Prozorov, and L. M. Rozenshtein (Moscow: Izd. Ul'ianskogo kombinata PPP, 1926), 12.

36. Professor A. A. Kapustin, "Nervnost' nashego vremeni i bor'ba s nei," *Meditsina* 5 (1927): 5. Nowhere in the reports on these studies is it explained how they were conducted or what factors determined the different designations of nervousness.

37. Kapustin, "Nervnost'," 5 (first two studies); A. B. Zalkind, "O zabolevaniiakh partaktiva," *Krasnaia nov'* 4 (1925): 196.

38. Kapustin, "Nervnost'," 5.

39. Prozorov, "Organizatsiia," 11.

40. Examples include Dr. R. Borisov, "Nevrasteniia," *Zhenskii zhurnal* 11 (1927): 26–27; Z. G. Lur'e, "Nevrasteniia," *Meditsina* 17–18 (1929): 6–8; A. Mendel'son, "Nevrasteniia," *Gigiena i zdorov'e rabochei sem'i* 15.22 (1924): 2–6, and 16.23 (1924): 2–6. David Joravsky refers to the condition as "Soviet exhaustion." See "The Construction of the Stalinist Psyche," in *The Cultural Revolution in Russia, 1928–1931,* ed. Sheila Fitzpatrick (Bloomington and Indianapolis: Indiana University Press, 1984), 113, and David Joravsky, *Russian Psychology: A Critical History* (Oxford and New York: Blackwell, 1989), 337.

41. V. V. Dekhterev, "Dispanserizatsiia kak osnova bor'by s istoshcheniem nervnoi sistemy," *Klinicheskaia meditsina* 19–20 (1930): 1095; A. B. Zalkind, *Revoliutsiia i molodezh'* (Moscow: Kommunisticheskii universitet, 1925): 21. Ironically, Soviet doctors' interpretation of the sources of neurasthenia corresponds to the diagnosis offered by conservative doctors in the wake of 1905; whereas radical psychiatrists attributed the illness to the repressive political regime and the lack of permissible outlets for the socially committed. Sirotkina, *Diagnosing Literary Genius,* 143.

42. E. N. Kameneva, *Chto kazhdomu nuzhno znat' o nervnosti* (Moscow: GMI, 1928), 11–12; Professor P. Gannushkin, "Ob okhrane zdorov'ia partaktiva," *Revoliutsiia i kul'tura* 4 (1930): 44; Zalkind, *Revoliutsiia i molodezh',* 20; Mendel'son, "Nevrasteniia," *Gigiena i zdorov'e* 15.22 (1924): 3; Z. G. Lur'e, "Nevrasteniia," 7; Borisov, "Nevrasteniia," 26.

43. Gannushkin, "Ob okhrane," 43; this is a republication of an article that appeared originally in 1926.

44. Zalkind, *Revoliutsiia i molodezh',* 21; also Dekhterev, "Dispanserizatsiia," 1095. For nervousness among students, see Fitzpatrick, "Sex and Revolution," 266–67; Joravsky, "Stalinist Psyche," esp. 113–14.

45. Gannushkin, "Ob okhrane," 44.

46. Joravsky, "Stalinist Psyche," 112–17; Joravsky, *Russian Psychology,* 336–42; Ernest R. Groves and Phyllis Blanchard, *Introduction to Mental Hygiene* (New York: Holt, 1930); Department of Philanthropic Information, Central Hanover Bank and Trust Company, *The Mental Hygiene Movement: From the Philanthropic Standpoint* (New York: Central Hanover Bank and Trust Company, 1939), 36; Sirotkina, *Diagnosing Literary Genius,* 156–61.

47. Kapustin, "Nervnost'," 5; Z. G. Lur'e, "Nevrasteniia," 6–7; Mendel'son, "Nevrasteniia," 15.22 (1924): 3.

48. Leonard Schapiro, *The Communist Party of the Soviet Union* (New York: Random House, 1971), 313–14; Merle Fainsod, *How Russia Is Ruled* (Cambridge: Harvard University Press, 1962), 244; von Hagen, *Soldiers in the Proletarian Dictatorship,* 150; Sheila Fitzpatrick, "The Bolsheviks' Dilemma: Class, Culture, and Politics in the Early Soviet Years," *Slavic Review* 47 (Winter 1988): 599–613.

49. Ken Pinnow, *Suicide and the Social Science State in Early Bolshevik Russia, 1921–1929* (manuscript in progress), ch. 1; Anne Nesbet, "Suicide as Literary Fact in the 1920s," *Slavic Review* 50.4 (Winter 1991): 827–35.

50. "Bibliografiia: Dr. med. L. Ia. Iakobzon, *Polovaia slabost'*," *Gigiena i zdorov'e* 7 (1928): 15.

51. The relationship between sexual and mental health is made explicit in the establishment of a consultation in Leningrad devoted specifically to these two problems. "K otkrytiiu konsul'tatsii," 9.

52. L. Ia. Iakobzon, "Sotsial'noe znachenie polovykh rasstroistv," *Gigiena i zdorov'e* 3 (1930): 5.

53. L. Ia. Iakobzon, *Voprosy pola*, 128–30.

54. Dr. A. M. Khaletskii, *Polovaia zhizn' i nevrasteniia* (Odessa: Svetoch, 1927), 8; Dr. L. I. Faingol'd, *Polovoe bessilie: Ego prichiny, preduprezhdenie i lechenie* (Odessa: Svetoch, 1926), 25.

55. Mendel'son, *Nervnaia sistema*, 16.

56. Dr. L. Ia. Iakobzon, *Onanizm* (Moscow and Leningrad: Gos. izd., 1929), 2nd ed., 19; Prof. R. M. Fronshtein, *Rasstroistvo polovoi deiatel'nosti muzhchiny* (Moscow and Leningrad: GMI, 1929), 28; Rozenshtein, *Nervnost' i bor'ba s nei*, 12.

57. Khaletskii, *Polovaia zhizn' i nevrasteniia*, 10.

58. See "Otvety na voprosy chitatelei" columns in *Gigiena i zdorov'e* 19 (1927): 17; 1 (1928): 17; 19 (1928): 17.

59. "Otvety na voprosy chitatelei," *Gigiena i zdorov'e* 13 (1928): 17.

60. Iakobzon, *Onanizm*, 9, 20, 26.

61. Mendel'son, *Nervnaia sistema*, 17–18; also Faingol'd, *Polovoe bessilie*, 25.

62. Iakobzon, *Voprosy pola*, 132; Khaletskii, *Polovaia zhizn' i nevrasteniia*, 7–9.

63. The only reference I have seen to the demographic implications of male impotence comes from one of the sex survey respondents cited by Sheila Fitzpatrick: "The half-starved and restless" condition of student life "threatens complete sexual impotence, so that there is very little chance that we Communists will leave descendants." Fitzpatrick, "Sex and Revolution," 265. This is a major difference between the Russian case and that of the French in the nineteenth century. See Robert A. Nye, "Honor, Impotence, and Male Sexuality in Nineteenth-Century French Medicine," *French Historical Studies* 16.1 (Spring 1989): 53, 55.

64. Faingol'd, *Polovoe bessilie*, 29; see also L. Ia. Iakobzon, "Sotsial'noe znachenie polovykh rasstroistv," 5–6.

65. Naiman, *Sex in Public*, ch. 6.

66. Khaletskii, *Polovaia zhizn' i nevrasteniia*, 27; Kameneva, *Chto kazhdomu nuzhno znat' o nervnosti*, 28; Z. G. Lur'e, "Nevrasteniia," 8.

67. Mendel'son, "Polovoe bessilie," *Gigiena i zdorov'e* 1.8 (1924): 6.

68. B. Gurvich, "Po povodu pisem o polovykh rasstroistvakh."

69. Naiman calls it "NEP Gothic." *Sex in Public*, ch. 4.

70. S. I. Gusev-Orenburgskii, *Kakova zhe nasha molodezh'. Sbornik statei* (Moscow and Leningrad: Gos. izd-vo, 1927); A. V. Lunacharskii and V. Knorin, *Upadochnoe nastroenie sredi molodezhi. Eseninshchina* (Moscow: Izd. Kommunisticheskoi Akademii, 1927); Pinnow, *Suicide and the Social Science State*, ch. 1.

71. Semashko, *Novyi byt i polovoi vopros*, 25–27; N. Shvarts, "Razvrashchena li nasha molodezh'," *Za zdorovyi byt* 5 (1929): 2.

72. Semashko, "Kak ne nado pisat'."

73. "Otvety na voprosy chitatelei," *Gigiena i zdorov'e* 7 (1927): back cover.

74. "Khronika-Polovaia konsul'tatsiia," *Gigiena i zdorov'e* 12 (1928): 14.

75. Mendel'son, *Nervnaia sistema*, 9.

76. Iakobzon, *Voprosy pola*, 108.

77. Ibid., 135.

78. Ibid., 104.

79. Fronshtein, *Rasstroistvo polovoi*, 37–38.

80. Iakobzon, *Polovaia kholodnost' zhenshchiny*, 67; Iakobzon, *Voprosy pola*, 135.

81. Iakobzon, *Voprosy pola,* 106.

82. Gurvich and Zalutskii, "Opyt konsul'tatsii," 234; B. Gurvich, "Polovaia slabost' muzhchin (Iz konsul'tatsii po polovoi gigiene)," 2. The responsibility placed on a husband for his wife's orgasm is a theme that also emerges in the European medical literature. See Lesley A. Hall, "'Somehow very distasteful': Doctors, Men, and Sexual Problems between the Wars," *Journal of Contemporary History* 20 (1985): 554; Nye, "Honor, Impotence, and Male Sexuality," 64.

83. Fronshtein, *Rasstroistvo polovoi,* 38; Iakobzon, *Polovaia kholodnost' zhenshchiny,* 73; Iakobzon, *Voprosy pola,* 105.

84. B. Gurvich, "Prostitutsiia, kak sotsial'no-psikhopatologicheskoe iavlenie (predvarite'noe soobshchenie)," in Miskinov, Prozorov, and Rozenshtein, *Sovetskaia meditsina v bor'be za zdorovye nervy,* 60–68. On lesbians, see for example N. P. Brukhanskii, *Materialy po seksual'noi psikhopatologii: Psikhiatricheskie ekspertizy* (Moscow: M. i S. Sabashnikovy, 1927), 62–65. For the medical approach to lesbianism during this period, see Healey, *Homosexual Desire,* esp. ch. 5.

4—Envisioning Health

1. A. V. Mol'kov, "Sanitarnoe prosveshchenie, ego zadachi i metody," *Sotsial'naia gigiena* 1 (1923): 42; N. A. Semashko, *Health Protection in the USSR* (London: Victor Gollancz, 1934), 37–38; Anna J. Haines, *Health Work in Soviet Russia* (New York: Vanguard Press, 1928), ch. 11.

2. For the political poster conveying Bolshevik ideology and iconography, see Stephen White, *The Bolshevik Poster* (New Haven and London: Yale University Press, 1988); Victoria E. Bonnell, *Iconography of Power: Soviet Political Posters under Lenin and Stalin* (Berkeley and Los Angeles: University of California Press, 1999). For political uses of visual images in medicine, see Daniel M. Fox and Christopher Lawrence, *Photographing Medicine: Images and Power in Britain and America since 1840* (New York: Greenwood Press, 1988); Lisa Cartwright, *Screening the Body: Tracing Medicine's Visual Culture* (Minneapolis: University of Minnesota Press, 1995).

3. Elise Kimerling, "Civil Rights and Social Policy in Soviet Russia, 1918–1936," *Russian Review* 41 (1982): 24–46; Sheila Fitzpatrick, "Ascribing Class: The Construction of Social Identity in Soviet Russia," *Journal of Modern History* 65 (December 1993): 745–70.

4. This follows an approach described by Ludmilla Jordanova in "Medicine and Visual Culture," *Social History of Medicine* 3.1 (April 1990): 94.

5. See Hutchinson, *Politics and Public Health,* esp. intro. The idea of making (something) healthy (*ozdorovlenie*) expressed as much a political and moral commitment as a professional vocation on the part of these doctors and explains why the term continued to be used by Soviet physicians.

6. Nancy Frieden, *Russian Physicians in an Era of Reform and Revolution, 1856–1905* (Princeton, N.J.: Princeton University Press, 1981), ch. 6, also pp. 182–85; Mol'kov, "Sanitarnoe prosveshchenie," 40–42.

7. The most noteworthy is A. V. Mol'kov, who served as the president of the Pirogov Commission for Popular Hygiene Education from 1907 to 1917 and continued to be closely involved in educational work after the Revolution.

8. Lenin cited in Semashko, *Health Protection,* 39.

9. For Narkomzdrav, see Haines, *Health Work,* 44–45; Solomon, "Social Hygiene," 178–79; M. I. Barsukov, *Velikaia Oktiabrskaia sotsialisticheskaia revoliutsiia i organizatsiia sovetskogo zdravookhraneniia* (Moscow: Medgiz, 1951); A. I. Nesterenko, *Kak byl obrazovan Narodnyi komissariat zdravookhraneniia RSFSR: Iz istorii Sovetskogo zdravookhraneniia* (Moscow: Meditsina, 1965). For the Division of Sanitary Enlightenment, see GARF, f. A482, op. 1, d. 118, l. 1. In 1922 Strashun replaced Isaev who then

worked at the newly established State Venereological Institute. For the Institute of Sanitary Culture, see GARF, f. 9636, op. 1, d. 47, l. 1; op. 5, d. 7, ll. 7–13; op. 5, d. 1, ll. 1–3.

10. For 1920s sanitary enlightenment work, see *Sanitarnoe prosveshchenie v rabochem klube*, ed. I. D. Strashun and A. S. Berliand (Moscow: Doloi negramotnost', 1925); Volkonskaia and Berman, *Teoriia i praktika sanitarnogo proveshcheniia* (Moscow: Izd. Moszdravotdela, 1925, 1926, 1928.)

11. Iazykov, "O blizhaishikh zadachakh komossii po rasprostraneniiu gigienicheskikh znanii v narode," *Zhurnal Pirogovskogo obshchestva* 1 (1900); A. V. Mol'kov, "Doklad Pirogovskoi komissii po rasprostraneniiu gigienicheskikh znanii v narode," *Trudy 9-go Pirogovskogo s"ezda*, vol. 4.

12. Mol'kov, "Sanitarnoe prosveshchenie," 43; L. O. Kanevskii, "Osnovnye momenty organizatsii sovremennoi gorodskoi museino-vystavochnoi raboty po sanitarnomu prosveshcheniiu," in Volkonskaia and Berman, *Teoriia i praktika*, issue 2 (1926), p. 92; GARF, f. A482, op. 1, d. 641, l. 649.

13. S. Volkonskaia, "Opyt Moskovskogo Sanprosveta," *Sanitarnoe prosveshchenie* 4–5 (1924): 62; A. V. Mol'kov, "Tezisy doklada: Sanitarnoe prosveshchenie, kak sotsial'naia gigienicheskaia problema i rol' vracha v nem," *Sanitarnoe prosveshchenie* 3 (1924): 16.

14. GARF, f. A482, op. 1, d. 641, l. 649. In contrast, Peter Kenez has located the reasons for the demise of (political) posters in the conditions of NEP: "Rosta windows and posters flourished in war conditions, as long as it was clear who the enemy was, as long as it was possible to draw simple juxtapositions, as long as the revolutionary enthusiasm of the artists was uncontaminated. The world of the NEP was too complex and too prosaic." *The Birth of the Propaganda State: Soviet Methods of Mass Mobilization, 1917–1929* (Cambridge and New York: Cambridge University Press, 1985), 118.

15. Mol'kov, "Sanitarnoe prosveshchenie," 42; Semashko, *Health Protection*, 17. For citizens' health obligations in other historical contexts, see Alfons Labisch, "Doctors, Workers, and the Scientific Cosmology of the Industrial World: The Social Construction of 'Health' and the 'Homo Hygienicus'," *Journal of Contemporary History* 20 (1985): 611; Dora B. Weiner, *The Citizen-Patient in Revolutionary and Imperial Paris* (Baltimore: Johns Hopkins University Press, 1993).

16. I. M. Katsenelenbogen, "Zadachi sovetskoi meditsiny," in *Sanitarno-prosvetitel'naia rabota v izbe-chital'ne* (Leningrad: Izd. Knizhnogo sektora LGONO, 1925), 9; Dr. L. Tomilov, "O podgotovke vrachei k sanitarnomu prosveshcheniiu i vospitaniiu krasnoarmeitsev," *Sanitarnoe prosveshchenie* 3 (1924): 10. A list of places where sanitary enlightenment posters hung is contained in GARF, f. A482, op. 1, d. 641, l. 649.

17. Stephen White, in "The Political Poster in Bolshevik Russia," *Sbornik: Study Group on the Russian Revolution* (1982): 28–37, has distinguished four native sources for the Bolshevik political poster: the *lubok* (an illustrated peasant broadsheet), Russian satirical journals, commercial posters, and icons. See also Victoria Bonnell, "The Iconography of the Worker in Soviet Political Art," in *Making Workers Soviet: Power, Class, and Identity*, ed. Lewis H. Siegelbaum and Ronald Grigor Suny (Ithaca: Cornell University Press, 1994), 343; Kenez, *Propaganda State*, 112–13. For more on the role of dichotomy in visual representations of health, pathology, and deviance, see Ludmilla Jordanova, *Sexual Visions: Images of Gender in Science and Medicine between the Eighteenth and Twentieth Centuries* (London: Harvester Wheatsheaf, 1989), ch. 2; Sander L. Gilman, *Disease and Representation: Images of Illness from Madness to AIDS* (Ithaca: Cornell University Press, 1988), ch. 1.

18. Kanevskii, "Osnovnye momenty," 112–13. See also Mol'kov, "Sanitarnoe prosveshchenie," 53.

19. For the 1920s distinction between sexual and nonsexual syphilis, see Susan Gross Solomon, "The Soviet-German Syphilis Expedition to Buriat Mongolia, 1928: Scientific Research on National Minorities," *Slavic Review* 52.2 (Summer 1993):

204–32; Solomon, "Innocence and Sexuality." Soviet doctors inherited their interpretive model for distinguishing between the forms of venereal disease from their prerevolutionary counterparts. Engelstein, *Keys to Happiness*, ch. 5.

20. Artistic editor A. A. Ioffe, "What every woman should know" (Leningrad: Okhmatmlad NKZ, 1920s). The print run was thirty thousand.

21. Elizabeth Waters, "The Female Form in Soviet Political Iconography, 1917–1932," in *Russia's Women: Accommodation, Resistance, Transformation*, ed. Barbara Evans Clements, Barbara Alpern Engel, and Christine D. Worobec (Berkeley and Los Angeles: University of California Press, 1991), 227, 232.

22. For the new Soviet world as an all-male utopia, see Eliot Borenstein, *Men without Women: Masculinity and Revolution in Russian Fiction, 1917–1929* (Durham: Duke University Press, 2000).

23. Elizabeth Waters, "Victim or Villain: Prostitution in Post-Revolutionary Russia," in *Women and Society in Russia and the Soviet Union*, ed. Linda Edmondson (Cambridge: Cambridge University Press, 1992), 160–77; Elizabeth Wood, "Prostitution Unbound: Representations of Sexual and Political Anxieties in Post-Revolutionary Russia," in Costlow, Sandler, and Vowles, *Sexuality and the Body*, 124–35.

24. Prerevolutionary health educators also vilified folk medicine in order to promote "modern" medicine. See Nancy Frieden, "Child Care: Medical Reform in a Traditionalist Culture," in *The Family in Imperial Russia*, ed. David L. Ransel (Champagne-Urbana: University of Illinois Press, 1978), 242.

25. Sander L. Gilman, *Sexuality, an Illustrated History: Representing the Sexual in Medicine and Culture from the Middle Ages to the Age of AIDS* (New York: John Wiley and Sons, 1989), 238.

26. See V. M. Bronner and A. I. Elistratov, eds., *Prostitutsiia v Rossii: Prostitutsiia v Rossii do 1917 goda i bor'ba s prostitutsiei v RSFSR*, (Moscow: Narkomzdrav, 1927), 97.

27. Bernstein, "Prostitutes and Proletarians"; Fanina Halle, *Women in Soviet Russia* (New York: Viking Press, 1933), 233–58.

28. The "Nepwoman" was the symbolic female companion to the "Nepman," the gluttonous, depraved private businessman/trader who personified the New Economic Policy.

29. Gilman, *Sexuality*, 240.

30. Judith R. Walkowitz analyzes the relationship between female independence, sexual danger, public space, and public order in *City of Dreadful Delight: Narratives of Sexual Danger in Late-Victorian London* (Chicago: University of Chicago, 1992); see also Griselda Pollock, *Vision and Difference: Femininity, Feminism, and the Histories of Art* (London and New York: Routledge, 1988), ch. 3.

31. Introduced into the 1926 Criminal Code of the RSFSR, article 150 replaced article 155 of the 1922 Code and the later addition of article 155-a. For the text of article 150 and the history of antivenereal legislation, see *Sobranie kodeksov RSFSR* (Ugolovnyi kodeks), 4th ed. (Moscow: Iuridicheskoe izd. NKIu RSFSR, 1927), 690; I. Ia. Bychkov and N. S. Isaev, *Ugolovnaia otvetstvennost' za zarazhenie venericheskoi bolezn'iu (st. 150 ugolovnogo kodeksa)* (Moscow and Leningrad: Gos. izd., 1931).

32. Semashko, "Meropriiatiia Narkomzdrava po lichnoi profilaktike," in Zelenin, *Polovoi vopros v svete nauchnogo znaniia*, 327.

33. Bychkov and Isaev, *Ugolovnaia otvetstvennost'*, 16.

34. In its presentation of different options and their ramifications, this poster has much in common with American and British anti-VD films produced during World Wars I and II. See Annette Kuhn, *The Power of the Image: Essays on Representation and Sexuality* (New York: Routledge, 1985), ch. 5; Brandt, *No Magic Bullet*.

35. On the debate surrounding the adoption of this code, see Goldman, *Women, the State, and Revolution*, ch. 5.

36. "Don't abandon your child" (Moscow: Moszdravotdel, 1920s). The print run was twenty thousand.

37. Other kinds of posters also lacked single female images, as noted by Waters and Bonnell. The situation changes in the early 1930s in relation to collectivization and the industrialization agenda of the Five-Year Plans. Victoria Bonnell, "The Peasant Woman in Stalinist Political Art of the 1930s," *American Historical Review* 98 (February 1993): 55–82.

38. It is informative to compare this aspect of health posters with the visual syntax of political posters: "Thus male peasants often appeared with male workers or female peasants; male and female peasants were depicted together or with workers. By contrast, the figure of the male worker did not depend for definition on a relationship of contiguity. The presence of the male worker conferred heroic status on those nearby. The worker himself, however, needed no other figure to establish his position in the hierarchy of heroes." Bonnell, "Iconography of the Worker," 352.

39. Kate Sara Schecter, "Professionals in Post-Revolutionary Regimes: A Case Study of Soviet Doctors" (PhD diss., Columbia University, 1992). For British doctors addressing similar threats, see Mary Poovey, "'Scenes of an Indelicate Character': The Medical 'Treatment' of Victorian Women," in *The Making of the Modern Body: Sexuality and Society in the Nineteenth Century,* ed. Catherine Gallagher and Thomas Laqueur (Berkeley and Los Angeles: University of California Press, 1987), 137–68; see also Ornella Moscucci, *The Science of Woman: Gynaecology and Gender in England, 1800–1929* (Cambridge and New York: Cambridge University Press, 1990).

5—*Conserving Soviet Power*

1. Donichev, *Zdorovaia i nezdorovaia,* 66–67. For Lenin, see Zetkin, *My Recollections of Lenin,* 67.

2. On the postrevolutionary afterlife of Fyodorov's ideas, see Irene Masing-Delic, *Abolishing Death: A Salvation Myth of Russian Twentieth-Century Literature* (Stanford: Stanford University Press, 1992), 76–97; Borenstein, *Men without Women,* 26–29; Svetlana Semenova, *Nikolai Fedorov: Tvorchestvo zhizni* (Moscow: Sovetskii pisatel', 1990), 346–81; Vladislav Todorov, *Red Square, Black Square: Organon for Revolutionary Imagination* (Albany: State University of New York Press, 1995), 59–61, 63–66.

3. David Herman, "Stricken by Infection: Art and Adultery in *Anna Karenina* and 'Kreutzer Sonata,'" *Slavic Review* 56.1 (1997): 15–36.

4. Edward H. Clarke, "Sex in Education: A Fair Chance for the Girls," in *Desire and Imagination: Classic Essays in Sexuality,* ed. Regina Barreca (New York: Meridian/Penguin, 1995), 157–87; Henry Maudsley, "Sex in Mind and Education," in ibid., 189–90.

5. See G. J. Barker-Benfield, *The Horrors of the Half-Known Life: Male Attitudes toward Women and Sexuality in Nineteenth-Century America* (New York and London: Routledge, 2000), esp. ch. 15; Raymond Lee Muncy, *Sex and Marriage in Utopian Communities: Nineteenth-Century America* (Bloomington and Indianapolis: Indiana University Press, 1973), chs. 11, 12.

6. Jonathan Coopersmith, *The Electrification of Russia* (Ithaca: Cornell University Press, 1992).

7. Uspenskii, *Polovaia zhizn',* 72; Vasilevskii, *Polovoe zdorov'e,* 8.

8. S. E. Moiseev, "Polovoi vopros i fizkul'tura," *Put' k zdorov'iu* 7–8 (1926): 31; Lass, *Zdorovaia polovaia zhizn',* 5.

9. Timofeev, *Kuda dolzhna napravliat'sia,* 10; Semashko, *Puti sovetskoi fizkul'tury,* 56; Rozenblium, *Kakoe znachenie imeet,* 18.

10. Timofeev, *Kuda dolzhna napravliat'sia,* 5–6, 9.

11. Dr. G. Uzhanskii, *Ob onanizme* (Saratov, 1926), 12. The 1922 and 1926 Criminal Codes rejected explicit age limits for consent, favoring instead the determination of sexual maturity on a case-by-case basis by a qualified (forensic) medical expert. Healey, *Homosexual Desire,* 116–22.

12. Vasilevskii, *K zdorovomu,* 26; Dr. S. A. Protoklitov, *Chto dolzhna znat' devushka* (Moscow and Leningrad: Gos. izd., 1930), 16–17.

13. Lass, *Zdorovaia polovaia zhizn'*, 13–14; Lemberg, *Chto neobkhodimo znat'*, 7, 36; Karov, *Chto dolzhny znat' muzhchina i zhenshchina*, 20.

14. Feigin, *Chto takoe normal'naia*, 13; Rozenblium, *Kakoe znachenie imeet*, 21.

15. V. E. Dembskaia, *Polovaia gigiena zhenshchiny* (Leningrad: Leningradskaia pravda, 1929), 10.

16. Glezer, *Polovaia zhizn'*, 39.

17. V. Kashkadamov, "Gigiena perioda polovogo sozrevaniia," *Gigiena i zdorov'e* 4 (1923): 10; Uspenskii, *O vrede*, 48; Vasilevskii, *K zdorovomu*, 30–31.

18. Glezer, *Polovaia zhizn'*, 39–41; Kashkadamov, "Gigiena perioda polovogo sozrevaniia," 10.

19. Lass, *Zdorovaia polovaia zhizn'*, 15; Ivanovskii, *Polovaia zhizn'*, 23.

20. Dr. M. F. Levi, "Polovaia zhizn' v brake i vne braka," *Za novyi byt* 19–20 (1928): 19.

21. Kaminskii, *Polovaia zhizn'*, 22.

22. Vasilevskii, *Polovoe zdorov'e*, 28–29.

23. Levi, "Polovaia zhizn' v brake i vne braka," 19; Vasilevskii, *Polovoe zdorov'e*, 29.

24. Rozenblium, *Kakoe znachenie imeet*, 50.

25. Naiman, *Sex in Public*, ch. 7. On hooliganism, see Gorsuch, *Youth in Revolutionary Russia*, esp. ch. 8.

26. Kaminskii, *Polovaia zhizn'*, 21–22; Vasilevskii, *Polovoe zdorov'e*, 17; Uzhanskii, *Ob onanizme*, 4; Iakobzon, *Onanizm*, 3.

27. Lass, *Zdorovaia polovaia zhizn'*, 17; Kaminskii, *Polovaia zhizn'*, 22.

28. Rozenblium, *Kakoe znachenie imeet*, 19; Vasilevskii, *K zdorovomu*, 26.

29. Engelstein, *Keys to Happiness*, 227–28, 237. Because the young (both boys and girls) and women, in addition to the adult men on whose behavior earlier codes of sexual ethics had focused, could so easily engage in this pleasurable activity, Thomas W. Laqueur has labeled masturbation "the first truly democratic sexuality." *Solitary Sex: A Cultural History of Masturbation* (New York: Zone Books, 2003), 18.

30. GARF, f. A579, op. 1, d. 861, l. 27.

31. Ibid., l. 27ob.

32. O. Feigin, *Vazhneishie nenormal'nosti polovoi zhizni* (Leningrad: Izd. avtora, 1927), 28; Lass, *Zdorovaia polovaia zhizn'*, 40; Glezer, *Polovaia zhizn'*, 41.

33. N. F. Al'tgauzen, A. Iu. Lur'e, and E. P. Melent'eva, *Besedy s devushkami o materinstve i mladenchestve* (Moscow and Leningrad: GMI, 1929), 82–83.

34. Dr. M. Z. Shpak, *Polovaia zhizn' zhenshchiny* (Odessa: Svetoch, 1927), 22.

35. Iakobzon, *Onanizm*, 8; Lass, *Zdorovaia polovaia zhizn'*, 17–18.

36. Ivanovskii, *Polovaia zhizn'*, 24; Uzhanskii, *Ob onanizme*, 8.

37. M. F. Levi, "Besplodnye braki," *Za novyi byt* 10 (1927): 16–17; M. F. Levi, "Gigiena braka," *Za novyi byt* 23–24 (1928): 17; Mendel'son, "O preduprezhdenii detskogo onanizma," *Gigiena i zdorov'e* 24 (1930): 11.

38. Iakobzon, *Onanizm*, 26; also Shpak, *Polovaia zhizn' zhenshchiny*, 22.

39. Uspenskii, *Polovaia zhizn'*, 95; Al'tgauzen et al., *Besedy s devushkami*, 83.

40. Anonymous, *Onania, or the heinous sin of self-pollution and all its frightful consequences (in both sexes) considered, with physical and spiritual advice to those who have already injured themselves by this abominable practice* (London: n.p., 1710[?]). Paula Bennett and Vernon A. Rosario II, eds., *Solitary Pleasures: The Historical, Literary, and Artistic Discourses of Autoeroticism* (New York and London: Routledge, 1995), esp. introduction; Lesley A. Hall, "Forbidden by God, Despised by Men: Masturbation, Medical Warnings, Moral Panic, and Manhood in Great Britain, 1850–1950," in *Forbidden History: The State, Society, and the Regulation of Sexuality in Modern Europe*, ed. John Fout (Chicago and London: University of Chicago Press, 1992), 293–315.

41. B. Sigal, "Polovaia zhizn' nashei molodezhi," *Gigiena i zdorov'e* 16.32 (1924): 2.

42. Uzhanskii, *Ob onanizme*, 8; Rozenblium, *Kakoe znachenie imeet*, 19.

43. Vasilevskii, *Polovoe zdorov'e,* 19–20; B. V. Tsukker, *Voprosy polovoi zhizni rabochei molodezhi* (Khar'kov: Kosmos, 1927), 18. Perhaps surprisingly, given the growing emphasis on surveillance during these years, the medical concern with masturbation as encouraging an uncontrollable erotic imagination is absent in the Soviet sources.

44. Feigin, *Vazhneishie nenormal'nosti,* 28; Al'tgauzen et al., *Besedy s devushkami,* 83.

45. Vasilevskii, *K zdorovomu,* 27. All of the incidents of indoctrination cited involve males only, suggesting that, as with nervousness, male public behavior is of greater therapeutic concern.

46. Laqueur, *Solitary Sex,* 210.

47. GARF, f. A579, op. 1, d. 861, ll. 27ob–28.

48. A. Mendel'son, "Ranniaia polovaia zhizn' ili vozderzhanie," *Gigiena i zdorov'e* 4 (1928): 8.

49. Rozenblium, *Kakoe znachenie imeet,* 22.

50. Dr. E. Zalutskaia, "Vred rannikh brakov," *Zhenskii zhurnal* 9 (1929): 20.

51. L. M. Vasilevskii, *Gigiena molodoi devushki* (Moscow: Novaia Moskva, 1926), 10.

52. Mendel'son, "Ranniaia polovaia zhizn'," 8; Lemberg, *Chto neobkhodimo znat',* 36.

53. Al'tgauzen et al., *Besedy s devushkami,* 69; I. K. Akimova, "O vrede rannikh brakov i rannei polovoi zhizni," *Okhrana materinstva i mladenchestva* 3–4 (1929): 10.

54. GARF, f. A579, op. 1, d. 861, l. 28.

55. Ibid., l. 28ob.

56. Lemberg, *Chto neobkhodimo znat',* 36.

57. Rozenblium, *Kakoe znachenie imeet,* 7; Donichev, *Zdorovaia i nezdorovaia,* 38; Feigin, *Chto takoe normal'naia,* 10.

58. Kalmanson, "Iz doklada na dispute," 4; Donichev, *Zdorovaia i nezdorovaia,* 38; S. V. Nikulin, "Onanizm, ego prichiny i bor'ba s nim," in Kalmanson, *Polovoi vopros,* 176.

59. Feigin, *Chto takoe normal'naia,* 14.

60. Kashkadamov, "Gigiena perioda polovogo sozrevaniia," 10; Sigal, *Polovoi vopros,* 48–49.

61. Prof. R. M. Fronshtein, "Vliianie polovogo vozderzhaniia na organizm," *Vrachebnoe delo* 12–14 (1925): 1009–11.

62. Golomb, *Polovaia zhizn',* 30; Rozenblium, *Kakoe znachenie imeet,* 24.

63. Rozenblium, *Kakoe znachenie imeet,* 14.

64. Feigin, *Chto takoe normal'naia,* 14.

65. M. F. Levi, "Vliianie polovogo vozderzhaniia na organizm," *Za novyi byt* 13–14 (1928): 22; Mendel'son, "Krainosti polovoi zhizni," *Gigiena i zdorov've* 6 (1923): 5.

66. Uspenskii, *O vrede,* 48.

67. Mendel'son, "O preduprezhdenii," 12; Bruk, *Chto takoe polovoe vlechenie,* 90.

68. Rozenblium, *Kakoe znachenie imeet,* 23; Karov, *Chto dolzhny znat' muzhchina i zhenshchina,* 15.

69. Lemberg, *Chto neobkhodimo znat',* 34–35; Lass, *Zdorovaia polovaia zhizn',* 24; Mendel'son, "Krainosti," 3.

70. Feigin, *Vazhneishie nenormal'nosti,* 23–24; Lemberg, *Chto neobkhodimo znat',* 38.

71. Mendel'son, *Nervnaia sistema,* 21–22; Feigin, *Chto takoe normal'naia,* 14. Quotes from Levi, "Vliianie polovogo vozderzhaniia," 22.

72. Uspenskii, *Polovaia zhizn',* 85–86; Bruk, *Chto takoe polovoe vlechenie,* 89.

73. Timofeev, *Kuda dolzhna napravliat'sia,* 37.

74. For the history of Soviet physical culture, see Irina Makoveeva, "Soviet Sports as a Cultural Phenomenon: Body and/or Intellect," *Studies in Slavic Cultures* 3 (July 2002): 9–32; James Riordan, *Sport in Soviet Society: The Development of Sport and Physical Education in Russia and the USSR* (Cambridge and New York: Cambridge University Press, 1977), esp. chs. 3–4; Robert Edelman, *Serious Fun: A History of Spectator Sports in the USSR* (New York: Oxford University Press, 1993), ch. 2; Frances Bernstein, "'What Everyone Should Know about Sex': Gender, Sexual Enlightenment, and the Politics of Health in Revolutionary Russia, 1918–1931" (PhD diss., Columbia University, 1998), 269–97; F. Samoukov, ed., *Istoriia fizicheskoi kul'tury* (Moscow, 1964).

75. Harvey Green, *Fit for America: Health, Fitness, Sport, and American Society* (New York: Pantheon, 1986), esp. ch. 9. Russian *fizkul'tura* advocates were not alone in their hostility toward competitive sports and "record-breaking." For Germany and France, see John M. Hoberman, "The Early Development of Sports Medicine in Germany," in *Sport and Exercise Science: Essays in the History of Sports Medicine*, ed. Jack W. Berryman and Roberta J. Park (Urbana and Chicago: University of Illinois, 1992), 245–46; Robert Nye, *Crime, Madness, and Politics in Modern France* (Princeton, N.J.: Princeton University Press, 1984), 325. On the *turnen* movement of nineteenth-century Germany, an important though unacknowledged precursor to the politicized vision of *fizkul'tura* advocated in the Soviet Union, see J. G. Dixon, "Prussia: Politics and Physical Education," in *Landmarks in the History of Physical Education*, ed. J. G. Dixon, P. C. McIntosh, A. D. Munrow, and R. F. Willetts (London: Routledge and Kegan Paul, 1957), 107–48.

76. Vasilevskii, *K zdorovomu*, 30; Semashko, *Puti sovetskoi fizkul'tury*, 56; B. A. Ivanovskii, *Sovetskaia meditsina i fizkul'tura* (Moscow: GMI, 1928), 33; Ivanovskii, *Polovaia zhizn'*, 32.

77. Moiseev, "Polovoi vopros i fizkul'tura," 31; B. F. Tsukker, *Fizkul'tura byta i polovoi vopros* (Khar'kov: Kosmos, 1927), 33, 38.

78. Feigin, *Chto takoe normal'naia*, 13.

79. Ivanovskii, *Polovaia zhizn'*, 18.

80. Kaminskii, *Polovaia zhizn'*, 18.

81. Uspenskii, *Polovaia zhizn'*, 87, 88. Ironically, one of the reasons given for Pushkin's self-imposed abstinence was a bout of venereal disease that resulted from his unrestrained sex life.

82. Rozenblium, *Kakoe znachenie imeet*, 19; Ivanovskii, *Polovaia zhizn'*, 15.

83. Feigin, *Chto takoe normal'naia*, 14 (quote); Golomb, *Polovaia zhizn'*, 30.

84. Karov, *Chto dolzhny znat' muzhchina i zhenshchina*, 9, 14; Bruk, *Chto takoe polovoe vlechenie*, 90.

85. Feigin, *Chto takoe normal'naia*, 13; Berman, "Garmoniia polovoi zhizni," 72–89; Mendel'son, "Ranniaia polovaia zhizn'," 6.

86. Ivanovskii, *Polovaia zhizn'*, 20; Semashko, "Voprosy polovogo vospitaniia," 22; Bruk, *Chto takoe polovoe vlechenie*, 69.

87. Uspenskii, *Polovaia zhizn'*, 89; Lass, *Zdorovaia polovaia zhizn'*, 5–6.

88. Faingol'd, *Polovoe sozrevanie*, 30; Glezer, *Polovaia zhizn'*, 39; Bruk, *Chto takoe polovoe vlechenie*, 91.

89. Ia. Lifshits, "Pravda o polovoi zhizni molodezhi," *Put' k zdorov'iu* 7–8 (1926): 9. All quotations in the following paragraphs are from this page.

6—Doctors without Boudoirs

1. Angus McLaren, *Twentieth-Century Sexuality: A History* (Oxford: Blackwell, 1999), ch. 3; Atina Grossmann, "The New Woman and the Rationalization of Sexuality in Weimar Germany," in *Powers of Desire: The Politics of Sexuality*, ed. Ann Snitow, Christine Stansell, and Sharon Thompson (New York: Monthly Review Press, 1983), 39–51; Porter and Hall, *Facts of Life*, ch. 9.

2. For instance, Max Hodann, a number of whose pamphlets were published in the USSR during this era, visited in 1927 and lectured at the Institute of Social Hygiene. GARF, f. A482, op. 10, d. 1496, l. 47ob.

3. Hoffmann, *Stalinist Values*, 120–23; Robert Service, *Lenin: A Political Life* (Bloomington and Indianapolis: Indiana University Press, 1985), 1:193. According to Gor'kii, Lenin claimed to be so affected by the beauty of Beethoven's *Appassionata* that, when listening to it, he forgot that violence was a necessary part of creating a new political order. G. N. Golikov et al., eds., *Vospominaniia o V. I. Lenine* (Moscow: Politizdat, 1968–1969), 2:161. For the mistrust of pleasure in other areas of expert advice during the 1920s, see Kelly, *Refining Russia*, esp. 268–71.

4. Uspenskii, *Polovaia zhizn'*, 54.

5. Lass, *Zdorovaia polovaia zhizn'*, 30–31. This assessment does not differ significantly from Kollontai's position; one gets the feeling that few of her ideological opponents actually read her work.

6. Lemberg, *Chto neobkhodimo znat'*, 24–27.

7. Dr. Bernatskii, "Chto nuzhno znat', vybiraia muzha i zheny," *Gigiena i zdorov'e* 15 (1928): 2; A. M. Mamutov, *Gigiena polovoi zhizni zhenshchiny* (Khar'kov: Kosmos, 1927), 4; Timofeev, *V chem proiavliaetsia*, 43.

8. Vasilevskii, *Polovoe zdorov'e*, 21–22.

9. Dr. A. Iu. Lur'e, *Gigiena devochki, devushki, zhenshchiny* (Moscow: Okhmatmlad, 1927), 17. Lur'e repeats this argument in a second publication, geared for the medical community rather than the public, identifying the British author Marie Carmichael Stopes as one of the many other educators who subscribed to this theory. Stopes was indeed a scientist, but her degree was in paleobotany, a fact Lur'e neglects to mention. Dr. A. Iu. Lur'e, *Metody raboty konsul'tatsii dlia zhenshchin* (Moscow and Leningrad: GMI, 1930), 68.

10. Berman, "Garmoniia polovoi zhizni," 82.

11. Uspenskii, *Polovaia zhizn'*, 32, 54; N. Mikulina-Ivanova, "Normal'naia i nenormal'naia polovaia zhizn' zhenshchiny," *Zhenskii zhurnal* 9 (1927): 14.

12. Feigin, *Chto takoe normal'naia*, 9.

13. Mendel'son, "Krainosti," 6–7.

14. Dembskaia, *Polovaia gigiena zhenshchiny*, 16; Uspenskii, *Polovaia zhizn'*, 49.

15. Vasilevskii, *K zdorovomu*, 34 (quote); Berman, "Garmoniia polovoi zhizni," 82.

16. Dr. N. Mikulina-Ivanova, "Polovaia zhizn' zhenshchiny," *Zhenskii zhurnal* 7 (1926): 18; Mikulina-Ivanova, "Normal'naia i nenormal'naia" 9 (1927): 15.

17. Vasilevskii, *Polovoe zdorov'e*, 35.

18. T. I. Iudin, *Zdorov'e, brak i sem'ia* (Moscow: Narkomzdrav, 1928), 37; Rozenblium, *Kakoe znachenie imeet*, 57.

19. I. G. Burlakov, *Kak dolzhny zhit' muzh s zhenoi* (Khar'kov: Nauchnaia mysl', 1929), 20; Donichev, *Zdorovaia i nezdorovaia*, 71–72.

20. Vasilevskii, *Polovoe zdorov'e*, 35.

21. "Ne zabyvaite," *Put' k zdorov'iu* 7–8 (1926): inside front cover.

22. Burlakov, *Kak dolzhny zhit'*, 19; Mikulina-Ivanova, "Polovaia zhizn' zhenshchiny," 18; Mikulina-Ivanova, "Normal'naia i nenormal'naia polovaia zhizn'," 9 (1927): 14.

23. Feigin, *Chto takoe normal'naia*, 22; Golomb, *Polovaia zhizn'*, 25; Lur'e, *Gigiena devochki*, 28; Dembskaia, *Polovaia gigiena zhenshchiny*, 20.

24. Berman, "Garmoniia polovoi zhizni," 84 (quote); Dr. N. Mikulina-Ivanova, "Preduprezhdenie beremennosti," *Zhenskii zhurnal* 6 (1926): 34; Donichev, *Zdorovaia i nezdorovaia*, 81; Bruk, *Chto takoe polovoe vlechenie*, 86.

25. Goldman, *Women, the State, and Revolution*, ch. 7.

26. E. N. Fedotova, "Preduprezhdenie beremennosti," *Put' k zdorov'iu* 7–8 (1926): 22; M. F. Levi, "Abort i bor'ba s nim," *Za novyi byt* 22 (1926): 14; M. F. Levi, "Protivozachatochnye sredstva," *Za novyi byt* 10 (1927): 14.

27. Prof. P. I. Liublinskii, "Protivozachatochnye sovety i okhrana materinstva," *Leningradskii meditsinskii zhurnal* 6 (1926): 62. According to Susan Solomon, demographic issues figured prominently in medical resistance to contraception; opposition to abortion centered on concerns for women's health. "The Demographic Argument in Soviet Debates over the Legalization of Abortion in the 1920s," *Cahiers du Monde Russe et Soviétique* 2 (1992): 59–82. In popular medical sex education, the issue of physical danger was foremost in discussions of both contraception and abortion; anxiety about the birthrate was voiced by only a few authors.

28. Donichev, *Zdorovaia i nezdorovaia*, 81; Dr. N. Mikulina-Ivanova, "Besplodie zhenshchiny: Mery preduprezhdeniia beremennosti," *Zhenskii zhurnal* 9 (1927): 18.

29. Dr. O. Feigin, *Abort i preduprezhdenie beremennosti* (Leningrad: Izd. avtora, 1927), 14; M. Z. Shpak, *Preduprezhdenie beremennosti* (Odessa: Svetoch, 1927), 28. For the individual methods under consideration, see Bernstein, "'What Everyone Should Know about Sex'," 363–74; Thomas, "International Intercourse," ch. 4.

30. Fedotova, "Preduprezhdenie beremennosti," 22–23.

31. Professor Khanzhinskii, "Abort i besplodie," *Put' k zdorov'iu* 3 (1927): 10.

32. Mamutov, *Gigiena polovoi zhizni zhenshchiny,* 31; Feigin, *Abort,* 8; L. A. Gabinov, "Abort (iskusstvennyi vykidysh)," *Put' k zdorov'iu* 3.6 (1926): 7.

33. A. Gens, "Abort-sotsial'noe zlo," *Meditsina* 7 (1927): 11. The idea of a woman's right to control her fertility was entirely absent in the medical literature; only women activists such as Inessa Armand and Nadezhda Krupskaia voiced this argument. Wood, *Baba and the Comrade,* 107–8; Solomon, "Soviet Legalization of Abortion," 460.

34. Vasilevskii, *K zdorovomu,* 73.

35. *Gigiena i zdorov'e rabochego i ego sem'i* (Stalingrad, 1925), 27. Given the political climate, opposition to abortion on moral grounds was extremely rare. I encountered only one such example: L. G. Lichkus, "Kak predokhranit' sebia ot beremennosti," *Gigiena i zdorov'e* 12 (1925): 2.

36. Rozenblium, *Kakoe znachenie imeet,* 62; Karov, *Chto dolzhny znat' muzhchina i zhenshchina,* 30; M. Z. Shpak, *Abort, ego posledstviia, i mery ego preduprezhdeniia* (Odessa: Svetoch, 1926), 4.

37. L. A. and L. M. Vasilevskie, *Abort kak sotsial'noe iavlenie* (Moscow and Leningrad: Izd. L. D. Frenkel', 1924), 112; Gens, "Abort-sotsial'noe zlo," 11; Khanzhinskii, "Abort i besplodie," 10.

38. Al'tgauzen et al., *Besedy s devushkami,* 96.

39. Glezer, *Polovaia zhizn',* 44; Fedotova, "Preduprezhdenie beremennosti," 23; Lichkus, "Kak predokhranit'," 2; Shpak, *Preduprezhdenie beremennosti,* 3–4.

40. Feigin, *Abort,* 6–7. See the illustration with the caption "One of the most serious complications during an abortion," in Al'tgauzen et al., *Besedy s devushkami,* 97.

41. Rozenblium, *Kakoe znachenie imeet,* 62; Levi, "Protivozachatochnye sredstva," 13; Protoklitov, *Chto dolzhna znat' devushka,* 29–30; Feigin, *Abort,* 6.

42. Al'tgauzen et al., *Besedy s devushkami,* 95.

43. Shpak, *Abort,* 8, 11.

44. Donichev, *Zdorovaia i nezdorovaia,* 77; Dembskaia, *Polovaia gigiena zhenshchiny,* 7–8.

45. Karov, *Chto dolzhny znat' muzhchina i zhenshchina,* 31; Mamutov, *Gigiena polovoi zhizni zhenshchiny,* 25; Iudin, *Zdorov'e, brak i sem'ia,* 37; Feigin, *Chto takoe normal'naia,* 15.

46. Al'tgauzen et al., *Besedy s devushkami,* 95. While the decision to recriminalize abortion was taken in 1934, it was not put into effect until 1936, codified in the "Stalin" constitution of that year. Goldman, *Women, the State, and Revolution,* 331–36.

47. A. Mendel'son, "Brachnyi vybor," *Gigiena i zdorov'e* 17–18 (1930): 13.

48. "Vstupaiushchim v brak," *Gigiena i zdorov'e* 16.23 (1924): 12, first printed in *Venerologiia i dermatologiia* 2 (1924).

49. Mark Adams, *The Wellborn Science: Eugenics in Germany, France, Brazil, and Russia* (New York: Oxford University Press, 1990), 153–216; Loren Graham, "Science and Values: The Eugenics Movement in Germany and Russia in the 1920s," *American Historical Review* 83 (1977): 1135–64.

50. Adams, *Wellborn Science,* 167, 176–77.

51. Graham, "Science and Values," 1147–50; Paul Weindling, "German-Soviet Cooperation in Science: The Case of the Laboratory for Racial Research, 1931–1938," *Nuncius: Annali di Storia della Scienza* 1.2 (1986): 103–9.

52. Graham, "Science and Values," 1152, 1155–56.

53. Adams, *Wellborn Science,* 182–83, 185; Graham, "Science and Values," 1156; G. A. Batkis, "Evgenika," *Bol'shaia sovetskaia entsiklopediia* (Moscow: Sovetskaia entsiklopediia, 1931), 23: 812–19.

54. Mark B. Adams, "Eugenics as Social Medicine in Revolutionary Russia: Prophets, Patrons, and the Dialectics of Discipline-Building," in Solomon and Hutchinson, *Health and Society,* 200–201.

55. Martin Pernick describes a similarly flexible interpretation of eugenics at work in early twentieth-century America, as evidenced in the eugenic, pro-euthanasia commercial film *The Black Stork.* Martin S. Pernick, *The Black Stork: Eugenics and the Death of "Defective" Babies in American Medicine and Motion Pictures since 1915* (New York and Oxford: Oxford University Press, 1996), esp. ch. 3.

56. See David Joravsky's discussion in *The Lysenko Affair* (Cambridge: Harvard University Press, 1971), 261–62.

57. N. Mikulina-Ivanova, "Brak i evgenika: O kontrole nad zdorov'em lits, vstupaiushchikh v brak," *Zhenskii zhurnal* 1 (1929): 22; T., "Obshchestvenno-nauchnyi podkhod k materinstvu," *Zhenskii zhurnal* 7 (1927): 13.

58. P. Rokitskii, "Evgenika i brak," *Zhenskii zhurnal* 6 (1930): 18.

59. Rozenblium, *Kakoe znachenie imeet,* 70.

60. Iudin, *Zdorov'e, brak i sem'ia,* 24; Vasilevskii, *K zdorovomu,* 88, 93, 103; Levi, "Gigiena braka," 17–18; Glezer, *Polovaia zhizn',* 46, 50. As with venereal disease, the battle against tuberculosis and alcoholism generated widespread public health and propaganda campaigns. See Kate Transchel, *Under the Influence: Working-Class Drink, Temperance, and Cultural Revolution in Russia, 1895–1932* (Pittsburgh, Pa.: Pittsburgh University Press, 2006); Laura A. Phillips, *Bolsheviks and the Bottle: Drink and Worker Culture in St. Petersburg, 1900–1929* (DeKalb: Northern Illinois University Press, 2000); Michael David, "The White Plague in the Red Capital: Tuberculosis and Its Control in Moscow and the RSFSR, 1900–1941" (PhD diss., University of Chicago, in preparation).

61. Mikulina-Ivanova, "Brak i evgenika," 22; Feigin, *Chto takoe normal'naia,* 21; Karov, *Chto dolzhny znat' muzhchina i zhenshchina,* 24.

62. Mamutov, *Gigiena polovoi zhizni zhenshchiny,* 13; Mendel'son, "Brachnyi vybor," 13. Aside from such cursory discussions, infertility becomes an issue in sexual enlightenment only when it has developed "unnaturally": as a result of either untreated venereal disease, the use of hazardous birth control methods, or the consequence of frequent or botched abortions.

63. Bernatskii, "Chto nuzhno znat'," 3.

64. Iudin, *Zdorov'e, brak i sem'ia,* 30–31; Adams, *Wellborn Science,* 174–76; Dr. N. Mikulina-Ivanova, "Oplodotvorenie i nasledstvennost'," *Zhenshkii zhurnal* 1 (1927): 14; Vasilevskii, *K zdorovomu,* 106; Shpak, *Preduprezhdenie beremennosti,* 30.

65. Iudin, *Zdorov'e, brak i sem'ia,* 31–32. The full text can be found in *Sobranie kodeksov (Kodeks zakonov o brake, sem'e i opeke),* 630, 646 (Moscow: Iuridicheskoe izdatel'stvo NKIU SSSR, 1937), 132.

66. Rokitskii, "Evgenika i brak," 18; Mendel'son, "Brachnyi vybor," 13; L. S. Gurvich, "Organy zdravookhraneniia i ZAGSy," *Zhurnal po izucheniiu rannego detskogo vozrasta* 7 (1929): 582; *Sobranie kodeksov (Kodeks zakonov o brake, sem'e i opeke),* 646.

67. GARF, f. A482, op. 1, d. 122, ch. 1, ll. 106–11; d. 174, ch. 1, ll. 501–501ob; d. 176, ll. 338–39; d. 176, l. 724.

68 Romanov, "O medosvidetel'stvovanii brachushchikhsia," *Biulleten' Narkomzdrava* 6 (1925): 13.

69. "Rezoliutsii pervogo vserossiiskogo s"ezda," 12–13; "Rezoliutsii, priniatye vtorym vsesoiuznym s"ezdom po bor'be s venericheskimi bolezniami, sostoiavshimsia v Khar'kove 13–19 maia 1925," *Venerologiia i dermatologiia* 3 (1925): 170.

70. Even worse, perhaps, was another writer's concern that the introduction of mandatory examinations would drive couples from civil back to religious ceremonies. Rozenblium, *Kakoe znachenie imeet,* 43.

71. V. M. Bronner, "K voprosy o meditsinskom osvidetel'stvovanii brachushchikhsia," *Biulleten' Narkomzdrava* 6 (1925): 13–14.

72. Rokitskii, "Evgenika i brak," 18; Lifshits, "Zakon o brake," 5; "Ne zabyvaite," inside front cover.

73. Iudin, *Zdorov'e, brak i sem'ia*, 30.

74. Al'tgauzen et al., *Besedy s devushkami*, 81; Feigin, *Chto takoe normal'naia*, 20; also Karov, *Chto dolzhny znat' muzhchina i zhenshchina*, 21; Burlakov, *Kak dolzhny zhit'*, 8.

75. Mikulina-Ivanova, "Oplodotvorenie i nasledstvennost,'" 14.

76. Rozenblium, *Kakoe znachenie imeet*, 67; Mikulina-Ivanova, "Oplodotvorenie i nasledstvennost'," 15.

77. Mikulina-Ivanova, "Brak i evgenika," 23.

78. Ibid.

79. Rokitskii, "Evgenika i brak," 18; Vasilevskii, *K zdorovomu*, 87; Burlakov, *Kak dolzhny zhit'*, 8.

80. "Postanovleniia VTsIK i SNK RSFSR ot 24/I-1927 goda, 'O merakh bor'by s venericheskimi bolezniami,'" republished in N. L. Rossiianskii, *Dispanserizatsiia v bor'be s venericheskimi bolezniami* (Moscow: Izd. NKZ RSFSR, 1928), 263–64.

81. "Instruktsiia o poriadke primeneniia postanovleniia VTsIK i SNK RSFSR ot 24/I-1927 goda, 'O merax bor'by s venericheskimi bolezniami,'" republished in Rossiianskii, *Dispanserizatsiia*, 264–66. For an extensive assessment of the article's and resolution's application, based on several years of practical experience, see Bychkov and Isaev, *Ugolovnaia otvetstvennost'*, pt. 2.

82. Rossiianskii, *Dispanserizatsiia*, chs. 4, 12; N. Semashko, "O vrachebnoi taine," *Biulleten' NKZ* 11 (1925): 12.

83. Rossiianskii, *Dispanserizatsiia*, 68–69, 257. I. M. Okun', "Sovremennoe zakonodatel'stvo v oblasti bor'by s venericheskimi zabolevaniiami i prostitutsieu." *Venerologiia i dermatologiia* 6 (1928): 986.

84. *Sobranie kodeksov (Ugolovnyi kodeks)*, 690, 698.

Conclusion

1. Z. Gurevich, "Polovoi vopros," in *Bol'shaia meditsinskaia entsiklopediia*, 1st ed. (Moscow: OGIZ RSFSR, 1933), 26: 313.

2. Eliot Borenstein, "'About That': Deploying and Deploring Sex in Post-Soviet Russia," *Studies in Twentieth-Century Literature* 24.1 (Winter 2000): 54; Igor S. Kon, *Seksual'naia kul'tura v Rossii: Klubnichka na berezke* (Moscow: OGI, 1997), 1.

3. These include Mendel'son, "Gigiena polovoi zhizni," *Gigiena i zdorov'e* 2 (1935): 6; 3 (1935): 6–7.

4. N. A. Torsuev, *Venericheskie bolezni i bor'ba s nimi* (Gor'kii: Gor'kovskoe izdatel'stvo, 1935).

5. Adams, *Wellborn Science*, 184; Graham, "Science and Values," 1154.

6. Adams, *Wellborn Science*, 184.

7. Solomon, "Social Hygiene," 189–90.

8. Ibid., 192, 199.

9. Unpublished interview with Semashko's widow conducted by Mark Borisovich Mirskii, the director of the Department of the History of Medicine at the Semashko Institute of Social Hygiene, Economics, and the Administration of Public Health.

10. "Ot redaktsii," *Venerologiia i dermatologiia* 1 (1931): 1.

11. GARF, Kniga prikazov po GVI, 9.X.29–30.IX.31, ll. 235, 236.

12. Ibid., l. 306.

13. V. M. Bronner, "Po novomu rabotat'," *Sovetskii vestnik venerologii i dermatologii* 3–4 (1932): 6.

14. "Ot redaktsii," *Sovetskii vestnik venerologii i dermatologii* 1–2 (1932): 1–2; Bronner, "Po novomu rabotat'," 1–12. For the most extensive attack on social venereology and on Bronner in particular for his leadership role, see Ia. I. Lifshits, "Zadachi rekonstruktsii sotsial'noi venerologii," *Sovetskii vestnik venerologii i dermatologii* 6 (1932): 1–23 (quote: 9).

15. GARF, f. A482, op. 24, d. 517, l. 141. For Zdravomyslov and Semashko, see Chapter 1.

16. Bronner was rehabilitated on April 28, 1956, at the initiative of his daughter, B. V. Bronner. I am extremely grateful to her for sharing his rehabilitation documents with me.

17. N. A. Kriachko, *Fizicheskaia kul'tura* (Moscow: Fizkul'tura i Sport, 1948), 29–31.

18. V. Vnukov, "Reshaiushchie zven'ia v okhrane zdorov'ia kadrov," *Revoliutsiia i kul'tura* 4 (1930): 40, 42.

19. N. I. Propper, "Itogi diskussii na estestvenno-nauchnom fronte i bor'ba na dva fronta v meditsine," *Zhurnal nevropatologii i psikhiatrii* 5 (1931): 7–18 (13, 15).

20. See also Joravsky's discussion of the Vnukov and Propper articles in *Russian Psychology*, ch. 12.

21. Miller, *Freud and the Bolsheviks*, 103–4, 198n21.

22. Semashko, "Na putiakh k novomu bytu," 3.

23. Timofeev, *Kuda dolzhna napravliat'sia*, 25, 27; Semashko, "Voprosy polovogo vospitaniia," 21–22.

24. Healey, *Homosexual Desire*, 174–75.

25. Lebina and Shkarovskii, *Prostitutsiia*, 153–63; Stites, *Women's Liberation Movement*, 405; Healey, *Homosexual Desire*, 185.

26. GARF, f. 2306, op. 69, d. 2291, ll. 49–67. This scandal occurred in a climate of increasingly brutal political conflicts within the educational sector, and many of the supposed ringleaders were children of leading Party and school officials. My thanks to Mark Johnson for telling me abut the case. See his "Russian Educators, the Stalinist Party-State, and the Politics of Soviet Education, 1929–1939" (PhD diss., Columbia University, 1995), 336–37.

27. Goldman, *Women, the State, and Revolution,* 331; Peter H. Solomon Jr., *Soviet Criminal Justice under Stalin* (Cambridge: Cambridge University Press, 1996), 212. David Hoffmann has shown that such pronatalist policies were pursued across Europe at this time in countries ranging from democratic to fascist, indicative of a "new type of population politics practiced in the modern era" that relied heavily on "state management of reproduction." David L. Hoffmann, "Mothers in the Motherland: Stalinist Pronatalism in Its Pan-European Context," *Journal of Social History* (Fall 2000): 35–54.

28. Healey, *Homosexual Desire*, 197–98.

29. See also Hoffmann, *Stalinist Values,* 107.

30. *Rabotnitsa i krest'ianka* 12 (1936): 2, cited in Hoffmann, "Mothers in the Motherland," 44.

31. Rebecca Balmas Neary, "Mothering Socialist Society: The Wife-Activists' Movement and the Soviet Culture of Daily Life, 1934–1941," *Russian Review* 58 (1999): 396–412; also Sheila Fitzpatrick, *The Cultural Front* (Ithaca: Cornell University Press, 1992), 216–37; Mary Buckley, "The Untold Story of *Obshchestvennitsa* in the 1930s," *Europe-Asia Studies* 48.4 (1996): 569–86.

32. Hoffmann, *Stalinist Values,* 105.

33. Semashko, "Nevezhestvo i pornografiia," 3.

34. Private conversation with Dr. Georgii Vladimirovich Arkhangel'skii, a Moscow psychoneurologist who attended the State Medical Publishers' meeting when the decision was made to publish a book on sexual hygiene.

Bibliography

Archival Sources

Archive of the "Medical Museum" Scientific Research Center of the Russian Academy of Medical Sciences (NITs "Meditsinskii muzei" RAMN): Poster and Photograph Collection.

Archive of the Semashko Institute of Social Hygiene, Economics, and the Administration of Public Health: Personal file of N. A. Semashko.

Moscow State Municipal Archive (GMAM): f. 2194, Institute for Methods of Work in the Schools.

State Archive of the Russian Federation (GARF; formerly TsGA RSFSR): f. A482, People's Commissariat of Public Health; f. A579, Personal file of G. A. Batkis; f. 2306, People's Commissariat of Enlightenment.

State Archive of the Russian Federation (GARF; formerly TsGAOR): f. 9636, Institute of Sanitary Culture; State Venereological Institute (GVI) Register of Directives, 1929–1930.

Published Primary Sources

Akimova, I. K. "O vrede rannikh brakov i rannei polovoi zhizni." *Okhrana materinstva i mladenchestva* 3–4 (1929): 8–11.

Al'tgauzen, N. F., A. Iu. Lur'e, and E. P. Melent'eva. *Besedy s devushkami o materinstve i mladenchestve.* Moscow and Leningrad: GMI, 1929.

Aroni, M. A. *Kak voznikaet i razvivaetsia chelovecheskii zarodysh. Obshchedostupnoe izlozhenie v sviazi s gigienoi beremennosti.* Khar'kov: Kosmos, 1926.

Bakaleinikov, P. G. *Polovoe znanie.* Leningrad: Izd. avtora, 1927.

Barreca, Regina, ed. *Desire and Imagination: Classic Essays in Sexuality.* New York: Meridian/Penguin, 1995.

Batkis, G. A. "Evgenika." *Bol'shaia sovetskaia entsiklopediia.* 1st ed. Vol. 23, 812–19. Moscow: Sovetskaia entsiklopediia, 1931.

———. "Polovoe vospitanie i prosveshchenie v usloviiakh sovetskogo stroia." *Venerologiia i dermatologiia* 6 (1925): 193–94.

———. "Soderzhanie i metody vneshkol'noi raboty po polovomu prosveshcheniiu." *Sotsial'naia gigiena* 6 (1925): 146–48.

Beard, George Miller. *American Nervousness: Its Causes and Consequences.* New York: G. P. Putnam's Sons, 1881.

———. "Neurasthenia, or Nervous Exhaustion." *Boston Medical and Surgical Journal* 3 (1869): 217–21.

Bekhterev, V. M. "Ob izvrashchenii i uklonenii polovogo vlecheniia." In Zelenin, *Polovoi vopros v svete nauchnogo znaniia,* 293–325.

———. *Obshchie osnovy refleksologii cheloveka.* Leningrad: Go. izd., 1926.

———. "O polovom izvrashchenii, kak osoboi ustanovke polovykh refleksov." In Simonov, *Polovoi vopros v shkole i v zhizni,* 166–80.

———. "Polovaia deiatel'nost' s tochki zreniia refleksologii." In Zelenin, *Polovoi vopros v svete nauchnogo znaniia,* 142–81.

———. *Znachenie polovogo vlecheniia v zhiznedeiatel'nosti organizma.* Moscow, Narkomzdrav RSFSR, 1928.

Berman, F. Iu. "Garmoniia polovoi zhizni." In Volkonskaia and Berman, *Teoriia i praktika* issue 4, 72–89. Moscow: Izd. Moszdravotdela, 1926.

———. *Sputnik sanlektora: Konspekt lektsii.* Krasnodar: Izd. sanprosveta IX Kubarmii, 1921.

Bernatskii, Dr. "Chto nuzhno znat', vybiraia muzha i zheny." *Gigiena i zdorov'e rabochei i krest'ianskoi sem'i* 15 (1928): 2–3; 16 (1928): 6.

"Bibliografiia. Chto chitat' po polovomu voprosu." *Gigiena i zdorov'e* 18 (1927): 16.

"Bibliografiia: Dr. med. L. Ia. Iakobzon, *Polovaia slabost'.*" *Gigiena i zdorov'e rabochei i krest'ianskoi sem'i* 7 (1928): 15.

Bol'shaia meditsinskaia entsiklopediia. 1st ed. 35 vols. Moscow: OGIZ RSFSR, 1928–1936.

Bol'shaia sovetskaia entsiklopediia. 1st ed. 65 vols. Moscow: Sovetskaia entsiklopediia, 1936–1947.

Borisov, R. "Nevrasteniia." *Zhenskii zhurnal* 11 (1927): 26–27.

Bronner, V. M. "Iazyk faktov." *Venerologiia i dermatologiia* 10 (1927): 895–98.

———. "K voprosy o meditsinskom osvidetel'stvovanii brachushchikhsia." *Biulleten' Narkomzdrava* 6 (1925): 13–14.

———. "Polozhenie i perspektivy bor'by s venericheskimi bolezniami v Respublike." In *Raspredelenie zaniatii,* 11–14.

———. "Po novomu rabotat'." *Sovetskii vestnik venerologii i dermatologii* 3–4 (1932): 1–12.

Bronner, V. M., and A. I. Elistratov. *Prostitutsiia v Rossii: Prostitutsiia v Rossii do 1917 goda i bor'ba s prostitutsiei v RSFSR.* Moscow: Narkomzdrav, 1927.

Bruk, G. Ia. *Chto takoe polovoe vlechenie.* Moscow and Leningrad: Gos. izd., 1929.

Brukhanskii, N. P. *Materialy po seksual'noi psikhopatologii: Psikhiatricheskie ekspertizy.* Moscow: M. i S. Sabashnikovy, 1927.

Bulgakov, Mikhail A. "Sobach'e serdtse." In *Sobranie sochinenii v piati tomakh,* 2:129–40. Moscow: Khudozhestvennaia literatura, 1989.

Burlakov, I. G. *Kak dolzhny zhit' muzh s zhenoi.* Khar'kov: Nauchnaia mysl', 1929.

Bychkov, I. Ia., and N. S. Isaev. *Ugolovnaia otvetstvennost' za zarazhenie venericheskoi bolezn'iu (st. 150 ugolovnogo kodeksa).* Moscow and Leningrad: Gos. izd., 1931.

Cherkes, M. I. "K voprosu ob organizatsii i metodike raboty sanitarno-prosvetitel'nykh kabinetov pri vendispanserakh i konsul'tatsii po voprosam polovoi zhizni i polovoi gigieny pri rabochikh klubakh." *Vrachebnoe delo* 3–4 (1931): 170–74.

Chuchelov, N. I. "Opyt raboty konsul'tatsii po polovoi gigiene v Tashkente." *Sovetskii vrach* 2 (1930): 76–78.

Clarke, Edward H. "Sex in Education: A Fair Chance for the Girls." In Barreca, *Desire and Imagination,* 157–87.

Consultation for Sexual Hygiene at the State Institute of Social Hygiene. "K ozdorovleniiu byta." *Za zdorovyi byt* 1 (1928): 2.

Dekhterev, V. V. "Dispanserizatsiia kak osnova bor'by s istoshcheniem nervnoi sistemy." *Klinicheskaia meditsina* 19–20 (1930): 1094–99.

Dembskaia, V. E. *Polovaia gigiena zhenshchiny.* Leningrad: Leningradskaia pravda, 1929.

Department of Philanthropic Information, Central Hanover Bank and Trust Company. *The Mental Hygiene Movement: From the Philanthropic Standpoint.* New York: Central Hanover Bank and Trust Company, 1939.

Donichev, N. *Zdorovaia i nezdorovaia polovaia zhizn'.* Moscow and Leningrad: Gos. izd., 1930.

Efimov, D. "Na puti k novoi sem'e." *Put' k zdorov'iu* 7–8 (1926): 2.

Faingol'd, L. I. *Polovoe bessilie: Ego prichiny, preduprezhdenie i lechenie.* Odessa: Svetoch, 1926.

———. *Polovoe sozrevanie cheloveka.* Odessa: Svetoch, 1927.

Fedotova, E. N. "Preduprezhdenie beremennosti." *Put' k zdorov'iu* 7–8 (1926): 22–23.

Feigin, O. *Abort i preduprezhdenie beremennosti.* Leningrad: Izd. avtora, 1927.

———. *Chto takoe normal'naia polovaia zhizn'.* Leningrad: Izd. avtora, 1927.

———. *Polovoe sozrevanie i polovoe vospitanie.* Leningrad: Izd. avtora, 1927.

———. *Vazhneishie nenormal'nosti polovoi zhizni.* Leningrad: Izd. avtora, 1927.

Fronshtein, R. M. *Rasstroistvo polovoi deiatel'nosti muzhchiny.* Moscow and Leningrad: GMI, 1929.

———. "Vliianie polovogo vozderzhaniia na organizm." *Vrachebnoe delo* 12–14 (1925): 1009–11.

Gabinov, L. A. "Abort (iskusstvennyi vykidysh)." *Put' k zdorov'iu* 3.6 (1926): 7–8.

Gannushkin, P. "Ob okhrane zdorov'ia partaktiva." *Revoliutsiia i kul'tura* 4 (1930): 43–46.

Gel'man, I. G. *Polovaia zhizn' sovremennoi molodezhi. Opyt sotsial'no-biologicheskogo obsledovaniia.* Moscow and Petrograd: Gos. izd., 1923.

Gens, A. "Abort-sotsial'noe zlo." *Meditsina* 7 (1927): 10–11.

Gigiena i zdorov'e rabochego i ego sem'i. Stalingrad, 1925.

Glezer, M. A. *Polovaia zhizn'.* Khar'kov: Nauchnaia meditsina, 1929.

Golomb, Ia. D. *Polovaia zhizn' normal'naia i nenormal'naia.* Odessa: Svetoch, 1926.

———. *Polovoe vozderzhanie (za i protiv).* Odessa: Svetoch, 1927.

Gremiatskii, M. *Chto takoe omolozhenie.* Moscow and Leningrad: Gos. izd., 1930.

Groves, Ernest R., and Phyllis Blanchard. *Introduction to Mental Hygiene.* New York: Holt, 1930.

Gumilevskii, Lev. *Sobachii pereulok.* 1927. Riga: Gramatu draugs, 1928.

Gurevich, Z. "Polovoi vopros." *Bol'shaia meditsinskaia entsiklopediia,* 26:302–17.

Gurevich, Z. A., and F. I. Grosser. *Voprosy polovoi zhizni.* Kiev: Gos. izd. USSR., 1929.

Gurvich, B. "Eshche o polovoi slabosti muzhchin (Iz konsul'tatsii po polovoi gigiene)." *Za zdorovyi byt* 6 (1929): 2.

———. "K ozdorovleniiu byta (Iz konsul'tatsii po polovoi gigiene) II." *Za zdorovyi byt* 2 (1928): 2.

———. "O polliutsiiakh." *Za zdorovyi byt* 6 (1929): 2.

———. "Polovaia slabost' muzhchin (Iz konsul'tatsii po polovoi gigiene)." *Za zdorovyi byt* 4 (1928): 2.

———. "Po povodu pisem o polovykh rasstroistvakh." *Za zdorovyi byt* 9 (1930): 2.

———. "Prostitutsiia, kak sotsial'no-psikhopatologicheskoe iavlenie (predvarite'noe soobshchenie)." In Miskinov, Prozorov, and Rozenshtein, *Sovetskaia meditsina v bor'be za zdorovye nervy,* 60–68.

Gurvich, B. R., and L. E. Zalutskii. "Opyt konsul'tatsii po polovoi gigiene." In *Psikhogigienicheskie i nevrologicheskie issledovaniia,* ed. L. M. Rozenshtein, 229–39. Moscow: Narkomzdrav, 1928.

———. "Opyt konsul'tatsii po polovoi gigiene." *Venerologiia i dermatologiia* 2 (1928): 574–75.

———. "Opyt postroeniia polovoi konsul'tatsii." *Sotsial'naia gigiena* 7 (1928): 136–37.

Gurvich, L. S. "O rabote konsul'tatsii po ozdorovleniiu byta." *Vestnik sovremennoi meditsiny* 10 (1929): 582–86.

———. "Organy zdravookhraneniia i ZAGSy." *Zhurnal po izucheniiu rannego detskogo vozrasta* 7 (1929): 581–84.

Gusev-Orenburgskii, S. I. *Kakova zhe nasha molodezh'*. *Sbornik statei*. Moscow and Leningrad: Gos. izd., 1927.

Haines, Anna J. *Health Work in Soviet Russia*. New York: Vanguard Press, 1928.

Halle, Fanina. *Women in Soviet Russia*. New York: Viking Press, 1933.

Hare, Norman, ed. *World League for Sexual Reform: Proceedings of the Third Congress*. London: Ken Paul, Trench, Trubner, 1930.

Iakobzon, L. Ia. *Onanizm*. 2d ed. Moscow and Leningrad: Gos. izd., 1929.

———. "Polovaia kholodnost' zhenshchiny." *Gigiena i zdorov'e rabochei i krest'ianskoi sem'i* 6 (1927): 2–7.

———. *Polovaia kholodnost' zhenshchiny dlia vrachei i studentov*. Leningrad: Praktich-eskaia meditsina, 1927.

———. "Polovaia zhizn' cheloveka." *Gigiena i zdorov'e* 18 (1929): 11.

———. "Sotsial'noe znachenie polovykh rasstroistv." *Gigiena i zdorov'e rabochei i krest'ianskoi sem'i* 3 (1930): 5–6.

———. *Voprosy pola*. 2nd ed. Moscow and Leningrad: GMI, 1929.

Iazykov. "O blizhaishikh zadachakh komissii po rasprostraneniiu gigienicheskikh znanii v narode." *Zhurnal Pirogovskogo Obshchestva* 1 (1900).

"Instruktsiia o poriadke primeneniia postanovleniia VTsIK i SNK RSFSR ot 24/I-1927 goda, 'O merax bor'by s venericheskimi bolezniami.'" In Rossiianskii, *Dispanser-izatsiia*, 264–66.

Ioffe, A. A., ed. "Chto dolzhna znat' kazhdaia zhenshchina." Leningrad: Okhmatmlad NKZ, 1920s.

Iordanskii, N. P., ed. *Biosotsial'naia priroda polovoi zhizni cheloveka*. Moscow: Prometei, 1930.

Iudin, T. I. *Polovoe vlechenie i nenormal'nosti polovogo povedeniia*. Moscow: Izd. Narkomzdrava RSFSR, 1928.

———. *Zdorov'e, brak i sem'ia*. Moscow: Narkomzdrav, 1928.

Ivanova, N. "Seksual'naia pedagogika." *Zhenskii zhurnal* 6 (1930): 15.

Ivanovskii, B. A. *Polovaiai zhizn' i fizkul'tura*. Moscow and Leningrad: Gos. izd., 1928.

———. *Sovetskaia meditsina i fizkul'tura*. Moscow: GMI, 1928.

Kalmanson, S. M. "Iz doklada vracha S. M. Kalmansona na dispute po polovomu vo-prosu v Kommunisticheskom universitete trudiashchikhsia vostoka, 20/V 1924 g." In Kalmanson, *Polovoi vopros*, 4.

———, ed. *Polovoi vopros*. Moscow and Leningrad: Molodaia gvardiia, 1924.

Kameneva, E. N. *Chto kazhdomu nuzhno znat' o nervnosti*. Moscow: GMI, 1928.

Kaminskii, Ia. I. *Polovaia zhizn' i fizicheskaia kul'tura*. Odessa: Svetoch, 1927.

Kanevskii, L. O. "Osnovnye momenty organizatsii sovremennoi gorodskoi museino-vystavochnoi raboty po sanitarnomu prosveshcheniiu." In Volkonskaia and Berman, *Teoriia i praktika*, 2:90–123.

Kapustin, A. A. "Nervnost' nashego vremeni i bor'ba s nei." *Meditsina* 5 (1927): 5–6.

Karov, A. N. *Chto dolzhny znat' muzhchina i zhenshchina vstupaiushchie v brak*. Odessa: Svetoch, 1927.

Kashkadamov, V. "Gigiena perioda polovogo sozrevaniia." *Gigiena i zdorov'e rabochei sem'i* 4 (1923): 10.

Katsenelenbogen, I. M. "Zadachi sovetskoi meditsiny." In *Sanitarno-prosvetitel'naia rab-ota v izbe-chital'ne*, 6–10. Leningrad: Izd. Knizhnogo sektora LGONO, 1925.

Khachatrian, V. A. *Polovye otkloneniia i polovoe vospitanie. Onanizm i bor'ba s nim*. Tbil-isi, 1929.

Khaletskii, A. M. *Polovaia zhizn' i nevrasteniia*. Odessa: Svetoch, 1927.

Khanzhinskii, Prof. "Abort i besplodie." *Put' k zdorov'iu* 3 (1927): 10.

Khol'stov, B. N. *Funktsional'nye rasstroistva muzhskogo polovogo apparata i funktsion-al'nye rasstroistva mochevykh organov nervnogo proiskhozhdeniia*. Leningrad: Prak-ticheskaia meditsina, 1926.

"Khronika-Polovaia konsul'tatsiia." *Gigiena i zdorov'e* 12 (1928): 14.

Kirov, Ia. I. "K voprosu o geterotransplantsii pri gomoseksualizme." *Vrachebnoe delo* 20 (1928): 1587–90.

Kol'tsov, N. K. "Opyty Shteinakha po omolozheniiu organizma." *Priroda* 1–3 (1921): 3–26.

Kollontai, A. "Dorogu krylatomu erosu." *Molodaia gvardiia* 3 (1923): 111–24.

———. *Liubov' pchel trudovykh.* Moscow and Petrograd, 1923.

"Konsul'tatsiia po polovoi gigiene." *Za zdorovyi byt* 1 (1925): 3.

"K otkrytiiu konsul'tatsii po voprosam nervno-psikhicheskogo zdorov'ia i polovoi zhizni." *Gigiena i zdorov'e rabochei sem'i* 9 (1925): 9.

Kushelevskii, A. "Venerologicheskii dispanser i rabochaia obshchestvennost'." *Voprosy zdravookhraneniia* 3–4 (1929): 64–68.

Lass, D. I. "Pervaia Moskovskaia konferentsiia po seksual'noi pedagogike." *Vrachebnoe delo* 4 (1930): 313–14.

———. *Sovremennoe studenchestvo. Byt, polovaia zhizn'.* Moscow and Leningrad: Molodaia gvardiia, 1928.

———. *Zdorovaia polovaia zhizn'.* Moscow: GMI, 1929.

Lemberg, M. *Chto neobkhodimo znat' o polovom voprose.* Leningrad: Priboi, 1925.

Levi, M. F. "Abort i bor'ba s nim." *Za novyi byt* 22 (1926): 13–14.

———. "Besplodnye braki." *Za novyi byt* 10 (1927): 16–17.

———. "Gigiena braka." *Za novyi byt* 23–24 (1928): 17–18.

———. "Polovaia zhizn' v brake i vne braka." *Za novyi byt* 19–20 (1928), 19.

———. "Protivozachatochnye sredstva." *Za novyi byt* 10 (1927): 14–15.

———. "Vliianie polovogo vozderzhaniia na organizm." *Za novyi byt* 13–14 (1928): 21–22.

Levillain, Fernand. *La Neurasthenie: Maladie de Beard.* Paris: A. Maloine, 1891.

Liberman. "Molodezh' i polovoe zdorov'e (K rabote konsul'tatsii po polovoi gigiene)." *Za zdorovyi byt* 6 (1929): 2.

Lichkus, L. G. "Kak predokhranit' sebia ot beremennosti." *Gigiena i zdorov'e rabochei sem'i* 12 (1925): 2–6.

Lifshits, Ia. I. "Pravda o polovoi zhizni molodezhi." *Put' k zdorov'iu* 7–8 (1926): 7–9.

———. "Zadachi rekonstruktsii sotsial'noi venerologii." *Sovetskii vestnik venerologii i dermatologii* 6 (1932): 1–23.

———. "Zakon o brake." *Put' k zdorov'iu* 3(6) (1926): 5–6.

Lipschütz, Alexander. *The Internal Secretions of the Sex Glands: The Problem of the "Puberty Gland."* Cambridge: W. Heffer, 1924.

Liublinskii, P. I. *Prestupleniia v oblasti polovykh otkloneniiakh.* Moscow and Leningrad: Izd. I. D. Frenkel', 1925.

———. "Protivozachatochnye sovety i okhrana materinstva." *Leningradskii meditsinskii zhurnal* 6 (1926): 60–83.

Lunacharskii, A. V. and V. Knorin. *Upadochnoe nastroenie sredi molodezhi. Eseninshchina.* Moscow: Izd. Kommunisticheskoi Akademii, 1927.

Lur'e. "Polovaia konsul'tatsiia." *Za zdorovyi byt* 10 (1930): 1.

Lur'e, A. Iu. *Gigiena devochki, devushki, zhenshchiny.* Moscow: Okhmatmlad, 1927.

———. *Metody raboty konsul'tatsii dlia zhenshchin.* Moscow and Leningrad: GMI, 1930.

Lur'e, A. Iu., Z. I. Baisheva, and E. S. Kushnirskaia. "Opyt raboty polovoi konsul'tatsii pri ZAGSE." *Zhurnal po izucheniiu rannego detskogo vozrasta* 3–4 (1930): 295–306.

Lur'e, Z. G. "Nevrasteniia." *Meditsina* 17–18 (1929): 6–8.

Mamutov, A. M. *Gigiena polovoi zhizni zhenshchiny.* Khar'kov: Kosmos, 1927.

Mandels, L. "Ozdorovlenie polovogo byta." *Gigiena i zdorov'e rabochei i krest'ianskoi sem'i* 2 (January 1927): 10–11.

Maudsley, Henry. "Sex in Mind and Education." In Barreca, *Desire and Imagination,* 188–209.

Mendel'son, A. "Brachnyi vybor." *Gigiena i zdorov'e rabochei i krest'ianskoi sem'i* 17–18 (1930): 12–13.

————. "Gigiena polovoi zhizni." *Gigiena i zdorov'e rabochei i krest'ianskoi sem'i* 2 (1935): 6; 3 (1935): 6–7.

————. "Krainosti polovoi zhizni." *Gigiena i zdorov've rabochei sem'i* 6 (1923): 2–7.

————. *Nervnaia sistema i polovaia zhizn'*. Leningrad: Leningradskaia pravda, 1929.

————. "Nevrasteniia." *Gigiena i zdorov'e rabochei sem'i* 15.22 (1924): 2–6; 16.23 (1924): 2–6.

————. "O preduprezhdenii detskogo onanizma." *Gigiena i zdorov'e rabochei i Krest'ianstkoi sem'i* 24 (1930): 11–12.

————. "Polovaia zhizn' cheloveka." *Gigiena i zdorov'e rabochei sem'i* 5 (1923): 2–8.

————. "Polovoe bessilie." *Gigiena i zdorov'e rabochei sem'i* 1.8 (1924): 2–6; 2.9 (1924): 7–8.

————. "Polovye izvrashcheniia v svete sovremennoi nauki." *Gigiena i zdorov'e rabochei sem'i* 23.30 (1924): 3–4; 24 (1924): 2–5.

————. "Polovye razlichiia v svete sovremennoi nauki." *Gigiena i zdorov'e rabochei sem'i* 10.17 (1924): 10; 11.18 (1924): 13–14.

————. "Ranniaia polovaia zhizn' ili vozderzhanie." *Gigiena i zdorov'e rabochei i krest'ianskoi sem'i* 4 (1928): 8; 5 (1928): 6.

Mikulina-Ivanova, N. "Besplodie zhenshchiny: Mery preduprezhdeniia beremennosti." *Zhenskii zhurnal* 9 (1927): 18–20.

————. "Brak i evgenika: O kontrole nad zdorov'em lits, vstupaiushchikh v brak." *Zhenskii zhurnal* 1 (1929): 22–23.

————. "Normal'naia i nenormal'naia polovaia zhizn' zhenshchiny." *Zhenskii zhurnal* 9 (1927): 13–15; 10 (1927): 14–16.

————. "Oplodotvorenie i nasledstvennost'." *Zhenshkii zhurnal* 1 (1927): 14–15.

————. "Polovaia zhizn' zhenshchiny." *Zhenskii zhurnal* 7 (1926): 17–18.

————. "Preduprezhdenie beremennosti." *Zhenskii zhurnal* 6 (1926): 34.

Miskinov, A. I., L. A. Prozorov, and L. M. Rozenshtein, eds. *Sovetskaia meditsina v bor'be za zdorovye nervy. Trudy 1 Vsesoiuznogo soveshchaniia po psikhiatrii i nevrologii i gosudarstvennogo nevro-psikhiatricheskogo dispansera*. Moscow: Izd. Ul'ianovskogo kombinata PPP, 1926.

Moiseev, S. E. "Polovoi vopros i fizkul'tura." *Put' k zdorov'iu* 7–8 (1926): 31.

Mol'kov, A. V. "Doklad Pirogovskoi komissii po rasprostraneniiu gigienicheskikh znanii v narode." *Trudy 9-go Pirogovskogo s"ezda*, Tom. 4.

————. "Sanitarnoe prosveshchenie, ego zadachi i metody." *Sotsial'naia gigiena* 1 (1923): 40–62.

————. "Tezisy doklada: Sanitarnoe prosveshchenie, kak sotsial'naia gigienicheskaia problema i rol' vracha v nem." *Sanitarnoe prosveshchenie* 3 (1924): 16–17.

Monikh, S. "Konsul'tatsiia po polovym i brachnym voprosam." *Za zdorovyi byt* 9 (1930): 4.

Muralevich, V. S. *Chto takoe starost' i omolozhenie*. Moscow: Moskovskii rabochii, 1923.

Nemilov, A. V. *Biologicheskaia tragediia zhenshchin*. Leningrad: Seiatel', 1927.

————. "O peresadke semennykh zhelez u mlekopitaiushchikh i cheloveka." *Priroda* 7–12 (1923): 77–84.

Nestrukh, M. *Polovoe vlechenie v prirode*. Moscow: Novaia Moskva, 1924.

"Ne zabyvaite." *Put k zdorov'iu* 7–8 (1926): inside front cover.

Nikulin, S. V. "Onanizm, ego prichiny i bor'ba s nim." In Kalmanson, *Polovoi vopros*, 165–76.

Okun', I. M. "Sovremennoe zakonodatel'stvo v oblasti bor'by s venericheskimi zabolevaniiami i prostitutsieu." *Venerologiia i dermatologiia* 6 (1928): 985–93.

Onania, or the heinous sin of self-pollution and all its frightful consequences (in both sexes) considered, with physical and spiritual advice to those who have already injured themselves by this abominable practice. 8th ed. London: n.p., 1710[?].

"O rabote konsul'tatsii po ozdorovleniiu byta." *Zhenskii zhurnal* 9 (1929): 22.

Osipov, V. P. "Dr. L. Ia. Iakobzon, *Polovoe bessilie*." *Kniga i revoliutstiia* 3–4 (1920): 76.

"Ot redaktsii." *Venerologiia i dermatologiia* 1 (1924): 3.

"Ot redaktsii." *Venerologiia i dermatologiia* 1 (1931): 1–2.

"Ot redaktsii." *Sovetskii vestnik venerologii i dermatologii* 1–2 (1932): 1–2.

"Otvety na voprosy chitatelei." *Gigiena i zdorov'e rabochei i krest'ianskoi sem'i* 10.17 (1924): back cover; 12.19 (1924): back cover; 7 (1927): back cover; 19 (1927): 17; 1 (1928): 17; 13 (1928): 17; 19 (1928): 17.

Perel'muter, Ts. *Nauka i religiia o zhizni chelovecheskogo tela.* N.p.: Bezbozhnik, 1927.

Perna, N. "Znachenie organov vnutrennei sekretsii." *Priroda* 8–9 (1922): 9–18.

Pisareva, L. V. "O polovoi probleme v sviazi s vyiavleniem novogo byta u komsomol'skoi i rabochei molodezhi." In *Programma zaniatii 2-go vsesoiuznogo s"ezda po bor'be s venerizmom,* 14–15. Khar'kov: Narkomzdrav USSR, 1925.

Platovskii, A. K. *Polovaia zhizn' sovremennogo studenchestva.* Rostov na Donu, 1926.

Polonskii, V. "Russkii revoliutsionnyi plakat." *Pechat' i revoliutsiia,* kn. 2 (1922): 56–77.

"Polovoi vopros." *Put' k zdorov'iu* 7–8 (1926): 1.

"Postanovleniia VTsIK i SNK RSFSR ot 24/I-1927 goda, 'O merakh bor'by s venericheskimi bolezniami.'" In Rossiianskii, *Dispanserizatsiia,* 263–64.

Propper, N. I. "Itogi diskussii na estestvenno-nauchnom fronte i bor'ba na dva fronta v meditsine." *Zhurnal nevropatologii i psikhiatrii* 5 (1931): 7–18.

Protoklitov, S. A. *Chto dolzhna znat' devushka.* Moscow and Leningrad: Gos. izd., 1930.

"Protokol zasedaniia plenuma organizatsionnogo biuro po sozyvu vsesoiuznogo s"ezda po bor'be s venericheskimi bolezniami." *Venerologiia i dermatologiia* 1 (1925): 88–94.

Protopopov, V. P. "Sovremennoe sostoianie voprosa o sushchnosti i proiskhozhdenii gomoseksualizma." *Nauchnaia meditsina* 10 (1922): 49–62.

Prozorov, L. A. "Organizatsiia nevro-psikhiatricheskoi pomoshchi v usloviiakh nastoiashchego vremeni, v chastnosti, psikhpomoshchi sel'skomu naseleniiu." In Miskinov, Prozorov, and Rozenshtein, *Sovetskaia meditsina v bor'be za zdorovye nervy,* 12–13.

Rakhmanov, A. "Konsul'tatsiia dlia zhenshchin." *Biulleten' Narkomzdrava* 9 (1926): 3–9.

Raspredelenie zaniatii i tezisy dokladov vserossiiskogo s"ezda po bor'be s venericheskimi bolezniami. Moscow, 1923.

"Rebenka ne podkidyvai." Moscow: Mozdravotdel, 1920s.

"Rezoliutsiia po voprosu o seksual'nom vospitanii." In *Rezoliutsii i postanovleniia 2-go vsesoiuznogo s"ezda po bor'be s venerizmom,* 5. Khar'kov: Narkomzdrav USSR, 1925.

"Rezoliutsii, priniatye vtorym vsesoiuznym s"ezdom po bor'be s venericheskimi bolezniami, sostoiavshimsia v Khar'kove 13–19 maia 1925." *Venerologiia i dermatologiia* 3 (1925): 168–72.

Rokitskii, P. "Evgenika i brak." *Zhenskii zhurnal* 6 (1930): 18.

Romanov. "O medosvidetel'stvovanii brachushchikhsia." *Biulleten' Narkomzdrava* 6 (1925): 13.

Rossiiskii, D. "Istoriia meditsinskogo obrazovaniia v dorevoliutsionnoi Rossii." In *Bol'shaia meditsinskaia entsiklopediia,* 17:651–62. Moscow: Sovetskaia entsiklopediia, 1936.

Rossiiskii, D. M. *Ocherk istorii razvitiia endokrinologii v Rossii.* Moscow, 1926.

Rossiianskii, N. L. *Dispanserizatsiia v bor'be s venericheskimi bolezniami.* Moscow: Izd. NKZ RSFSR, 1928.

———. "Vrachebnaia etika i venericheskie bolezni." In *Raspredelenie zaniatii,* 42.

Rozenblium, G. *Kakoe znachenie imeet brak dlia zdorov'ia liudei.* Khar'kov: Kosmos, 1926.

Rozenshtein, L. M. *Nervnost' i bor'ba s nei.* Moscow: Izd. Narkomzdrava, 1928.

Sakharov, G. P. "Chelovecheskii polovoi dimorfizm." In Iordanskii, *Biosotsial'naia priroda,* 72–73.

———. "Proizvol'noe izmenenie pola u zhivotnykh." In Iordanskii, *Biosotsial'naia priroda,* 59–63.

———. "Vnutrenniaia sekretsiia i omolozhenie." In Iordanskii, *Biosotsial'naia priroda,* 64–71.

Semashko, N. A. *Health Protection in the USSR*. London: Victor Gollancz, 1934.

———. "Kak ne nado pisat' o polovom voprose." *Izvestiia*, January 1, 1925, 5.

———. "Meropriiatiia Narkomzdrava po lichnoi profilaktike." In Zelenin, *Polovoi vopros v svete nauchnogo znaniia*, 326–28.

———. "Na putiakh k novomu bytu." *Gigiena i zdorov'e rabochei i krest'ianskoi sem'i* 22 (1930): 2–3.

———. "Nevezhestvo i pornografiia pod maskoi prosveshcheniia, nauki i literatury." *Izvestiia*, April 8, 1927, 3.

———. *Novyi byt i polovoi vopros*. Moscow and Leningrad: Gos. izd., 1926.

———. "Nuzhna li 'zhenstvennost'?" *Molodaia gvardiia* 6 (1924): 205–6.

———. "O biologicheskom podkhode k postanovke polovogo vospitaniia." *Zvezda* 5 (1924): 150–53.

———. "O vrachebnoi taine," *Biulleten' NKZ* 11 (1925): 12.

———. "Predislovie." In Miskinov, Prozorov, and Rozenshtein, *Sovetskaia meditsina v bor'be za zdorovye nervy*, 3–4.

———. *Puti sovetskoi fizkul'tury*. Moscow: Izd. vysshego soveta fizkul'tury, 1926.

———. "Voprosy polovogo vospitaniia." In *Polovoi vopros*, ed. Em. Iaroslavskii, 17–23. Moscow: Izd. GIZh, 1925.

Shapiro, Ia. S. *Polovoe vospitanie detei v sem'e*. Moscow: Izd. Narkomzdrava RSFSR, 1928.

Shchukin, N. I. *Muzhchina i zhenshchina v polovoi zhizni*. Moscow and Leningrad: Gos. izd., 1928.

Shereshevskii, N. A. "Ocherk istorii endokrinologii v SSSR." *Problemy endokrinologii* 4 (1937): 452–58.

Shpak, M. Z. *Abort, ego posledstviia, i mery ego preduprezhdeniia*. Odessa: Svetoch, 1926.

———. *Polovaia zhizn' zhenshchiny*. Odessa: Svetoch, 1927.

———. *Preduprezhdenie beremennosti*. Odessa: Svetoch, 1927.

Shvarts, N. "Biologicheskii ocherk." In Kalmanson, *Polovoi vopros*, 17–38.

———. "Razvrashchena li nasha molodezh'." *Za zdorovyi byt* 5 (1929): 2.

Sigal, B. S. "Ozdorovite svoi polovoi byt." *Gigiena i zdorov'e rabochei i krest'ianskoi sem'i* 15 (1929): 13.

———. "Polovaia zhizn' nashei molodezhi." *Gigiena i zdorov'e rabochei sem'i* 16.23 (1924): 1–2.

———. *Polovaia zhizn' rabochei molodezhi*. Moscow and Leningrad: Molodaia gvardia, 1926.

———. *Polovoi vopros*. Moscow and Leningrad: Molodaia gvardiia, 1925.

Simonov, I. S., ed. *Polovoi vopros v shkole i v zhizni*. Leningrad: Brokgauz Efron, 1927.

Slovtsov, B. I., E. S. London, and I. I. Kryzhanskii. "Omolozhenie i izmenenie pola." In *Novoe v voprosakh pola*, ed. L. V. Blumenau et al., 8–48. Leningrad: Obrazovanie, 1924.

Sobranie kodeksov RSFSR (Ugolovnyi: kodeks RSFSR). 4th ed. Moscow: Iuridicheskoe izd. NKIu RSFSR, 1927.

Sorokhtin', G. N. *Obshchie osnovy polovogo vospitaniia dlia pedologov, vrachei i pedagogov*. Moscow: Prometei, 1930.

S.P. "Chto chitat' po polovomu voprosu." *Put' k zdorov'iu* 7–8 (1926): 33–34.

Steinach, Eugen. "Feminierung von Männchen und Maskulierung von Weibchen." *Zentralblatt für Physiologie* 27 (1913): 717–23.

———. "Pubetätsdrüsen und Zwitterbildung." *Archiv für Entwicheklungsmechanik* 42 (1917): 307–32.

———. *Sex and Life: Forty Years of Biological and Medical Experiments*. New York: Viking, 1940.

———. *Verjüngung durch experimentelle Neubelebung der alternden Pubertätsdrüse*. Berlin: Springer, 1920.

———. "Willkürliche Umwandlung von Säugetier-Männchen in Tiere mit ausgeprägt weiblichen Geschlechtscharakteren und weiblicher Psyche." *Pflügers Archiv für die gesammte Physiologie* 144 (1912): 71–108.

Strashun, I. D. "Sanitarnoe prosveshchenie v dele bor'by s venericheskimi bolezniami (Zadachi i metody)." In *Raspredelenie zaniatii*, 35–36.

Strashun, I. D., and A. S. Berliand, eds. *Sanitarnoe prosveshchenie v rabochem klube.* Moscow: Doloi negramotnost', 1925.

T. "Obshchestvenno-nauchnyi podkhod k materinstvu." *Zhenskii zhurnal* 7 (1927): 13.

Timofeev, A. *Kuda dolzhna napravliat'sia polovaia energiia molodezhi.* Khar'kov: Kosmos, 1927.

———. *V chem proiavliaetsia polovaia zhizn' muzhchiny i zhenshchiny.* Khar'kov: Kosmos, 1926.

Tkachenko, I. M. *O polovom voprose.* Kiev, 1926.

Tomilov, L. "O podgotovke vrachei k sanitarnomu prosveshcheniiu i vospitaniiu krasnoarmeitsev." *Sanitarnoe prosveshchenie* 3 (1924): 10–11.

Torsuev, N. A. *Venericheskie bolezni i bor'ba s nimi.* Gor'kii: Gor'kovskoe izdatel'stvo, 1935.

Trudy Vysochaishe razreshennogo s"ezda po obsuzhdeniiu mer protiv sifilisa v Rossii. St. Petersburg, 1897.

Tsukker, B. F. *Fizkul'tura byta i polovoi vopros.* Khar'kov: Kosmos, 1927.

———. *Voprosy polovoi zhizni rabochei molodezhi.* Khar'kov: Kosmos, 1927.

Uspenskii, A. *O vrede rannikh polovykh snoshenii.* Khar'kov: Kosmos, 1927.

———. *Polovaia zhizn' i ee otkloneniia.* Khar'kov: Kosmos, 1926.

Uzhanskii, G. *Ob onanizme.* Saratov, 1926.

Vasilevskie, L. A. and L. M. *Abort kak sotsial'noe iavlenie.* Moscow and Leningrad: Izd. L. D. Frenkel', 1924.

———. "Polovaia zhizn' cheloveka." In Kalmanson, *Polovoi vopros*, 39–86.

Vasilevskii, L. M. *Gigiena molodoi devushki.* Moscow: Novaia Moskva, 1926.

———. *K zdorovomy polovomu bytu.* Moscow: Zdorovaia Moskva, 1926.

———. *Polovoe zdorov'e.* Moscow: Izd. G. F. Mirimanova, 1925.

———. *Polovye izvrashcheniia.* Moscow: Novaia Moskva, 1924.

Veselovskaia, K. P. *Pedologicheskie osnovy polovogo vospitaniia.* Moscow, 1928.

Vnukov, V. "Reshaiushchie zven'ia v okhrane zdorov'ia kadrov." *Revoliutsiia i kul'tura* 4 (1930): 40–43.

Volkonskaia, S. "Opyt Moskovskogo Sanprosveta." *Sanitarnoe prosveshchenie* 4–5 (1924): 61–64.

Volkonskaia, S. N., and F. Iu. Berman, eds. *Teoriia i praktika sanitarnogo proveshcheniia.* Moscow: Izd. Moszdravotdela. Issue 1 (1925), issue 2 (1926), issue 4 (1926), issue 6 (1928).

Voronoff, Serge A. *Rejuvenation by Grafting,* trans. Fred F. Imianitoff. New York: Adelphi, 1925 [1924].

"Vserossiiskii s"ezd po bor'be s venericheskimi bolezniami." *Biulleten' Narkomzdrava* 16 (1923): 9–13.

"Vstupaiushchim v brak." *Gigiena i zdorov'e rabochei sem'i* 16.23 (1924): 12.

Zalkind, A. B. "O zabolevaniiakh partaktiva." *Krasnaia nov'* 4 (1925): 187–203.

———. "Polovoi vopros s kommunisticheskoi tochki zreniia." *Na putiakh k novoi shkole* 6 (1924): 47–57.

———. *Polovoi vopros v usloviiakh sovetskoi obshchestvennosti.* Leningrad: Gos. izd., 1926.

———. *Revoliutsiia i molodezh'* (Moscow: Kommunisticheskii universitet, 1925).

Zalutskaia, E. "Vred rannikh brakov." *Zhenskii zhurnal* 9 (1929): 20.

Zalutskii, Dr. "Ozdorovlenie byta." *Zhenskii zhurnal* 11 (1930): 21.

Zavadovskii, B. M. *Estestvoznanie i religiia.* Moscow: Bezbozhnik, 1925.

Zavadovskii, M. M. "Issledovanie semennika gomoseksualista." *Trudy po dinamike razvitiia (Prodolzhenie "Trudov laboratorii eksperim. biologii Mosk. Zooparka")* 6 (1931): 65–70.

———. *Pol i razvitie ego priznakov.* Moscow: Gos. izd., 1922.

———. *Pol zhivotnykh i ego prevrashchenie (mekhanika razvitiia pola).* In *Izbrannye Trudy.* Moscow: Agropromizdat, 1990.

Zdravomyslov, Ia. I. *Voprosy polovoi zhizni.* Leningrad: P. P. Soikin, 1926.

Zelenin, V. F., ed. *Polovoi vopros v svete nauchnogo znaniia.* Moscow and Leningrad: Gos. izd., 1926.

Zetkin, Klara. *My Recollections of Lenin.* Moscow: Foreign Languages Publishing House, 1956.

Zhbankov, D. N. "O polovoi zhizni uchashchikhsia zhenshchin." *Vrachebnoe delo* 10–12 (1922): 225–34.

Zhizhilenko, A. A. *Polovye prestupleniia (St. st. 166–171 Ugolovnogo Kodeksa).* Moscow: Izd. Pravo i Zhizn', 1924.

Zil'berg, Ia. F. "Chto chitat' po polovomu voprosu." *Za novyi byt* 23–24 (1928): 24.

———. "Chto chitat' po polovomu voprosu: Nepravil'nosti polovoi zhizni." *Za novyi byt* 7–8 (1929): 24.

Zoshchenko, Mikhail. *Nervous People and Other Satires,* tr. Maria Gordon and Hugh McLean. London: Victor Gollancz, 1963.

Secondary Sources

Adams, Mark B. "Eugenics as Social Medicine in Revolutionary Russia. Prophets, Patrons, and the Dialectics of Discipline Building." In Solomon and Hutchinson, *Health and Society,* 200–223.

———. *The Wellborn Science: Eugenics in Germany, France, Brazil, and Russia.* New York: Oxford University Press, 1990.

Ball, Alan M. *Russia's Last Capitalists: The Nepmen, 1921–1929.* Berkeley and Los Angeles: University of California Press, 1987.

Barker-Benfield, G. J. *The Horrors of the Half-Known Life: Male Attitudes toward Women and Sexuality in Nineteenth-Century America.* New York and London: Routledge, 2000.

Barsukov, M. I. *Velikaia Oktiabrskaia sotsialisticheskaia revoliutsiia i organizatsiia sovetskogo zdravookhraneniia.* Moscow: Medgiz, 1951.

Bennett, Paula, and Rosario, Vernon A., II, eds. *Solitary Pleasures: The Historical, Literary, and Artistic Discourses of Autoeroticism.* New York and London: Routledge, 1995.

Bernstein, Frances L. "Prostitutes and Proletarians: The Labor Clinic as Revolutionary Laboratory in the 1920s." In *The Human Tradition in Modern Russia,* ed. William Husband, 113–28. Wilmington, Del.: Scholarly Resources, 2000.

———. "'What Everyone Should Know about Sex': Gender, Sexual Enlightenment, and the Politics of Health in Revolutionary Russia, 1918–1931." PhD diss., Columbia University, 1998.

Bernstein, Laurie. *Sonia's Daughters: Prostitutes and Their Regulation in Imperial Russia.* Berkeley and Los Angeles: University of California Press, 1995.

Bershtein, Evgenii. "Tragediia pola: dve zametki o russkom veiningerianstve." *Novoe literaturnoe obozrenie* 1.65 (2004): 208–28.

———. "Psychopathia sexualis v Rossii nachala veka: politika i zhanr." In *Eros and Pornography in Russian Culture,* ed. M. Levitt and A. Toporkov, 414–41. Moscow: Ladomir, 1999.

Bland, Lucy and Doan, Laura, eds. *Sexology in Culture: Labelling Bodies and Desires.* Chicago: University of Chicago Press, 1998.

———. *Sexology Uncensored: The Documents of Sexual Science.* Chicago: University of Chicago Press, 1998.

Bonnell, Victoria E. *Iconography of Power: Soviet Political Posters under Lenin and Stalin.* Berkeley and Los Angeles: University of California Press, 1999.

———. "The Iconography of the Worker in Soviet Political Art." In *Making Workers Soviet: Power, Class, and Identity,* ed. Lewis H. Siegelbaum and Ronald Grigor Suny, 341–76. Ithaca: Cornell University Press, 1994.

———. "The Peasant Woman in Stalinist Political Art of the 1930s." *American Historical Review* 98 (February 1993): 55–82.

———."The Representation of Women in Early Soviet Political Art." *Russian Review* 50 (1991): 267–88.

Borenstein, Eliot. "'About That': Deploying and Deploring Sex in Post-Soviet Russia." *Studies in Twentieth-Century Literature* 24.1 (Winter 2000): 51–83.

———. *Men without Women: Masculinity and Revolution in Russian Fiction, 1917–1929.* Durham: Duke University Press, 2000.

Brandt, Allan M. *No Magic Bullet: A Social History of Venereal Disease in the United States since 1880.* New York and Oxford: Oxford University Press, 1987.

Brooks, Jeffrey. "The Breakdown in Production and Distribution of Printed Material, 1917–1927." In *Bolshevik Culture: Experiment and Order in the Russian Revolution,* ed. Abbott Gleason, Peter Kenez, and Richard Stites, 151–74. Bloomington: Indiana University Press, 1985.

Brown, Julie. "Revolution and Psychosis: The Mixing of Science and Politics in Russian Psychiatric Medicine, 1905–1913." *Russian Review* 46.3 (1987): 283–302.

Bryson, Norman, Holly, Michael Ann, and Moxey, Keith, eds. *Visual Culture: Images and Interpretations.* Hanover and London, 1994.

Buckley, Mary. "The Untold Story of *Obshchestvennitsa* in the 1930s." *Europe-Asia Studies* 48.4 (1996): 569–86.

Cartwright, Lisa. *Screening the Body: Tracing Medicine's Visual Culture.* Minneapolis: University of Minnesota Press, 1995.

Cavanaugh, Cassandra Marie. "Backwardness and Biology: Medicine and Power in Russian and Soviet Central Asia, 1868–1934." PhD diss., Columbia University, 2001.

Clark, Katerina. *Petersburg: Crucible of Cultural Revolution.* Cambridge: Harvard University Press, 1995.

Clements, Barbara Evans. "The Effects of the Civil War on Women and Family Relations." In *Party, State, and Society in the Russian Civil War: Explorations in Social History,* ed. Diane P. Koenker, William G. Rosenberg, and Ronald Grigor Suny, 105–22. Bloomington: Indiana University Press, 1989.

Coopersmith, Jonathan. *The Electrification of Russia.* Ithaca: Cornell University Press, 1992.

Costlow, Jane T., Stephanie Sandler, and Judith Vowles, eds. *Sexuality and the Body in Russian Culture.* Stanford: Stanford University Press, 1993.

Darby, Robert. "Circumcision as a Preventive of Masturbation: A Review of the Historiography." *Journal of Social History* 36 (Spring 2003): 737–58.

David, Michael. "The White Plague in the Red Capital: Tuberculosis and Its Control in Moscow and the RSFSR, 1900–1941." PhD diss., University of Chicago, in preparation.

David-Fox, Michael. *Revolution of the Mind: Higher Learning among the Bolsheviks, 1918–1929.* Ithaca: Cornell University Press, 1997.

Dijkstra, Bram. *Idols of Perversity: Fantasies of Feminine Evil in Fin-de-Siècle Culture.* New York: Oxford University Press, 1986.

Dixon, J. G. "Prussia: Politics and Physical Education." In *Landmarks in the History of Physical Education,* ed. J. G. Dixon, P. C. McIntosh, A. D. Munrow, and R. F. Willetts, 107–48. London: Routledge and Kegan Paul, 1957.

Drinka, George Frederick. *The Birth of Neurosis: Myth, Malady, and the Victorians.* New York: Simon and Schuster, 1984.

Edelman, Robert. *Serious Fun: A History of Spectator Sports in the USSR.* New York: Oxford University Press, 1993.

Engelstein, Laura. *Castration and the Heavenly Kingdom: A Russian Folktale.* Ithaca: Cornell University Press, 1999.

———. "Combined Underdevelopment: Discipline and the Law in Imperial and Soviet Russia." *American Historical Review* 98.2 (1993): 338–53.

———. *The Keys to Happiness: Sex and the Search for Modernity in Fin-de-Siècle Russia.* Ithaca: Cornell University Press, 1992.

———. "Soviet Policy toward Male Homosexuality: Its Origins and Historical Roots." In *Gay Men and the Sexual History of the Political Left,* ed. Gert Hekma, Harry Oosterhuis, and James D. Steakley, 155–78. New York: Haworth Press, 1995.

Etkind, Aleksandr. *Eros nevozmozhnogo: istoriia psikhoanaliza v Rossii.* Moscow: Gnozis, 1994.

———. *Khlyst: Sekty, Literatura i Revoliutsiia.* Moscow: Novoe Literaturnoe Obozrenie, 1998.

Fainsod, Merle. *How Russia Is Ruled.* Cambridge: Harvard University Press, 1962.

Fitzpatrick, Sheila. "Ascribing Class: The Construction of Social Identity in Soviet Russia." *Journal of Modern History* 65 (December 1993): 745–70.

———. "The Bolsheviks' Dilemma: Class, Culture, and Politics in the Early Soviet Years." *Slavic Review* 47 (Winter 1988): 599–613.

———. *The Cultural Front.* Ithaca: Cornell University Press, 1992.

———. "Sex and Revolution: An Examination of Literary and Statistical Data on the Mores of Soviet Students in the 1920s." *Journal of Modern History* (June 1978): 252–78.

Foucault, Michel. *The History of Sexuality.* Vol. 1, *An Introduction.* Translated by Robert Hurley. New York: Pantheon, 1978.

Fox, Daniel M., and Christopher Lawrence, eds. *Photographing Medicine: Images and Power in Britain and America since 1840.* New York: Greenwood Press, 1988.

Frieden, Nancy. "Child Care: Medical Reform in a Traditionalist Culture." In *The Family in Imperial Russia,* ed. David L. Ransel, 236–59. Champagne-Urbana: University of Illinois Press, 1978.

———. *Russian Physicians in an Era of Reform and Revolution, 1856–1905.* Princeton, N.J.: Princeton University Press, 1981.

Gilman, Sander L. *Difference and Pathology, Stereotypes of Sexuality, Race, and Madness.* Ithaca: Cornell University Press, 1985.

———. *Disease and Representation: Images of Illness from Madness to AIDS.* Ithaca: Cornell University Press, 1988.

———. *Sexuality, an Illustrated History: Representing the Sexual in Medicine and Culture from the Middle Ages to the Age of AIDS.* New York: John Wiley and Sons, 1989.

Golden, Janet Lynne. *Pictures of Health: A Photographic History of Health Care in Philadelphia, 1860–1945.* Philadelphia: University of Pennsylvania, 1991.

Goldman, Wendy Z. *Women, the State, and Revolution: Soviet Family Policy and Social Life, 1917–1936.* Cambridge and New York: Cambridge University Press, 1993.

Golikov, G. N., et al., ed. *Vospominaniia o V. I. Lenine.* Moscow: Politizdat, 1968–1969. Vol. 2.

Golub, Spencer. *The Recurrence of Fate: Theatre and Memory in Twentieth-Century Russia.* Iowa City: University of Iowa Press, 1994.

Gorsuch, Anne. "Flappers and Foxtrotters: Soviet Youth in the 'Roaring Twenties.'" *Carl Beck Papers in Russian and East European Studies* 1102 (March 1994): 1–33.

———. "'A Woman Is Not a Man': The Culture of Gender and Generation in Soviet Russia, 1921–1928." *Slavic Review* 55.3 (Fall 1996): 636–60.

———. *Youth in Revolutionary Russia: Enthusiasts, Bohemians, Delinquents.* Bloomington: Indiana University Press, 2000.

Graham, Loren. "Science and Values: The Eugenics Movement in Germany and Russia in the 1920s." *American Historical Review* 83 (1977): 1135–64.

Green, Harvey. *Fit for America: Health, Fitness, Sport, and American Society.* New York: Pantheon, 1986.

Grossmann, Atina. "The New Woman and the Rationalization of Sexuality in Weimar Germany." In *Powers of Desire: The Politics of Sexuality,* ed. Ann Snitow, Christine Stansell, Sharon Thompson, 39–51. New York: Monthly Review Press, 1983.

———. *Reforming Sex: The German Movement for Birth Control and Abortion Reform, 1920–1950.* New York: Oxford University Press, 1995.

Groves, Ernest R. and Blanchard, Phyllis. *Introduction to Mental Hygiene.* New York: H. Holt and Company, 1930.

Haley, Bruce.*The Healthy Body and Victorian Culture*. Cambridge: Harvard University Press, 1978.

Hall, Lesley A. "Forbidden by God, Despised by Men: Masturbation, Medical Warnings, Moral Panic, and Manhood in Great Britain, 1850–1950." In *Forbidden History: The State, Society, and the Regulation of Sexuality in Modern Europe*, ed. John Fout, 293–315. Chicago and London: University of Chicago Press, 1992.

———. "'Somehow very distasteful': Doctors, Men, and Sexual Problems between the Wars." *Journal of Contemporary History* 20 (1985): 553–74.

Healey, Dan. *Homosexual Desire in Revolutionary Russia*. Chicago: University of Chicago, 2001.

———. "A Social History of Homosexuality in Soviet Russia, 1917–1934." MA thesis, University of London, 1991.

Herman, David. "Stricken by Infection: Art and Adultery in *Anna Karenina* and 'Kreutzer Sonata.'" *Slavic Review* 56.1 (1997): 15–36.

Hoberman, John M. "The Early Development of Sports Medicine in Germany." In *Sport and Exercise Science: Essays in the History of Sports Medicine*, ed. Jack W. Berryman and Roberta J. Park, 233–82. Urbana and Chicago: University of Illinois, 1992.

Hoffmann, David L. "Mothers in the Motherland: Stalinist Pronatalism in Its Pan-European Context," *Journal of Social History* (Fall 2000): 35–54.

———. *Stalinist Values: The Cultural Norms of Soviet Modernity, 1917–1941*. Ithaca: Cornell University Press, 2003.

Hoffmann, David L., and Yanni Kotsonis, eds. *Russian Modernity: Politics, Knowledge, Practices*. New York: St. Martin's Press, 2000.

Husband, William B. *"Godless Communists": Atheism and Society in Soviet Russia, 1917–1932*. DeKalb: Northern Illinois University Press, 2000.

Hutchinson, John F. *Politics and Public Health in Revolutionary Russia, 1890–1918*. Baltimore: Johns Hopkins University, 1990.

Ingerflom, Claudio Sergio. *La secte russe des castrates*. Paris: Les Belles Lettres, 1996.

Johnson, Mark. "Russian Educators, the Stalinist Party-State, and the Politics of Soviet Education, 1929–1939." PhD diss., Columbia University, 1995.

Joravsky, David. "The Construction of the Stalinist Psyche." In *The Cultural Revolution in Russia, 1928–1931,* ed. Sheila Fitzpatrick, 105–20. Bloomington and Indianapolis: Indiana University Press, 1984.

———. *The Lysenko Affair*. Cambridge: Harvard University Press, 1971.

———. *Russian Psychology: A Critical History*. Oxford and New York: Blackwell, 1989.

Jordanova, Ludmilla. "Medicine and Visual Culture." *Social History of Medicine* 3.1 (April 1990): 89–99.

———. *Sexual Visions: Images of Gender in Science and Medicine between the Eighteenth and Twentieth Centuries*. London: Harvester Wheatsheaf, 1989.

Kelly, Catriona. *Refining Russia: Advice Literature, Polite Culture, and Gender from Catherine to Yeltsin*. Oxford: Oxford University Press, 2001.

Kenez, Peter. *The Birth of the Propaganda State: Soviet Methods of Mass Mobilization, 1917–1929*. Cambridge and New York: Cambridge University Press, 1985.

Kimerling, Elise. "Civil Rights and Social Policy in Soviet Russia, 1918–1936." *Russian Review* 41 (1982): 24–46.

Kon, Igor S. *Seksual'naia kul'tura v Rossii: Klubnichka na berezke*. Moscow: OGI, 1997.

———. *The Sexual Revolution in Russia*. New York: Free Press, 1995.

Konecny, Peter. *Builders and Deserters: Students, State, and Community in Leningrad, 1917–1941*. Montreal: McGill-Queens University Press, 1999.

Kriachko, N. A. *Fizicheskaia kul'tura*. Moscow: Fizkul'tura i Sport, 1948.

Kuhn, Annette. *The Power of the Image: Essays on Representation and Sexuality*. New York: Routledge, 1985.

Labisch, Alfons. "Doctors, Workers, and the Scientific Cosmology of the Industrial World: The Social Construction of 'Health' and the 'Homo Hygienicus'," *Journal of Contemporary History* 20 (1985): 599–615.

Laqueur, Thomas. *Making Sex: Body and Gender from the Greeks to Freud.* Cambridge: Harvard University Press, 1990.

———. *Solitary Sex: A Cultural History of Masturbation.* New York: Zone Books, 2003.

Lebina, N. B., and M. V. Shkarovskii. *Prostitutsiia v Peterburge.* Moscow: Progress-Akademiia, 1994.

Lutz, Tom. *American Nervousness, 1903: An Anecdotal History.* Ithaca and New York: Cornell University Press, 1991.

Makoveeva, Irina. "Soviet Sports as a Cultural Phenomenon: Body and/or Intellect." *Studies in Slavic Cultures* 3 (July 2002): 9–32.

Martin, Emily. "The Egg and the Sperm: How Science Has Constructed a Romance Based on Stereotypical Male-Female Roles." *Signs: Journal of Women in Culture and Society* 16.3 (1991): 485–501.

Masing-Delic, Irene. *Abolishing Death: A Salvation Myth of Russian Twentieth-Century Literature.* Stanford: Stanford University Press, 1992.

Massell, Gregory J. *The Surrogate Proletariat: Moslem Women and Revolutionary Strategies in Soviet Central Asia, 1919–1929.* Princeton, N.J.: Princeton University Press, 1974.

McLaren, Angus. *Twentieth-Century Sexuality: A History.* Oxford: Blackwell, 1999.

McNeal, Robert H. *Bride of the Revolution.* Ann Arbor: University of Michigan Press, 1972.

Micale, Mark S. *Approaching Hysteria: Disease and Its Interpretations.* Princeton, N.J.: Princeton University Press, 1994.

Michaels, Paula A. *Curative Powers: Medicine and Empire in Stalin's Central Asia.* Pittsburgh, Pa.: University of Pittsburgh Press, 2003.

Miller, Martin A. *Freud and the Bolsheviks: Psychoanalysis in Imperial Russia and the Soviet Union.* New Haven: Yale University Press, 1998.

Moscucci, Ornella. *The Science of Woman: Gynaecology and Gender in England, 1800–1929.* Cambridge and New York: Cambridge University Press, 1990.

Muncy, Raymond Lee. *Sex and Marriage in Utopian Communities: Nineteenth-Century America.* Bloomington and Indianapolis: Indiana University Press, 1973.

Naiman, Eric. "Historectomies: The Metaphysics of Reproduction in a Utopian Age." In Costlow, Sandler, and Vowles, *Sexuality and the Body in Russian Culture,* 255–76.

———. *Sex in Public: The Incarnation of Early Soviet Ideology.* Princeton, N.J.: Princeton University Press, 1997.

Nathans, Benjamin. *Beyond the Pale: The Jewish Encounter with Late Imperial Russia.* Berkeley and Los Angeles: University of California Press, 2002.

Neary, Rebecca Balmas. "Mothering Socialist Society: The Wife-Activists' Movement and the Soviet Culture of Daily Life, 1934–1941." *Russian Review* 58 (1999): 396–412.

Nesbet, Anne. "Suicide as Literary Fact in the 1920s." *Slavic Review* 50.4 (Winter 1991): 827–35.

Nesterenko, A. I. *Kak byl obrazovan Narodnyi komissariat zdravookhraneniia RSFSR: Iz istorii Sovetskogo zdravookhraneniia.* Moscow: Meditsina, 1965.

Nye, Robert. *Crime, Madness, and Politics in Modern France.* Princeton, N.J.: Princeton University Press, 1984.

———. "The History of Sexuality in Context: National Sexological Traditions." *Science in Context* 4 (1991): 387–406.

———. "Honor, Impotence, and Male Sexuality in Nineteenth-Century French Medicine." *French Historical Studies* 16.1 (Spring 1989): 48–71.

Oosterhuis, Harry. "Homosexual Emancipation in Germany before 1933: Two Traditions." *Journal of Homosexuality* 22.1–2 (1992): 1–27.

Oudshoorn, Nelly. *Beyond the Natural Body: An Archeology of Sex Hormones.* London and New York: Routledge, 1994.

Pernick, Martin S. *The Black Stork: Eugenics and the Death of "Defective" Babies in American Medicine and Motion Pictures since 1915.* New York and Oxford: Oxford University Press, 1996.

Phillips, Laura L. *Bolsheviks and the Bottle: Drink and Worker Culture in St. Petersburg, 1900–1929.* DeKalb: Northern Illinois University Press, 2000.

Pinnow, Kenneth M. "Cutting and Counting: Forensic Medicine as a Science of Society in Bolshevik Russia, 1920–1929," in Hoffmann and Kotsonis, *Russian Modernity,* 115–37.

———. *Suicide and the Social Science State in Early Bolshevik Russia, 1921–1929.* Manuscript in progress.

Pollock, Griselda. *Vision and Difference: Femininity, Feminism, and the Histories of Art.* London and New York: Routledge, 1988.

Poovey, Mary. "'Scenes of an Indelicate Character': The Medical 'Treatment' of Victorian Women." In *The Making of the Modern Body: Sexuality and Society in the Nineteenth Century,* ed. Catherine Gallagher and Thomas Laqueur, 137–68. Berkeley and Los Angeles: University of California Press, 1987.

Porter, Roy, and Lesley Hall. *The Facts of Life: The Creation of Sexual Knowledge in Britain, 1650–1950.* New Haven and London: Yale University Press, 1995.

Rabinbach, Anson. *The Human Motor: Energy, Fatigue, and the Origins of Modernity.* New York: Basic Books, 1990.

Reich, Wilhelm. *The Sexual Revolution: Toward a Self-Governing Character Structure,* trans. Theodore P. Wolfe. New York: Orgone Institute Press, 1945.

Riordan, James. *Sport in Soviet Society: The Development of Sport and Physical Education in Russia and the USSR.* Cambridge and New York: Cambridge University Press, 1977.

Roberts, Mary-Louise. *Civilization without Sexes: Reconstructing Gender in Postwar France, 1917–1927.* Chicago: University of Chicago Press, 1994.

Samoukov, F., ed. *Istoriia fizicheskoi kul'tury.* Moscow, 1964.

Schapiro, Leonard. *The Communist Party of the Soviet Union.* New York: Random House, 1971.

Schecter, Kate Sara. "Professionals in Post-revolutionary Regimes: A Case Study of Soviet Doctors." PhD diss., Columbia University, 1992.

Semenova, Svetlana. *Nikolai Fedorov: Tvorchestvo zhizni.* Moscow: Sovetskii pisatel', 1990.

Sengoopta, Chandak. "Glandular Politics: Experimental Biology, Clinical Medicine, and Homosexual Emancipation in Fin-de-Siècle Central Europe." *Isis* 89 (1998): 445–73.

Service, Robert. *Lenin: A Political Life,* vol. 1. Bloomington and Indianapolis: Indiana University Press, 1985.

Showalter, Elaine. *The Female Malady: Women, Madness, and English Culture, 1830–1980.* New York: Pantheon, 1985.

Sirotkina, Irina. *Diagnosing Literary Genius: A Cultural History of Psychiatry in Russia, 1880–1930.* Baltimore and London: Johns Hopkins University Press, 2002.

Solomon, Peter H., Jr. *Soviet Criminal Justice under Stalin.* Cambridge: Cambridge University Press, 1996.

Solomon, Susan Gross. "The Demographic Argument in Soviet Debates over the Legalization of Abortion in the 1920s." *Cahiers du Monde Russe et Soviétique* 2 (1992): 59–82.

———. "Innocence and Sexuality in Soviet Medical Discourse." In *Women in Russia and Ukraine,* ed. Rosalind Marsh, 121–30. Cambridge: Cambridge University Press, 1996.

———. "Social Hygiene and Soviet Public Health, 1921–1930." In Solomon and Hutchinson, *Health and Society,* 175–99.

———. "The Soviet-German Syphilis Expedition to Buriat Mongolia, 1928: Scientific Research on National Minorities." *Slavic Review* 52.2 (Summer 1993): 204–32.

———. "The Soviet Legalization of Abortion in German Medical Discourse: A Study of the Use of Selective Perceptions in Cross-Cultural Scientific Relations." *Social Studies of Science* 22.3 (1992): 455–87.

Solomon, Susan Gross, and John Hutchinson, eds. *Health and Society in Revolutionary Russia.* Bloomington: Indiana University Press, 1990.

Starks, Tricia Ann. "The Body Soviet: Health, Hygiene, and the Path to a New Life in the Soviet Union in the 1920s." PhD diss., Ohio State University, 2000.

Stites, Richard. *Revolutionary Dreams: Utopian Vision and Experimental Life in the Russian Revolution*. New York: Oxford University Press, 1989.

———. *The Women's Liberation Movement in Russia: Feminism, Nihilism, and Bolshevism, 1860–1930*. Princeton, N.J.: Princeton University Press, 1978.

Thomas, Julie L. "International Intercourse: Establishing a Global Discourse on Birth Control, 1914–1939." PhD diss., Indiana University, in progress.

Tikhonova, Z. *Narodnyi komissar zdorov'ia (o N. A. Semashko)*. Moscow: Gos. izd. politicheskoi literatury, 1960.

Timasheff, Nicholas. *The Great Retreat: The Growth and Decline of Communism in Russia*. New York: Dutton, 1946.

Todorov, Vladislav. *Red Square, Black Square: Organon for Revolutionary Imagination*. Albany: State University of New York Press, 1995.

Transchel, Kate. *Under the Influence: Working-Class Drink, Temperance, and Cultural Revolution in Russia, 1895–1932*. Pittsburgh, Pa.: Pittsburgh University Press, 2006.

Usborne, Cornelie. *The Politics of the Body in Weimar Germany*. London: Macmillan, 1992.

"V. M. Bronner." In *Vrachi-bol'sheviki: Stroiteli sovetskogo zdravookhraneniia*, ed. E. I. Lotovaia i B. D. Petrov, 241–51. Moscow: Meditsina, 1970.

von Hagen, Mark. *Soldiers in the Proletarian Dictatorship*. Ithaca: Cornell University Press, 1990.

Wagner, William G. *Marriage, Property, and Law in Imperial Russia*. Oxford: Clarenden Press, 1994.

Walkowitz, Judith R. *City of Dreadful Delight: Narratives of Sexual Danger in Late-Victorian London*. Chicago: University of Chicago Press, 1992.

Waters, Elizabeth. "The Female Form in Soviet Political Iconography, 1917–1932." In *Russia's Women: Accommodation, Resistance, Transformation*, ed. Barbara Evans Clements, Barbara Alpern Engel, and Christine D. Worobec, 225–42. Berkeley and Los Angeles: University of California Press, 1991.

———. "Victim or Villain? Prostitution in Post-Revolutionary Russia." In *Women and Society in Russia and the Soviet Union*, ed. Linda Edmondson, 160–77. Cambridge: Cambridge University Press, 1992.

Weeks, Jeffrey. *Coming Out: Homosexual Politics in Britain from the Nineteenth Century to the Present*. London and New York: Quartet Books, 1977.

Weindling, Paul. "German-Soviet Cooperation in Science: The Case of the Laboratory for Racial Research, 1931–1938." *Nuncius: Annali di Storia della Scienza* 1.2 (1986):103–9.

Weiner, Dora B. *The Citizen-Patient in Revolutionary and Imperial Paris*. Baltimore: Johns Hopkins University Press, 1993.

Weissman, Neil B. "Origins of Soviet Health Administration: Narkomzdrav, 1918–1928." In Solomon and Hutchinson, *Health and Society*, 97–120.

White, Stephen. *The Bolshevik Poster*. New Haven and London: Yale University Press, 1988.

———. "The Political Poster in Bolshevik Russia." *Sbornik: Study Group on the Russian Revolution* (1982): 28–37.

Wood, Elizabeth. *The Baba and the Comrade: Gender and Politics in Revolutionary Russia*. Bloomington: Indiana University Press, 1997.

———. *Performing Justice: Agitation Trials in Revolutionary Russia*. Ithaca and New York: Cornell University Press, 2005.

———. "Prostitution Unbound: Representations of Sexual and Political Anxieties in Post-revolutionary Russia." In Costlow, Sandler, and Vowles, *Sexuality and the Body*, 124–35.

Zolotonosov, Mikhail. "Masturbanizatsiia. 'Erogennye zony' sovetskoi kul'tury 1920–1930-kh godov." *Novoe literaturnoe obozrenie* 11 (1991): 93–99.

Index